Achieving the Single European Sky

Aviation Law and Policy Series

Volume 8

Series Editor

Pablo Mendes de Leon

International Institute of Air and Space Law, Leiden University

The global liberalization regime of the past two decades has fundamentally affected the operation of international air transport services.

This process calls for reflection and analysis across a wide range of legal and policy areas, including but not limited to public international air law and policy, with special reference to safety, security and environmental concerns, liability, competition law regimes, company law, and the complex relationship between European Community law and public international law.

The *Aviation Law and Policy Series* critically examines developments around liberalization of air services internationally resulting in the establishment of Open Aviation Areas; institutional questions such as the external powers of the European Community and the relationship between international organizations such as ICAO and EUROCONTROL; the coming into force of unlimited liability regimes and related case law; the granting of antitrust immunity to international airline alliances; and cooperation between competition authorities. Attention will also be paid to topical safety and security issues, and the growing impact of aviation in relation to the environment, dictating the design of emission trade systems. Last but not least, commercially oriented subjects such as aircraft financing and leasing will be addressed, both from the perspective of national and international legal regimes, taking into account practical cases and case law.

The objective of the *series* is to make a contribution to legal thinking on the multifaceted aspects of this important field of law. The publications are designed to document and anticipate the evolution of aviation law and policy in the twenty-first century.

The titles published in this series are listed in the back of this volume.

Achieving the Single European Sky

Goals and Challenges

Editors-in-Chief

Daniel Calleja Crespo

and

Pablo Mendes de Leon

Wolters Kluwer
Law & Business

Published by:
Kluwer Law International
PO Box 316
2400 AH Alphen aan den Rijn
The Netherlands
Website: www.kluwerlaw.com

Sold and distributed in North, Central and South America by:
Aspen Publishers, Inc.
7201 McKinney Circle
Frederick, MD 21704
United States of America
Email: customer.service@aspenpublishers.com

Sold and distributed in all other countries by:
Turpin Distribution Services Ltd.
Stratton Business Park
Pegasus Drive, Biggleswade
Bedfordshire SG18 8TQ
United Kingdom
Email: kluwerlaw@turpin-distribution.com

DISCLAIMER: The Editors regard this book as an academic publication which is designed to promote the understanding of the Single European Sky regime and not to make commercial profits. The opinions expressed in this book only reflect the authors' views and do not necessarily bind the institutions they work for.

Printed on acid-free paper.

ISBN 978-90-411-3730-2

Printed and Bound by CPI Group (UK) Ltd, Croydon, CR0 4YY.

To the memory of Loyola de Palacio who continues to inspire us to achieve the Single European Sky

Table of Contents

Foreword

An integrated cross border transport sector is essential for a well-functioning internal market. At the same time transport by land, sea and air has traditionally been characterized by heavy state intervention. For that reason the original EEC Treaty foresaw the establishment of a European common transport policy to replace and complement the large variety of national legislations in Europe. This has proven to be a formidable task. It has taken decades before a European policy has taken shape in the various transport sectors.

In particular European air transport policy has been governed for many years by liberal bilateral agreements between individual EU Member States and third parties, the so-called *Open Skies* Agreements. The jurisprudence of the Court of Justice of the EU has been of decisive influence in overcoming national fragmentation. Hundreds of discriminatory agreements between national and third states have been replaced by a more transparent European framework.

In the same vein, the creation of a Single European Sky regime has been decided in 2004. This regime already has produced a useful European legislative framework. It has formed the starting point of a wide range of measures designed to improve efficiency in air traffic management in Europe. National borders have been adapted by European measures in order to achieve a Single European Sky. The concept of absolute sovereignty over national skies has been abandoned and is replaced by legal and political structures facilitating a common air space in the whole of Europe. This comprises not only the territories of the EU states, but also the western Balkan states, as well as Norway, Iceland and Switzerland.

The legislation of 2009 is designed to increase cross-border coordination, to remove administrative and organizational bottlenecks in decision-making and to enhance enforcement in air traffic management in Europe. Since air transport is basically a global activity, it will also facilitate a common European voice in the worldwide management of airspace.

Against this background the publication of *Achieving the Single European Sky (SES): Goals and Challenges* is very timely. The editors-in-chief, Daniel Calleja Crespo and Pablo Mendes de Leon, each have a wealth of experience both in policy-making and academia. They have succeeded in selecting a team of highly competent collaborators who together represent a great variety of skills on the management of the Single European Sky. The publication gives a thorough explanation of what has been achieved so far, not only in theory, but also in practice. Moreover, it also covers a catalogue of future challenges, such as technological, environmental and safety concerns. In short, it is an indispensable tool for students and practitioners alike; hence, it is a welcome addition to an important field of European policy.

Laurens Jan Brinkhorst
Professor of Law, Leiden University, the Netherlands
Chairman of the International Institute of Air and Space Law

List of Abbreviations

ACAS	Airborne Collision Avoidance System
ACC	Area Control Centers
ACI	Airports Council International
AEA	Association of European Airlines
AESA	Agencia Estatal de Seguridada Aérea
AIRE	Atlantic Interoperability initiative to Reduce Emissions
AIS	Aeronautical Information Services
ANP	Air Navigation Plan
ANS	Air Navigation Services
ANSB	Air Navigation Services Board
ANSP	Air Navigation Service Provider
ASAS	Airborne Separation Assistance System
ASM	Air Space Management
ASNP	Air Navigation Services Provider
ATC	Air Traffic Control
ATFM	Air Traffic Flow Management
ATM	Air Traffic Management
ATM SD	Air Traffic Management Social Dialogue
ATS	Air Traffic Services
BoD	Board of Directors
CAA	Civil Aviation Authority
CAD	Computer-Aided Design
CANSO	Civil Air Navigation Service Organization
CDA	Continuous Descent Approaches
CDG	Charles De Gaulle
CDO	Continuous Descent Operations
CE	Central Europe

CEATS	Central European Air Traffic Services
CEO	Chief Executive Officer
CFMU	Central Flow Management Unit
CMG	Crisis Management Group
CMIC	Military Interface Standing Committee
CO2	Carbon Dioxide
CONOPS	Concept of Operations
CRD	Comment Response Document
CRS	Computerized Reservation System
DoD	Department of Defense
EACCC	European Aviation Crisis Coordination Cell
EANPG	European Air Navigation Planning Group
EASA	European Aviation Safety Agency
EATMS	European ATM System
ECA	European Cockpit Association
ECAA	European Common Aviation Area
ECAC	European Civil Aviation Conference
ECIP	European Convergence and Implementation Plan
ECJ	European Court of Justice
EDA	European Defence Agency
EEA	European Economic Area
EEC	European Economic Community
ENAC	Italian Civil Aviation Authority
ERA	European Regions Airlines
ESPI	European Space Policy Institute
ETF	Eurocontrol Task Force
EVITA	Crisis Visualization Interactive Tool for AFTCM
FAA	Federal Aviation Administration
FAB	Functional Airspace Block
FABEC	FAB Europe Central
FASID	Facilities and Services Implementation Document
FDPS	Flight Data Processing Systems
FEP	Flight Efficiency Plan
FIR	Flight Information Region
FRY	Federal Republic of Yugoslavia
FYROM	Former Yugoslav Republic of Macedonia
GASP	Global Aviation Safety Plan
GNSS	Global Navigation Satellite System
HF	High Frequency
HLG	High Level Group
IATA	International Air Transport Association
ICANN	Internet Corporation for Assigned Names and Numbers
ICAO	International Civil Aviation Organization
ICB	Industry Consultation Body
IETF	Internet Engineering Task Force

IFATCA	International Federation of Air Traffic Controllers Associations
IP	Internet Protocol
IPCC	Intergovernmental Panel on Climate Change
ISOC	Internet Society
IVATF	International Volcanic Ash Task Forced
LCIP	Local Convergence and Implementation Plan
MBE	Model-Based Enterprise
MoC	Means of Compliance
MUAC	Maastricht Upper Area Control
NASA	National Aeronautics and Space Administration
NATO	North Atlantic Treaty Organization
NEFAB	North European FAB
NGMT	Next Generation Manufacturing Technologies
NMB	Network Management Board
NOP	Network Operations Portal
NSA	National Supervisory Authority
PLM	Poduct Lfe-cycle Mnagement
PRAC	Council and the European Parliament
PRB	Performance Review Body
PRC	Performance Review Commission
QoS	Quality of Service
RM	Resource Management
RNP	Required Navigation Performance
RPA	Remotely Piloted Aircraft
RPAS	Remotely Piloted Aircraft System
SARP	Standards and Recommended Practice
SEAC	SESAR European Airports Consortium
SES	Single European Sky
SESAR	Single European Sky ATM Research
SJU	SESAR Joint Undertaking
SLA	Service Level Agreements
SME	Small and Medium Enterprise
SMS	Safety Management System
SRC	Safety Regulation Commission
SSC	Single Sky Committee
SWIM	System Wide Information Management
TCAS	Traffic Collision Avoidance System
TFEU	Treaty of the Functioning on the European Union
UAS	Unmanned Aerial System
UAV	Unmanned Aerial Vehicles
UGC	User Generated Contents
UNCLOS	UN Convention on the Law of the Sea
VAAC	Volcanic Ash Advisory Centre
VoIP	Voice on Internet Protocol
WG	World Group
WSIS	World Summit on the Information Society

Preface

The International Civil Aviation Organization (ICAO) was formed on 7 December 1944 with the signing of the Convention on International Civil Aviation. From the outset, its mission has been to foster the development of international civil aviation in a 'safe and orderly manner' and to make sure that international air transport services are 'established on the basis of equality of opportunity and operated soundly and economically'.[1]

As the forum for cooperation among its now 190 Member States, ICAO has always provided leadership in the evolution of aviation as a modern, efficient, affordable and safe mode of transport. Today, ICAO further demonstrates its ability to tackle daunting challenges in the areas of safety, security and environmental protection, as well as operational performance and overall sustainability of the global air transport system.

In this wide-ranging collaborative effort, Europe continues to play a determinant role. On the one hand, it provides the aviation community with systems and equipment on the leading edge of technological progress. On the other, its unique political and geographical configuration offers many lessons. Europe is composed of a fragmented patchwork of nations of medium to relatively small size, with many different languages and cultures. It has one of the world's densest airspaces in terms of traffic and related operational requirements. Many capital cities are not more than a few hundred kilometres from each other. The intensity and complexity of the aviation challenges in Europe, and mostly the way they are being addressed, have made the 'old continent' into a kind of laboratory where cross-border and international solutions can be developed and tested. The experience gained can be taken on board at ICAO, for adaptation and adoption in other parts of the world.

1. Preamble of the Convention on International Civil Aviation ('Chicago Convention').

The European Union's Single European Sky (SES) initiative is a prime example. It seeks to fundamentally transform the way air transport is organized and operated in Europe, by putting into place a 'more sustainable and better performing aviation'.[2] With its distinct network and gate-to-gate approaches, it also aims to extend beyond the borders of the EU, in partnership with its many neighbouring countries.

To achieve these results, the European Union's Single Sky legislation explicitly and systematically refers to ICAO's vast body of rules and regulations. Article 1 of Regulation (EC) No. 549/2004 (the so-called 'Framework Regulation'), as amended by Regulation (EC) No. 1070/2009 states:

> The application of this Regulation and of the measures referred to in Article 3[3] shall be without prejudice to the rights and duties of Member States under the 1944 Chicago Convention on International Civil Aviation (the Chicago Convention). In this context, an additional objective of this Regulation is, in the fields it covers, to assist Member States in fulfilling their obligations under the Chicago Convention, by providing a basis for a common interpretation and uniform implementation of its provisions, and by ensuring that these provisions are duly taken into account in this Regulation and in the rules drawn up for its implementation.

ICAO welcomes the SES initiative. It will monitor and, where it can, contribute to the development of the concept.

This is in line with our Organization's policy of encouraging regional approaches to aviation issues which is more likely to reduce fragmentation, improve safety and generate economies of scale. In Europe, these purposes were initiated decades ago with the creation of EUROCONTROL and the Joint Aviation Administrations. The time has come to speed up the process and provide more support to it, given the SES undertaking and the development and implementation of associated concepts: the European-wide performance target setting, cross-border Functional Airspace Blocks, network management functions, SESAR for a pooling of the European R&D, leading to harmonized and synchronized technological choices and EASA entrusting to a single regional entity the responsibility of the entire aviation safety chain.

In this contexts, ICAO and the European Union share common goals. Not surprisingly, there exists a permanent and fruitful interaction between work carried out in Europe and within ICAO.

In the performance area, Europe's input was a key success factor in ICAO Conferences on the Economics of Airports and on Air Navigation Services – ANSConf 2000 of June 2000 and CEANS of September 2008, respectively.

2. Communication from the Commission to the European Parliament, the Council, the European Economic and Social Committee and the Committee of the Regions – Single European Sky II: Towards More Sustainable and Better Performing Aviation {SEC(2008) 2082}
3. I.e. all the Regulations adopted for the creation of the Single European Sky.

This latter event was linked to a 'Worldwide Symposium on Performance of the Air Navigation System', which in turn led to a revision of ICAO Documents 9082 and 9161 aimed at incorporating the performance element in the provision of airport and air navigation services. I am confident that Europe's experience in performance target setting will prove very useful in the development by ICAO of a performance-based ATM system in the coming years.

On the technology side, and with the aim of supporting improvement on a worldwide basis, ICAO hosted in November 2008 the 'Forum on Integration and Harmonization of NextGen and SESAR into the Global ATM Framework', during which various national and regional initiatives were presented. ICAO follows with great interest the developments of SESAR and similar programmes from other regions as useful contributions to the Global ATM concept. It cooperates with Europe and other regions in the preparation of the 12th Air Navigation Conference in November 2012, designed to update the ICAO Global Air Navigation Plan (GANP) and prepare the aviation world for the future ATM system concepts in a globally harmonized manner.

Civil/military coordination and in particular the concept of Flexible Use of Airspace are the key elements of the SES package to improve the use of available airspace and thus generate efficiency gains. The need for strengthened civil/military cooperation and coordination was discussed at ICAO's 36th Session of the Assembly in September 2007. This resulted in the decision to prepare guidance material for identifying best practices and defining steps to support the establishment of national and regional airspace management plans that meet the needs of all civil and military airspace users. A civil/military forum was held at ICAO in 2009 to enhance airspace organizations and management.

The Eyjafjallajökull ash cloud crisis of 2010 generated real-time intensive cooperation between Europe and ICAO aiming at mitigating disruption to air transport. ICAO now works, with valuable input from Europe, on the establishment of tools and standards that will make it possible to tackle the next crises in a more efficient way.

On the institutional side, following the establishment of an office in Montréal to represent the EU at ICAO, the signature of a Memorandum of Cooperation (MoC) between the European Union and ICAO is the next step in intensifying cooperation between the two institutions. This MoC also reflects ICAO's efforts to promote the establishment of regional safety oversight organizations, much like EASA in the European Union. The agreed exchange of safety-related data between ICAO and the EU is another example of fruitful cooperation leading to concrete safety improvements. The MoC also covers security, air traffic management and environmental protection.

At the regional level, the ICAO office for the EURNAT region has an observer seat in the Single Sky Committee, the Comitology body assisting the European Commission in the implementation of the SES. This allows ICAO to ensure that its requirements are taken into consideration and that it stays abreast in real time of SES progress. In return, the European Commission has observer status in the ICAO European Air Navigation Planning Group (EANPG).

With such coordination and cooperation, ICAO and the EU advance hand in hand to ensure a coordinated approach to the main challenges facing an ever evolving aviation world, for the benefit of international civil aviation, and thus for the global economy and the travelling public.

I would like to end this contribution with a personal note. In my previous professional capacity as Executive Secretary of ECAC, I had the honour to meet the late Mrs Loyola de Palacio several times. Apart from her warm personality, I was each time struck by her determination to reach concrete outcomes and bring improvements wherever she focused her attention. For her, this made the creation of a single European sky a formidable, yet logical challenge to take up. This unrelenting focus on tangible results is a great source of motivation for me at the helm of ICAO.

Raymond Benjamin
Secretary General of the International Civil Aviation Organization

PART I
REGULATORY DEVELOPMENTS

Chapter 1

The Single European Sky (SES): 'Building Europe in the Sky'

*Daniel Calleja Crespo** *and Timothy Fenoulhet***

1 AIR TRAFFIC MANAGEMENT IN EUROPE PRE-1999: HIGH FRAGMENTATION

The European Union's (EU) Single Market came into being in 1992. Ten years later, in 2002, EU citizens were for the first time exchanging banknotes and coins in the new single currency, the Euro.

Also for over ten years now, we have been enjoying the benefits of a single market for air transport services. Although not fully achieved in 1992, by 1997 the removal of national barriers for air transport services and establishment of the associated harmonized regulatory framework, leading ultimately to full liberalization, had been achieved.

However, the picture 'on the ground' was not at all reflected in the sky. Indeed air navigation services have traditionally been provided by government departments and today by corporate entities known as 'air navigation service providers' (ANSPs), which enjoy – at least for the core air traffic services – a natural monopoly.

---

* Daniel Calleja Crespo, European Commission, former Head of Cabinet of Loyola De Palacio and Director for Air Transport (2005-February 2011).

** Timothy Fenoulhet, European Commission, Head of EU Liaison Office at Eurocontrol. Any opinions expressed in this chapter only reflect the authors views and do not bind the institution they work for.

Daniel Calleja Crespo & Pablo Mendes de Leon, *Achieving the Single European Sky: Goals and Challenges*, pp. 3–9.

Furthermore, ANSPs are generally responsible for an area which typically coincides with the territory of their Member States and any high seas that may have been entrusted to the State. This nationally based organization of airspace management is sub-optimal on at least two accounts. Firstly, the territory of States may be too small to allow for efficient and cost-effective air traffic management (ATM), and secondly, a territorially based organization does not accommodate easily the actual air traffic flows.

So the overall picture in Europe has been one of high fragmentation. For example, in Europe twenty-nine ANSPs with fifty-eight en route centres are managing a similar geographical area and less than half the traffic volume managed by the U.S. Federal Aviation Administration (FAA) with only twenty-one centres. This goes some way into explaining that the unit cost of the European system is between 60% and 70% higher than in the US. This fragmentation in the European air traffic system is largely to blame for the unacceptable level of delays.

In many ways the initiative to create a 'Single European Sky' can be considered the 'last frontier' in European aviation.

2 THE START OF EU INVOLVEMENT IN AIR TRAFFIC MANAGEMENT: THE FIRST SINGLE EUROPEAN SKY LEGISLATIVE 'PACKAGE'

So even though the EU's air transport policy developed considerably from the 1980s onwards, ATM remained mostly outside the ambit of EU legislation. Efforts to better coordinate air navigation services in Europe had been entrusted to Eurocontrol, an intergovernmental organization based on its own treaty. In 1999, however, this approach started to change. Indeed, it was felt that the pursuit of a Community approach to complement the traditional Eurocontrol activities was necessary to achieve genuine reform of ATM in Europe. The vision, commitment and extraordinary energy of Ms de Palacio, member of the Prodi Commission responsible for transport policy, were undoubtedly instrumental in bringing about these changes. In particular, she argued that its political mandate, effective decision-making and enforcement mechanisms made the Community better-equipped to deliver results than Eurocontrol, which was perceived as being too slow in its decision-making and was being criticized for its inability to transform agreements into actions.

Early on in its term, by the end of 1999, the Commission had obtained endorsement from the EU Transport Ministers on the 'creation of the single European sky', which emphasized the need for structural reforms with a view to integrating management of airspace and developing new concepts and procedures for ATM. To support it in the preparation of concrete policy proposals, the Commission established a high level group composed of senior representatives of civil and military air traffic authorities in the Member States.

By the end of the year 2000, the high level group had completed its report, which emphasized the need to consider airspace as a common resource, managed as a continuum. Progress was necessary on several fronts, including joint civil and military management of air traffic, the development and deployment of new technology and the interoperability of equipment. The group also recommended the involvement of professional and trade union organizations in the Community social dialogue. It confirmed that reform of ATM required the intervention of a strong Community regulator, but expected the Community's involvement to be supported by Eurocontrol's technical expertise.

On this basis, the Commission set about developing its legislative proposals. The regulations, including a framework regulation setting out the principles and working methods to be followed in the Single Sky, and specific regulations on air navigation service provision, airspace, and equipment, were adopted in December 2003 and entered into force in April 2004.

3 THE NEED FOR A NETWORK AND PERFORMANCE-BASED APPROACH: THE HIGH-LEVEL GROUP FOR THE FUTURE EUROPEAN AVIATION REGULATORY FRAMEWORK

The adoption of the first Single European Sky legislation in 2004 was a real breakthrough. The rigorous and binding Community framework gave rise to much progress in harmonizing air navigation service provision. It brought about the establishment of new players, such as corporatized ANSPs and national supervisory authorities. Service provision in the Community became subject to a process of certification. However, two years into the Barroso Commission, it became clear that a truly single sky was still not being achieved. The system remained fragmented. Regional initiatives of service integration ('Functional Airspace Blocks' (FABs)) were diverse in scope and in ambition, and the prospect of a serious 'capacity crunch' was looming in the light of forecast traffic growth. Furthermore, little progress had been achieved in improving cost efficiency. This situation was placing the future competitiveness of the European aviation industry at risk. A highly competitive aviation industry required the best possible infrastructure with the highest level of safety and best possible cost efficiency.

With climate change at the top of the political agenda and aviation identified as one of the fastest-growing emitters, the urgent need to reduce ATM delays and inefficiencies resulting in unnecessary emissions, was also gathering political momentum.

Indeed, the significant role played by the air transport sector in the European economy as a whole, meant that it was also acknowledged that there could be negative consequences for the wider economic, social and environmental goals of the EU, embodied in the 'Lisbon Strategy' objectives.

So it was in response to strong demands from industry, EU Member States and other stakeholders to simplify and increase the effectiveness of the regulatory framework for aviation in Europe that in November 2006, Jacques Barrot, Vice-President of the Commission responsible for transport, appointed the 'High Level

Group for the Future of the European Aviation Regulatory Framework'. Vice-President Barrot asked the High Level Group to present a vision for the development of the aviation regulatory framework with a particular focus on ATM, and to provide a roadmap with practical next steps.

In its report, published in July 2007, the High Level Group came forward with ten recommendations. These included establishing the EU as the driving force in aviation regulation in Europe through a strengthening of the role of the 'Community method' as the sole vehicle to set the regulation agenda for European aviation. The objective would be to use the EU institutional and legal machinery to drive improved performance through regulatory intervention by setting performance targets within overriding safety objectives. This new framework would also introduce economic regulation for ATM services and incentives for ANSPs to achieve objectives at the European (network) level and address the hurdles to implementing FABs. Eurocontrol would be empowered to focus on performing pan-European functions and ATM network design, providing support to regulation for the EU. Responsibility for safety regulatory activities would be transferred to EASA, which would become the single EU instrument for aviation safety covering the entire aviation safety chain including airports and ATM. Finally a more systematic implementation of existing commitments by EU Member States, in particular the defragmentation targeted by the Single European Sky initiative, would be required.

In short, the overriding objective was to overcome the patchwork structure and go for a consolidated air traffic control system offering seamless services across the European network as a whole. The central goal was performance, which could only be achieved by replacing overlapping regulatory structures, a heritage of the past, by one single Community framework. According to this approach, it would be possible to put the genuine needs of aviation stakeholders, including military and general aviation, at the core of the system, ultimately bringing benefits for passengers through lower fares and reduced delays.

4 PLACING PERFORMANCE AT THE HEART OF THE SYSTEM: THE SECOND SINGLE EUROPEAN SKY LEGISLATIVE 'PACKAGE'

So over the five years following the launch of SES I, the situation had changed to a certain extent. While capacity was still a cause for concern, greater emphasis began to be placed on aviation's impact on the environment – and the fuel crisis made airlines focus even more on cost efficiency.

As a response to these demands and inspired by the recommendations of the High Level Group, in 2009 the EU updated the Single European Sky legislation in a'second package'. The reform of the Single European Sky is based on certain key pillars: performance, single safety framework, new technologies and managing capacity on the ground. Of course, all these pillars have an over-arching element which is absolutely crucial: the human factor.

4.1 First Pillar: Regulating Performance

Three measures have been agreed under this pillar:

(1) *Driving the performance of the air traffic control system*: an independent performance review body (PRB) monitors and assesses the performance of the system and proposes Community-wide targets for delays, cost reduction and the shortening of routes. These objectives are then approved by the Commission and passed on to national supervisory authorities who organize consultations to agree binding national and regional objectives.
(2) *Facilitating the integration of service provision*: the aim is to turn the current initiatives for functional airspace blocks into genuine instruments of regional integration to achieve performance targets. These blocks must be created by the end of 2012 at the latest.
(3) *Strengthening the network management function*: this function completes the performance framework and comprises a range of tasks, including European route network design, slot coordination and allocation and management of the deployment of the Single European Sky ATM Research (SESAR) technologies, to be carried out by different actors.

4.2 Second Pillar: A Single Safety Framework

The growth in air traffic, the congestion of air space and aerodromes, as well as the use of new technologies justifies a common approach to the development and application of harmonized regulation in order to improve safety levels in air transport. Following this approach the competence of the European Aviation Safety Agency (EASA) has been extended to include the remaining key safety fields: aerodromes, ATM and air navigation services.

4.3 Third Pillar: Opening the Door to New Technologies

The present air traffic control system is being pushed to its limits, working with obsolescent technologies and suffering from fragmentation. As a consequence, Europe must accelerate the development of its air traffic control system by implementing SESAR in order to increase safety levels and traffic control capacity, and deliver environmental benefits.

4.4 Fourth Pillar: Managing Capacity on the Ground

The European Commission has insisted that investment is necessary to ensure that airport capacity remains aligned with air transport management capacity and to preserve the overall efficiency of the network. Airports will need to be fully integrated into the EU's ATM performance scheme in order to ensure gate-to-gate performance improvements.

The European Commission has set up an Observatory, composed of Member States, relevant authorities and stakeholders, to exchange and monitor data and information on airport capacity as a whole, as well as to provide advice on the development and implementation of EU transport legislation.

4.5 Fifth Pillar: The Human Factor

However, the most important dimension is the human factor. Nothing will be achieved without the commitment and full involvement of the excellent professionals which Europe has in the aviation sector. They will benefit from the SESAR technological developments, but they will also be able to enjoy the freedom derived from the Community license which will allow them to provide services in other Member States in a truly internal market. It is essential to reinforce social dialogue to allow them to fully participate in the process.

5 THE CONTRIBUTION OF EUROCONTROL TO THE SINGLE EUROPEAN SKY

The European Commission is giving the political lead in implementing the Single European Sky and establishing the legal framework, which is binding on the EU Member States; Eurocontrol – widely acknowledged as Europe's principal repository of ATM experience and expertise – is providing the technical support.

A joint founding member, together with the European Commission, of the SESAR Joint Undertaking, Eurocontrol is making an important contribution to the construction of the single sky.

Eurocontrol is involved in the development of those implementing rules which fall within its remit, on the basis of mandates from the European Commission.

It also provides technical support to EASA, the European Aviation Safety Agency, in the area of ATM safety regulations and oversight activities.

Eurocontrol has recently restructured, so as to align itself with the Single European Sky's goals, notably by drawing clear lines between its various functions (separation of regulatory activities from service provision), and by becoming more pro-active in relations with stakeholders and more transparent.

There are now three new directorates in the Agency: Single Sky (which gives regulatory support and oversight); Network Management and SESAR Research.

On 29 July 2010, Eurocontrol was designated by the EU as the Performance Review Body (PRB), which will assist the European Commission in establishing and managing the performance scheme for air navigation services.

It is expected that the European Union will invite Eurocontrol to take on the role of Network Manager. The Network Manager will expedite decision-making and draw up detailed plans for achieving performance objectives – a key feature of the second SES package. The Network Manager will also be responsible for monitoring progress and addressing difficulties, from an operational perspective.

6 CIVIL-MILITARY COOPERATION

Another key issue is to consolidate civil-military cooperation within an effective framework. The Single European Sky fully guarantees this through the military participation in the SES Committee. The military are also fully represented in SESAR and EUROCONTROL. The challenge ahead will be to continue successfully pursuing this process. The commitment of the military and the excellent progress made so far is very encouraging.

7 THE NEXT STEPS

Looking forward to the implementation of the 'SES II' package, therefore, the main milestones will be the realization of a performance-based and network approach to ATM in Europe on a gate-to-gate basis, the establishment and effective operation of the Functional Airspace Blocks (FABs) in 2012, the deployment of SESAR, and the development of a framework defining the relationships between the different European aviation bodies, notably the European Commission, EASA and an institutionally reformed Eurocontrol, taking into account the pan-European dimension of the Single European Sky and the need for civil-military coordination. Last but not least, the human factor remains essential. Effective dialogue and appropriate involvement of the social partners must be ensured within the new framework which SESAR and the FABS will provide.

On the basis of the above objectives, all the necessary elements to deliver the Single European Sky are now in place. The challenge clearly is to successfully implement in a coherent manner the various components of this policy. We are confident that in the coming years, working in very close partnership with the Member States, the other European bodies and all interested parties, Europe shall succeed in bringing down the remaining barriers in the sky. By the end of this decade, we should be celebrating not only twenty years of the single market for air transport services and of the single currency, but also overcoming our last remaining frontier with the achievement of the Single European Sky!

Chapter 2

Single European Sky: The Challenge of Managing Change

Jacqueline Tammenoms Bakker[*]

1 ESTABLISHMENT OF THE HIGH LEVEL GROUP IN 2007

In July 2007 the High Level Group for the Future European Aviation Regulatory Framework presented its recommendations and report to Vice-President Barrot. Vice-President Barrot had asked the High Level Group to present a vision for the development of the aviation regulatory network in Europe – with a particular focus on Air Traffic Management (ATM) – and to provide a roadmap with practical next steps.

At the time it was very clear that the implementation of the High Level group proposals would require a wide ranging and complex change management programme. The purpose of this chapter is to share the experience of building commitment to change within the High Level Group and to offer some thoughts for managing the change process associated with achieving the objectives of the Single European Sky.

* Jacqueline Tammenoms Bakker, Director General Civil Aviation and Freight Transport, Ministry of Transport, The Netherlands 2004–2007; Chairperson, High Level Group, Single European Sky (2007).

Daniel Calleja Crespo & Pablo Mendes de Leon, *Achieving the Single European Sky: Goals and Challenges*, pp. 11–16.

2 SUMMARY OF HIGH LEVEL GROUP RECOMMENDATIONS AND THEIR RELEVANCE TODAY

The High Level Group made ten recommendations:

(1) Strengthen the role of the EU as the driving force in aviation regulation in Europe.
(2) Give greater responsibilities to industry in line with the liberalization of the internal market.
(3) Apply the principles of Better Regulation.
(4) Drive improved performance (including safety) as the core objective of all regulatory interventions.
(5) Accelerate the delivery of the Single European Sky and SESAR, focusing on implementing Functional Airspace Blocks (FABs).
(6) Empower Eurocontrol to play a key role in delivering the Single European Sky and SESAR and focus its activities on pan-European functions and ATM network design.
(7) Address the forthcoming airport capacity crunch.
(8) Deliver continuously improving safety, facilitating the uniform application of 'just culture' principles.
(9) Deliver improvement in the environmental performance of aviation.
(10) Commit the member states to deliver.

Each recommendation was supported by a set of proposed policies and actions. The Roadmap at the end of the document laid out a timetable for change.

Four years later the recommendations are still totally relevant. The economic crisis since 2007 has temporarily reduced the pressure of increasing traffic on airport and ATM systems. However, the opportunity to reduce the costs of inefficient routes and multiple national ATM service providers has become even more important for the competitive position of European aviation. Implementing the Single European Sky remains the single most effective action to reduce the operating costs and environmental emissions of aviation in Europe.

Significant progress has been made towards more efficient ATM systems, infrastructures and organizations in Europe, as is clear from the contributions in this book. Examples are:

- the concrete objectives in the SES II package agreed by Member States in 2008;
- alignment between the objectives of Eurocontrol, the EU Commission and the Member States;
- greater accountability for ATM performance by Member States to the EU;
- increased responsibilities for Eurocontrol to monitor performance and improve network coordination;

- new institutional arrangements for ATM cooperation between states such as the treaty to set up FABEC (Germany, Belgium, France, Luxemburg, The Netherlands and Belgium – 2010);
- more structured dialogue between states, military users, service providers and regulators in various fora as well as new platforms for involving the aviation industry.

The progress to date is very much in line with the conviction of the High Level Group that 'the challenge for Europe is not to embark on new system changes but to focus on accelerating the effective delivery of the existing initiatives and to strengthen the capabilities of the key players to deliver them'.

However, the promise of the Single European Sky remains elusive. The 'volcanic ash' crisis of April 2010 highlighted very clearly the limitations of current decision-making mechanisms in relation to cross-border European ATM.

Significant issues still need to be addressed, many of them centred round the role and responsibilities of individual Member States and the national ATM service providers.

The Member States have to adjust their traditional views of airspace as a primarily national responsibility linked to self-defence. They need to define agreements with military users and neighbouring states to optimize airspace within and across borders. They also need to align the expectations of 'their' (still mostly government owned) ATM service providers.

Key objectives for the ATM service providers are to stimulate cross-border network management, share services to reduce operating costs, address the legitimate concerns of the social partners involved in the potential organizational restructuring, and commit to a coordinated roll out of SESAR systems.

The High Level Group analysed very carefully whether there were any potential 'show stoppers' – related to international law and the Chicago Convention – for the states to move forward in this way, but did not identify any. The key question is one of 'will'. And that is something that follows from *commitment* to shared objectives and *confidence* in the parties involved to deliver their part of the changes required. The commitment to the objectives of the Single European Sky does not appear to be a bottleneck. The challenge is to build the confidence of all the parties involved in the required change programme.

3 BUILDING CONFIDENCE WITHIN THE HIGH LEVEL GROUP

Building confidence within the High Level Group was a real challenge. The journey towards a unanimously supported report may offer some 'lessons learned'.

The High Level Group was composed of the Directors General for Civil Aviation of France, Germany, the Netherlands, the UK and Switzerland (as a non-EU Member State), the Directors General of Eurocontrol and ACI Europe, the Secretary General of CANSO, the Chairman of the Industry Consultation Body and the Director of IATA. The European Commission had observer status during the High Level Group discussions.

Although the members were selected by Vice-President Barrot on the basis of their individual qualifications and not as representatives of specific organizations, the divergence of visions and interests around the table was very clear.

At the outset of the High Level Group discussions there was no shared view on many key issues, for instance:

- the extent to which the EU should intervene in European ATM;
- the role that Eurocontrol should play to support EU ATM ambitions, being an intergovernmental organization with thirty-seven members at that time;
- the degree to which ATM service providers should be subject to market forces;
- how to align EU Member State ambitions with the interests of the broader global and regional aviation community represented in ICAO and ECAC.

However, the High Level Group found common ground in the shared ambition to improve the performance of ATM in Europe. 'Performance' became the touchstone for all ideas. This was also the reason that the High Level Group rapidly decided not to pursue a 'grand design' approach but to build commitment to a set of feasible steps that would contribute rapidly to improved performance.

The process of opinion-forming within the High Level Group was highly structured. Key elements were:

(1) *Identify the key issues that needed to be addressed* and resolve each issue one by one. Each meeting was devoted to addressing a limited number of specific issues so that each meeting could complete a part of the total puzzle. Issues were discussed until agreement was reached. Remaining questions were identified to be resolved at a later meeting.
(2) *Build shared understanding and knowledge.* Stakeholders and experts were invited to brief the High Level Group on specific issues so that members operated from a shared knowledge base. Examples were briefings by social partners, SESAR experts, the military and non-EU Member States.
(3) *Work in teams of two or three* to prepare short papers on the specific issues. These papers were written by the members themselves and ensured the group benefited from the broad range of expertise available.
(4) *Invest significant time early in the process to understand the objectives and concerns* of each member and to define a set of guiding principles that were accepted by all. These were:
   (a) focus on performance, aligning growth, environment, safety and cost objectives;
   (b) improve governance, addressing patchwork of responsibilities and regulatory structures;
   (c) give industry greater responsibilities;

   (d) better engage non-EU states;
   (e) better engage key stakeholders;
   (f) apply the 'Total system approach' to all recommendations to ensure consistency.

(5) *Work with scenarios for different solutions* until such time as the High Level Group could support one direction. This was key to ensuring the richness of debate and keeping everyone committed to the process.
(6) *Actively seek out stakeholders* to secure input to and feedback on emerging conclusions. These conversations were conducted by the Chairman of the High Level Group and at least one member to ensure rapid sharing of information within the group.
(7) *Acknowledge the importance of personal confidence amongst the members.* It was extremely helpful that many members had strong professional relationships with each other, built in other contexts such as EU Transport Councils and working groups, Eurocontrol, ECAC and EASA. Without that starting point, it is doubtful that the appropriate level of confidence in each other could have been developed in the short period of time available. During the period of the High Level Group work, informal 'team' dinners also helped foster the required confidence at a personal level.

Without this process – focused on building common ground while recognizing different interests – it is unlikely that the High Level Group could have produced its recommendations within the time available (November 2006–July 2007).

4 MANAGING CHANGE

The experience of the High Level Group is an example of how the design of the process helped achieve commitment to change. The scope of change facing European ATM is obviously on a completely different scale but that only increases the need to reflect on the design of the change programme at every level of complexity.

The current process can continue productively to prepare the conditions for the Single European Sky. However, in the absence of another crisis such as the 'ash cloud,' it is not obvious at the moment where the 'will' to resolve remaining important issues will come from.

Examples of these issues are new pricing systems for ATM services affecting service providers and airlines, the division of responsibilities between different national service providers at a regional level in a FAB, and redefining the relationship between national service providers and the Member States.

At the heart of these issues lie significant and sometimes diverging social, economic, national and political interests. For instance, the concerns of the social partners involved in the potential restructuring of service providers merit particular attention.

5 MECHANISMS FOR ACHIEVING SES OBJECTIVES

Looking forward to the many challenges outlined in the Single European Sky programme including the deadlines for delivering FABs and important elements of the SESAR project in the period 2012–2014, the following three mechanisms may be helpful to achieve the objectives:

(1) *Visible role for the airlines as the chief beneficiaries of the SES.* ATM costs represent 'only' about 8% of the airlines' costs, but the airlines are the chief beneficiaries of the potential reduction in operating costs and emissions. The airlines also play a crucial role in building political commitment at the national and EU levels to resolve the issues indicated above. In fact, it is hard to see where the 'will' to resolve these issues could come from in the absence of strongly articulated demands from the airlines to deliver the Single European Sky.
(2) *Clarity about the different interests involved.* 'More haste, less speed' will apply to the Single European Sky programme if the interests and concerns of the different stakeholders are not made very transparent. Only then can each issue be filleted to its component parts and can a discussion take place on how to address the concerns. This is particularly important because technical, economic and social issues are interwoven and each aspect needs a different solution. History shows many examples of how breakthrough negotiation results have been achieved by leaders who are both highly articulate about the interests they represent as well as understanding of the interests of others.
(3) *Even the highest mountain is climbed with single steps.* Just as the top of a mountain is often not visible to climbers, so the end result of the Single European Sky is in some ways shrouded in mist. The solutions to many of the issues are not known yet. The key requirement now is to progress step by step, ensuring that each step is a building block for improved ATM performance. Improving performance will build legitimacy and confidence to overcome more complex hurdles in the future. In the absence of a crisis, shortcuts are very unlikely to lead to success in the longer term.

The EU has brought many benefits to aviation passengers in Europe by liberalizing markets, improving safety and security, and protecting consumers. Many of these improvements could be achieved by regulation preceded by appropriate fact-gathering, analysis and dialogue.

The challenge of the Single European Sky is of a different order because of the number of different interests involved. Only by ensuring that these interests are understood and addressed with a high degree of specificity will progress be made. And that will require a very explicit change programme, focused on reinforcing *commitment* and *confidence* at every step.

Chapter 3

FABEC: Structure Follows Performance or Performance Follows Structure?

*Bianca de Wit, Jeroen Fukken, Paul Riemens and Raymond Deleu**

1 INTRODUCTION

Performance improvement in Air Traffic Management (ATM) is necessary to cope with the challenges the air transport sector is facing. Air traffic in Europe is expected to almost double in 2030 as compared to 2009.[1] At the same time the requirements of military air traffic also change with new aircraft flying faster and requiring larger volumes of airspace.

The Single European Sky (SES) II Regulations focus on measures to improve performance. A Functional Airspace Block (FAB) is a crucial tool in this effort. Through the establishment of FAB's airspace design will improve, shortening routes and reducing delays and emissions. Also the efficiency of air navigation service providers (ANSPs) can improve by economies of scale.

---

* Bianca de Wit, Paul Riemens and Raymond Deleu, Air Traffic Control, The Netherlands. Jeroen Fukken, Ministry of Infrastructure and Environment.

1. Eurocontrol long-term forecast flight movements 2010–2030, Statfor Eurocontrol, 2010 (most likely scenario growth to 16.9 million IFR-movements).

Daniel Calleja Crespo & Pablo Mendes de Leon, *Achieving the Single European Sky: Goals and Challenges*, pp. 17–31.

FAB Europe Central (FABEC) is one of the most complex FABs in the core area of Europe. Both States and ANSPs within FABEC are convinced that a new governance model is needed to come to the performance improvements which are required by the SES II package.

This chapter describes in an illustrative way two possible institutional models to reach performance improvements, a (top-down) institutional model and a (more bottom up) performance driven model. These models do not directly refer to the models which are subject to discussion at the moment within FABEC [spring 2011]. This chapter also explores the pros and cons of these two illustrative models and comes to a conclusion. Both the institutional and the performance driven model can evolve towards a single ANSP. The chapter ends with an analysis on how to cope with local and regional interests within a single ANSP.

2 ARRANGEMENTS FOR THE CREATION OF FABs

The Single European Sky (SES) II regulations oblige Member States to establish functional airspace blocks,[2] by 2012. FABs are an essential tool to enhance performance: reduce airspace fragmentation so as to enhance current safety standards and overall efficiency, to optimize the steadily growing capacity requirements of all airspace users (including military) and to minimize delays by managing the traffic more dynamically. These objectives can only be achieved through an increase of the scale of operations, regardless of national borders.

The definition of a FAB, derived from SES regulations, is:

> an airspace block based on operational requirements and established regardless of State boundaries, where the provision of air navigation services and related functions are performance-driven and optimized with a view to introducing, in each functional airspace block, enhanced cooperation among ANSPs or, where appropriate, an integrated provider.

Member States have to ensure that these FABs realize a number of objectives. They have to enable optimal use of airspace, ensure a smooth and flexible transfer of responsibility for air traffic control between air traffic units and ensure compatibility between different airspace configurations also in a broader European context. FABs must prove their added value by making optimal use of technical and human resources, on the basis of cost benefit analyses.[3]

The European Commission has set binding EU-wide targets for EU Member States on the basis of the Performance Scheme regulation for the period

2. Regulation (EC) No. 549/2004 of the European Parliament and of the Council of 10 Mar. 2004 laying down the framework for the creation of the single European sky, as amended by Regulation (EC) No. 1070/2009 which entered into force 4 Dec. 2009.
3. Regulation 550/2004 of the European Parliament and of the Council of 10 Mar. 2004 on the provision of air navigation services in the single European sky (the service provision Regulation) as amended by Regulation (EC) No 1070/2009 which entered into force 4 Dec. 2009.

2012–2014.[4] Targets have been set in the area of environment, airspace capacity and cost efficiency. This is a further stimulus for States and ANSPs participating in each FAB to join their forces to deliver the required performance, for example by improving airspace design and intensifying civil-military cooperation across national borders (Figure 3.1).

3 FAB EUROPE CENTRAL (FABEC)

3.1 DESCRIPTION

Figure 3.1 Airspace of FAB Europe Central

Several FABs throughout Europe are in the process of implementation. One of the more complex FABs is the FAB Europe Central (FABEC) (Figure 3.1), which covers the airspace of six states (Belgium, France, Germany, Luxembourg, the Netherlands and Switzerland) and lies at the heart of Europe. From an ATM

4. Regulation (EU) No. 691/2010 of 29 Jul. 2010 laying down a performance scheme for air navigation services and network functions and amending Regulation (EC) No. 2096/2005 laying down common requirements for the provision of air navigation.

perspective this area is often referred to as the 'core area' of Europe. It encompasses several major European airports, generating dense traffic flows, and accounts for more than half of all European air traffic.

Apart from civil air traffic, the military also make extensive use of the same airspace, which contributes to its overall complexity. Civil and military air traffic routes are closely interlaced and several military training areas are situated within major pan-European air traffic flows. Owing to its size, air traffic volume and central position in Europe, the success of FABEC will be important for the overall success of SES.

The partners within FABEC are not only the six Member States, but also include seven civil and three separate military ANSPs. This often results in complex negotiations among partners with different (national) interests.

The ANSPs all have different legal forms, for example the French ANSP forms part of the Ministry, while the German ANSP is a limited company with the State as shareholder.

Within FABEC, the Member States are responsible for the legal and institutional arrangements, including oversight. The ANSPs are responsible for initiating and implementing studies and projects for performance improvements, for example in the areas of airspace optimization and intensification of civil-military cooperation. A five-year work plan, which describes all activities, is set up each year.

3.2 Arrangements

As a first step the FABEC partners decided to perform a Feasibility Study on the creation of FABEC. This study was finished in 2008 and showed that most benefits could be gained by improvements in the airspace: shortening routes and diminishing delays. Furthermore, efficiency gains were held possible by working closely together in different areas like Communication, Navigation, Surveillance Services (CNS) and Aeronautical Information Services (AIS) and Training (Figure 3.2).

On 18 November 2008 the FABEC Member States signed a Declaration of Intent to jointly build up FABEC. In parallel, the civil ANSPs of FABEC signed a cooperation agreement for the implementation and operation of FABEC.

On 2 December 2010, the six Member States signed the FABEC Treaty relating to the establishment of a FAB. The FABEC Treaty is expected to be ratified by 2012. With this FABEC Treaty, the Member States put a framework in place for the States to cooperate and take decisions for FABEC and for ANSPs to improve their performance. A FABEC Council composed of civil and military representatives with a clearly defined decision-making process will be set up. Based on decisions of the FABEC Council, the Member States will establish the necessary national rules and procedures.

In January 2011, the National Supervisory Authorities (NSAs) of the six FABEC Member States signed a Memorandum of Cooperation. This document covers aspects such as the supervision of ANSPs and the establishment of a FABEC performance management system. As a first step, FABEC States are

Figure 3.2 Cost Benefits of FABEC as Estimated during the Feasibility Study

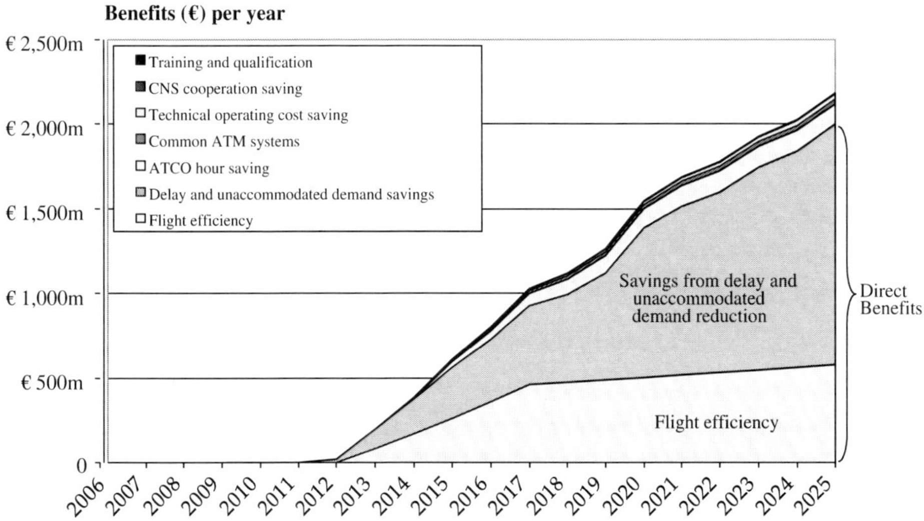

preparing a common FABEC performance plan to assess the concrete targets for the year 2012–2014 set by the European Commission.

3.3 Performance Improvements

Although not formally created yet, FABEC has already achieved some results, increasing capacity, reducing delays and emissions and lowering costs. Examples are:

(1) AMRUFRA: the first major cross border airspace design under the aegis of FABEC in the east of the Netherlands and the west of Germany. Civil air traffic flows to/from Frankfurt and Amsterdam airports have been optimized, balancing civil and military airspace requirements in the Netherlands and Germany.
(2) Night network: a night route network has been implemented. Shorter routes are offered to airlines during the night. This is possible due to the fact that air traffic decreases significantly at night and that military training areas are mostly inactive.
(3) Volcanic ash cloud situation: cooperation within FABEC and growing trust between the partners made it possible in 2010 to find innovative solutions for reopening the airspace for air traffic in the volcanic ash cloud situation.

However, the real performance bottlenecks still have to be tackled to reach the agreed performance targets within FABEC.

4 GOVERNANCE MODELS

All FABEC partners agree that future governance of FABEC is a major underlying enabler to improve FABEC performance and to carry FABEC further. Therefore, the FABEC partners have put the issue of Air Navigation Services (ANS) governance on the agenda.

Two possible governance models are described: a top-down institutional model and a more bottom-up performance driven model. Despite the difference in approach there is a common denominator in both governance models: they both require a common mindset change from 'thinking national' to 'thinking FABEC'. Both models are illustrative and do not refer to models which are subject of discussion.

4.1 Institutional Model: Performance Follows Structure

The first governance model is a top-down institutional model. The concept of this governance model is that a so-called FABEC Entity is created by Treaty by the States. This FABEC Entity will be established in a relatively short time-frame as a single ANSP. Governance control is vested in an accountable FABEC Council in which the States are represented. The States have indirect joint control of the ANSPs via the FABEC Entity.

The FABEC Entity will initially be set up with accountability for a limited set of functions like programme management, performance management, but also for instance some airspace redesign responsibilities. The amount of functions can gradually be expanded. ANSPs are initially represented in the Board of Directors (BoD), the Supervisory Body of the FABEC Entity. Member States, including Military, will also be represented there. This means that Member States will not only be able to direct the results, but also be able to direct the more common process/content (Figure 3.3).

Through the creation of the FABEC Entity, ANSPs will be dissolved evolutionary. This process starts with shifting most of their support functions to *the central organisation* of the FABEC Entity, while Air Traffic Control services will remain in centres. These centres will act as divisions of the FABEC Entity. In this model the first centre to be placed under the FABEC Entity is likely to be Maastricht Upper Area Control (MUAC) Centre that handles traffic in the upper airspace of Belgium, The Netherlands, Luxembourg and part of Germany. Currently MUAC is part of the Eurocontrol organization. An evolutionary consolidation of centres can follow later.

This FABEC Entity will have an executive management which is responsible for conducting day-to-day business. It organizes Air Navigation Services (ANS) functions centrally in a common way. In the end this FABEC Entity will be designated as single ANSP within the FABEC area.

An important aspect of this governance model is that the initial effort is directed at building the structure. The performance improvement can then be achieved from within this new structure. Hence this approach could be characterized as 'performance follows structure'.

Figure 3.3 Institutional Governance Model

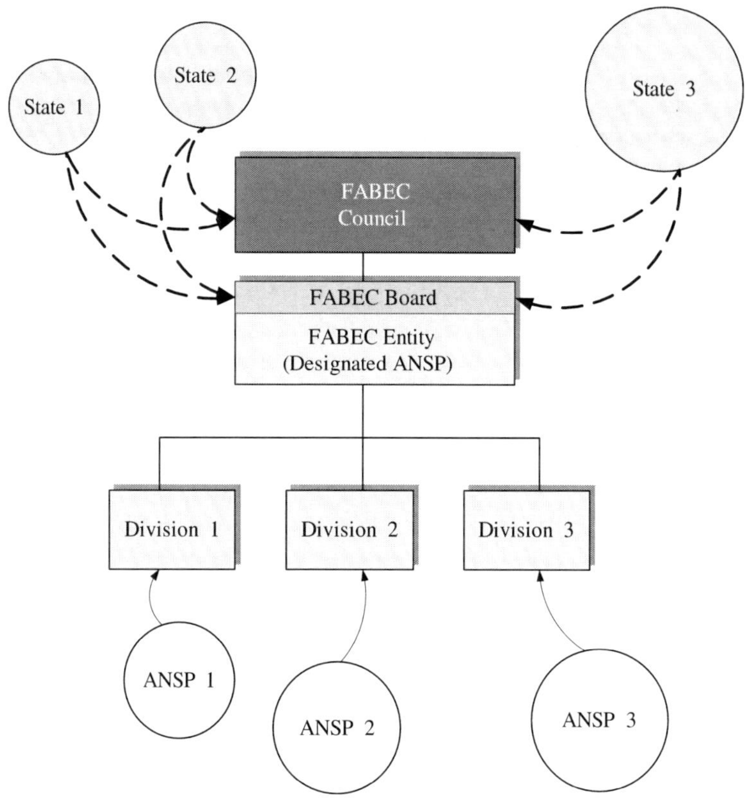

4.2 Performance Driven Model: Structure Follows Performance

The second governance model is a performance driven model. This governance model is characterized by a more organic, bottom-up growth. It is expected to stimulate an entrepreneurial spirit within the ANSPs. Since the ANSPs are experts in Air Navigation Services it makes sense that the ANSPs – and not the Member States – are responsible for finding the required solutions to come to the required performance improvement within FABEC. Various approaches are allowed, for example setting up bilateral or multilateral organizations in different areas, on the basis of cost benefit analyses. In this way the ANSPs have the possibility to come to de-fragmentation.

The governance model will change gradually depending on the choices made to enhance performance. This can best be illustrated by an example (see Figure 3.4). The assumption is that Communication, Navigation and Surveillance (function A) is taken out of the ANSPs and put for instance into a separate company. This Air

Navigation Services Company can then be made responsible for delivering part of the performance improvement within FABEC. The CEO of this company joins the FABEC Board and the decision-making process there. In this way the governance changes step-by-step.

The process to come to joint organisations implies taking small steps in co-operation. Steps that evolve 'naturally', for example from historic bonds or geographic characteristics. From this starting point on joint organizations can further develop; either in number of participants (more ANSPs) or in number of tasks and functions.

FABEC Member States within the FABEC Council are responsible for setting performance targets and in some areas more specific goals for the ANSPs in the FABEC Board. The FABEC ANSPs within the FABEC Board are responsible for finding the required solutions. In implementing these solutions they also need legal and institutional arrangements from the Member States. The FABEC Board will ask the FABEC Council to deliver these arrangements. In this way, performance improvement is achieved through co-makership between the Member States and ANSPs.

Essential element of this performance driven model is that the way the governance structure is organized, is not – at least not in detail – set out in advance. It

Figure 3.4 Performance Driven Governance Model

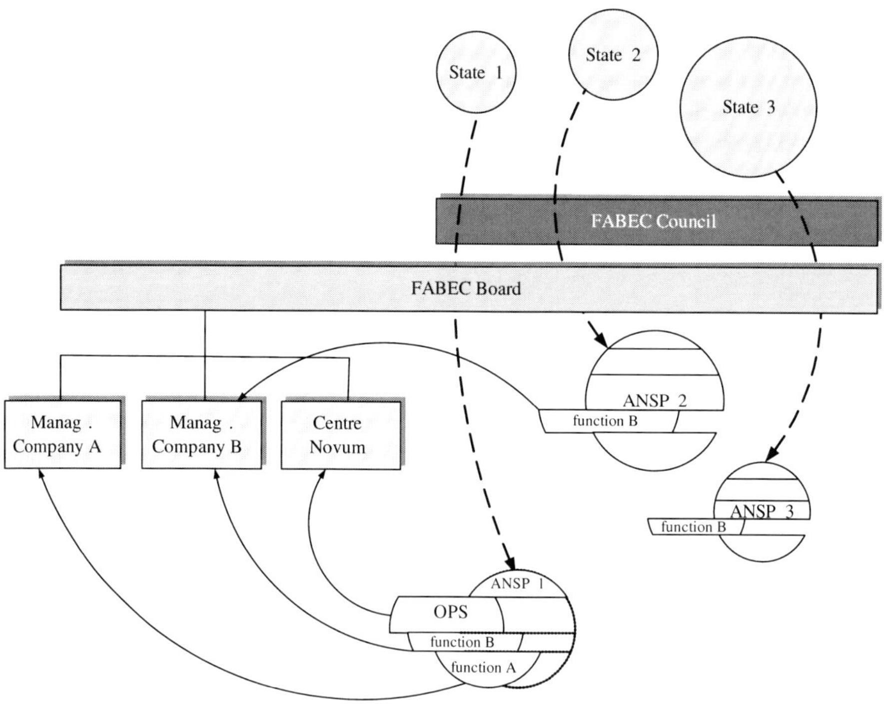

follows the performance strategy; the steps in which the evolutionary performance improvement is reached.

4.3 Examples of the Performance Driven Approach

Two step-by-step examples of creating bilateral or multilateral joint ventures with the performance driven approach are elaborated: Navigation Services and Air Traffic Services.

Within FABEC the performance driven approach can imply gradually setting up bilateral or multilateral joint ventures. In some functions ultimately commercial competition would be possible (but not obligatory). The SES Service Provision Regulation mentions Communication, Navigation, Surveillance (CNS) and Aeronautical Information Services (AIS, provision of aeronautical information and data). Also, common training and/or common training facilities are possibilities.

4.3.1 Navigation Services

While merging navigation services, different questions will pop up in a natural way. Participating parties will have to choose for a certain governance model, deal with European procurement rules and receive a SES-certificate. These are institutional and legal aspects. But also financial questions will be raised: making a cost-benefit analysis, solving fiscal issues. The same is true for challenges in the area of human resources; how can personnel smoothly shift to a (daughter) company and how can parties come to joint labour conditions?

The following steps could be envisaged that can ultimately lead to a commercial operator of navigation infrastructure.

Step 1

Contractual cooperation between two ANSPs is usually the first step in a bilateral cooperation. For instance, one ANSP takes care of training courses for personnel of the other ANSP and/or they arrange contractually to make use of each other's specific tools. This cautious start of cooperation opens the possibility for growing trust from both sides.

Step 2

In a second step the two ANSPs decide to take their alliance to a higher level. They agree on a common vision and strategy in the area of navigation. They establish a so-called management company. Such a management company only delivers navigation services to the two 'mother organizations'. The infrastructure (for instance radars) and most personnel remain within the mother organizations; the management company mainly encompasses the management layer. The management company 'pools' infrastructure and personnel of the mother organizations. It receives the mandate to give instructions to employees of both mother organizations and to optimize the infrastructure. For new tasks the company employs personnel. Mutual trust can grow and personnel can be trained to enable the alliance to take the next step. Other FABEC ANSPs can join the management company. If all ANSPs have joined, the company can fall under the responsibility of the FABEC Board.

Step 3

In step 3 a NAV Company is set up, with personnel and infrastructure. Shareholders are the participating ANSPs. Navigation service provision is still limited to the participating ANSPs. Arrangements about service provision, for instance quality and safety, are laid down in Service Level Agreements (SLAs), which in this way guarantee the service provision. The participating ANSPs can also take a seat in the Supervisory Board and/or appoint the management of the NAV Company.

Step 4

In step 4 the NAV Company is a commercial organization. The NAV Company delivers its services not only to the participating ANSPs, but also on a broader scale to the market. Private commercial companies can take a (minority) share in the NAV Company to stimulate innovation. The level of service provision to the participating ANSPs can still be guaranteed by SLAs and/or by participation in management or Supervisory Board.

The joint delivery of Navigation services can be further expanded with Communication and Surveillance services.

4.3.2 Air Traffic Services

The provision of Air Traffic Services will always remain a public task. Public authorities will need to regulate these services. The provision of Air Traffic Services is not of an economic nature. That is why in most cases it will be one of the last tasks to be taken out of existing ANSPs.

The number of Air Traffic Control (ATC) centres could be consolidated in the medium to long term (centre consolidation). The average size of an ATC centre in Europe, expressed in number of sectors within the centre, falls well below the average centre size in the United States (respectively 16 against 50). In this context efficiency gains are necessary. Moreover, centre consolidation is also a key enabler for airspace design. The two aspects are interconnected and influence one another. The choice of airspace design influences the optimal location for centres and the situation of centres for its part influences the airspace design.

The following approach could be followed to defragment the provision of Air Traffic Services.

Step 1

In step 1 a number of ATC centres are combined under one Joint Operational Officer. An example could be joining the centres of Amsterdam (civil), Nieuw Milligen (military), Bremen (civil), Brussels (civil), Semmerzake (military) en Maastricht (civil-military). This cluster of centres could be joined under one operational officer. In this way more clusters of centres can develop within FABEC. Although the centres within a cluster remain geographically divided, the cooperation will stimulate the thinking across organizations and borders. The centres can adopt each other's best practices and human development, procedure design and technical support could be arranged or purchased centrally if applicable.

Step 2

In the meantime a window of opportunity can occur that could bring the cooperation to a next level. For instance, two or more centres have to replace their systems. In that case the FABEC Board can decide on the basis of a cost-benefit analysis whether it is expedient to build a new centre and/or expand or close one or more existing centres.

In this cost-benefit analysis the following aspects are taken into account:

- safety compliance: will safety remain at the same level or improve?
- support for SES implementation through de-fragmentation and harmonization;
- improvement of operational performance (capacity, flight efficiency and impact on environment through an improved airspace design);
- military compliance: fulfilment of military requirements;
- stakeholder acceptance and ANSP acceptance;
- improvement of financial performance.

5 ASSESSING THE TWO TYPES OF GOVERNANCE MODELS

5.1 Performance Driven Model

In the performance driven model there is a clear division of tasks between the Member States, responsible for oversight and regulation and the ANSPs responsible for performance improvements.

It offers room for entrepreneurial spirit within the ANSPs, it stimulates initiatives, mutual respect, effectiveness and innovation. Entrepreneurial spirit means that ANSPs consider themselves not as monopolistic providers but as a vital and integral part of the value chain with airlines and airports. ANSPs continuously improve their services and lower exploitation costs for the benefit of their customers. By taking small steps to reach performance improvements the new organization can grow in an evolutionary manner. It is likely to expect that this approach delivers results that are durable. Also because the experiences made with the first steps are fed back to the steps that follow.

The performance driven model creates room for the participants to seek for a win-win solution. As it is not required that all actors participate in all joint ventures or cooperations, it may be expected that agreements can be reached in shorter amounts of time than if all partners are needed from the outset.

However, in the performance driven model the participating States have to be prepared to adapt their regulation in a more flexible way to facilitate the defragmentation activities.

5.2 Institutional Model

The described institutional governance model has the advantage that the desired structure is realized almost from the outset. However, the process is paved with numerous challenges in terms of organization models, legislation, governance, human resources management and financial models.

It is essential that consensus is reached on a lot of different subjects. This will be very difficult, as there are many actors, with many different backgrounds and interests. Strong existing beliefs within Member States about the merits of central steering, public and/or private partnership and freedom for ANSPs do not ease realization. It requires enormous steps in merging all ANSPs at once, even changing national laws, and has huge consequences for all parties involved. Inevitably the proposed structure will be unacceptable for some actors. These opponents will try to block the process, hoping for a more acceptable compromise. The fact that so many elements are at stake at once, makes the possibility of having many opponents (for different reasons) almost a certainty. In a situation in which the Member States are in the lead, this is a perfect recipe for long-term political debate (in analogy with the long discussions about the new EU Treaty).

5.3 Comparing the Models: Project and Process Management

An interesting view on the comparison between the institutional and the performance driven governance model can be derived from a (rather quick) comparison between project management and process management (see Table 3.1). The institutional model can best be compared to project management because from the outset the concrete results, targets, approach and structure are defined. The performance driven model has more similarities with process management since the only elements that

Table 3.1 Comparison between Project Management and Process Management

Aspect	*Project Management*	*Process Management*
Core issue	Defining a solution	Defining a process to solve the issue
Activities	Analysing the issue itself, identifying possible solutions	Analysing the actors that should be involved in solving the issue, their interests, goals and relations. Activities are aimed at getting the actors together.
Getting support	By defining a solution that is so attractive that all actors are willing to participate	Actors are allowed to participate in the definition of the solution, resulting in a win-win solution
Solving dynamics	Rapid decision making reduces the influence of changing circumstances	Offering options, so that each actor can adapt the initiative to maintain the attractiveness of the solution
Communication	Aimed at 'announcing and defending' the solution	Aimed at listening and understanding, resulting in decision making

Source: Vrij - Project- versus procesmanagement in PPS-projecten: welke stijl levert het meeste op?; J. Edelenbos, Bestuurskunde, et al., vol. 14 (Radboud Universiteit Nijmegen, 2007 issue 1), 66–79.

are defined at the start are the direction and the performance targets. During the process the results and structures will develop (mostly step by step).

The process management model[5] and the project management model are not mutually exclusive but rather complementary. As long as there is no agreed solution the process management approach can be used to define the solution. Once the solution is clear and agreed, the project management approach can be used to implement it. An analysis of eighteen infrastructure-related projects in the Netherlands by Edelenbos et al.[6] showed that process management in many cases leads to better results.

5.4 Comparing the Models: Concession and Partnership Model

Another interesting way to look at the two governance models is by making a side step towards a comparison between two types of models which are often at stake

5. Procesmanagement. Over procesontwerp en besluitvorming J.A. de Bruijn, E.F. ten Heuvelhof en R.J. in 't Veld (1998) Academic Service, Schoonhoven.
6. J. Edelenbos, E.H. Klijn, M. Kort, M. van Twist Bestuurskunde, 2007 issue 1.

for public private partnerships: the concession model and the partnership model. The institutional model can then be compared to the concession model and the performance driven model to the partnership model. In the concession model, the solution is defined completely by the public partner, which then tenders in a competition to come to a contract with the private partner for implementing the solution. There is a hierarchical client-contractor relationship between the public and the private partner.

In the partnership model the private parties are allowed to participate in the definition of the solution. The partner is selected first, then the solution is defined. The public and private partners' often start a joint venture which then acts as the principal to tender the implementation.

In this case the partnership model is regarded as a better solution. First of all because a concession model fits best in a competitive situation. In this case the 'private' partners are already selected, as the ANSPs are all already appointed by their states. So there is no competition.

Secondly, the 'private' actors in this case possess the expert knowledge needed to define the solution. Apart from raising private investments the introduction of innovations is the main reason for starting public private partnerships.

5.5 Assessment of the Governance Models

The analysis of the performance driven and the institutional model indicate that the performance driven model seems to have some important advantages, because:

- it is based on a clear division of responsibilities between States and ANSPs;
- it stimulates entrepreneurial spirit within ANSPs;
- it is based on a step-by-step approach where lessons can be learned from each step;
- it does not require consensus on the whole structure and all elements from the outset.

Of course the institutional model has some advantages as well. This model supplies more clarity from the start (but it is always the question how long this clarity can sustain). Another reason which favours the institutional model is that the leadership of States in complex playing fields can help overcome market imperfections (but it does not always bring forth the most effective solution).

From the limited analogy of the governance models with project versus process management, it seems that as long as an agreed solution is not available, the performance driven governance model could be preferred. The other illustrative analogy with the concession model versus the partnership model shows that the performance driven model seems to offer better possibilities to gather participants and to find innovative solutions. The institutional model can be risky as long as there is no agreement by all partners on the complete structure and all important underlying elements.

The overall conclusion is therefore that the performance driven model is better suited to bring FABEC forward.

6 TOWARDS A SINGLE ANSP?

Although the processes differ, both in the institutional and in performance driven model the end-point may well be the same: a single ANSP.

In the institutional model the single ANSP is almost the starting point, with a framework that is gradually filled in. In the performance driven model a single ANSP will come into place when in the end state nearly all functions are taken out of the existing ANSPs and an almost empty shell remains.

Of course in both models some questions still need to be resolved. For instance, in both models a solution must be found for the organization of the functions that are important for safeguarding local and regional interests. Examples are negotiations with the surrounding communities of airports about possibilities for noise abatement and finding a possibility for growth of smaller airports within the different countries. If safeguarding these local and regional interests can be firmly rooted within the FABEC organization, a single ANSP is the endpoint. The ANSPs in that case cease existing.

Another solution to cope with these interests could be to divide the airspace into upper and a lower airspace. Responsibility for and control over the lower airspace remains with the Member States and the local ANSP, whereas the upper airspace will be the responsibility of FABEC (of course respecting the sovereignty and including the Member States). In this case the FABEC organization is the single ANSP, but only in the upper airspace.

These types of questions still need thorough analysis and attention before the end-stage: a single ANSP can be reached.

Chapter 4

The ANSP Certification Process

*Guenter Martis**

1 HARMONIZING AIR TRAFFIC MANAGEMENT IN EUROPE

The air transport sector counts several stakeholders, airspace users and airports being the most known ones. There is another important player in this aviation industry which is the air navigation service provider. On behalf of the State or a group of States, this organization keeps control on the air traffic movements and flow both on the ground and in flight within a defined block of airspace.

The United Nations created a specific agency to coordinate and regulate international air travel. The Convention on International Civil Aviation signed in 1944, henceforth also referred to as the Convention, established this specialized agency: the International Civil Aviation Organization (ICAO). The convention lays down the main features of international aviation regulation with regard to airspace, aircraft registration, safety and traffic rights between States.

The Convention defines that every State has complete and exclusive sovereignty over airspace above its territory and has the subsequent obligation to set the appropriate framework for providing safe air traffic services.[1] Each signatory State developed its own legal regime and sometimes notified a difference to Standards

* Guenter Martis, Director General Civil Air Navigation Services Organisation (CANSO).

1. See Art. 28 of the Convention: Art. 28 *Air navigation facilities and standard systems*

Daniel Calleja Crespo & Pablo Mendes de Leon, *Achieving the Single European Sky: Goals and Challenges*, pp. 33–38.

and Recommended Practices (SARPs) drawn up by ICAO and laid down in Annexes to the Convention.[2] This led to a patchwork of national safety legislations.

This was the situation for the Air Traffic Management (ATM) system in European States, at least until 2004. The air navigation service providers in almost all European States were integrated into the organizational structures of the State and reported to the competent Transport Minister. There was no formal separation between the unit providing services and the department ensuring oversight. In order to cope with the European air traffic growth, it was then considered necessary to restructure the ATM which includes air traffic services in Europe.

The Single European Sky (SES) set the scene to coordinate the design, management and regulation of airspace at European level and, in particular, imposed a strict functional separation between the service provider and the oversight authority of a State and also the granting of a certificate by a National Supervisory Authority (NSA) for the provision of the air navigation services.

Several additional regulations had to be introduced to support the SES package of 2004. One key implementing rule was the 2005 regulation laying down the common requirements for the provision of air navigation services.[3] The EU Member States had to reorganize their structure to establish the NSA – ensuring the oversight of the activities of the Air Navigation Service Provider (ANSP) against this set of essential requirements. This regulation requested all ANSPs to hold a certificate issued by their individual NSA by 22 December 2006.

Each contracting State undertakes, so far as it may find practicable, to:

(a) provide, in its territory, airports, radio services, meteorological services and other air navigation facilities to facilitate international air navigation, in accordance with the standards and practices recommended or established from time to time, pursuant to this Convention;
(b) adopt and put into operation the appropriate standard systems of communications procedure, codes, markings, signals, lighting and other operational practices and rules which may be recommended or established from time to time, pursuant to this Convention;
(c) collaborate in international measures to secure the publication of aeronautical maps and charts in accordance with standards which may be recommended or established from time to time, pursuant to this Convention.

2. Pursuant to Art. 38 of the Convention:

> Any State which finds it impracticable to comply in all respects with any such international standard or procedure, or to bring its own regulations or practices into full accord with any international standard or procedure after amendment of the latter, or which deems it necessary to adopt regulations or practices differing in any particular respect from those established by an international standard, shall give immediate notification to the International Civil Aviation Organization of the differences between its own practice and that established by the international standard. In the case of amendments to international standards, any State which does not make the appropriate amendments to its own regulations or practices shall give notice to the Council within sixty days of the adoption of the amendment to the international standard, or indicate the action which it proposes to take.

3. See Commission Regulation (EC) No. 2096/2005 of 20 Dec. 2005 laying down common requirements for the provision of air navigation services.

2 REQUIRED CHANGES

The Common Requirements Regulation brought indubitably changes which forced the European ANSPs and NSAs to adapt their national system in the course of 2005. In order to ease the setting-up of this new mechanism, the European organization for the Safety of Air Navigation – EUROCONTROL – fulfilling its'support-to-regulation' role, developed guidance material assisting NSAs and ANSPs in the context of certification. It provides an overview of the roles and responsibilities of each player (Member State, NSA, ANSP), includes a description of what the certification process should cover and how to assess compliance with the common requirements on the basis of evidence. This document is not binding material but provides guidelines regarding the certification process.

The compulsory functional separation between the service provider and the oversight function within the national State organization and the subsequent creation of a formal national supervisory authority were some of the major changes introduced in the SES Package I. This presented a major challenge for some Member States.

The Common Requirements Regulation foresees the essential parameters of the peer review procedure of the NSAs. The NSAs have been encouraged to exchange information and experiences. This, combined with the EUROCONTROL Guidelines, helped to set the new institutional framework for the oversight function. However, some NSAs are still understaffed today which causes problems for the SES implementation.

In some countries there were procedures to audit the national ANSP that had been well defined before 2004, which helped to enter into the new system imposed by the SES Package I. Nonetheless, being forced to develop a clear safety and quality management system, the ANSPs had to modify their operational and management procedures to comply with the new legal requirements laid down in the Common Requirements Regulation.

3 THE EXAMPLE OF THE SPANISH PROVIDER AENA

For AENA, this led to important adaptations of almost all parts of the company (from an operational/technical/business/human resources point of view and also regarding the management systems, the organizational structure, etc.).

The majority of the required adaptations occurred in the following areas:

- systems of quality management plus operational and physical safety;
- planning/checking/reporting tools and mechanisms;
- organization, dispatch of the roles and responsibilities;
- mechanisms in place for selecting, training and when required, ensuring the supervisory and accreditation of the personnel;
- operations manuals (regarding CNS, AIS and ATS) and working methods;
- financial viability and transparency.

Once having received all details about the inspection and certification process, AENA gathered the required documents providing the evidence of its compliance with the common requirements. The certification process included various supervisory proceeding steps and questionnaires. The Spanish NSA checked the compliance of AENA with the common requirements through a meticulous analysis of the provided documentation and through in-site inspections in order to verify if the service was provided exactly as described in the documentation. AENA was certified within the deadline imposed by the Common Requirements Regulation.

4 THE COMMON PROJECT OF FOUR STATES

One of the ANSPs to be certified in Europe was the Maastricht Upper Area Centre (MUAC) providing air navigation services for the upper airspace of four States: Belgium, Germany, Luxembourg and the Netherlands. These four States decided to develop a common set of rules and measures to demonstrate compliance against the Common Requirements Regulation and ensuring the certification of MUAC, rather than setting parallel national approaches.

The four States set up a working structure for developing these rules to break down the common requirements into various manageable areas including project management, organizational management covering business planning and reporting, liability and insurance coverage, safety management, quality management, human resources management and so forth. This process of the four States was successful and MUAC was certified within the deadline imposed by the Common Requirements Regulation.

5 ADDED-VALUE OF THE CERTIFICATION PROCESS

Whereas the air transport market for the airspace users has been liberalized,[4] a complete liberalization of the ATM sector was hardly possible in particular considering sensitivities pertaining to sovereign competencies. The SES package, however, brought a relative liberalization of the air navigation service provision by stating that 'the issue of certificates shall confer on air navigation service providers the possibility of offering their services to other air navigation service providers, airspace users and airports within the Community'.[5]

In essence, the Common Requirements Regulation is applicable all across the EU. Hence, it provides the guarantee that all certified ANSPs will provide the same quality of service.

4. Pursuant to the 'Third Package' of 1992, and now by EC Regulation 1008/2008.
5. Regulation (EC) No. 550 /2004 of 10 Mar. 2004, on the provision of air navigation services in the Single European Sky, Art. 7; 2 ATCO – Air Traffic Controller.

6 SES AND FURTHER CHANGES

The European institutional ATM situation has been a constant path of change and development since the introduction of the SES Package I.

The second SES legislative package adopted in October 2009 brought additional major changes in the way to deal with the ATM business in Europe.

The amendment to the regulation, which sets common rules in the field of civil safety and the European Aviation Safety Agency (EASA), marked a step in this direction. With the extension of the competence of EASA to ATM/ANS, the common requirements for the ANSPs and the rules on the NSA oversight are under review by the Safety Agency. The new rules replacing the Common Requirements Regulation and the safety oversight regulation are expected to be adopted and published by mid 2011. Even if these new regulations will faithfully reflect the existing SES legislation in terms of requirements for the air navigation service provision and safety oversight, this transposition into the EASA legal system is essential. This will be the basis for EASA to propose further rules. The adoption of these rules by mid-2011 is, therefore, only a first step. The Safety Agency is already working on more detailed requirements. The aviation stakeholders (national civil aviation authorities and the industry, including ANSPs) are consulted and actively contributing to the second stage of the legislative development. EASA created three working groups composed of aviation stakeholders (including CANSO) to help preparing the ATM safety rulemaking with following areas of work:

- Requirements for the ANSPs
- Requirements for the ATCOlicensing
- Requirements for the competent authorities

A fourth group should be set in the coming weeks to deal with the requirements for systems and constituents.

It will take few more months to finalize the whole set of rules.

Requirements for the ANSPs will be reinforced. The ANSP management systems in the future would have to cover other elements than the safety and quality aspects, as defined in the existing version of the Common Requirements. Another example which constitutes a priority for the European Commission is the establishment of a competency scheme for Air Traffic Safety Electronics Personnel.

The certificate is issued for a limited period of time. ANSPs have to renew it on a regular basis. In case an ANSP was not to be granted a certificate, it would not be able to provide services any longer. Up to now this has not happened.

The extension of the EASA remit to ATM/ANS also impacts NSAs. Since 2005, the peer review procedure of the NSAs is the norm (as set in the Common Requirements Regulation). In the future, EASA might be tasked to proceed to the inspections of the NSAs.

These few examples mentioned above illustrate the extent to which the ATM sector has been and still is under deep reform.

7 TOWARDS THE ESTABLISHMENT OF A PERFORMANCE SCHEME

The SES II also brought major changes on the financial aspects of ATM/ANS services. It introduced the performance scheme with an incentive scheme. The performance scheme will force the ANSP to reorganize its structure and business differently. This will have indubitably an impact on the certification process since an ANSP has to demonstrate its financial strength to get a certificate. Until now, the ANSPs have been applying the 'total cost recovery system' which permits them to recover from the unit rate charged to airspace users, any kind of costs they consider necessary to spend to do their business – costs of operations or capital investment costs. The national authority has always been checking the accounting system and reasons justifying the costs. In the total cost recovery system, the ANSPs have also been consulting the airspace users to know their views in particular on the investment planning. This system is, however, not firmly pushing for achieving performance goals and keeping costs under control.

The performance scheme set by the SES Package II will replace the 'total cost recovery system' by a 'determined cost mechanism'. Key performance indicators and targets will be defined for a certain period of time (so-called reference period). ANSPs will have also to determine at the beginning of the reference period, the costs associated to the objectives they will have to achieve. The European Member States will have to endorse the ANSP plans, which will represent a contribution to the performance plans the European Member States will present at European level against European-wide targets. This is a major change in the way to do ATM business.

The certification of the ANSPs is only a part of the SES legislation. The whole SES edifice tackles much more elements: the performance scheme as presented above, the ATM technological (SESAR), the reform of the European Organisation for the Safety of Air Navigation – EUROCONTROL, the establishment of the Functional Airspace Blocks (FABs), the better consideration of the human factor and so forth. All these facets compose the SES project and reflect the unprecedented changing ATM institutional environment occurring in Europe.

The transformation will obviously not happen overnight and will take some more years to complete. Initially the SES was launched to solve delays but the objectives became more ambitious. The transition from the situation before 2004 to the completion of the SES project will cost a lot and, therefore, needs to be well defined before being implemented at full speed.

The CANSO European Regional Office plays a major role as being the European ANSPs focal point for their involvement in all the above described institutional changes. CANSO ensures coordination to prepare the views of the ANSPs and representing them in all important fora and meetings.

Chapter 5
Single European Sky: The Airlines' Perspective

Ulrich Schulte-Strathaus[*]

1 TOWARDS A MORE RATIONALIZED REGIME

The Single European Sky project can trace its origins back to a study produced by the Association of European Airlines in August 1989 entitled 'Towards a Single Air Traffic Control System in Europe'. This study responded to an unprecedented increase in the incidence of delays reported by AEA members in their regular data submissions to the Association's statistical reporting system.

Whilst being supported by a similar exercise subsequently undertaken by IATA, the proposal gathered little official recognition, and indeed encountered strong opposition within the EU Member States, represented by EUROCONTROL, who individually managed their airspaces in an imperfectly coordinated system, commonly characterized as 'fragmented' or 'patchwork'. The airlines' arguments at the time would typically refer to the number of national service providers, of control centres, of hardware suppliers, of operating systems and of programming languages.

The reality dawned that Europe's airway network did not consist of routes between hubs, but rather routes from hubs to border crossing points, which joined end-to-end with routes from the border crossings to other hubs. In the majority of

* Ulrich Schulte-Strathaus, Secretary General, General, Association of European Airlines (AEA).

Daniel Calleja Crespo & Pablo Mendes de Leon, *Achieving the Single European Sky: Goals and Challenges*, pp. 39–43.

cases the handover from one centre to another, of an aircraft travelling at perhaps 600km/h, was conducted by telephone.

The concept of a rationalized system, whilst pursued by the airspace users through the 1990s (during which time AEA coined the slogan 'A Single Sky for Europe'), did not achieve solid political support until Romano Prodi assumed the Presidency of the European Commission in 1999, and promoted ATM reform as a key priority, as a project with a truly pan-European dimension which offered tangible consumer benefits.

Consequently, we may reasonably ask, more than eleven years later, why we are still awaiting the implementation of the Single Sky and the realization of its well-documented benefits. Again, the timeline is well-enough known. In 2004, we had the first package of regulations which provided the legislative framework for the project but delivered very little in terms of onward momentum, requiring a second package (SES II) which entered into force at the end of 2009 – twenty years after the initial AEA proposal.

2 BENEFITS FOR AIRLINES

What are the benefits which the airline community hopes to realize through SES? In the first place, a reduction in cost. According to EUROCONTROL studies, the inefficiencies inherent in the current system amount to approximately EUR 5 billion annually. Part of this can be attributed to the inflated operating cost of the fragmented system, part to the delay it generates, and part to the sub-optimal routings which aircraft are obliged to follow, avoiding military zones, avoiding congestion choke points, or simply following a disjointed route map.

This last shortcoming of the current system highlights another headache for the airlines; unnecessary flying means unnecessary fuel burn. Unnecessary fuel burn means additional greenhouse-gas emissions. It is estimated that a fully functioning Single Sky could reduce European airlines' carbon footprint by 12%.

This is particularly significant, as the airlines gear up for the inclusion of aviation into the EU Emissions Trading Scheme. From 2012, carbon credits will become a scarce and valuable resource; it will be a bitter pill for the airlines to swallow, that they will be using up a significant proportion of their credits flying circuitous routings or sub-optimal flight profiles.

The delay inherent within the present system evidently jeopardizes the integrity of airline scheduling and obliges major carriers to have spare aircraft standing by to cover for service disruptions – a very expensive option. Delay also affects passengers directly, not only in terms of frustration and apprehension, but materially by affecting travel decisions – taking an earlier flight to ensure a connection is made, even travelling the evening before an urgent appointment, just to be sure of making it.

It is also a feature of the complexity of the current system, and its sensitivity to disturbance, that short delays can very quickly become long ones, if a'slot' is missed. Recent rulings in the field of passenger rights have opened the spectre of compensatory payments for long delays which could amount to a quarter of a million Euro for a fully booked intercontinental flight.

3 THE ESTABLISHMENT OF FABs

The process of tackling fragmentation has already begun, with the creation of the nine Functional Airspace Blocks which will overlay the thirty-one national airspaces covered by the Single Sky. I suppose the first thing one notices about the 'new' map of European airspace is that the FABs continue to be delineated by national boundaries, and as such their functionality is constrained. There has been no concession to the principle of designing the FABs around the major traffic flows, although evidently the number of 'handovers at the frontier' will be very much reduced.

Of course, we expect the FABs to work more closely together in rationalizing the airway network, and can expect airspace design within each FAB to be substantially enhanced. But such improvements need to be driven by targets, and the targets need to be ambitious, and enforceable.

We have seen, in the latter half of 2010, the first machinations of the target-setting process, and the signs were less than wholly encouraging. For the three years 2012–2014, cost efficiency improvements of 3.5% annually, over the whole Single Sky, were proposed. While these targets are relatively modest, they still proved hard to swallow by the participating States, who initially rejected them before, with some reluctance, agreeing to accept them under strong pressure from the European Commission.

But that was just a preliminary phase to establish system-wide goals. The next stage will be to refine targets down to the level of individual FABs, and individual States within FABs, and at this point the determination to make the system work will be more severely tested. It goes without saying that the more inefficient components of the system will be where the most challenging targets are aimed, and the exercise will be an indicator of the FABs' ability to govern their internal affairs.

4 THE POSITION OF ANSPs

Modest improvements or not, the mandated efficiency improvements will provide the airspace users with the first tangible financial benefits of the Single Sky as they see unit rates – the charging basis for navigation services – begin heading downward from 2012. It will also mean an end to the detested cost-recovery model, whereby Air Navigation Service Providers have been protected from economic reality by the ability to recover all costs, including any accumulated under-recovery, through the price mechanism. Up to now, ANSPs have not been able to make either a profit or a loss, but they have had the certainty that any extravagance on their part would be funded by their customers. In future, efficient ANSPs will be rewarded with the ability to generate a surplus.

It should not come as a surprise that resistance to the Single European Sky has manifested itself amongst the air traffic controller community. It is inevitable that those employed in any sector which is recognized as inefficient, and is tasked with eliminating inefficiency, will feel threatened. It is true that a fully functioning Single Sky will allow controllers to be more productive, as the workload involved in handling an individual aircraft from one point to another on the network will be reduced. This does not necessarily mean fewer controllers – air transport is a growth sector – but it should mean that the intensity of work in what has always been a high-stress occupation will be diminished.

5 FLEXIBLE USE OF AIRSPACE

When speaking of the Single Sky programme, the topic of civil/military cooperation will inevitably arise. Civil users cannot claim unrestricted privileges in European airspace; military aviation has, and will continue to have, a need to access airspace sufficient to meet its operational and training needs. Flexibility is a priority, and of course integrating two very different kinds of aerial activity places an additional priority on safety.

The key concept here is 'flexible use of airspace', and without prejudice to the needs of military aviation, most of the potential to achieve flexibility lies on the military side. Do military zones need to be situated where they are? If they encroach upon civilian flows, are there some times when their use is less appropriate than others? Whatever the outcome, it is certainly true that a greater degree of cooperation and coordination is achievable under the FAB structure of the Single Sky than under the fragmented system.

6 THE ROLE OF SESAR

Looking beyond the structural reorganization of European airspace, the FABs and the performance targets, brings us to SESAR, the technological component of the Single Sky, the electronical wizardry which will allow aircraft to make use of the potential of the upgraded airspace, the increased capacity and flexibility.

SESAR stands for the Single European Sky ATM Research programme, although I think this is a case of the title being tailored to fit the acronym. In fact the programme was originally called SESAME, which was a very good name, with its echoes of opening doors into unimagined treasure-houses, but unfortunately it was found that another project had prior claim to the name. So SESAR it became.

No matter. What is important is the substance, and having undergone a four-year Definition Phase, the project is currently just over halfway through the Development Phase, with implementation scheduled to begin from 2014.

The project is enormous and, as may be imagined, big-budget. For the airlines there will be the long-term benefits associated with the successful realization of the

Single Sky potential, and indeed without SESAR the Single Sky would have only a limited effect.

There is a problem, however. SESAR will require a complete new set of installed technologies, on the ground and on-board aircraft. Since aircraft flying in proximity will be in automatic communication with each other, a prerequisite for the effectiveness of the new equipment is that everybody has it. It is not enough that it is installed on new-built aircraft and comes on-stream in a gradual process, it needs to be retro-fitted to the existing fleets, at a cost in excess of EUR 1 million per aircraft.

Investment on this scale is, frankly speaking, beyond the capability of the airlines in today's – or tomorrow's – business climate. SESAR is a European technology project supporting a European infrastructure project, with benefits for citizens, businesses and the environment. It is an ideal candidate for public funding. Without support, SESAR could fail and the Single European Sky be severely compromised.

7 SAFETY

It would be negligent to discuss Air traffic Management and the Single Sky without a proper reference to safety. After all, that is the primary role of air traffic management. When we speak of the inefficiencies inherent in the current system, we do not refer to concerns of safety; Europe's exemplary record speaks for itself. And yet, we expect the Single Sky to deliver a further step-change in safety, accounted for within the target-setting system. A combination of a strong and effective safety regulator, in the shape of the European Aviation Safety Agency, a robust and capable technology base, as delivered by SESAR, and a controller community which functions in a lower-stress working environment will, I confidently hope, maintain Europe's pre-eminent position in the air safety league.

Chapter 6

Enforcement Measures, the Tasks of National Supervisory Authorities*

*Isabel Maestre**

1 INTRODUCTION

According to Article 2 of the Regulation (EC) 550/2004 of the European Parliament and of the Council, of 10 March 2004, modified by the Regulation (CE) 1070/2009:

> The national supervisory authorities shall ensure the appropriate supervision of the application of the Regulation, in particular with regard to the safe and efficient operation air navigation service providers....

Law enforcement, after inspections and oversight tasks have been conducted, will depend on the size of the Air Navigation Service Provider (ANSP) and the separation between the regulator and service provider. Hence, each government of an EU State has two tasks: rule-making and oversight. The authorities of EU States have come up with different approaches to this duality.

The mission of the regulator has been assumed by either a governmental department or a public entity dependent on the government. On the other hand, oversight tasks have been attributed to NSA authorities, pursuant to the provisions of the Single European Sky (SES).

---

* Isabel Maestre, Agencia Estatal de Seguridada Aérea (AESA).

Daniel Calleja Crespo & Pablo Mendes de Leon, *Achieving the Single European Sky: Goals and Challenges*, pp. 45–49.

2 ANSPs Influence

As for the ANSP's functions, there is an unclear line between its role as service provider and as regulator. In fact, they sometimes converge. ANSPs as service providers may handle their own budgets; it makes the difference.

Despite the fact the ANSPs form a larger organization and ANSP staff is often better paid than National Supervisory Authority (NSA) staff, they, are also more skilled and have more expertise than NSA staff as they are operating the system on a day-to-day basis The credibility of the NSA inspectors and hence, the acceptance of the findings and corrective actions, would be improved when better qualified NSA staff could be considered, consequently, enforcement would be easier.

The ANSP size and the importance of the service which is provided are other relevant factors. The more relevant these two factors are, the more difficultie the ANSP has to implement corrective actions, because they are bound to affect its capabilities and facilities, leading to higher costs. Smaller service providers are more flexible and easier to adapt, hence, they can accept and implement faster corrective actions.

3 STRATEGIC LAW ENFORCEMENT

Although the NSA has legal and enforcement powers, including the prosecution and punishment of ANSPs, it is deemed more valuable to establishing a good working relationship between them. NSA and ANSP should try to reach an agreement rather than the NSA using its 'authority'.

The strategic question of how to use this authority is an important and not always an easy issue. Continuity of the services is another important goal that people sometimes tend to rank higher. The NSA staff is often in a dilemma. They have to assess the effect of their decisions and actions on safety, bearing in mind that it is easy to endanger the continuity of the service

Communication is considered one of the most powerful tools to achieve an appropriate relationship between NSA and ANSP. Here are some communication techniques which may be used:

- Guidelines for NSA and ANSP staff setting out the process of how to conduct the inspections and how to meet legal requirements will help to achieve the appropriate communications, and, therefore, the working relationship that will prevent the NSA from enforcing via prosecuting and punishing. However, as a father with his songs, there must be always a 'distance' to avoid that the 'friendship' could jeopardize the independence and objectivity of the NSA.
- As different areas of activities of NSAs and ANSPs are involved in the oversight process, and therefore involve many departments of both entities, the communications need a clear flow of information laid down in agreements, also identifying the representatives from the two organizations. This will prevent errors and misunderstandings.

- Frequent meetings between the two organizations will also help to coordinate oversight aspects, from the annual planning to the proposal to the acceptance of corrective actions.

In case of several service providers, it is difficult to organize the supervision activities of the NSAs, who must review every requirement during inspections. The Safety Management System (SMS) is a key element of a service provider certification. Assessing the ANSP, SMS could be done in specific inspections or through particular studies. Overseeing the SMS can be managed by focusing on the risk assessment, which is an essential part of the safety degree of the service provision and on the Notifications System.

Focusing on the SMS is a preventive measure rather than a corrective one. Detecting SMS weaknesses gives the NSA the possibility to make the appropriate arrangements with the ANSP in order to correct deviations that could cause future incidents.

4 ENFORCEMENT IN A MULTINATIONAL CONTEXT

As to enforcement, and in particular enforcement of the Air Navigation Service Providers, Regulation (EC) No 549/2004 provides the following:

> 'air navigation services' means air traffic services; communication, navigation and surveillance services; meteorological services for air navigation; and aeronautical information services;

We are in a transitional period proceeding from the present situation where the ANSPs are giving the service in the same State that has issued the certificate, to a new environment where the ANSPs will be giving the service in a State that is not the one that has issued the certificate.

In the new context, that is foreseen by the SES legislation, arrangements will be needed between the two NSAs, that is, the one that issued the certification and the one where the service is provided. This new approach must be implemented in the coming years in specific documents but it is not a simple track. The first cases will probably pave the way for the following questions. Which part of the certified system is associated with one NSA, and which one is associated with the other? Which are the limits of the enforcement measures of the issuing NSA, and which are the ones of the NSA where the service is?

If these questions have been correctly answered, further thought has to be given to these questions taking into account the continuity of the service according to SES:

> If a national supervisory authority finds that the holder of a certificate no longer satisfies such requirements or conditions, it shall take appropriate measures while ensuring continuity of services.

This is a complex subject, especially in the context of enforcement measures adopted by an NSA affecting service continuity in another State. In such cases, letters of agreement between the two NSA are obviously needed.

5 THE NATIONAL LEGAL CONTEXT

The ANSP is entitled to appeal the decision taken by the NSA to other legal entities. The NSA should reassess the proposals from the ANSP. This is also a quality management system tool. If there are too many questions regarding the inspection reports, something must be done.

A legal national framework must provide for the settlement of cases for which no agreement is possible. National Decrees or equivalent rules are needed for solving such disagreements before they are taken to court, while taking into account the objective pertaining to the continuity of the service. The NSA should balance the safety concerns and the continuity of the service with a minimum safety service level.

The National Decrees should lay down the responsibilities and the penalties of aeronautical personnel in, accordance with the degree to which the alleged conduct affected safety.

Since the ongoing supervision of the certified ANSPs is more or less stabilized, we may be facing a dilemma since there is no automatically fine for non-compliance with the regulations for certification that are drawn up in the inspection reports: Is this a matter of consultancy, internal audits or NSA audits to resolve? What would we think if the police stops our car and gives us a report saying what we have done wrong and asking for corrective actions without having given us a fine in Euros?

6 UNIT TRAINING PLANS

Unit Training Plans play an important role in the relation between ANSP's and NSA's relation. Directive 2006/23/EC defines a Unit Training Plan as:

> an approved plan detailing the processes and timing required to allow the unit procedures to be applied to the local area under the supervision of an on-the-job-instructor.

EUROCONTROL Guidelines for the development of Unit Training Plans provides the following definitions:

- Unit Training Plans: 'a Training Plan for the Unit Training Phase'.
- Unit Training: 'as training comprising transitional training, pre-on-the-job training and OJT which results in a learner obtaining an air traffic control (ATC) license with appropriate rating and with appropriate rating endorsement and unit endorsement'.
- Training Plan: 'a plan which specifies how an entity will provide training to fill as identifies training gap. It include syllabi, training events, timing, staff responsibilities and assessment mechanisms'.

NSAs are assigned a variety of tasks which include the provision of approval of training courses, Unit Training Plans and unit competence schemes. The role of NSAs in terms of law enforcement needs to be addressed in this context.

The process of Unit Training Plans' approval requires the following:

- Proper coordination with ANSPs
- Continuous feedback on both sides
- Mutual understanding
- Reciprocal trust
- Clearly coordinated procedures.

Although law enforcement is on the NSA side while national authorities may impose criteria for this, we cannot ignore that ANSPs hold a great deal of experience in terms of air service provision, and accumulate many hours of air traffic control in different scenarios. Drafting Unit Training Plans is, therefore, a process which demands common sense and to some extent confidence with respect to the work of ANSPs.

The above does not imply that ANSPs may work at their own discretion without being subject to control. It only highlights the necessity of looking for channels providing coordination.

Once the proper channels have been set, the line must keep a permanent flow of messages and constant feedback. A given NSA approving procedures for the drafting of Unit Training Plans without relying on the ANSP's expertise will be deemed to failure. Therefore, ANSP's experience in operational units needs to be considered by the NSA when approving Unit Training Plans.

The mentioned procedure does not promote ANSP's freedom of movement while considering the NSA as a mere observer; it only underlines the need for cooperation. What is more, NSA's role in the approval process of Unit Training Plans is crucial to enhance safety, and security based on uniform and client-oriented plans.

NSA's role to promote safety must be reinforced by creating procedures which are flexible enough for each unit while accommodating safety standards.

Finally, as mentioned above, the size of ANSP's and NSA's staff will modulate the result of the equation resulting in the development of Unit Training Plans. At the same time regardless of such variable factors the result should prove as productive.

Chapter 7

The Liability of Air Navigation Services Providers: Some Lessons from the Single European Sky

*Francis Schubert**

1 INTRODUCTION

There is presently no global or regional convention, ruling the liability of Air Navigation Service Providers (ANSPs). With some rare exceptions,[1] the liability of these organizations is governed by the provisions of national laws, which have usually offered a satisfactory framework. In the light of that observation, International Civil Aviation Organization (ICAO) has consistently concluded to the absence of any need for an international convention on the liability of air traffic control agencies, comparable to the Montreal Convention of 1999 for the Unification of Certain Rules for International Carriage by Air, ever since it was confronted with the subject in the early 1960s.

---

* Dr Francis Schubert is Chief Corporate Officer for skyguide, Swiss Air Navigation Services Ltd, in Geneva. He is also Adjunct Professor at the Institute of Air & Space Law of McGill University in Montreal and Lecturer at the Faculty of Law of the University of Lausanne.

1. The exceptions relate to the few ANSPs such as ASECNA COCESNA and the EUROCONTROL MUAC, which have been established in the form of international organizations to serve specific regional needs. The constituting arrangements of these entities contain provisions regarding their liability, but also often refer to relevant rules of the national laws of the participating States.

Daniel Calleja Crespo & Pablo Mendes de Leon, *Achieving the Single European Sky: Goals and Challenges*, pp. 51–63.

The overwhelming majority of Air Navigation Services (ANS) liability cases, however, relate to damages occurring over the territory of the State from where the service provider involved is established. But, the few existing examples of accidents involving a cross-border service provision dimension show that such occurrences raise complex legal problems which can hardly be resolved through the application of domestic legislations alone.[2] Cross-border service provision still remains a practice of limited numerical and geographical magnitude, since States have historically organized the provision of ANS within the boundaries of their sovereign airspace. But planned developments, both at global and regional levels, are expected to significantly increase the number and scope of such situations.

In particular, a departure from the traditional alignment of the limits of air traffic control sectors on political borders is an essential success factor of the Single European Sky (SES) initiative. In effect, the implementation of the SES is based on the creation of Functional Airspace Blocks (FABs):

> established regardless of State boundaries, where the provision of air navigation services and related functions are performance-driven and optimised with a view to introducing, in each functional airspace block, enhanced cooperation among air navigation service providers or, where appropriate, an integrated provider.[3]

This chapter addresses the need for appropriate arrangements to govern the liability of ANSPs in the Single European Sky, in the light of the increasing risk of occurrences involving a cross-border service provision element. It draws in particular on the legal research which supported the drafting of the State Treaty for the FAB Europe Central (FABEC).

2 THE LIABILITY OF ANS PROVIDERS

In spite of the diversity of applicable domestic liability laws, the national legislations that govern the liability of ANSPs in Europe show a significant amount of commonality.

First, ANS qualify as a sovereign function in a vast majority of countries. States derive the sovereign status of ANS from their obligations under Article 28 of the Chicago Convention as well as from the eminent public service character of this activity, especially from a public safety perspective. The sovereign status of ANS

2. The complexity of the concrete legal challenges raised by such situations was highlighted in the aftermath of the midair collision over Ueberlingen, Germany, on 1 Jul. 2002.
3. Regulation (EC) No. 549/2004 of the European Parliament and of the Council of 10 Mar. 2004 laying down the framework for the creation of the Single European Sky [hereinafter, the Framework Regulation], Art. 2, Definitions, such as amended by Regulation1070/2009 of the European Parliament and of the Council of 21 October 2009 amending Regulations (EC) No. 549/2004, (EC) No. 550/2004, (EC) No. 551/2004 and (EC) No. 552/2004 in order to improve the performance and sustainability of the European aviation system [hereinafter Regulation (EC) No. 1070/2009].

is also reflected in the organizational models put in place by States for the purpose of establishing ANS. Although the SES Regulations require that the regulatory function be separated from the service provision function,[4] some States still directly provide ANS through a governmental agency. Most European States, however, have established public or private corporations, of which they retain full or a majority ownership.[5] In one case, four States have created a common service provider in the form of a public intergovernmental agency.[6]

Second, no European State currently claims either sovereign immunity or immunity of jurisdiction for damages caused by their air traffic control agencies. All European States accept the principle of being accountable for damages caused by a failure of their ANS and formal legal channels have been established under their domestic laws to allow claimants to present their case in court. The liability of ANS is usually subject to a fault-based regime[7] and the liability is unlimited. This implies that, regardless of the perceived adequacy of the arrangements in place, there is presently no vacuum to be filled in Europe as far as the existence of legal means to raise liability claims is concerned.

Another common feature of European ANS liability regimes is that, irrespective of the legal status of the service provider, the liability remains, ultimately, a State liability.[8] The sovereign qualification of ANS is directly reflected in the regime that applies to the entities in charge of their provision. In those countries where the State provides ANS[9] through a governmental agency, the liability of this entity is governed by the same rules as those that apply to the liability of the State itself.

ANS liability in States where the responsibility for service provision has been entrusted to autonomous entities, is inspired by two different legal doctrines which emphasize different aspects of the ANS activity. The *primary State liability* doctrine focuses on the sovereign character of ANS. In the States which follow this approach, the State remains primarily liable for the reparation of damages caused by the provider.[10] The State may retain the right to seek reimbursement for any compensation paid, from the effective service provider. The *effective service provider* doctrine reflects the practical and functional nature of ANS operations. In the States which have adopted this approach, the autonomous service provider is

4. Framework Regulation, Art. 4.2, such as amended by Regulation (EC) No. 1070/2009.
5. NATS (UK) is currently the only case of privatized provider in Europe.
6. The Maastricht Upper Air Traffic Control Center (MUAC) is in charge of providing services in the upper airspace of Belgium, Luxembourg, the Netherlands and a part of German airspace. It is operated by EUROCONTROL.
7. The only exception appears to be Switzerland, where a regime of strict liability is applied to the State, and consequently to the service provider.
8. The only exception is the United Kingdom, where ANS have been technically privatized. In that country, the service provider is subject to the same liability rules as any ordinary private company. The State has no legal duty to compensate damages that would exceed the financial capacity of the provider. Outside of Europe, the situation is the same in Canada.
9. For example, France.
10. The doctrine of the primary liability of the State is applied for instance in Germany and in Austria.

primarily liable for any damage caused, but the State retains a subsidiary obligation to compensate any damage that exceeds the insurance coverage or financial capacity of the service provider.[11]

Finally, the national regimes applicable to ANS liability offer little discretion for the claimants regarding the selection of a competent jurisdiction. The possibilities for practices such as forum shopping offered by the liability regimes applicable to other actors in the air transportation system, in particular the Montreal Convention, are normally not available for claims brought against an ANS agency. Because of the sovereign status of the activity, all claims must be brought exclusively to the courts of the State over the territory of which the accident occurred, which will decide the case under the terms of that State's liability law. When an ANSP is involved, claims against different defendants can often not be merged into a single case and need to be submitted to different courts, sometimes in different countries.

3 CROSS-BORDER SERVICE PROVISION AND ANS LIABILITY

Whereas the existing national liability regimes offer a satisfactory framework to address claims related to events occurring over the territory of the State from where the ANSP is operating, cases involving a cross-border element raise complex legal issues which cannot always be solved in a satisfactorily manner through the application of national legislations alone. Cross-border service provision is defined as a situation where an ANSP located on the territory of one State, provides services across the national boundary of that State, into the sovereign airspace of the neighbouring country.

Liability cases involving cross-border service provision raise concrete difficulties for both the claimants and the States concerned. From a victim's perspective, the issues relate first to possibility of negative or positive conflicts of laws and jurisdictions. In the absence of clear resolution rules, agreed between the various States involved, the determination of the competent courts and applicable law may significantly prolong the duration of litigation, putting the principle of prompt compensation at risk. In addition, the lack of clear resolution rules jeopardizes legal certainty. Then, cases of cross-border service provision may also raise problematic issues for the States themselves. Because of the direct or indirect public status of service providers, a foreign ANSP may be tempted to oppose sovereign jurisdiction to escape litigation in front of the courts of the territorial State. Appropriate safeguards may need to be formalized. Then, under the terms of its own national laws, a State may be compelled to compensate damages occurring over its territory because of a failure of a foreign ANSP, but, in the absence of adequate arrangements, it may be deprived of any legal

11. The doctrine of the subsidiary liability of the State is applied, for instance, in Switzerland.

mechanism to successfully recover the amounts paid to compensate the damages, from the foreign ANSP concerned.

A deeper analysis, however, points out that the difficulties associated with liability cases involving cross-border service provision often derive more from flaws in the arrangements supporting a particular instance of cross-border service provision than from limitations in the respective domestic legislation of the concerned countries. For example, the legal debate to determine the competence of either the German or the Swiss courts in the case of the midair collision over Ueberlingen on 1 July 2002 was primarily focused on the legality of the agreements upon which the Swiss service provider was operating over parts of the German territory. In effect, in practice, existing cross-border service provision agreements have often been concluded directly between service providers without the formal involvement of their parent States. They have remained essentially of operational and technical nature and have rarely addressed legal aspects such as liability considerations.

The liability regime applicable to situations of cross-border service provision is consequently closely linked to the legal validity and contents of the institutional arrangements supporting each particular instance. Until the advent of the SES, most cases of cross-border service provision took the form of 'delegations of the responsibility to provide Air Traffic Services' or 'ATS delegations'. ATS delegations are agreed at State level, in accordance with Annex 11 to the Chicago Convention which specifies that 'a State may delegate to another State the responsibility for establishing and providing air traffic services'.[12]

The liability arrangements found in existing ATS delegation agreements reflect two different legal doctrines, which are strongly correlated to the legal models developed at the domestic level.

The predominant doctrine is the *territorial State doctrine*, which stipulates that, regardless of the identity, status, nationality and operative location of the organization in charge of providing the service, the State over the territory of which the damage occurs is primarily liable. All claims are to be directed against that State, in front of its national courts, and are to be decided in accordance with its national laws. The applicable arrangements may prescribe that the territorial State is entitled to obtain the reimbursement from the effective service provider (or from its parent State) of the compensation paid to the claimants.

An alternative doctrine, the *effective service provider doctrine*, is intended to allocate the primary liability to the effective wrongdoer. Under this model, all claims are to be addressed against the ANSP providing the cross-border service. The arrangements may however allow actions against the territorial State, in front of its own courts, in order to avoid depriving the right for the citizens of the territorial State to obtain compensation from their national courts.

12. Annex 11 to the *Chicago Convention*, Air Traffic Services, 13th edn (2001), § 2.11, Establishment of authority.

4 THE LIABILITY OF AIR NAVIGATION SERVICES UNDER THE SINGLE EUROPEAN SKY

The subject of the liability of ANSPs is not covered by any provision of general European law, and only marginally within the specific regulations governing the SES. These regulations foresee neither the establishment of a common material regime, nor the definition of rules to resolve potential conflicts of laws or jurisdiction.

The SES Regulations implicitly reflect the belief that domestic laws are sufficient to address claims which relate to accidents occurring within the national boundaries of the service provider involved. They, however, explicitly recognize the difficulties likely to arise from cases involving cross-border service provision, as a consequence of the diversity of existing national liability regimes, but they assume that these constraints can be resolved by the means of appropriate liability arrangements agreed between service providers.[13]

The only provisions on liability in the SES Regulations consequently establish an obligation for ANSPs to carry adequate insurance to cover potential damages arising from their activities. This obligation is laid down among the conditions prescribed for service providers to obtain their SES certification.[14]

Article 6 of the Regulation on Service Provision[15] prescribes in that respect that, for the purpose of certification:

> common requirements for the provision of air navigation services shall be established in accordance with the procedure referred to in Article 5(3) of the framework Regulation. The common requirements shall include the following: . . . liability and insurance cover, ...

The Common Requirement Regulation specifies that:

> [a]n air navigation service provider shall have in place arrangements to cover its liabilities arising from applicable law. The method employed to provide the cover shall be appropriate to the potential loss and damage in question, taking into account the legal status of the air navigation service provider and the level of commercial insurance cover available.[16]

---

13. 'Different national arrangements as to liability should not prevent an air navigation service provider from entering into agreements on the cross-border provision of services, once they [*sic*] have set up arrangements to cover losses for damages arising from liabilities under the applicable law', Commission Regulation (EC) No. 2096/2005 of 20 Dec. 2005 laying down common requirements for the provision of air navigation services [hereinafter Common Requirements Regulation], recital 15.
14. The Common Requirements Regulation also require States which 'allow the provision of air navigation services in all or part of the airspace under their responsibility without certification . . . should cover the liabilities of those providers', *ibid.*
15. Regulation (EC) No. 550/2004 of the European Parliament and of the Council of 10 Mar. 2004 on the Provision of Air Navigation Services in the Single European Sky [hereinafter '*Service Provision Regulation*'].
16. Common Requirements Regulation, Art. 7.

The competence to decide that the insurance coverage subscribed is adequate belongs to the certifying State (i.e. the State where the ANSP has its principal place of operation).[17] The certificate, including the validation of the adequacy of the level of insurance coverage, must be recognized by all other States.[18]

In the absence of specific rules governing ANS liability in the SES, except for a requirement to carry appropriate insurance coverage, the liability regime applicable to service providers engaged in cross-border service provision will depend on the contents of the legal arrangements which formalize their mandate to operate.

The SES Regulations foresee two models for the establishment of cross-border service provision, which differ in essence from the historical ATS delegations described by ICAO:

- the designation of a foreign service provider;
- the sub-contracting of the functional responsibility for service provision by a designated service provider to a foreign ANSP.

The SES Regulations prescribe a designation process under which a certified ANSP is entrusted with the responsibility to provide ANS within a particular block of airspace, on an exclusive basis.[19] Whereas most States have, so far, designated their 'national' provider to operate within the limits of their sovereign airspace, a State may also designate a foreign ANSP to provide services over its territory or over parts thereof. The mandate given to a service provider is formalized by the means of the designation instrument, which will need to include provisions governing the liability of the service provider. Alternatively, in the context of a FAB, the participating States are required to jointly designate the service providers operating within the FAB.[20] In that case, general liability arrangements can be defined in the constituting treaty supporting the creation of the FAB. In the absence of explicit liability rules, the risk exists that the liability will be channelled solely against the territorial State, with no possibility for the latter to recover the expenses paid to the claimants, from the effective service provider.

Then, Article 10 of the Service Provision Regulation authorizes a designated service provider to avail itself of the services of another service provider.[21] This construction is meant, among other purposes, to allow a service provider to subcontract the provision of services in a part of the airspace for which it has been designated to a foreign provider, operating from beyond the common national boundary, where such arrangements are expected to improve the performance of service provision. The so-called Article 10 arrangements take the form of a

17. 'Applications for certification shall be submitted to the national supervisory authority of the Member State where the applicant has its principal place of operation and, if any, its registered office', Service Provision Regulation, Art. 7.2.
18. 'A Member State shall recognize any certificate issued in another Member State in accordance with this Article', Service provision Regulation, Art. 7.8.
19. Service Provision Regulation such as amended by Regulation (EC) No. 1070/2009, Art. 8.
20. *Ibid.*, Art. 8.5
21. 'Air navigation service providers may avail themselves of the services of other service providers that have been certified in the Community', Service Provision Regulation, Art. 10.1.

contractual agreement between both ANSPs. While these arrangements must be approved by the concerned States[22], the designated ANSP retains the responsibility for service provision, as well as the corresponding liability, towards the designating State, regardless of the existence of any sub-contracting arrangements. Specific arrangements need to be agreed between the service providers involved, in order to ensure that the designated provider can obtain the reimbursement of any compensation paid to third parties, because of a failure of its sub-contractor. The Common Requirements Regulation consequently prescribes that:

> An air navigation service provider which avails itself of services of another air navigation service provider shall ensure that the agreements cover the allocation of liability between them.[23]

5 THE LIABILITY OF SERVICE PROVIDERS IN FUNCTIONAL AIRSPACE BLOCKS

The concept of FABs is a fundamental pillar of the SES initiative. The very purpose of FABs is to reorganize the fragmented European airspace, where control sectors are delineated primarily along political boundaries, into large airspace blocks, where sectors are delimited according to operational and technical needs, irrespective of national boundaries.[24]

The SES Regulations do not lay down any particular requirement in respect of the liability of service providers within FABs. However, because FABs are foreseen to become the main institutional vehicles for cross-border service provision, the various FAB projects have emerged as the natural forum to discuss the need for a common liability framework. Most FAB projects are still in the development phase and the maturity of their supporting arrangements remain to be tested but the first attempts to formalize common liability rules at sub-regional level have already highlighted a number of trends. In particular, the State Treaty supporting the FAB Europe Central (FABEC)[25] offers an illustration of the manner in which liability is likely to be addressed within FABs.

The early efforts to produce common liability rules remain timid and confirm the traditional scepticism of States towards multilateral liability arrangements. The development of such arrangements within the FABEC State Treaty is in itself a remarkable achievement, in the light of the diversity of national sensitivities and cultures to be reconciled, even among a small number of countries. These first attempts consequently tend to focus on the most acceptable common denominators.

---

22. Service Provision Regulation, Art. 10.3. The approval of the States concerned is only required in cases involving the provision of Air Traffic Services.
23. Common Requirements Regulation, Art. 7 (Liability and Insurance Cover).
24. Although this is not explicitly required by the SES Regulations, all current FAB projects cover the airspace of several countries. Further, no individual State is committed to more than one FAB States are required to formally establish FABs until 4 Dec. 2012.
25. Service Provision Regulation, such as amended by Regulation (EC) No. 1070/2009, Art. 9a.

The minimalist approach adopted by States shows through several of the underlying principles of the FABEC State Treaty.

First, the FABEC State Treaty confirms the assumption that liability cases which involve no cross-border service provision element are to treated on the basis of the domestic legislation of the State over the territory of which the damage occurred. These cases remain outside of the scope of the FABEC agreement. The liability regime prescribed in the FABEC Treaty applies exclusively to cases of cross-border service provision, in other words to damages caused by a service provider over the territory of a State other than the country from the territory of which it is operating. Further, the FABEC liability rules applies only within the outer boundaries of the FABEC airspace and is not applicable to cases involving inter-FAB cross-border service provision

Then, the compensation model established in the FABEC Treaty is a subsidiary liability regime. It requires the victims of an accident arising from a failure in the provision of ANS to first exhaust all remedies available under '*specific national or international laws or regulations*' before they can seek compensation on the ground of the FABEC Treaty.[26] Concretely, this article prescribes that the victims must first bring their claims against the concerned air carrier or the aircraft operator, in accordance with the Montreal Convention of 1999,[27] respectively under the Rome Convention of 1952, or any other applicable national legislation. The generic wording used in the FABEC Treaty does not prevent a claimant from presenting his case against the territorial State or its designated ANSP, in front of their domestic courts, in accordance with the applicable national legislation. But such direct actions are treated outside of the scope of the FABEC Treaty. It is only in the absence of compensation, sanctioned by a final judicial decision in the direct cases brought against an air carrier, an aircraft operator or any other defendant, that claimants can trigger the compensation mechanism enshrined in the FABEC Treaty. Such requests must be submitted within two years after the issuance of the final judicial decision denying compensation.[28]

Further, the regime laid down in the FABEC Treaty applies only in cases where a State designates a foreign ANSP to provide service over its territory or parts thereof, in other words, when the cross-border service provision is established through formal designation under Article 8 of the Service Provision Regulation.[29]

---

26. FABEC State Treaty, Art. 33.
27. Or the Warsaw system, if applicable.
28. 'The right to compensation . . . shall be extinguished if an action is not brought within a period of two years as from the date of the definitive judicial decisions . . . ', FABEC State Treaty, Art. 30.3.

    'Compensation . . . may be claimed only for damage which has not been compensated under any definitive judicial decision taken according to specific national or international laws or regulations.' FABEC State Treaty, Art. 30.4
29. 'A Contracting State shall compensate any damage . . . when this damage:

    a. has occurred in the airspace over its territory or under its responsibility according to ICAO rules, and

Cases where a State has designated its national ANSP to operate over its territory, and the designated ANSP has sub-contracted the responsibility for service provision within a particular sector to a foreign ANSP, in accordance with Article 10 of the Service Provision Regulation, are considered as domestic events and treated accordingly. In such cases, depending on the contents of the applicable national legislation, the territorial State or its national ANSP will be primarily liable for any damage. The principle and extent of any obligation for the foreign ANSP acting on the basis of the sub-contracting arrangement will depend on the contents of the agreement between the service providers involved.

The compensation mechanism defined in the FABEC Treaty confirms the predominance of the doctrine of the liability off the territorial State.[30] It requires the State over the territory of which the damage occurred to compensate the damage caused by the negligence of the foreign provider. That State is granted a right to seek reimbursement from the foreign service provider designated for the particular sector of foreign airspace where the accident occurred.[31] The State of the responsible ANSP is required to bring its assistance to ensure the effective reimbursement of the territorial State. In the event of a default by that service provider (inability or unwillingness to pay), the State of the defaulting ANSP is required reimburse itself the cost incurred by the territorial State.[32]

6 CONCLUSION

The deployment of the SES raises numerous fundamental questions associated with the provision of ANS, among which those pertaining to the liability of the organizations in charge of providing these services. The core issue relates to the evaluation of the need for a common liability regime for ANS Providers. Neither the general provisions of European Law, nor the specific regulations supporting the SES establish such a common European framework. However, the various FABs initiatives are starting to play an important role in the formalization of common multilateral liability rules at sub-regional level. Subject to appropriate coordination among the different FABs, a harmonized European liability regime could arise from these efforts.

---

b. has been caused by the fault of any air traffic service provider designated in accordance with Article 12 or that of its agents or any other person acting on its behalf other than the provider whose principal place of operation is located on the territory of the Contracting State concerned', FABEC State Treaty, Art. 30.1.

30. *Ibid.*
31. 'The effective air traffic service provider shall reimburse the Contracting State concerned for any compensation paid or costs incurred by this Contracting State .... The Contracting State of the effective air traffic service provider shall ensure the enforcement of this obligation and, in case of default of the effective air traffic service provider, shall take its place at first request as to reimburse the Contracting State concerned', FABEC State Treaty, Art. 30.6.
32. *Ibid.*

The FABs are still in the development phase, but the work performed, in particular within the FAB Europe Central, has already delivered valuable conclusions in respect of ANS liability, most of which confirm earlier theoretical assumptions.

First, the early efforts confirm both the complexity and the sensitivity of the topic. Forms of cross-border human activity are countless. Aviation itself is largely founded on the principle of internationality. However, few of these activities generate as delicate liability issues as ANS. A considerable amount of the sensitivity associated with the liability of ANS derives from the sovereign qualification of the activity. The first attempts to establish common liability rules have also consolidated the focus on the sovereign dimension of ANS, over its technical and operational aspects. If other FABs are to follow the example of the FABEC, it is likely that the doctrine of the liability of the territorial State will prevail over the doctrine of the effective service provider.

Then, the debate has confirmed the earlier belief that the need for a common liability framework is limited to cross-border service situations. The purpose of a liability regime is to ensure that victims obtain an effective, prompt and adequate compensation for their losses. Early studies into the liability of ANSP have concluded that the existing national laws offer satisfactory solutions, as long as the occurrences from which liability claims arise are confined to domestic events. From a victim perspective, the primary interest of common liability arrangements to address cross-border service provision is not to fill a legal vacuum, but to provide for legal certainty in respect of complex potential conflicts of laws and jurisdiction. The absence of clear rules of conflict resolution puts the prospect of a prompt reparation in serious jeopardy. But States themselves will find an interest in formal liability arrangements for cross-border service provision, in the sense that such arrangements will be necessary to secure the reimbursement from a foreign service provider operating from outside of its jurisdiction, of any compensation they may be asked to pay to third parties.

The first efforts to produce a common framework remain timid and focused on the effectiveness of the compensation. Their main purpose is to guarantee that no victim is denied reparation, following an accident attributable to a failure of ANS. They are, however, ineffective in expediting the resolution of liability cases, in the sense that common liability for cross-border service provision are subsidiary and will require that all means available under domestic law, in particular those against air carriers and aircraft operators are exhausted, before a request for compensation is submitted under the ANS liability arrangements.

In addition to elements pertaining to the need or desirability of European liability rules for ANS, a key conclusion of this research is that, before the definition of proper liability arrangements, it is the appropriate formalization of each specific instance of cross-border service provision which is of outmost importance. The difficulties experienced in the resolution of existing cross-border service provision were often more the result of questionable legal grounds for the cross-border service provision itself, than of the lack or unsatisfactory contents of applicable liability rules. The existence of a clear mandate, in the form of a direct designation or a sub-contracting agreement, in accordance with the terms of the SES Regulation is a first prerequisite for an adequate liability regime. The instruments formalising each case of cross-border service provision must then specify the applicable liability rules.

In this respect, the first discussions on liability under the umbrella of the SES seem to have highlighted a potential conceptual flaw in the principles underlying the SES Regulations. Indeed, in the light of the debate on cross-border service provision, it is questionable whether requirements for adequate insurance coverage should be defined at the level of the certification of ANSPs, or whether they would not be better addressed at the level of the designation of service providers. The insurance arrangements taken by an ANSP normally relate to damages arising over the territory of the certifying State, which is primarily concerned. But a foreign State may have different requirements in terms of insurance coverage, dictated by the specificity of its own political, social or economic environment. Since States retain the discretion to designate any certified provider to operate over their territory or parts thereof, an insurance coverage deemed too low may deter a State to designate a foreign service provider to operate within a part of its airspace, even if the establishment of a cross-border control sector would make full sense from an operational point of view. Embedding insurance requirements in the designation process, instead of in the certification procedure would offer a better framework for liability. The correlation between the insurance coverage and the designation process is for instance established in the FABEC Treaty which states that '[t]he designated air traffic service providers shall maintain adequate coverage for the liability incurred under this Treaty . . . '[33]

The final conclusion to this chapter will significantly defuse the sensitivity of the debate over the liability of ANS. While common liability arrangements are necessary to address cases of cross-border service provision, other developments in the field of ANS liability tend to make the controversial debate over ANS liability increasingly theoretical and, possibly, irrelevant. The separation of regulatory and service provision function, a requirement under the SES Regulations, has led to the establishment of autonomous ANS entities, most often in the form of corporatized companies.[34] A condition for the creation of autonomous service providers has often been that the newly independent company was compelled to carry sufficient insurance coverage to compensate any damage caused by its activities. States have prescribed this as a legal requirement, in order to limit their own exposure for activities occurring beyond their operational control. The requirement to carry adequate insurance coverage has been further strengthened by the certification requirements under the SES Regulations. The generalization of insurance coverage has fundamentally modified the way ANS liability cases are being addressed.

33. FABEC State Treaty, Art. 30.11.

34. A corporatized service provider is to be understood as a provider which is established in the form of a company under the private law of the country of registration, but whose share capital remains, in whole or in majority, in the hands of the parent State. Corporatization is opposed to privatization, where a majority of the capital is sold to private investors.

The common practice for insurance companies is to achieve out of court settlement, instead of pursuing lengthy, uncertain and costly formal litigation. Such practices prove to be beneficial for all parties. It is foreseeable that most future cases of ANS liability will be resolved without any judicial decision. Whereas they will be needed in the event of a failure to negotiate a settlement, formal legal arrangements are likely to acquire a subsidiary character.

PART II

THE INSTITUTIONAL FRAMEWORK

Chapter 8
EUROCONTROL and the EU Single European Sky

*David McMillan and Roderick van Dam**

1 INTRODUCTION

The performance, management and regulation of Air Traffic Services[1] (ATS) represent one of those functions that are an absolute condition for the very existence of safe and efficient air transport all over the world. It is also typically an activity that remains generally invisible and will not make the news until something happens that disrupts that infrastructure and affects commercial air transport. The spring 2010 volcanic ash crisis that started in Europe and quickly expanded to global proportions is a recent example. But that quiet is deceptive;

* Respectively Director General and General Counsel of EUROCONTROL

1. In addressing activities related to EUROCONTROL, different activities related to Air Traffic will be referred to. The most important ones are:
   - *Air Traffic Management* (ATM) encompasses the functions needed to ensure safe and efficient movement of aircraft during all phases of operation: air traffic services, airspace management and air traffic flow management;
   - *Air Traffic Services* (ATS), which is a part of ATM, is a generic term meaning variously flight information service, alerting service, air traffic advisory service and air traffic control service.
   - *Air Traffic control* (ATC) is a service operated by the appropriate authority to promote the safe, orderly and expeditious flow of air traffic.

Daniel Calleja Crespo & Pablo Mendes de Leon, *Achieving the Single European Sky: Goals and Challenges*, pp. 67–78.

behind the scenes there is a constant stream of activities ongoing to improve the provision of Air Traffic Management (ATM) and to assure full interaction with the users of the ATS infrastructure. Nowadays, both EUROCONTROL and the EU are in the centre of those activities.

ATM in Europe has traditionally been determined by, at global level, the Convention on International Civil Aviation signed at Chicago on 7 December 1944 (hereinafter the Chicago Convention) and by the national regulatory frameworks of the States. However, a third level of ATM regulation emerged in Europe through the establishment, in the sixties, of the European Organisation for the Safety of Air Navigation, EUROCONTROL, and more recently since the European Union (EU) activities in this field.

Last December 2010, EUROCONTROL modestly celebrated the 50th anniversary of its contribution to the ATM business. Fifty years of serving the interests of its, to date, thirty-nine contracting Parties. That is a long period and it is therefore not surprising that the EUROCONTROL of today is quite different from the one created in 1961. EUROCONTROL has consistently demonstrated its potential to adapt to the needs of its members and those of the providers and users of the ATM infrastructure and the tasks of the organization have evolved throughout the years. As a matter of fact, the organization has changed its goals and functions at least three times during that period but one of EUROCONTROL's most important goals was and remains the development of coherent and coordinated ATM for its thirty-nine European Member States of which twenty-six are currently also members of the (EU).[2]

EUROCONTROL activities span the entire range of gate-to-gate air navigation service operations – from strategic and tactical air traffic flow management to controller training; from regional air traffic control (ATC) to development and implementation of leading-edge safety-proofed technologies, procedures and regulations. EUROCONTROL furthermore has developed a highly sophisticated common route charges system under which the organization regulates, bills and collects the charges for the provision of air navigation services by its Member States and third parties.

In the EU context, by adopting the Single European Sky (SES) regulations in 2004, the European Union has established exclusive competence in the ATM field and, in doing so, also triggered an in-depth reform of ATM in Europe. While the EU has reinforced its competences in the ATM domain, it has also recognized the complementary nature of the expertise within EUROCONTROL. The SES is a European Union initiative, but with a wider perspective, so it should be implemented in a way that safeguards the interests of the full pan-European ATM community. All EU Member States are bound by the SES legislation but, in the context of its external aviation policy, the EU has concluded various types of agreements with third States, aiming to establish a common aviation area with its neighbours. As a result, many European States which are not members of the EU

2. Estonia is presently not (yet) a member of EUROCONTROL.

have now agreed to be subject to EU law in the Aviation and ATM domains or are in the process of doing so.

The process of reform of ATM in Europe is underway. The main partners on the ATM scene in Europe, EUROCONTROL and the EU, are currently in the process of further defining the future role and functions of both organizations on the European ATM scene on the basis of their respective strengths, know-how and experience.

After a brief description of EUROCONTROL, this article will, in particular, address the organization's current relationship with the EU in the context of the Single European Sky, the need for change and the future relationship between both organizations.

2 EUROCONTROL, THE EUROPEAN ORGANIZATION FOR THE SAFETY OF AIR NAVIGATION

EUROCONTROL is an international organization with full legal personality created by six European States (Germany, Belgium, France, United Kingdom and Northern Ireland, Luxembourg and the Netherlands) through an instrument of Public International Law: the EUROCONTROL International Convention relating to Co-operation for the Safety of Air Navigation signed at Brussels on 13 December 1960 and which entered into force on 1 March 1963.

The initial EUROCONTROL Convention of 1960 was principally directed at the joint organization and provision of air traffic services in the upper airspace of the signatory States, and, for those States which so wished, also in all or part of their lower airspace. In view of the reservations relating to national sovereignty voiced by the United Kingdom and France, the Member States at the time (France, the Federal Republic of Germany, Belgium, the United Kingdom, the Netherlands, Luxembourg, and Ireland which joined in 1965) limited the application of the Convention as far as operational air traffic control activities were concerned.[3]

Consequently and to reflect this limitation, the Member States sought to amend the scope of the Convention in order to focus it to a greater extent on study, research and coordination activities rather than the provision of air traffic control services, with the organization retaining the possibility of exercising direct operational responsibilities at the express request of Member or non-Member States. As a result, the scope of the EUROCONTROL Convention of 1960 was extended mainly to cover research and development, coordination activities and to consolidate the route charges system in place at that time. The deliberations of the States within the numerous technical, financial, legal, political and diplomatic working groups responsible for drafting the Protocol amending the EUROCONTROL Convention of 1960 (hereinafter referred to as the Amended Convention) turned out to be rather difficult and it took over ten years from the beginning of this work

3. The EUROCONTROL Maastricht Upper Airspace Control Center presently handles more than 1.2 million movements per year – it is the second largest ATC centre in Europe.

in 1975 before the Amended Convention as well as a Multilateral Agreement relating to Route Charges signed at Brussels on 12 February 1981 entered into force on 1 January 1986.

In the early nineties and in view of the air traffic increase and ATM capacity shortages, the EUROCONTROL Member States agreed to further amend the 1981 EUROCONTROL Convention. To that effect, the EUROCONTROL Member States signed, on 27 June 1997, the Protocol consolidating the EUROCONTROL Convention (hereinafter referred to as the Revised Convention). The ratification of this Convention is still ongoing to date but the EUROCONTROL membership agreed on the early implementation of most of the provisions contained in the Revised Convention. At present, thirty-nine European States (including twenty-six EU Member States) are members of the organization.[4]

The activities of the organization and the budget of the Agency are financed through the annual contribution of each Contracting Party to the budget: 30% of the contribution is calculated in proportion to the value of the Gross National Product of the Contracting Party and 70% is calculated in proportion to the value of the route facility cost-base of the Contracting Party. In view of the present economic situation, steps have been taken to introduce significant savings and to stabilize the budget.

The EUROCONTROL organization comprises currently two organs, the Permanent Commission and the Agency. The Permanent Commission, composed of representatives of the Member States, is responsible for formulating the organization's general policy and represents the sole decision-making organ that can take decisions that bind the EUROCONTROL membership, e.g. in the rulemaking domain. The Agency is the organ responsible for the performance of the tasks set out in the Convention or entrusted to it by the Permanent Commission. It functions under the exclusive management responsibility of the Director General. A Provisional Council was created early 1998 for the period until the entry into force of the Revised Convention. It adopts for the Permanent Commission's final approval, all measures to be taken for the accomplishment of the organization's tasks and forms the general forum for the discussion and implementation of the work of the organization.

The Revised Convention has introduced the possibility for the accession to EUROCONTROL organization by 'regional economic integration organizations'. The European Commission, on behalf of the European Community, applied in 1998 for European Community membership in EUROCONTROL organization. As a result, a Protocol on the Accession of the European Community to the EUROCONTROL Convention (hereinafter referred to as the EU Accession Protocol) was signed on 8 October 2002, which is still in the process of being ratified

4. Albania, Germany, Armenia, Austria, Belgium, Bosnia and Herzegovina, Bulgaria, Cyprus, Croatia, Denmark, Spain, Finland, France, United Kingdom and Northern Ireland, Greece, Hungary, Ireland, Italy, FYROM, Latvia, Lithuania, Luxembourg, Malta, Moldova, Monaco, Montenegro, Norway, the Netherlands, Poland, Portugal, Romania, Serbia, Slovak Republic, Slovenia, Sweden, Switzerland, Czech Republic, Turkey and Ukraine.

by the EU and EUROCONTROL Member States. Pending the entry into force of the Revised Convention, the EUROCONTROL Member States and the European Community decided to provisionally apply, pending their entry into force, most of the provisions of the EU Accession Protocol.

The revised Convention has introduced three significant innovations:

The Performance Review Commission (PRC), independent from the Contracting Parties and from the Agency, provides advice to the Permanent Commission, through the Provisional Council, in order to ensure the effective management of the European ATM system through a strong, transparent and independent performance review and target setting system.

The Safety Regulation Commission (SRC) equally provides independent advice in order to ensure consistent high levels of safety in ATM in Europe. The SRC is responsible for developing safety regulation proposals as part of the present mandatory rulemaking functions of EUROCONTROL. The SRC is increasingly cooperating with EASA in the context of support to SES.

Finally, the Civil/Military Interface Standing Committee (CMIC), composed of high-level civil and military officials of the Member States, advises the Provisional Council on issues having a civil/military interface. For example, the CMIC examines and advises on the military implications of the organization's programmes and interacts with competent organizations relating to military matters (e.g., National States and NATO). This confirms the widely recognized role of EUROCONTROL as unique platform for civil-military coordination.

3 THE CURRENT RELATIONSHIP BETWEEN EUROCONTROL AND THE EUROPEAN UNION

Various legal instruments define at this moment in time the relationship between EUROCONTROL and the European Union.

As referred to above, a Protocol on the Accession of the European Community to the EUROCONTROL Convention was signed on 8 October 2002, and is to date not yet in force but provisionally applied. As a result, the EU, represented by the European Commission, now already exercises most of rights and duties specified under the revised Convention and the Protocol. It fully participates in the different steps of the tasks related processes and has a strong position in it in view of its associated competencies.

On 22 December 2003, a Memorandum of Co-operation was signed between EUROCONTROL and the European Commission. This Memorandum for Co-operation establishes a framework for mutual cooperation and support between the two Parties on the development and implementation of the Single European Sky and other joint activities and responsibilities, in accordance with their respective roles and obligations. Its provisions aim at facilitating cooperation between the Parties at the administrative and technical level in the domains foreseen in the revised Convention and the SES regulations, with the aim of making the best use of the EUROCONTROL experience, expertise and competencies in ATM and making sure that duplication of effort is avoided. A 1st Framework Financial Agreement was concluded in 2005 between the European Community and EUROCONTROL as the financial tool to implement the Memorandum of Cooperation. It was replaced by the Framework Financial Agreement of 19 November 2009 which is still in force to date.

On the basis of these arrangements, the European Commission has issued numerous requests for support to EUROCONTROL which cover various subject matters such as support to SES annual reporting, support to NSA Coordination Platform and to FABs Focal Point Group, support to international cooperation, support to public relations, etc.

Last but not least, the four basic Single European Sky Regulations (the Framework Regulation No 549/2004, the Service Provision Regulation No 550/2004, the Airspace Regulation No 551/2004 and the Interoperability Regulation No 552/2004) were adopted in 2004 by the European Parliament and the Council of the European Union on a proposal from the European Commission and amended in 2009. In several instances, the SES Regulations expressly address the relationship between the EU and EUROCONTROL. The Single European Sky Regulations explicitly acknowledge the institutional relationship between the EU and EUROCONTROL and recognize the obligations, under international law, of the EU and its Member States as Members of EUROCONTROL. They also confirm that EUROCONTROL has the appropriate expertise to support the EU in its role as regulator.

One of the best examples of such support is the development of implementing rules by EUROCONTROL on the basis of a mandate from the European Commission. EUROCONTROL has accepted and delivered many mandates in various areas covered by the four SES Regulations: charging scheme, flexible use of airspace, coordination and transfer, flight message transfer protocol, initial flight plan, data link services, air ground voice channel spacing, mode S, aeronautical data quality, air traffic flow management, etc.

Another example is the development, by EUROCONTROL and at the request of the European Commission, of EUROCONTROL specifications as Means of Compliance (MoC) for specific SES regulatory material. These relate to various matters: flexible use of airspace, flight message transfer protocol, initial flight plan, online data interchange, ATS data exchange presentation, ATS message handling system.

A landmark in the interaction with the EU was, in 2010, the designation by the European Commission of EUROCONTROL, acting through its Performance Review Commission, as the Performance Review Body (PRB) for the Single European Sky. In October 2010, the Director General of EUROCONTROL accepted that function on behalf of the organization.

This confirms EUROCONTROL's position as a preferred partner for the implementation of the Single European Sky. It underlines the growing confidence between the two organizations and is an express recognition of the work EUROCONTROL has been doing in the field of performance review for more than ten years. The work of the PRB, which reports directly to the European

Commission, includes the setting of EU-wide performance targets, initially in the areas of cost efficiency, capacity and the environment. It also involves assessing national or Functional Airspace Blocks (FABs) performance plans for consistency with the targets set and subsequent monitoring.

The Single Sky Committee issued on 15 February 2011 a positive opinion on the nomination of EUROCONTROL as Network Manager, as foreseen in the Airspace Regulation No. 551/2004 and in the Regulation laying down the detailed rules for the implementation of ATM network functions. The European Commission intends to formally adopt the nomination decision by June 2011. This will constitute another landmark in the EUROCONTROL-EU relationship.

4 TIME FOR CHANGE: TOWARDS A REFORM OF ATM IN EUROPE

The provision of Air Traffic Services traditionally has been a part of the public domain. States, under the aegis of Article 28 of the Chicago Convention, accepted and exercised their sovereign responsibility for the ATS provision and related functions over their sovereign territory. The services were organized by and imbedded in the relevant civil service entities such as Ministries of Transport, Civil Aviation Authorities that formed part of the Public Function. Often the ATC function was exercised in close liaison with or even under the control of the relevant Defence or Military authorities.

As a result of the introduction of the Single European Sky, the institutional future of ATM in Europe is currently under full discussion. The actual ATM developments raise numerous legal and institutional issues, fuelled in particular by the interaction between the role of the new players, such as supranational and intergovernmental organizations, corporatized/privatized air navigation service (ANS) providers and users' organizations and the traditional sovereign functions and responsibilities of the European States.

The Europe-wide implementation of a fully harmonized ATM system must encompass effective instruments to ensure the highest levels of safety regulation and management, aimed at implementation and application by regulators as well as the service providers. It will have to establish an optimized and harmonized airspace design and management system that satisfies the needs of both military and civil users. It has to be designed to provide the users with a safe, efficient and economic ATM infrastructure in which they can offer their services to the flying public in a competitive manner.

The European ATM system will furthermore have to reconcile the above principles with the demands of the corporatized or even privatized ANS providers that will increasingly exercise their functions in specially designated functional blocks of airspace (FABs) that no longer depend on the delineation of their airspace by sovereign States. The system will therefore have to absorb and allow the creation of private consortia of service providers that will operate in a growing competitive environment.

The overriding challenge for a new institutional approach to ATM in Europe is the need to realistically maintain the guarantee for a continued quest to provide the highest possible safety levels in a domain that is expected to double its volume over the next twenty years. That target will have to be met with all the efforts both EUROCONTROL and the European Union can muster and both organizations find themselves now jointly committed to a series of tasks of Herculean proportions.

This approach will have to combine the public function elements that still govern the regulation and provision of ATM services with demands created by the corporatization and privatization of the ANS providers and the diminishing role of the national States that remain bound by provisions of public international law such as, but not limited to, their responsibilities under e.g. Article 28 of the Chicago Convention. There is a general recognition that the need for change is driven by issues such as the future relation between the EU and EUROCONTROL, recognition of the changing role of States under SES and the need to enhance stakeholder governance as well as ensure a rigorous separation between regulatory and service provision functions.

The unquestionable merit of the SES Regulations and generally the involvement of the EU in ATM is that the four basic parts of SES Regulations constitute a decisive and, in certain parts, innovative step forward towards fundamental changes in the domain of European ATM. It is equally clear that the effective implementation of these changes will depend on the timely availability of effective and mature implementing rules. EUROCONTROL and its Member States will fulfil a crucial role in that process. At the same time, EUROCONTROL, as a public body, will be expected to continue to assist and support its Member States in the exercise of its functions in the civil and military domains and in the exercise of State public functions such as Central Flow Management, a centralized route charges system and managing a central aeronautical database (EAD), to name a few.

5 THE FUTURE RELATIONSHIP BETWEEN EUROCONTROL AND THE EUROPEAN UNION

It would probably be an overstatement to hold that the future of ATM in Europe solely depends on the successful integration of both organizations, but it is now widely recognized that they both will play a decisive role in that process. That means that the many synergies between EUROCONTROL and the EU need to be carefully sorted out and established for the longer term.

That need was also recognized at the High-Level Conference on the SES implementation which took place at Budapest on 3 and 4 March 2011. The 'Budapest Charter for the implementation of the Single European Sky', endorsed by the participants at the end of the Conference, invited the European institutions/organizations to:

- help to rationalize the institutional architecture of the European ATM system to deliver the Single European Sky objectives, interconnect the existing

aviation bodies and create synergies to make the best use of available expertise;
- in particular, to revise the relations between the European Union and EUROCONTROL, to recognize the latter as the'implementing arm' of the Single European Sky and consolidate these relations, possibly in the form of a High-Level Agreement.

EUROCONTROL and the EU are currently in the process of further defining their future role and functions in the new European ATM environment. The challenges of making both worlds meet should not be underestimated and will require realistic, workable steps and solutions with mutual respect for the positions of those involved and a common determination to succeed.

The potential synergies between EUROCONTROL and the EU are obvious: a pan-European ATM domain in which the role of the EU is recognized in the political and legislative domains, with EUROCONTROL as the pan-European technical support and management arm (e.g., development of implementing rules, of specifications, performance of PRB tasks).

The reason for addressing the ATM reform in Europe at the pan-European level is the fact that all the key functions required to bring about a safe and efficient European ATM domain will have to be available in at least the EUROCONTROL or ECAC airspace. It would be difficult to imagine any other credible foundation for the future ATM domain. Restricting the European ATM area to, for example, the EU airspace would discriminate between beneficiaries of a harmonized EU neighbourhood and those outside that area, who would be deprived of obvious safety, economic and efficiency benefits of an ATM institutional reform in their part of Europe.

The pan-European area is not a static one. An important argument for a harmonized pan-European ATM domain is its potential to expand further. Both EUROCONTROL and ECAC as regional European organizations have steadily grown since their creation, providing new European States, under objective conditions, with the benefits from membership in neutral and independent organizations that are driven by the need to enhance safety and efficiency of ATM in Europe. The ECAC Transport Ministers agreed in the late Nineties on a standing policy to align the ECAC participation with the EUROCONTROL membership and that process is presently ongoing.

The pan-European issue is not only relevant for the EUROCONTROL membership. The EU, apart from its membership of twenty-seven States (twenty-six of which are EUROCONTROL Members), has concluded or is in the process of concluding agreements with several non-EU States. In the context of its external aviation policy, the EU has concluded different types of agreement, aiming to establish a Common Aviation Area with its immediate neighbours.[5] These

5. Various agreements have been concluded: EEA Agreement, bilateral Agreement with Switzerland, multilateral ECAA agreement with South Eastern and Northern European States, Euro Mediterranean Air Transport Agreement with Morocco. In addition, the EU has concluded

agreements do in effect oblige the States involved to implement and apply the relevant EU aviation and ATM legislation.

The EU has now acquired full legislative competence in ATM, predominantly through the SES regulations. A number of EUROCONTROL functions, in particular in the regulatory field, overlap with those of the EU. This situation could potentially lead to undue conflict and liability which needs to be addressed. As long as the rules of EUROCONTROL and the legal rights and obligations of the Member States are respected in the process of change, there are no basic impediments for the introduction of one central ATM legislative function as an essential part of the ATM reform at the pan-European level.

EUROCONTROL represents a unique body of knowledge, experience and support resources that will serve the various demands in the European ATM domain and perform in an independent and cost effective manner. EUROCONTROL currently provides these functions and services at the pan-European level, as a civil and military intergovernmental organization with presently thirty-nine Member States.

EUROCONTROL is now in the process of reforming its core activities and strengths with a view to becoming the organization dedicated to the successful achievement of the Single European Sky at the pan-European level, ensuring that its benefits are shared amongst all Member States of the organization and following the principles of separating service provision from regulatory tasks in combination with the strong wish from airspace users to finance only those services that directly support their operations. Its tasks will include wide support for the implementation of EU legislation at the pan-European level (in particular SES-related functions, PRB, rule drafting and implementation support, support to EASA) as well as continued support to its Member States in the exercise of their ATM activities and provision of public domain functions/services (such as central flow management, a common route charges system and EAD) entrusted to it by its membership since more than twenty years and conducted at the European level on an independent basis at an optimal cost-benefit ratio.

The future governance of the new EUROCONTROL should also reflect the role of key stakeholders as presently represented in the Air Navigation Services Board (ANSB)[6] as well as the responsibilities of the States in relation to civil-military coordination, presently represented through the Civil/Military Interface Standing Committee (CMIC) and the Military ATM Board (MAB).[7]

In view of the substantial public interest component of the activities as well as the common interest of all ATM network actors, the organization would continue to operate in an impartial way in a spirit of partnership in order not to jeopardize the

---

horizontal agreements for the provision of certain air services in order for all existing bilateral air services agreements between Member States and a given third country to be in line with EU law.

6. The purpose of the ANSB is to increase the involvement of air navigation stakeholders in the preparation of decisions and aligning the business planning and budgetary processes at different levels in the organization, while respecting the decision-making responsibilities of the Member States.
7. The MAB gives advice and military views to the Director General on ATM matters.

benefits for the whole network. It has to ensure safety, quality of service, continuity of service, security, cost-effectiveness, confidentiality of information.

Introducing new functions for EUROCONTROL, abolishing existing ones and including stakeholder governance functions will require amendments to the Convention or an entirely new legal instrument. For the continuity of the many ongoing tasks and functions, changes to the existing institutional framework might be preferred. A number of options regarding the status of EUROCONTROL could be considered but that would be for the present Member States of the organization to decide.

Much will depend upon the joint commitment of the two main players in this field, the EU and EUROCONTROL, to realize an effective ATM reform for Europe. The complementary nature of the activities of the two organizations should therefore be formally acknowledged through a high-level agreement between the EU and the EUROCONTROL Member States, offering clarity over the relationship and working arrangements, and providing sound basis for a renewed EUROCONTROL institutional framework.

In terms of timing, a first step would be the agreement on the purpose and concept of such a high-level agreement. This could be achieved at relatively short notice. It would be followed by the need for both organizations to get negotiating mandates from their respective Member States – this would have to be coordinated and reflect the objectives set forward by the Member States regarding the future of EUROCONTROL.

The agreement would serve as the stepping stone to initiate the necessary changes to the current EUROCONTROL institutional framework. A joint commitment between the two organizations for implementing the reform of EUROCONTROL under agreed principles would be a major step forward towards the establishment of the new EUROCONTROL. It would be part of the impetus for the institutional reform of the EUROCONTROL organization which now needs to adapt itself to the new environment. It would furthermore be the driver for further amending the present EUROCONTROL institutional framework.

6 CONCLUSION

Two main actors, EUROCONTROL and the European Union, cooperate nowadays on the ATM scene in Europe, for the sake of safety of ATM in the whole of Europe geographical area.

The process of establishing a Single European Sky has led to an in-depth reform of the architecture of European ATM to meet future capacity, safety and performance needs. Profound changes to the landscape of ATM have taken place: a new regulatory framework established by the SES legislation, the introduction of SESAR and the setting up of a SESAR Joint Undertaking together with the extension of EASA competence to the ATM domain. The drive to reform EUROCONTROL forms a central component of this European ATM process; it is based on key elements such as recognizing the benefits of having the EU as a single driver for European legislation as an important enabler for a unified and harmonized European ATM domain, while acknowledging the pan-European nature of EUROCONTROL and its role in providing support to the EU in its different functions.

The current Agency reform process is focused on the management and organization of the Agency, establishing it as the technical arm to enable the successful implementation of a single pan-European ATM system. The next step will be to reflect this change at the level of the EUROCONTROL organization. EUROCONTROL should now adapt itself, directing its core values and strengths to become the organization dedicated to enable the successful achievement of the Single European Sky at the pan-European level, ensuring that its benefits are shared amongst all present and future Member States of the organization. The institutional, financial and operational enablers for such developments now have to be discussed, developed and agreed upon by the full EUROCONTROL membership.

A reformed institutional environment should provide EUROCONTROL with the tools to better exercise its new functions, fully exploit its expertise and reflect the changes which have taken place with respect to, *inter alia*, the European ATM landscape and the implementation of the Single European Sky. It should serve and benefit all of EUROCONTROL present and future Member States as well as its stakeholders and consolidate its supporting role with respect to the EU.

Chapter 9

ICAO and the Pan European Dimension: The Single European Sky from a Global Perspective

*Luis Fonseca de Almeida**

1 INTRODUCTION

It is not my intention here to analyse the first and the second package of the Single European Sky (SES) Programme or to go through its technical aspects which are being covered in-depth in tonnes of dedicated publications. Neither do I need to add comments on SES's goals of achieving better aviation safety, capacity as well as financial and environmental sustainability, through the implementation of an ambitious reform of air traffic management in Europe.

All aviation initiatives succeeding in these areas are welcome and encouraged by the International Civil Aviation Organization (ICAO), for all of them – starting from Safety – coincide with the institutional strategic objectives of the Organization.

Being SES, as per the European Commission definition, an 'initiative to reform the architecture of European air traffic control to meet future capacity and safety needs', I wish to focus instead on what does this mean in terms of

* Luis Fonseca de Almeida, Regional Director, ICAO European and North Atlantic Office.

Daniel Calleja Crespo & Pablo Mendes de Leon, *Achieving the Single European Sky: Goals and Challenges*, pp. 79–89.

international civil aviation harmonization goals and legally binding international obligations undertaken by States.

Namely, how does a regional Single European Sky initiative fit into a global ICAO framework?

In order to answer this question, I first need to delve into the history and geography of international civil aviation in order to explain ICAO's role in pursuing the safety and sustainability of it, as well as the regional weight of this important initiative promoted by the European Union.

2 ICAO: THE 'GLOBAL DIMENSION' OF AVIATION GUIDING 'REGIONAL ONES'

Echoing the words of the then President of the United States, Franklin Delano Roosevelt, we can say that the goal of the Chicago Conference on International Civil Aviation, held in Chicago in 1944 towards the end of the Second World War, was for all nations to 'work together, so that the air may be used by humanity, to serve humanity'. By keeping this broad but constitutional goal in mind as an evergreen one, it will be easier to understand how and why any regional initiative involving aviation safety and sustainability needs to be implemented within the International Civil Aviation Organization (ICAO) framework.

How have nations been pursuing this goal globally so far since the signing of the Chicago Convention which, in addition to the international legal framework for aviation safety regulation, also established an institutional tool to fulfil the aims of the Convention? Indeed, the above-mentioned tool is the International Civil Aviation Organization which, since its inception, provides both a global forum for its Member States to take concerted action on safety matters, as well as an institutional mechanism allowing members to reach such goal.

The pillars of ICAO's role in ensuring the safety and sustainability of international civil aviation have remained unchanged from those described in the early Memoranda of the Organization (to which reference will be made in the next paragraphs). This role cannot change for no international aviation activity would be even conceivable without ICAO and this because no 'global' aviation safety would be even conceivable without ICAO.

To ensure the safety, regularity and efficiency of international civil aviation operations, international standardization is essential in all matters which affect them: operation of aircraft, aircraft airworthiness and the numerous facilities and services required in their support such as aerodromes, telecommunications, navigational aids, meteorology, air traffic services, search and rescue, aeronautical information services and aeronautical charts.

To achieve the highest practicable degree of uniformity wherever this will facilitate and improve air safety, efficiency and regularity, the ICAO Council – formed by thirty-six countries out of 190 Member States – adopts or amends (when necessary) international standards and recommended practices, and approves appropriate procedures.

In short, since ICAO came into being in 1947, a main feature of the technical work of the Organization has been the achievement of agreement by contracting States on the necessary level of standardization for the operation of safe, regular and efficient air services. As widely known, this standardization is directed towards ensuring a high level of safety and that error and accident will not occur because of flight crew incompetence or incompatibility of operating tasks or environments with human skills or physiological tolerances. Or by cause of unfamiliarity with equipment procedures, human fatigue, actual or potential medical condition or any other human factor problem.

It goes without saying that the well-being of passengers and crews is safeguarded also through the development of aircraft design and equipment requirements as well as through operational procedures and future aviation concepts factoring in technological improvements and ensuring harmonization at a global level. Indeed – as will be examined in more depth below – most SES-related developments fall into one of the above-mentioned categories.

The necessary standardization has been achieved by ICAO primarily through the creation, adoption and amendment by the Council of specifications known as *International Standards and Recommended Practices* (SARPs), reflected in the eighteen Annexes to the Convention on International Civil Aviation, also referred to as the Chicago Convention (1944).

Should a particular specification be an aviation international standard? Otherwise stated: Is its uniform application by all contracting States necessary? If the answer is 'yes' then that specification has to become a standard.

So far ICAO has adopted more than 10,000 safety provisions, aimed at protecting passengers' lives, which are listed not only in the eighteen Annexes to the Convention but also in more than 300 Circulars and 150 Documents/Manuals, namely guidance material covering all technical, operational, procedural and human aspects. From the duration of radars' reply pulsed to the integrity level of critical aeronautical data, from the bearing strength of a pavement intended for aircraft to the minimum radius of a turnoff curve to be applied when designing a rapid exit taxiway, there are basically no safety-related issues on which the 190 Member States are left without reference standards or recommended practices.

But what happens at a Regional level? What if there is a need for specifications to meet particular aspects of certain areas of the world? In fact, dealing with international civil aviation, there may well be requirements that need to be dealt with at a regional level. From an ICAO perspective the world is divided into nine Air Navigation Regions: Africa-Indian Ocean, Asia, Caribbean, Middle-East, North American, North Atlantic, Pacific, South American and last but not least the European Region.

To facilitate detailed planning of facilities and services, the formulation of supplementary procedures, or the operational designing needed to accommodate traffic growth or other aviation priorities, regional air navigation meetings have been held periodically to consider these requirements in the relevant areas. The results of these meetings are reflected in the nine regional Air Navigation Plans (ANPs) covering the corresponding nine ICAO Regions of the world.

The provisions of these Plans are meant to, when implemented by the States, lead to an INTEGRATED international air navigation system adequate for the foreseeable future.

In 1997, Member States of the ICAO Council decided that the regional Air Navigation Plans should be published in two volumes: a Basic ANP and a Facilities and Services Implementation Document (FASID). While the latter sets forth the facilities and services required for international air navigation within the specified area, the Basic ANP contains stable plan material such as the geographical description of the Flight Information Regions (FIRs) covered by the plan.

This contribution will explain why this is relevant for the appropriate implementation of the Single European Sky.

3 A PAN-EUROPEAN DIMENSION: DEFINITIONS

No 'pan'-European dimension can be defined without having agreed in advance on what do we mean by 'Europe' from an international aviation point of view. Since the Second World War there has been a strengthening of regional arrangements in the aviation field in response to the need for international cooperation. A number of organizations were established worldwide. This flourishing of aviation organizations has been especially active in Europe. Some of them were aimed at dealing with all aspects of aviation matters, in close coordination with ICAO and receiving assistance from it. This is the case of the European Civil Aviation Conference (ECAC) that was established in 1954.

Other organizations were given more specialized mandates as is the case for Eurocontrol which was established in 1960 by the International Convention for the Safety of Air Navigation.

The early 1970s saw the birth of the Joint Aviation Authorities which gradually disappeared and was finally replaced in 2009 by the European Aviation Safety Agency (EASA), which is designed to be 'the centrepiece for the European Union's strategy on aviation safety'.

Regardless of the specific cooperation agreements with a few third-party States, all the above-mentioned important aviation organizations mark different borders in drawing Europe. ECAC counts 44 Member States, Eurocontrol 39, the European Union 27 and EASA 31. The North Atlantic Treaty Organization (NATO) in geographical Europe counts 26 Member States out of 28.

All these organizations perform tasks of paramount importance for the safety and the sustainability of air navigation in Europe. However, is the abundance and richness of aviation provisions and inputs emanating from these organizations sufficient to ensure aviation harmonization in Europe? Unfortunately not. For example, only eighteen States are simultaneously represented in all the above-mentioned organizations while the rest of the European countries are represented in a non-homogeneous manner. On top of this, all of them have an area of competence falling within the borders of Western/Central Europe.

On the other hand, the ICAO European Region has fifty-two Member States. Within this area of responsibility, stretching from the North Pole to the Mediterranean Sea and from the Atlantic to the Pacific Rim (and to the borders of China), ICAO has to promote, on a European regional level, a harmonized implementation of its policies and safety standards, the development of air navigation plans as well as the planning and implementation of air navigation facilities and services.

The ICAO European Region, which includes the Russian Federation and all countries of the former Soviet Union, is not only huge; it is also extremely heterogeneous. It must be kept in mind that, from an aviation point of view, Europe is a club made of fifty-two States, not just twenty-seven.

On top of this, the European and North Atlantic Office, which I have the honour to lead, is accredited to fifty-six contracting States and two non-contracting States in the European, North Atlantic and Africa-Indian Ocean (AFI) Regions, some of which are involved in the nine Functional Airspace Blocks being envisaged in the SES initiative.

The European and North Atlantic Office is also working closely with Canada and USA on North Atlantic issues and cooperates with eleven international organizations. This renders our tasks extremely challenging for we must take into account a wide spectrum of different needs in terms of traffic type and density, different degrees of aviation maturity, financial means as well as cross-border diplomatic issues having an impact on aviation.

A chain is only as strong as its weakest link. This is why ICAO considers of paramount importance any effort focusing on cross-border support and cooperation, aiming at harmonizing international civil aviation within the ICAO global regulatory framework. Having specified what 'Europe' is from an ICAO point of view, we can still affirm that the EU's Single European Sky initiative is one the most ambitious aviation coordination and harmonization programmes taking place in the Region. Like all initiatives taken by each of the 190 ICAO Member States affecting international civil aviation, the SES Programme is required to pursue effective global harmonization, be consistent with international legislation and pre-existing obligations undertaken by States and to be notified by States in conformity with ICAO current procedures.

4 SES' PLACE WITHIN THE ICAO FRAMEWORK

What was previously said on ICAO's history and role in pursuing the safety and sustainability of international civil aviation, as well as the clarification of what Europe stands for from an aviation point of view, are of paramount importance in order to understand SES' place within the ICAO framework.

SES' targets – perfectly matching in terms of principles ICAO's strategic objectives – have indeed to be implemented not only within the current international legal framework but also through harmonized operational and procedural specifications. When trying to pursue harmonization for the EU twenty-seven

Member States, the SES initiative should ensure that it is harmonized with ICAO's global provisions and other international projects. This has many implications. For instance we have to make sure that the technological pillar of the second Single European Sky package, namely the SESAR Programme, is compatible with its US counterpart and that both of them are compatible not only with the ICAO Global Air Navigation Plan but also with the rest of the other ATM upgrade programmes in the world.

ICAO has already set up the framework allowing all parties involved to meet the global harmonization goal. The ICAO NextGen-SESAR Gap Analysis which started in 2008 was one of the first steps taken by ICAO to ensure that the advances of NextGen and SESAR would be transferable to and compatible with the global civil aviation system. ICAO Gap Analysis reviewed more than 1500 entries finding over 300 differences in respect to ICAO Documents and Annexes to the Chicago Convention. As already highlighted by ICAO Headquarters, both NextGen and SESAR are huge and have aggressive schedules and both aim at implementing hundreds of operational improvements and enablers in terms of policy, technology and procedures. ICAO's role is to ensure that they are compatible with the rest of the world.

In 2009 ICAO presented the results of its GAP Analysis and the related challenges to a formal Standard Roundtable meeting attended by FAA, Eurocontrol, the SESAR Joint Undertaking and the International Standards-Making bodies. The meeting identified twenty primary focus areas for standardization many of which corresponding to ICAO's own analysis and mainly coming from those Programme areas still requiring concept development. The high priority focus areas ranged from Navigation Capability (VNAV, RNAV, GBAS) to 4D Trajectory Exchange and from Procedures for Delegation (ATC/Pilots) to Air Traffic Flow Management. This first formal meeting triggered a positive cooperation effort which is still in place. As an example, on 3–4 March 2011, during the high-level conference on 'Implementing the Single European Sky' organized by the EU Hungarian Presidency, the European Union and the United States signed a memorandum of cooperation in the field of aviation research promoting interoperability between the European and US ATM modernization programmes, namely SESAR and NextGen.

In addition to this, it is of paramount importance that the future SES implementation be able to set up easy steps allowing harmonization with the civil aviation of third-party States, regardless which segment of the wide 'Aviation Europe' they belong to. As already highlighted in many documents published by the ICAO European and North Atlantic (EUR/NAT) Office, it is positive that the European Commission (EC) has entered into or is negotiating agreements with non-EU Member States on the so-called European Common Aviation Area (ECAA). Under such agreement, a non-EU Member State will accept the obligation, *inter alia*, to transpose the Single European Sky Regulations and the associated implementing rules into nationally applicable legislation. Such approach has recently been reinforced in the Declaration of Madrid containing the Conclusion of the high level Conference on the Roadmap towards implementing the Single European Sky (held in the Spanish capital on 25–26 February 2010). The declaration states the following:

> Bearing in mind the importance of the network dimension, the participants agreed on the importance of extending the single European sky to neighbouring States of the European Union for the benefit of airspace users, stressing its strong pan-European dimension, in accordance with the ICAO regional approach. This extension shall be achieved through the conclusion of agreements or participation in functional airspace blocks.

In order to comply with EU Regulations, initiatives have been taken by all EU Member States – as well as by some non-EU Members – to establish the so-called Functional Airspace Blocks (FABs) before 4 December 2012. For the EU twenty-seven Member States this date is legally binding in application of the SES regulations) whilst for the non-EU Member States the implementation may be beneficial as they involve an implementation of elements from the SES concept.

The FAB concept purposes to battle fragmentation of European airspace through the restructuring of Flight Information Regions in line with operational criteria of homogeneity but ignoring national boundaries or constraints to traffic flows not relevant to ATM needs. This aspect, together with the appropriate procedures to be applied in order to notify the SES' Programme and its developments to the rest of the world, is the one on which States have increasingly started to ask for guidance.

Most of the States currently engaged in the establishment of FABs are either members of or observers of the ICAO European Air Navigation Planning Group (EANPG), namely the pan-European club of fifty-two States belonging to the ICAO EUR Navigation Region and therefore sharing the same Regional Air Navigation Plan (ANP). As already said in the previous sections, a Regional Air Navigation Plan sets forth facilities, services and regional supplementary procedures to be provided or applied by Member States.

That is why some EANPG Member States recently raised the question with the ICAO EUR/NAT Office Secretariat whether the establishment of FABs, especially when they include airspace over the High Seas, would be subject to the formal procedure for the update and amendment of Regional ANPs. This question is not a trivial one given that, under Article 28 of the Chicago Convention[1], each contracting State is responsible for the provision, in its territory, of facilities, services and the application of appropriate procedures and given that, according to the ICAO

1. Article 28(a) of the Chicago Convention:

> *Air navigation facilities and standard systems*
> Each contracting State undertakes, so far as it may find practicable, to:
>
> Provide, in its territory, airports, radio services, meteorological services and other air navigation facilities to facilitate international air navigation, in accordance with the standards and practices recommended or established from time to time, pursuant to this Convention.

Assembly, all of those set forth in Regional ANPs constitute facilities, services and procedures to be provided pursuant to Article 28. Indeed, the Plan may include services to be provided in a portion of airspace over the High Seas for which a State has accepted the responsibility for providing such services.

Regional ANPs are composed of two volumes: Volume 1 – Basic ANP and Volume II FASID. While the latter can be modified with a lighter procedure and, in case of consensus, with a decision process that remains at a regional level, the Basic ANP needs to be approved by the ICAO Council.

According to the Procedure for the Amendment of the Basic ANP – which was approved by the Council on 25 February 1998 – if any contracting State or Group of States of a Region as it would be in the case of FABs wishes to amend the Basic ANP for that Region, it should present an appropriate and documented proposal to the Secretary General of ICAO. This proposal has to be made through the Regional Office accredited to the State, in our case the EUR/NAT Office which is located in Paris. The Secretary General will then circulate the proposal with a request for comments to all provider and user States of the Region considered affected, as well as to user States outside the Region and to international organizations which may be invited to attend suitable ICAO meetings. If no objection is raised against the proposed amendment, the latter shall be submitted to the President of ICAO who can approve it on behalf of the Council. On the contrary, should any objection be raised, the matter will be documented for formal consideration by the Air Navigation Commission which will decide on the action to be taken on the proposal. Indeed, like all provisions for which consensus is needed at a State level, the process might be a little bit time-consuming. This is also why increased awareness on this issue is of paramount importance.

5 EU MEMBER STATES AND THIER RESPONSIBILITIES TOWARD ICAO

With regard to the questions on SES's implementation procedures raised by the EANPG member States, the EUR/NAT Secretariat has recently issued some documents aimed at clarifying this issue.

We do believe that EU Regulations regarding the Single European Sky in general, and the implementation of FABs in particular, seem to be in conformance with and meet the spirit of ICAO provisions. For example, the EU Regulations on SES explicitly establish the relationship with the Chicago Convention. Since the SES inception, the Framework Regulation (594/2004), in its fourth clause of the *Whereas*, states that:

> The single European sky initiative should be developed in line with the obligations stemming from the membership of the Community and its Member States of Eurocontrol, and in line with the principles laid down by the 1944 Chicago Convention on International Civil Aviation.

Indeed, those principles stated in the Convention are nothing less than international obligations undertaken by contracting States. Moreover, according to the SES Airspace Regulation (551/2004):

> Member States shall retain their responsibilities toward the ICAO within the geographical limits of the upper flight information regions and the flight information regions entrusted to them by ICAO on the date of entry into force of this Regulation.

The other issue to be considered is ICAO's position regarding the provision of services in the High Seas. According to Article 12 of the Convention:

> Each contracting State undertakes to keep its own regulations in these respects uniform, to the greatest possible extent, with those established from time to time under this Convention. Over the high seas, the rules in force shall be those established under this Convention. Each contracting State undertakes to insure the prosecution of all persons violating the regulations applicable.

In addition to this, the Foreword to Annex 2 *Rules of the Air*, clearly states that over the High Seas the *Rules of the Air* apply without exceptions. States' obligations stemming from the Chicago Convention highlighted so far are a few examples of those taken into consideration by the EUR/NAT Secretariat's analysis. Its outcome was presented to the EANPG Member States in December 2009.

On the basis of the above-mentioned considerations, the EUR/NAT Secretariat has highlighted that a State having the responsibility of the provision of air navigation services will maintain it not only within its sovereign airspace but also within the airspace over the high seas for which it has accepted the same responsibility. Initially, it is understood that there is no intention to seek modification of either the Flight Information Region (FIR) boundaries or the facilities and services currently listed in the Regional Air Navigation Plan.

Therefore we can conclude that:

(a) The establishment of FABs in accordance with the EU Regulations on the Single European Sky is not in itself subject to the process for amendment of ANPs. However, should changes to the FIR boundaries or to the facilities or services provided be required at a later stage, such changes might be subject to the ANP amendment procedure and should therefore be examined on a case-by-case basis.
(b) Pursuant to Article 83 of the Chicago Convention, agreements or arrangements for FABs are subject to registration with ICAO in accordance with the applicable rules in ICAO Doc 6685 (Rules for registration with ICAO of Aeronautical Agreements and Arrangements).[2]

---

2. Article 83 of the Chicago Convention:

> *Registration of new arrangements*
>
> Subject to the provisions of the preceding Article, any contracting State may make arrangements not inconsistent with the provisions of this Convention. Any such arrangement shall be forthwith registered with the Council, which shall make it public as soon as possible.

Both concepts highlighted in points (a) and (b) are being echoed by the European Commission in the Regulation 176/2011 *on the information to be provided before the establishment and modification of functional airspace blocks* that was published on 24 February 2011.

As an example, Preamble 12 of the Regulation's states that:

> The establishment of FABs which would result in changes to the ICAO flight information region (FIR) boundaries or to the facilities and services provided within those boundaries should continue to be the subject of the ICAO air navigation planning process and the procedure for amendment of the ICAO air navigation plans.

With regard to point (b) above, also echoed by the above-mentioned Regulation in the 11th Preamble, it has to be noted that only States, rather than international organizations including the European Union, are members of ICAO. In short, this means that any supra-national agreement as is customarily done by States also for the notification of departures from international standards has to be notified to ICAO through the appropriate and relevant 'national' authorities.

In short, Functional Airspace Blocks implementation should be consistent with the provisions of the Chicago Convention and, as far as airspaces over the High Seas are concerned, with the UN Convention on the Law of the Sea (UNCLOS III). They must also respect the conditions stemming from ICAO regional air navigation Agreements and have to ensure the safe, interoperable and seamless operation for all users during all phases of flight.

6 CONCLUSIONS

By adhering to the Chicago Convention ICAO Member States have pledged to'serve humanity'. The goal set was very high but, to that end, each contracting State undertook 'to collaborate in securing the highest practicable degree of uniformity in regulations, standards, procedures and organization'.[3]

The SES Programme promoted by the twenty-seven Member States of the European Union which are also ICAO Member States aims at improving future air trafficking management for better Safety and Sustainability of the international civil aviation within a portion of Europe. So far, excellent cooperation among EU and ICAO has allowed parties involved to identify in advance, as it should happen for all initiative of comparable dimensions, some critical areas and

3. See Art. 37 of the Chicago Convention:

> *Adoption of international standards and procedures*
>
> Each contracting State undertakes to collaborate in securing the highest practicable degree of uniformity in regulations, standards, procedures, and organization in relation to aircraft, personnel, airways and auxiliary services in all matters in which such uniformity will facilitate and improve air navigation.

issues for which there is still room for improvement. A lot has been done so far but nothing should be left to chance in the future for, as we all know, the devil is in the details.

ICAO supports the SES' inspiring principles and – with the support of all stakeholders involved – will continue to do its best to make sure that this ambitious reform of air traffic management will benefit the 'global aviation community' starting, indeed, with the 'pan-European one'.

Annex: ICAO Air Navigation Regions

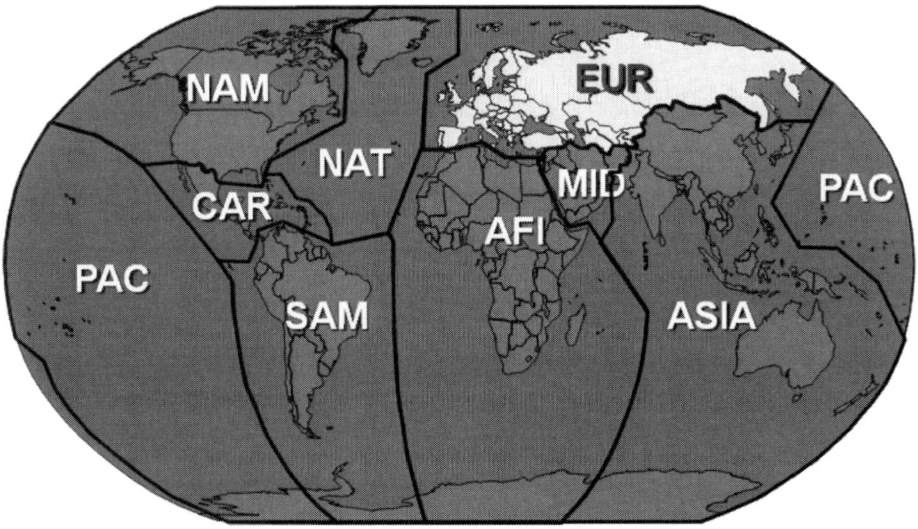

Chapter 10

European Safety Regulatory System and the Single European Sky

*Patrick Goudou**

1 THE EUROPEAN APPROACH TOWARDS AIR TRAFFIC MANAGEMENT (ATM)

A basic principle underlying the aviation policy of the EU has been that a high and uniform level of safety can be best achieved through common action at European level. High and uniform protection of the citizens will be ensured by the adoption of common safety rules and by ensuring that products, persons and organizations involved in the execution of safety critical functions comply with such rules. This was the main foundation for the European legislator to establish a European safety regulatory system and as a central element of it to set up the European Aviation Safety Agency (EASA) as an independent safety regulator. This objective was achieved by the adoption of the Regulation (EC) No 1592/2002, which entered into force in September 2002.

As a first step the EASA system included provisions necessary to ensure the airworthiness and environmental compatibility of aircraft, including personnel and organizations involved in their design, production and maintenance. Further work was then undertaken to properly address all other fields of aviation safety,

* Patrick Goudou, Executive Director, EASA.

Daniel Calleja Crespo & Pablo Mendes de Leon, *Achieving the Single European Sky: Goals and Challenges*, pp. 91–94.

including air traffic management and air navigation services (ATM/ANS). The aviation system behaves as a chain of activities with different elements interacting with each other – fragmentation at any level would be a significant impediment to the efficient functioning of the overall system. Therefore, the high and uniform level of safety could in the future only be achieved through progressively harmonizing certain requirements applicable across all domains of aviation safety. Thus, also the responsibilities in the EASA system were, therefore, to be extended progressively to cover all aspects of safety, building on a *total system approach.*

In November 2006, Vice-President Barrot of the European Commission appointed the High-Level Group for the Future European Aviation Regulatory Framework in response to a strong demand from industry, EU Member States and other stakeholders to simplify and increase the effectiveness of the regulatory framework for aviation in Europe. Vice-President Barrot asked the High-Level Group to present a vision for the development of the aviation regulatory framework – with a particular focus on ATM – and to provide a roadmap with practical next steps. The High-Level Group final report concluded its work in July 2007 through several recommendations, one of which called to bring together responsibility for safety regulation under the EASA umbrella through a total system approach.

When preparing the extension of the EASA system to cover ATM/ANS, the Single European Sky (SES) framework already established EU competence in the field and had conducted a significant effort – not only related to safety, but also on economic regulation and rationalization of service provision. It was, therefore, obvious that this further step in complementing the EU aviation safety regulatory system had to be implemented in a close coordination and building on SES. The EU legislative process to extend the EASA system – and to establish the safety pillar of SES was prepared by EASA. The related Opinion by EASA was published and issued to the Commission after an extensive consultation process in April 2008, followed by the Commission SES II Package in June 2008. Through the co-decision process by the EU Council and the European Parliament, the amendment to the EASA basic regulation covering, for example, ATM/ANS entered into force in December 2009. It stipulates that the rules for its implementation in the SES field shall enter into force latest by 2012.

2 TOTAL SYSTEM APPROACH

The total system approach is based on the fact that the aviation system components; products, operators, crews, aerodromes, ATM/ANS – on the ground, in the air or even in space – are part of a single aviation network, which will be more and more integrated through the implementation of new technologies and concepts of operations. In order to ensure a high and uniform level of safety, uniformity is achieved by common implementing rules adopted by the Commission. The total system approach aims at eliminating the risk of safety gaps or overlaps, and seeks to avoid conflicting requirements and confused responsibilities between different aviation activities. Regulations are interpreted and applied in a standardized manner and best practices are provided. At the same time, such uniformity means to protect citizens and to provide the level playing field for the functioning of the internal market. Furthermore, it will allow for the realization of increased interoperability of products and services. The total system approach has also an objective to streamline the certification processes and reduce the burden on regulated persons and organizations.

The total system approach has become an important and continuous rulemaking policy for EASA – with an aim to develop safety rules building on the most efficient mitigation of safety risks through a holistic network approach. Its main target is to implement the aviation policy of the EU on a high and uniform level of aviation safety to be maintained or improved in the evolving aviation system through common action at European level. Although this systemic approach in regulation is well on its way, the structure of ATM governance in Europe still needs to follow.

3 THE BUDAPEST CHARTER AND ITS OBJECTIVES ON SAFETY

It has become customary for many EU Presidencies to arrange High-Level Conferences on Aviation. Hungary holding the EU presidency over the first half of 2011 took its chance to arrange such an event on the very topical issue on the implementation of the SES, including its safety pillar. This conference took place at Budapest on 3 and 4 March 2011 and was jointly organized by the Vice-President of the European Commission, Mr Siim Kallas and the Minister of State for Infrastructure, Ministry of National Development of Hungary, Mr Pál Völner.

The conference established a most interesting programme including all different pillars of the implementation of SES and gathered a broad participation by the most important aviation stakeholders; The EU Commission, EASA, FAA, EUROCONTROL, States, industry (air operators, ANSPs, airports and manufacturers) and different aviation end-user staff representatives. The conference concluded its main results through the 'Budapest Charter', containing several important and actual recommendations and inviting consequently participants to the Conference and the next EU Presidencies to assess the progress made on the concrete measures proposed by the Charter and to review – and as necessary to revise – this Charter. One of the most interesting and crucial recommendations in the Charter fitting very well under this headline is the following:

> Ensure all European safety ATM/ANS tasks under the responsibility of a single framework (EASA).

It seems like a plea – '*all safety tasks under the responsibility of a single framework*' – this is nothing new and is so logical but yet there is much to do to achieve it.

4 CONCLUSION

Safety tasks in ATM/ANS are sometimes subject to reappearing discussions and even debates about what is safety and what is non-safety, or which activities should be subject to safety regulation and which ones to economic (or performance) regulation. This may not bring much added value in the safety challenges of the future European ATM system, when the main purpose of such debates is to show inertia in the tasks and mandates of the various European institutions or other bodies that are concerned with ATM/ANS. But such a debate is most welcome and necessary in defining the most efficient ways and means to tackle the safety challenges related to the new concepts of operations of our future ATM system. Although Europe has already made a significant effort in addressing the European ATM patchwork, this work has to continue – with efficient governance on the actions taken, including clear responsibilities in guiding towards the safest ATM/ANS environment. Safety tasks under the EASA umbrella is definitely one of the key pillars to address this challenge.

Safety is for the citizens (EASA's mission; your safety is our mission). In terms of European laws it is the EU, and its executive arms the EU Commission and EASA, which have a broad competence in leading the development and in setting up the regulatory tools necessary for the aviation safety. Transparency and clear goal setting are the ingredients to success with this leadership.

Chapter 11

Governance of the Single European Sky: The Single Sky Committee (SSC) and the Involvement of the Industry Consultation Body (ICB)

*Luc Tytgat**

1 INTRODUCTION

> The Union is founded on the values of democracy and the rule of law. The EU institutions shall maintain an open, transparent and regular dialogue with representative associations and civil society.

By these statements in its Articles 2 and 11, the Treaty on European Union defines not only the values guiding the policies of the EU but also the functioning of its institutions.

In the exercise of the Union's legislative and regulatory responsibilities, these values are translated into shared decision-making powers which never lie with a single institution. While the Commission takes the initiative and submits legislative or regulatory proposals, the Council and the European Parliament jointly adopt them.

Where implementing powers are conferred on the European Commission, mechanisms of control by the Member States of the Commission's powers are

* Luc Tytgat, Director Single Sky in EUROCONTROL-Former Head of Unit at the European Commission. The views expressed in this chapter are the author's own and are not necessarily endorsed by EUROCONTROL or its senior management.

Daniel Calleja Crespo & Pablo Mendes de Leon, *Achieving the Single European Sky: Goals and Challenges*, pp. 95–106.

established: this systematic and institutionalized mechanism is particular and used to be commonly referred to as 'comitology' until the recent changes introduced by the Lisbon Treaty (section 2).

The governance of the Single European Sky (SES) is primarily based on the legislative and regulatory mechanisms which led to the adoption of two successive packages. In line with the rules in force at the time, the regulations of the Council and the Parliament which created the SES in 2004 provided also for such control by the Member States through the establishment of a 'Single Sky Committee' (SSC), in charge of assisting the Commission and delivering opinions on its proposals.[1] Beyond this obligation, the legislators went further by establishing an additional forum for the consultation of other stakeholders: the Industry Consultation Body.

These two structures are an essential part of the SES implementation machinery and have been key success factors in the adoption of a comprehensive and solid legislative package containing more than forty regulatory Acts (section 3).

But governing a Single Sky, by definition vast and borderless, is proving to be much more than a simple regulatory procedure. Translating such regulations into effective implementation also requires interaction with social and political forces, as well as coordination and/or consultation with other competent organizations. Furthermore, due account has to be taken of the constantly evolving context, resulting from crises, the economic situation or technological progress. The further development of the EU policy/competence in air traffic management, the close links with other Union policies and the need to associate new actors, whether national or international, call for an assessment and possibly re-examination of the functioning of the committees. Ideas on possible innovative approaches to the governance of the Single Sky should help make it an even better performing instrument for the benefit of the European air transport industry and passengers (see section 4, below).

2 COMITOLOGY AND CONTROL BY THE MEMBER STATES

2.1 The Former 'Comitology' Mechanism

The comitology procedure is not defined in the original treaties of the European Community. It was established by practice in the 1960s, and since then has constantly been defined through the European construction. This innovation responds to a need for greater efficiency and to the necessity for the Council, which lacked the necessary resources to make all the necessary implementing rules, to control the executive powers delegated to the Commission. To this end, it established administrative committees composed of representatives of Member States, and experts in the respective policy areas, chaired by the Commission. The first

1. Article 5 of Regulation (EC) No. 549/2004 of the European Parliament and of the Council of 10 Mar. 2004 laying down the framework for the creation of the Single European Sky.

committees were the management committees for the implementation of agriculture regulations.

In its Köster case of 17 December 1970, the European Court of Justice (ECJ) acknowledged that these committees do not affect the institutional balance and that if the Council was free to delegate executive powers to the Commission, it was also free to control them. The number of committees grew rapidly until the entry into force of the Single European Act designed to achieve a single market and the adoption of Decision 87/373/EEC, which led to the codification of these comitology procedures. Pressure by the European Parliament and the need to address the opacity and complexity of the comitology mechanisms led to the adoption of a new comitology decision in 1999.[2]

Thus, before the entry into force of the Lisbon Treaty on 1 December 2009, the comitology system was governed by the Council Decision of 17 July 2006[3] amending Decision 1999/468/EC. At the time, comitology had spread so rapidly that almost all policy areas of the EU made use of comitology.

According to Article 202 of the Treaty establishing the European Community, there were five different committee procedures: the advisory procedure, the management procedure, the regulatory procedure, the regulatory procedure with scrutiny by the Council and the European Parliament (known as the 'PRAC') and the safeguard procedure. The applicable procedures were usually defined in the basic legislation adopted by the Council and the Parliament, and delineated the powers of the Commission to implement the said legislation, through the executive measures also laid down in the basic Act, for example, implementing rules, decisions, communications and so forth. The adoption of rules on composition, functioning and procedure was left to the discretion of each committee.[4]

In delegating to the Commission powers to implement the SES, the Council and the European Parliament established a committee in charge of assisting the Commission through the advisory procedure, the regulatory procedure and the regulatory procedure with scrutiny.

2.2 The New Comitology after Lisbon

2.2.1 The Provisions of the Lisbon Treaty

Following the numerous criticisms relating to its lack of transparency and lack of democratic control, the comitology procedure has been abolished by the Lisbon Treaty. Articles 290 and 291 of the Treaty on the Functioning of the European Union (TFEU) have 'split' the old comitology procedure and introduced two new legal

2. Council Decision 1999/468/EC of 28 Jun. 1999 laying down the procedures for the exercise of implementing powers conferred on the Commission.
3. Council Decision 2006/512/EC of 17 Jul. 2006.
4. Guided, however, by the Standards Rules of Procedure adopted by the Commission on 31 Jan. 2001.

bases. There are now two ways to delegate powers to the Commission: delegations of authority to adopt and update the technical implementing measures of a legislative Act and delegations of implementing powers.

While individual measures are always implementing Acts under Article 291, measures of a general scope can be delegated or implementing Acts. Implementing Acts are intended only to give effect to the existing rules of a basic Act. Delegated Acts modify the basic regulation by amending its normative rules or by adding new obligations to it.

2.2.2 Delegated Acts

Delegated Acts as referred to in Article 290 of the TFEU cover almost the same type of measures as those adopted previously under the 'regulatory procedure with scrutiny', introduced in the comitology decision in 2006. Pursuant to Article 290 of the TFEU, the EU legislators (the Council and the European Parliament) may delegate to the Commission the power to adopt non-legislative Acts supplementing or amending certain non-essential elements of a legislative Act. They may also decide to revoke such delegation or make objections to a delegated Act of the Commission. The objectives, content, scope and duration of the specific delegation will be defined explicitly in each legislative Act (or basic Act) at the origin of a delegation. The committees will no longer exist, but the Commission may consult experts from national authorities of all Member States. The delegated Act may enter into force if, within the time frame fixed by the legislative Act, the European Parliament (by an absolute majority vote) or the Council (by a qualified majority vote) does not express any objections.

In its Communication of 9 December 2009, the Commission proposed an interpretation of Article 290 for its practical implementation. The basic Acts will gradually be revised, meaning that the regulatory procedure with scrutiny will still be used in existing committees, but will disappear slowly over the years. The Commission is committed to completing this alignment exercise by the end of 2012 and finalizing the legislative amendments to replace the regulatory procedures with scrutiny by the procedure for adoption of delegated Acts by the end of June 2014.

2.2.3 Implementing Acts

Implementing Acts are the second category of measures that can be delegated to the Commission. They correspond to the 'traditional comitology procedures' applicable prior to the Lisbon Treaty which have undergone some changes. They are used where uniform conditions for implementing legally binding Union Acts are needed.

The application of Article 291 of the TFEU expressly requires a regulation framing the new committee procedures. To this end, the European Parliament and the Council adopted by a joint decision Regulation No. 182/2011 of 16 February 2011, laying down the rules and general principles concerning mechanisms for control by Member States of the Commission's exercises of implementing powers. It replaces Comitology Decision No. 1999/468/EC as amended in 2006.

This regulation establishes a simplified system compared to the old system of comitology. Indeed, only two procedures are laid down: the advisory procedure, which corresponds to the former advisory procedure, and a new procedure called the examination procedure replacing the existing management procedure and regulatory procedure.

Both types of procedures will be implemented as before with the help of committees composed of Member States' representatives and chaired by the Commission. Referral to the Council in the event of differences of opinion is done away with, and the European Parliament no longer has an institutional role. The procedure retains the voting system of the old regulatory procedure, so that the Commission must obtain a positive qualified majority vote of the committee to adopt the implementing Act. In the opposite case, if the committee issues a negative opinion, the Commission may submit its proposal to an Appeal Committee[5] for further examination or modification. Finally, in a limited number of cases, and when so provided for in the basic regulation, the Council and the Parliament may retain a right of scrutiny which entitles them to notify the Commission at any time that the proposed implementing Act is considered as exceeding the powers granted to the Commission.

Thus, under the new procedures, the European Parliament and the Member States keep hold of all European legal instruments. The right of scrutiny of the European Parliament and the Council, democratic control and the transparency requirements in decision-making procedures are increased, while the advantages of the former comitology procedures are maintained as the new procedures still allow for regular updating of legislation based on technical progress.

3 EUROPEAN COMITOLOGY APPLIED TO THE SINGLE EUROPEAN SKY

3.1 Added Value of EU Governance in Air Traffic Management

The need for the EU to act in this new domain of air traffic management resulted from the following observations:

- European airspace is highly fragmented and has more than sixty area control centres managing half of the volume of traffic flying in United States airspace, for insatnce. The Member States remain the key actors responsible for the implementation of the measures adopted.
- Air routes are 'zigzagging' to avoid massive military areas in the heart of Europe (a relic of the cold war), where the density of traffic is the highest.
- Air traffic control in Europe is twice as costly as control in the United States.

In addition, the sole regulatory activities in this domain were at the time performed in the framework of the European Organisation for the Safety of Air Navigation

5. Article 6 of Regulation No. 182/2011.

(EUROCONTROL), with solid legal, technical and industrial expertise in air traffic management but with weak regulatory powers. The decision-making process within EUROCONTROL was indeed heavily reliant on unanimous votes by its Member States and required lengthy prior consultation mechanisms to achieve consensus before the formal and final vote. The attempt by EUROCONTROL to improve its decision-making process by the revision of its amended Convention in 1997 never became fully effective in the absence of ratification of the amending protocol by the Member States. Some provisions are implemented on a provisional basis but do not allow a change of rules at the highest decision-making level (Permanent Commission). The subsequent Protocol of 2002 on the accession of the European Community to the EUROCONTROL Convention was not ratified either, thus depriving the Community of the possibility to exercise within EUROCONTROL, through voting rights cumulating the votes of the Community Member States, the competence conferred on it by the treaties. Finally, although the decisions adopted by the bodies of EUROCONTROL are binding on the Member States, they are not always complied with and applied. With the only means to resolve disputes between the organization and its Member States being arbitration,[6] it was felt that EUROCONTROL was lacking efficient and powerful enforcement powers.

The Commission's Communication on the 'creation of the Single European Sky' published at the end of 1999[7] noted the limitations of the traditional working methods, based thus far on inter-governmental cooperation within EUROCONTROL, as insufficient to address the structural problems of the air traffic control sector and recommended both urgent measures and 'new decision-making processes'.

The De Palacio vision of a single, defragmented and efficient sky for Europe materialized in 2004 with the extension of the competence of the EU to air transport. Immediate benefits resulted from the application to air traffic management of the EU decision-making process and of majority voting for the adoption of legislative and regulatory Acts, thus breathing new life into the congested and fragmented European skies.

Its right of initiative allowed the Commission to become the political driving force in moving towards the modernization of air traffic control and the development of an integrated and ambitious Single Sky.

The two successive SES legislative packages delivered more than forty regulatory acts:

- Four basic regulations[8] which laid down the foundations and principles of the SES (the 'Framework Regulation', the 'Service Provision Regulation', the 'Airspace Regulation' and the 'Interoperability Regulation');

6. Article 31 of the International Convention relating to Co-operation for the Safety of Air Navigation of 13 Dec. 1960, as amended on 12 Feb. 1981.
7. COM/99/0614/final.
8. Respectively Regulation No. 549/2004, No. 550/2004, No. 551/2004 and No. 552/2004 of 10 Mar. 2004 amended by Regulation No. 1070/2009 of 21 Oct. 2009.

- One directive on the licensing of air traffic controllers;[9]
- Twenty-Two Implementing Rules adopted as Commission Regulations between December 2005 and February 2011;
- Three Commission Decisions;[10]
- Seven Commission Communications.

3.2 Single European Sky Comitology Procedures and Achievements

3.2.1 Basic Role of the Commission

The basic Single Sky regulations entrusted the Commission with a large number of implementing tasks, which in addition to its powers of initiative gave it substantial power to drive the development and implementation of the Single Sky. However, the contributions of the Single Sky Committee (SSC) and the Industry Consultation Body (ICB) were essential for the successful achievement of this intensive legislative and regulatory work.

3.2.2 The Industry Consultation Body

The ICB was established by Article 6 of the Framework Regulation to exclusively advise the Commission on the implementation of the SES. It comprises representatives of stakeholders not represented by States: air navigation service providers, associations of airspace users, airports, the manufacturing industry and professional staff representative bodies.

The creation of this body was not an obligation under European legislation, and its establishment reflects the willingness of the legislator to mark the importance of stakeholders in the specific domain of air traffic management. While the initial text of Regulation No. 549/2004 limited the advice by the ICB to technical matters only, the amendment made by Regulation No. 1070/2009 ended this restriction. Today the ICB provides advice of a strategic nature on all aspects relating to the implementation of the SES, including for instance institutional and regulatory matters. The ICB acts as a forum of the major stakeholders of European industry to enable their views to be represented and discussed in an open and constructive manner to facilitate the establishment of balanced and consolidated advice to the Commission.

---

9. Repealed by Regulation No. 1108/2009 of 21 Oct. 2009 amending Regulation (EC) No. 216/2008 – about to be adopted as a Commission Regulation after limited re-drafting by EASA.
10. Commission Decision of 29 Jul. 2010 on the designation of the Performance Review Body of the Single European Sky, Commission Decision of 12 Aug. 2010 on the designation of a functional airspace block system coordinator, Commission Decision of 21 Feb. 2011 setting the EU-wide performance targets and alert thresholds for the provision of air navigation services for the years 2012–2014. Another Commission Regulation and a Commission Decision are expected to be adopted soon (on network functions).

It is composed of representatives of air traffic service providers, CNS providers,[11] meteorological service providers, airspace users, manufacturing industry, airports and professional staff representative bodies.[12] The US Federal Aviation Administration is also invited. This list illustrates the challenge faced by the ICB in delivering a single and consolidated opinion to the Commission despite the sometimes contradictory interests of its members. It is indeed difficult, on subjects such as the performance scheme and its targets for instance, to achieve the consensus required by the Terms of Reference, when the airspace users call for ambitious targets while air navigation service providers subject to these targets would like to keep them at the minimum level. However, throughout its thirty-nine meetings, the ICB has always managed so far to provide sound and expert advice to the Commission but also to the Single Sky Committee, which it usually precedes.

3.2.3 The Single Sky Committee

The Single Sky Committee (SSC) was convened and met for the first time even before the adoption of the basic Regulation No. 549/2004 of 10 March 2004, which officially established it in its Article 5, in accordance with Council Decision 1999/468/EC. Since 2004, the Committee has met forty-one times and it is estimated that it has provided on average one formal opinion after a voting procedure per meeting.

The SSC assists the Commission by providing opinions on the Commission's proposals for implementing measures, rules or decisions, under three *procedures*: advisory,[13] regulatory,[14] or regulatory procedures with scrutiny.[15] Simple majority voting is required under the advisory procedures and qualified majority voting is required for regulatory procedures. It may happen that the SSC is requested to provide various levels of opinions on the same subject: advisory for guidance documents and regulatory for implementing rules. The Committee can vote during sessions or adopt a position via written procedure.

The Lisbon Treaty and the new system for delegated or implementing Acts is at this stage having little impact on the SSC: existence, composition and procedure remain[16] for former advisory and regulatory procedures, but the permanent right of scrutiny of the Council and the Parliament no longer automatically entails a suspension of the decision-making process, which should make the process faster. Uncertainty remains, however, with regard to the future of the regulatory

---

11. *C*ommunication-*N*avigation-*S*urveillance providers.
12. Observers may also be invited on a case-by-case basis: EUROCONTROL and organizations representing non-EU interests are usually invited.
13. Example: Arts 8, 11.3(c) of the Framework Regulation, Art. 9a8 of the Service Provision Regulation.
14. Example: Arts 11.3 and 11.6 of the Framework Regulation, Arts 6 and 9a9 of the Service Provision Regulation, Arts 6.4 and 6.7 of the Airspace Regulation.
15. The first package of SES legislation did not provide for comitology under the regulatory procedure with scrutiny. The only example was introduced in the second package, in the amended Art. 6.3 of Regulation 551/2004 ('Airspace Regulation').
16. Until 31 Oct. 2014 the voting rights will remain the same.

procedure with scrutiny: the basic Act (Airspace Regulation) will probably need to be amended, but the exact timeline and modalities are still to be defined. The possible establishment of an appeal committee has not yet been clarified either.

The *composition* of the SSC, always chaired by the Commission, is specific in comparison with other comitology bodies. Here again, the legislator went beyond the usual requirements of the standard rules of procedure for committees in force at the time and enlarged the membership to two representatives per State: 'The Commission shall be assisted by the Single Sky Committee . . . composed of two representatives of each Member State'.[17]

The objective of this double representation was to reflect the specific nature of air traffic management and the importance of civil-military cooperation in this domain. Most of the States are, therefore, represented by a civil official and a military one. However, this double representation does not lead to double votes. The rules of procedure provide that the two representatives count as a single delegation: 'Each Member State delegation is considered to be one committee member. Each committee member can be represented by two Member State officials'.[18]

To ensure consistency of the policies beyond the EU's borders and adequate synergies with other European bodies, SSC membership can be extended to observer States or organizations.[19] Norway, Liechtenstein, Iceland, Switzerland and representatives of the contracting parties of the European Common Aviation Area are invited to attend the meetings of the Committee without voting rights. Representatives of EUROCONTROL, the ICAO Regional Office in Paris, the European Aviation Safety Agency and the SESAR Joint Undertaking (SESAR JU) can also be invited to participate by the Chairman of the SSC. Finally, the Chairman can also decide to invite experts to provide information on specific matters. All these observers and experts must withdraw when the Committee takes a formal vote.

The Committee exists because comitology was mandatory, but its *role* is wider. For all aspects not specifically provided for in the regulations as requiring a formal vote, the Commission is free to seek advice from the SSC. The adoption of a common position before participation on other institutions' bodies[20] is an example. The Committee is also kept informed about matters managed by the Commission in relation to the implementation of the SES and may comment as appropriate.

With the successful adoption of more than forty regulatory acts, the comitology system has proved its effectiveness in the context of the SES. However, both the practice followed and the evolution of the Single Sky needs highlight the necessity to seriously assess the suitability of the Committee as it exists today for fulfilling the SES policy objectives.

---

17. Article 5.1 of Regulation No. 549/2004.
18. Article 6 of the Rules of Procedure of the Single Sky Committee.
19. Article 8 of the Rules of Procedure of the SSC.
20. For example, before participation of the Commission on the SESAR JU Administrative Board.

4 TOWARDS A MORE INNOVATIVE GOVERNANCE OF SES

4.1 Limitations of SES Comitology

The constraints inherent to the current comitology concern the following aspects.

Difficulty in reaching consensus on highly strategic and political issues – Experience showed that while the SSC system worked very well in technical domains, such as the adoption of rules on interoperability, decision-making was more difficult in matters involving political sensitivities. The adoption of performance targets for air navigation services almost led to a crisis and the blocking of decision-making in winter 2010. Despite broad political support in Europe on the principle of a performance scheme, the detailed application did not trigger sufficient favourable voting in the successive attempts to formalize these very sensitive measures in the Committee. It was the first time that the next step of the comitology procedure was envisaged, that is, referral to the Council.[21]

The reasons behind this lie in the sometimes limited powers of States' representatives, who lack the freedom to manoeuvre during sessions, as well as in the often highly specialized and technical profiles of these representatives. In addition, independence from industry interests is not always ensured by the Member States.

Formal and pre-established decision-making and consultation are not sufficient to address all components of SES – SES governance includes a political dimension which goes beyond the regulatory aspects. The Commission has an essential role to play in ensuring that there is enough « oil in the machine » through informal political interaction. It ensures that sufficient liaison is established with other institutions, Member States, key stakeholders and social partners. This need is even more evident in times of crisis, as during the ash cloud crisis in spring 2010, the 'snow crisis' in December 2010 and the 'summer delay' potential crisis in 2011.

Furthermore, SES foundations are built on five pillars: in addition to the regulatory pillar, which of course involves comitology, the SES policy includes four other pillars: a safety pillar, a technological pillar, an airport pillar and a human factor pillar. While the SSC and the ICB are informed of developments in all these pillars, they do not formally decide on them. In this regard also, the Commission plays a central role in coordinating all aspects.

Insufficient association of the pan-European dimension – The sky has no limits: air traffic management problems and possible solutions extend beyond the strict borders of the twenty-seven EU Member States. The admission as observers of European Economic Area (EEA) and European Common Aviation Area (ECAA) States on the Single Sky Committee is already a first step. But any sound approach to effective ATM requires consideration of bringing the benefits of SES to a larger geographical area, particularly since many SES mechanisms and schemes rely on EUROCONTROL.[22] Eastern and Southern European, Middle-Eastern and North

21. Article 5.4 of Decision 2006/512/CE.
22. EUROCONTROL has 39 Member States, 26 of which are members of the EU (as of 1.4.11).

African States which are neighbours of the EU area are essential partners and should in some way be associated with EU decision-making.

Need to adjust to a new European ATM organizational landscape – The implementation of the SES is creating new actors on the European scene: Functional Airspace Blocks (FABs), joint State initiatives to achieve better ATM capacity and efficiency between their respective borders.[23] These new actors will have a definite impact on SSC decision-making since they may represent a blocking minority. The role of FABs is going to be taken into account for the first time in the composition of the Network Management Board (NMB) of the Network Manager (NM), but greater efforts will have to be made to take proper account of these emerging forces. Furthermore, the European ATM landscape is composed of various organizations and entities (EU institutions including the European Aviation Safety Agency (EASA), the Single European Sky ATM Research Joint Undertaking (SESAR JU), EUROCONTROL, the International Civil Aviation Organization (ICAO) Regional Office, etc.), whose competences need to be adequately coordinated to deliver the best synergies. For the first time, the meetings of the EASA Committee and the SSC have been aligned and held back to back in order to facilitate coordination, particularly on the innovative 'fast-track' procedures.[24]

Need to interconnect with related domains – The SES will deliver better if it takes proper account of domains which may have a connection with or an impact on it: the extension of SES to new pillars, in particular the airports and human factors pillars, is already an illustration of this added value. A link with environmental, satellite, and European standardization policies, for instance, would also bring interesting benefits.

4.2 Innovative Proposals on SES Governance

Several options could be investigated to overcome the above shortcomings.

The first option would consist in further extending membership of the SSC to non-EU States in order to participate in the preparation of regulation, for instance in the context of the network management functions which will potentially involve all EUROCONTROL Member States. This would enable a concerted approach at global European level facilitating synchronized investment and infrastructures.

Another possibility would be to align as far as possible the agendas and sessions of the SSC and EASA Committee; for the first time, in 2010, the meetings of the EASA Committee and the SSC were held back to back in order to facilitate coordination, particularly on the innovative 'fast-track' procedures.[25] It might also

23. The creation of FABs is provided for in Art. 9a of Regulation No. 550/2004. They have to be established by 4 Dec. 2012, and currently 9 projects have been completed or are under way.
24. The 'fast-track' procedures designed to change the legal basis of former Commission Regulations into regulations under the EASA format, while maintaining their substance. Based on a 'gentleman's agreement' with the Member States, this procedure allows a full consultation process to be avoided.
25. The 'fast-track' procedures designed to change the legal basis of former Commission Regulations into regulations under the EASA format, while maintaining their substance. Based on a 'gentleman's agreement' with the Member States, this procedure avoids a full consultation process. It is applied for instance to the changing of the ATCO Directive 2006/23/EC or the Common Requirements Regulation (No. 2096/2005).

be possible for the two bodies to align their agendas, not only on ATM matters, but also on other domains such as airworthiness. This would also allow for instance a more integrated approach to upgrades of on-board ATM equipment and ground systems.

In the same spirit, and based on the model of the joint committee created at ministerial level associating representatives of the EU and the European Space Agency, the EU would benefit from adopting a similar approach associating EUROCONTROL via its Permanent Commission with the sessions of the EU Transport Council, enabling a single political decision-making structure for as large as possible a European area.

Such synergies with other European organizations could in particular help in developing a regional overture to the ICAO, facilitating verification by the Organization that international standards are uniformly applied in the European region.

The Single Sky Committee would certainly deliver enhanced benefits if the States' participation also included representatives in charge of political issues with the appropriate level of decision-making powers. In addition, participation should be strictly independent of national industry interests and should be capable of capturing the strategic challenges at continental rather than local level.

Optimization of the current role of the SSC would also bring benefits and would for instance be a means of ensuring that the deliverables of the technological research and development carried out in common are actually deployed in a centralized and coordinated manner.

Finally, the central role of the Commission in the governance of the SES could produce more added-value: in its capacity as Chairman of the SSC, the Commission always has the possibility of placing on the agenda developments in other domains, or of liaising with other EU policies, in view of the potential impact of ATM on these policies, for example, the environment, noise at and around airports, consumer and passenger protection, intermodal transport. The Commission could make better use of this power through the horizontal internal adoption procedures, that is, inter-service consultations or collegiate adoption, and could demonstrate how air traffic management can respond to society's needs.

5 CONCLUSION

The actual need to reassess and possibly revise the governance of the SES will be highly dependent on the success of the implementation of the second package, which will be measured at the end of 2012 *inter alia* through verification of the compliance of FABs with regulatory criteria, the functioning of the performance scheme and the network functions, the development of EASA capabilities in ATM and the progress towards high-level formalized cooperation between EUROCONTROL and the EU.

If implementation is not successful, a third SES package would provide an opportunity to readjust the governance of the SES to ensure a more integrated and possibly top-down approach.

Chapter 12

A US Point of View on European ATM Developments

*Brian F. Havel**

1 INTRODUCTION

US Federal Aviation Administration (FAA) regulators are immersed in a multi-billion dollar project to modernize the US air traffic management (ATM) system by replacing terrestrial navigation aids and analogue communications with satellite solutions and digital systems.[1] The benefits of NextGEN,[2] a modern ATM system that will include reduced vertical separation minima, required navigation performance, free routing, and utilization of the full capabilities of modern in-aircraft navigation technology,[3] are compelling from multiple perspectives including cost efficiencies and environmental impact. It is scarcely surprising that, as this monumental effort to dismantle and supersede a legacy architecture proceeds, the

* Brian F. Havel, Distinguished Research Professor of Law & Director, International Aviation Law Institute, DePaul University College of Law, Chicago; Keeley Visiting Fellow, University of Oxford, Wadham College (2011–2012).

1. The current system operates primarily with 1940s technology, resembling 'something that was used to guide the Beatles during their first trip to America'. Justin T. Barkowski, *Managing Air Traffic Congestion*, 37 Pepp. L. Rev. 247, 249 (2010).
2. NextGEN is the appealing acronym for Next Generation Air Transportation System.
3. See *generally* FAA, Next Generation Air Transportation System (NextGEN), <www.faa.gov/nextgen/>.

Daniel Calleja Crespo & Pablo Mendes de Leon, *Achieving the Single European Sky: Goals and Challenges*, pp. 107–117.

FAA's specialists are interested in similar ambitious transformations that are planned or already occurring in other jurisdictions. The European Union's Single European Sky ATM Research (SESAR) programme provides a simultaneously evolving technical platform as well as an object for mutual intellectual emulation. The level of US interest is not purely a matter of seeking shared technical or engineering expertise, however. There is a much broader policy goal that is evidently motivating the FAA and US stakeholders, namely, the achievement of global interoperability among *all* ATM systems.[4]

If passenger air traffic does indeed double in the next fifteen to twenty years (a projection disputed geologically or emotionally by peak oil adherents[5] and anti-aviation environmentalists,[6] respectively), current air navigation services will require substantial upgrades. Flight delays and airport congestion in both the United States and Europe have already breached acceptable limits and exacerbated aviation's notoriety as a climate change offender.[7] But a multiplicity of ATM standards is also a huge cost imposition on an industry which operates on narrow margins and is always prey to exogenous natural or economic risks. A proliferation of standards as well as localized technology solutions and equipage requirements forecloses the full potential of advanced technologies that would operate across borders and ensure seamless aircraft transitions.

In the long term, the prospects for seamlessness and interoperability appear favourable (assuming that fiscal resources can be galvanized). At certain times the airline industry has evolved fissiparously, as with its 'spaghetti bowl' of bilateral air services treaties.[8] But at other times an international perspective has prevailed, especially in technical areas and notably through the regulatory harmonization initiatives of the International Civil Aviation Organization (ICAO). The danger of the parallel evolution of separate ATM initiatives (e.g., in Australia, Canada, China, and several EU countries)[9] is precisely what the industry's worldwide trade association, the International Air Transport Association (IATA), fears in its

---

4. In the view of the International Air Transport Association (IATA), the international airline industry's leading trade group, a modernized global ATM system 'will result in environmental benefits (i.e. reduced emissions), and lower overall costs for the airlines through operational improvements, efficiency, avionics equipage and equitable user charges'. IATA, ONE SKY...GLOBAL ATM–THE WAY FORWARD 1 (2003) [hereinafter IATA, ONE SKY].
5. See Alex Kuhlman, *Peak Oil–Impacts on Commercial Aviation*, AERLINES, at 1, <www.aerlines.nl/issue_38/38_Kuhlman_Peak_Oil_Collapse_Commercial_Aviation.pdf>.
6. See Ben Webster, *Aircraft Emissions to Double by 2030 Despite Hi-Tech Jets*, TIMES (London), 21 Jun. 2005, <www.timesonline.co.uk/tol/news/uk/article535686.ece>.
7. See *generally Environmentalists Less Than Impressed with Aviation Industry's Commitment to Reducing Aircraft Emissions*, GREENAIR, 23 Sep. 2009, <www.greenaironline.com/news.php?viewStory=603>.
8. See Brian F. Havel & Gabriel S. Sanchez, *Restoring Global Aviation's 'Cosmopolitan* Mentalité', 29 B.U. INT'L L.J. 1, 11–22 (2011) (assessing the development and implications of the international aviation trade system).
9. See Jad Mouawad, *Air Traffic System Update Encountered Turbulence*, N.Y. TIMES, 1 Apr. 2011, <www.nytimes.com/2011/04/02/business/02air.html>.

position paper on global ATM reform – the absence of an international perspective.[10] The question addressed in this Chapter is whether that international perspective is best obtained through aprioristic reliance on ICAO or through the evolution of a regional US/EU interoperability that evolves technical standards for later globalized application. It is submitted that the US 'point of view' is to favour ICAO but to rely in the first instance on US/EU regionalism.

2 REJECTING AN 'APRIORISTIC' ICAO APPROACH

The US perspective, therefore, looks to SESAR but also looks to ICAO's potential leadership role. It is not surprising that this apparently bifurcated approach has prevailed. The scale of the proposed global collaboration is unprecedented, exceeding the trans-border partnerships needed to build the Airbus 380 or, even more tellingly, the international space station.[11]

ICAO has invested considerable effort in developing the planning methodology that will lead to global harmonization. Its Global Air Navigation Plan is a 'living document' that has emerged through several iterations, consultations and conferences.[12] The current version of the Plan is anchored to a definitional premise describing a global ATM system as 'a worldwide system that, on a global basis, achieves interoperability and seamlessness across regions for all users during all phases of flight; meets agreed levels of safety; provides for optimum economic operations; is environmentally sustainable; and meets national security requirements'.[13] This impressively ambitious proposal, studded with complex diagrammatic blueprints, seeks to establish a structure of homogeneous ATM areas and major traffic flows and routing areas.[14] These areas and flows, the Plan envisages, 'tie together the various elements of the worldwide aviation infrastructure into a global system'.[15] While it lies outside the scope of this Chapter to examine the

10. See IATA, One Sky, *supra* n. 4, at 1–5.
11. *Ibid.*, at 11; see *also* ICAO, *Global Air Navigation Plan*, App. C, at 5, ICAO Doc. No. 9750 (3rd ed. 2007) ('[S]ince the global system will be a seamless one, it will require an unprecedented degree of cooperation among international organizations, States, service providers and users at all levels: local, national, regional and global').
12. *Ibid.*, App. A, at 3–4 (summarizing history of the Plan including involvement of the ICAO Air Navigation Commission).
13. *Ibid.*, at 1.
14. *Ibid.*, Ch. 1, at 1.
15. *Ibid.* There are 66 of these homogeneous ATM areas and major traffic flows/routing areas identified in Appendix I of the Plan, distributed among seven major global regions. The Plan defines a homogeneous ATM area as 'an airspace with a common ATM interest, based on similar characteristics of traffic density, complexity, air navigation system infrastructure requirements or other specified considerations'. *Ibid.* A major traffic flow refers to 'a concentration of significant volumes of air traffic on the same or proximate flight trajectories'. *Ibid.*, Ch. 1, at 2. Thus, major traffic flows may cross several homogeneous ATM areas with different characteristics. *Ibid.*

twenty-three 'initiatives' that form the Plan's logistical bedrock,[16] there is no doubting ICAO's ambition. The Organization unabashedly proclaims itself to be 'the only international organization in a position to effectively coordinate global ATM implementation activities leading to the realization of' a global ATM system.[17]

ICAO's chief contribution, in US eyes, will be to address the institutional challenges to an efficient and effective global ATM system. IATA, similarly, wants ICAO to 'orchestrate implementation efforts at a worldwide level'.[18] In this setting, if NextGen/SESAR are to become the twin supports for an arch of interoperability, then ICAO's leadership will ultimately be the keystone. But globalizing ATM beyond NextGEN/SESAR will not be a straightforward task, irrespective of the multiple benefits of a modernized, unified system. ICAO, IATA, and the United States advocate that a single multilateral institution should take custody of the matter and impose, through the powers vested in the Organization by the Chicago Convention, 'Standards and Recommended Practices' (SARPs) mandating a global ATM system.[19]

The success of such a major initiative cannot be guaranteed, however, for a number of reasons. First, a top-down mandate is likely to be met with displeasure by many, if not most, ICAO members. Since ICAO does not function as an autonomous supranational legislative body with the authority to 'bind and loose' its State parties without their express consent, any SARPs perceived as onerous or contrary to national policy would be stillborn.[20] Second, even if one were to concede (as some commentators have) that there is an undeniable legislative component to the SARP,[21] ICAO possesses highly circumscribed enforcement powers with respect to State disregard or non-implementation of SARPs. Thus, ICAO Member States are at liberty to reject newly promulgated SARPs so long as they timely notify their fellow members. There are no embedded repercussions for such defections in the

16. *Ibid.*, Ch. 1, at 6–7 (including, for example, flexible use of airspace, reduced vertical separation minima, alignment of upper airspace classifications, air traffic flow management, collaborative airspace design and management, functional integration of ground systems with airborne systems, etc.).
17. *Ibid.*, App. A, at 3.
18. IATA, One Sky, *supra* n. 10, at 8. 'Proper international standards, procedures and guidance are required to prevent the emergence of diverging national or regional solutions that could impose additional burdens on service providers and, in turn, on airlines'. *Ibid.*
19. See Convention on International Civil Aviation Arts 37, 54(1), & Ch. VI, *opened for signature* 7 Dec. 1944, 61 Stat. 1180, 15 U.N.T.S. 295 (entered into force 4 Apr. 1947) [hereinafter Chicago Convention]. IATA has certainly encouraged ICAO to assume a leadership position. See IATA, One Sky, *supra* n. 10, at 9. Thus, IATA brackets its own ATM Implementation Roadmap with the ICAO Global Air Navigation Plan. See *ibid.*
20. Moreover, optimal airspace allocation will require accommodation of military operations, thereby implicating national security issues. ICAO's remit under the Chicago Convention specifically excludes military (or State) aircraft and the Organization has been careful not to intrude into the regulation of military air operations. See Chicago Convention, *supra* n. 19, arts. 3(a)–(b) & 9(a).
21. See, *e.g.*, Michael Milde, *The Chicago Convention—After Forty Years*, 9 Annals Air & Space L. 119, 121 (1984).

Chicago Convention itself.[22] Finally, ICAO's handling of a multilateral scheme for airline carbon emissions has caused some reputational compression with respect to 'top-down' policymaking. Having won exclusive authority to develop a harmonized approach to reduction of international aviation emissions under the Kyoto Protocol to the U.N. Framework Convention on Climate Change, the Organization has failed to deliver effectively on this mandate.[23] In the meantime, the European Union has adopted internal legislation to begin unilateral regulation of all aircraft emissions by any airline entering or departing EU airspace.[24] The European Union's Emissions Trading Scheme (ETS) may have a negative cascading effect as other States adopt similar schemes or retaliatory measures. While ICAO continues to serve a crucial role as a forum to consider key issues in air transport liberalization, safety, and security, it is questionable whether it is (as of now) equal to the task of managing a transition to global ATM interoperability.

3 THE BILATERAL APPROACH: NEXTGEN/ SESAR COOPERATION

While interoperability and seamlessness on a global scale certainly call for a one-stop multilateral agency, the magnitude of the task almost defies credulity. As was obvious from the tortuous course of negotiations leading to the 2007 US/EU Air Transport Agreement (and its 2010 Protocol),[25] maintaining the optimal political and policy conditions for any multilateral aviation initiative – let alone one of this magnitude – would be a gargantuan undertaking.[26]

The discussion in Section 1 explains, therefore, the political and operational context that drives bilateral collaboration between US and EU aeronautical regulators (and engineers). The primary response of US aviation authorities to the emergence of the SESAR initiative has been one of interest in achieving bilateral collaboration as a precursor to ICAO standardization. The harmonization goals embraced in SESAR, in the US view, demonstrate a profound act of political will

22. See Gabriel S. Sanchez, *The Impotence of the Chicago Convention's Dispute Settlement Provisions*, 10 Issues Aviation L. & Pol'y 27, 36 n.39 (2010); see *also* Chicago Convention, *supra* n. 19, art. 38.
23. See Kyoto Protocol to Amend the U.N. Framework Convention on Climate Change art. 2(2), *opened for signature* 11 Dec. 1997, 37 I.L.M. 32. Thus far, ICAO has only been able to induce a non-binding resolution from its membership to undertake modest steps to offset aviation carbon emissions. See ICAO, *Consolidated Statement of Continuing ICAO Policies and Practices Related to Environmental Protection—Climate Change*, Assemb. Res. A-37/19, *compiled in Resolutions Adopted by the Assembly: Provisional Edition*, at 58, para. 4 (2010).
24. See *generally* Martin Staniland, *Air Transport and the EU's Emissions Trading Scheme: Issues and Arguments*, 8 Issues Aviation L. & Pol'y 153 (2009).
25. See Air Transport Agreement, US-EU, 30 Apr. 2007, 46 I.L.M. 470, *as amended by* Protocol to Amend the Air Transport Agreement, US-EU, 24 Jun. 2010, 2010 O.J. (L 223) 3.
26. The assertion in the main text humbly paraphrases the original statement by former US Department of Transportation Under Secretary for Policy, Jeffrey N. Shane, in *Aviation Deregulation: A Work in Progress*, Speech to the International Aviation Club, Washington, D.C. (8 Nov. 2005), <http://ostpxweb.dot.gov/aviation/Speeches/Intl%20Aviation%20Club.pdf>.

(as all prominent systemic reforms in aviation inevitably must).[27] But US officials understand that, even bilaterally, converting political will into technical accomplishment will require coordination mechanisms of great complexity.[28] For US federal aviation regulators, therefore, leveraging the virtually simultaneous EU experience offers the potential for a joint vehicle to create international technical standards in satellite-based ATM reform that can eventually be transmitted worldwide through ICAO. At the 2011 EU Forum on Transatlantic Aviation Competitiveness in Washington, D.C.,[29] at least one prominent EU regulator referred in passing to the 'dirty little secret' that ICAO will always follow the United States and European Union on the setting of global regulatory standards.[30] But that statement was not really a release of clandestine intelligence – it is a matter of demonstrable history.[31]

As well as technical coordination, the quest for universal interoperability also raises issues of State sovereignty over airspace and whether airspace can be addressed both collaboratively and multilaterally rather than in the piecemeal exchanges of traffic rights which characterized the bilateral treaties of the 'Chicago system'.[32] The ICAO Global Air Navigation Plan explicitly provides that airspace sovereignty

---

27. See ICAO, *Forum on Integration and Harmonization of NextGEN and SESAR into the Global ATM Framework*: *Summary*, at 2 (September 2008), <www.icao.int/inexses/docs/Forum_Summary.pdf>.
28. *Ibid.*
29. See Press Release, Eur. Comm'n, EU Forum on Transatlantic Competitiveness Confirms Strong Cooperation Between the US and EU (12 Apr. 2011).
30. While the speaker's identity could certainly be revealed, perhaps an *ex post facto* application of Chatham House rules would encourage similar bursts of candour in the future. In any event, the audience's reception of the remark (in a discussion on US/EU regulatory convergence) revealed general acquiescence in its sentiment.
31. For instance, ICAO has been pressured to calibrate its SARPs related to aircraft noise to the regulatory demands of both aeropolitical superpowers, though not always to the other's liking. See *generally* Benedicte A. Claes, *Aircraft Noise Regulation in the European Union: The Hushkit Problem*, 65 J. Air L. & Com. 329 (2000). Arguably, also, US and EU efforts to export their respective visions of air transport liberalization has prompted ICAO to shift its stance on civil aviation's market order from benign acceptance of the restrictive bilateral trade system to an active promoter of expansive commercial freedom for airlines. See Brian F. Havel, Beyond Open Skies: A New Regime for International Aviation 229 n. 543 (2009).
32. IATA, One Sky, *supra* n. 4, at 12. Note, however, that neither the Chicago Convention nor general international law presents any inherent objection to a collaborative restructuring of airspace responsibilities. ICAO, *Global Air Navigation Plan*, *supra* n. 11, App. C, at 1. General international law, as viewed through a contemporary lens, is similarly indifferent to how States implicitly forego claims of sovereignty as they pursue economic self-interest. Traditional *noli me tangere* ('do not touch me') sovereignty has been superseded by the view that in contemporary international law a State has an inherent right to regulate its economy and the actors within that economy. See M. Sornarajah, The International Law on Foreign Investment 199 (3rd edn 2010) (citing sources to support this proposition). Sovereignty, in this sense, performs as a perfectly rational paradox: its existence is defined by its capacity to be given away. See Brian F. Havel, *The Constitution in an Era of Supranational Adjudication*, 78 N.C. L. Rev.. 257, 328 (2000). States regularly take on positive and negative obligations to foster cooperation with one or more States on matters no single country can adequately address on its own, such as establishing uniform rules governing air transport.

must be compromised by implementation of a structure that extends 'over States, specific portions of States, or groupings of States'.[33] The juristic (and political) challenge of compromising sovereignty, in the US view, can be reconciled bilaterally with the European Union before the global implications of that challenge are tested in ICAO. Interoperability, after all, will effectively remove existing 'borders' in the sky, just as the SESAR 'airspace blocks' are intended to do within the European Union.[34]

Thus, in an authentically globalized ATM system, States will need to engage in a fundamental reassessment of how they organize their airspace.[35] Functional blocks of airspace will need to be created for both upper and lower airspace and managed in an integrated way, replacing the traditional airspace structure based along national borders.[36] Air navigation service providers will need autonomy and transnational (and even supranational) partnerships, although State supervision to monitor monopolies will also be required. A principle of universal accessibility without discrimination will need to be adopted and applied.[37] The sovereignty dimensions of this problem of collaboration are profound. If States, for example, become reliant on satellite systems that may be provided and operated by foreign entities (public or private) which are outside their sovereign control, there will need to be specific international guarantees ensuring the permanent availability and reliability of satellite signals. And non-discriminatory access to these signals will also feature in international guarantees.[38]

---

33. *Ibid.*, Ch. 1, at 2.
34. Thus, the European Union has 29 civil en route air navigation service providers compared to one (the FAA) in the United States. Europe's duplication and multiple authorities contribute to a 60%–70% cost increase of air navigation services compared to the United States. IATA, ONE SKY, *supra* n. 4, at 7.
35. See *supra* n. 32 (discussing how neither the Chicago Convention nor general international law presents objections to a collaborative restructuring of airspace responsibilities). See *also* ICAO, *Global Air Navigation Plan*, *supra* n. 11, App. C, at 1.
36. IATA, ONE SKY, *supra* n. 4, at 7. '[T]he implementation of [satellite-based ATM systems] requires that a balance be struck between the need to respect State sovereignty and the need to promote the use of advanced air navigation and ATM technology. A necessary compromise may involve flexibility in the exercise of certain sovereign rights, in particular by entrusting tasks of signal provision and augmentation to foreign States and/or joint agencies or operating structures[.]' ICAO, *Global Air Navigation Plan*, *supra* n. 11, App. C, at 3–4.
37. *Ibid.* App. C, at 2; *Charter on the Rights and Obligations of States Relating to GNSS Services* art. 3(2), Assemb. Res. A-32/19, *reprinted in* ICAO, *Global Air Navigation Plan*, *supra* n. 11, App. C, at 6 [hereinafter *Charter*]. The Charter preserves each State's traditional authority and responsibility to control operations of aircraft and to enforce safety and other regulations within its sovereign airspace. *Ibid.*, Art. 3(a). (Given that Art. 28 of the Chicago Convention, *supra* n. 19, explicitly assigns intra-territorial responsibility for air navigation to the sovereign, the Charter could hardly do otherwise.) The non-discrimination principle will have particular resonance in a satellite-based system where reliance on foreign State technology is likely to predominate. See ICAO, *Global Air Navigation Plan*, *supra* n. 11, App. C, at 2. Commercial competition (with multiple service providers) does not yet exist on a sufficient scale to provide effective alternatives. *Ibid.*
38. IATA, ONE SKY, *supra* n. 4, at 6. Extraterritorial reliance on satellites is just one (albeit critical) aspect of a global harmonization that will demand compatibility and interoperability of service providers, procedures, and on-board and ground equipment. If interoperability is to be

To steer past each of the foregoing technical, legal, and political hazards, it is clear that the United States has favoured perfecting a regional approach before seeking a comprehensive ICAO standardization. Channels of communication have been kept open with ICAO, but the more detailed collaborative plans have been executed with the European Union. Moreover, although neither the 2007 US/EU Air Transport Agreement nor its 2010 amending Protocol[39] contains a separate provision to organize and implement US/EU cooperation on ATM reform, the Protocol implicitly recognizes that, since the Agreement's adoption, collateral progress on such cooperation has clearly been made. The culmination of a separate US/EU ATM discourse was the signing of a formal US/EU Memorandum of Cooperation virtually simultaneously with the execution of the 2010 Protocol.[40]

---

economically meaningful, airlines will need to move from one global navigation satellite system to another without requiring separate onboard equipage to access each system. *Ibid.* Once these technical challenges are overcome, States will have to turn their attention to tackling the host of institutional and legal questions which are likely to arise, including State liability for malfunctions within the system. While ICAO has promulgated a Charter spelling out the rights and duties of its members with respect to a global air navigation system, see *supra* n. 37, a more formal, legally binding agreement may be necessary to maintain stability in the system.

39. The eighth meeting of the US/EU Joint Committee, the consensus body that monitors implementation of the 2007 Agreement, took place in Washington, D.C. on 17 Nov. 2010. As part of its proceedings, the Joint Committee welcomed the development by its Legal Working Group of a consolidated text of the 2007 Agreement as amended by the 2010 Protocol. The Committee approved the text for use as a non-binding reference document. See *Air Transport Agreement [As Amended By] Protocol to Amend the Air Transport Agreement Between the United States of America and the European Union and its Member States, Signed on April 25 and 30, 2007*, *reprinted in* US Dep't of State, *Eighth Meeting of the US-EU Joint Committee: Record of Meeting*, Attachment 2 (17 Nov. 2010), <www.state.gov/documents/organization/151670.pdf> [hereinafter US/EU Agreement]. All subsequent references to the Agreement in this Chapter will be to the consolidated text.

40. The Memorandum of Cooperation, NAT-I-9406, US-EU, 17 Jun. 2010, 2011 O.J. (L 89) 3 [hereinafter US/EU MOC], is a 'protean' agreement that provides for a broad spectrum of collaboration in civil aviation and research and development including safety, security, environment, performance, alternative fuels, aircraft design, unmanned aircraft systems, and satellite-based communications and related ATM applications. See Press Release, Eur. Comm'n, Commission and US Agree to Cooperate on Civil Aviation Research and Development (18 Jun. 2010). The Memorandum is to be implemented through specific Annexes and Appendices. At the time of writing, only one such technical instrument has been adopted, namely Annex I on SESAR-NextGEN Cooperation for Global Interoperability. Annex I was executed on 16 Jun. 2010 and includes opportunities for participation in consultative fora of each party's ATM modernization programme. See Press Release, *supra*. The European Council of Ministers authorized both the Memorandum and Annex on 28 Feb. 2011. According to the Council, the Memorandum and Annex replace a 2006 Memorandum of Understanding (MOU) and a 2009 update to the 2006 Memorandum. Neither of those instruments, in the Council's view, created 'the required legally binding framework' for US/EU cooperation on ATM interoperability. See Press Release, Council of the EU, Cooperation in Civil Aviation Research and Development with the US (28 Feb. 2011). The European Union's reticence concerning the legal effect of its MOU with the United States may have been motivated by the tendency of some States, including the United Kingdom, to view such accords as being on a par with 'gentleman's agreements' rather than with binding treaties governed by international law. See *generally* John H. McNeill, *International Agreements: Recent US-UK Practice Concerning the Memorandum of Understanding*, 88 AM. J. INT'L L. 821 (1994).

Two of the original Articles in the Agreement were amended in the Protocol in an apparent effort to acknowledge this orchestration of a more formal consultation and collaboration process on ATM interoperability.[41] Article 15, the 'Environment' provision, was expanded (through intercalation of a new Paragraph 6) to endorse and encourage the exchange of information and dialogue on mitigating international aviation's environmental impact through ATM innovation.[42] More specifically, the Protocol enlarged the mandate of the Joint Committee under Article 18 of the 2007 Agreement to include (under a new subparagraph (f)) cooperation to optimize the interoperability and compatibility of the parties' respective ATM systems.[43]

For the moment, despite the broader language of the 'economic' agreements in 2007 and 2010, the pursuit of ATM interoperability cooperation rests with the FAA and the European Commission.[44] Annex I to the 2010 Memorandum of Cooperation[45] anticipates a multipronged programme of technical collaboration that, according to Article IV(a), will lead to 'global interoperability'.[46] The 'scope of work' delineated in Article IV of the Annex can be mapped to similar protocols in the ICAO and IATA frameworks for multinational interoperability.[47] The Annex permits (for the first time) direct cooperation between the technical experts

---

41. Curiously, the Protocol and the Memorandum of Cooperation, although signed just a week apart from one another in 2010, omit any explicit mention of the other's existence. While one might be tempted to attribute these omissions to institutional *amour-propre*, in fact the US Department of State designated the Federal Aviation Administration as the negotiating party on behalf of the United States. See Council of the EU, *Agreement with the US-FAA on Interoperability Between SESAR and Next-Gen*, Information Note No. 1134/10 (22 Jun. 2010). Under US federal law, the State Department is only required to *advise and consult* with the FAA 'about negotiations for an agreement with a government of a foreign country to establish or develop air navigation'; it does not have to cede any control over the negotiations, however. See 49 USC. § 40105(a). Further, in this entire series of instruments only the Agreement/Protocol dyad appears to have enforceability through the arbitration arrangements in Art. 19 of the US/EU Agreement, *supra* n. 39; the Memorandum provides for resolution of disagreements only through party consultations and expressly prohibits referral to a third party (including an international tribunal). See US/EU MOC, *supra* n. 40, art. XI.
42. See US/EU Agreement, *supra* n. 39, art. 15(6).
43. *Ibid.*, Art. 18(f). Subparagraph (k) of Art. 18 (formerly subparagraph (h) in the 2007 Agreement) seeks to foster consultation on air transport issues dealt with in international organizations and in relations with third countries, including whether to adopt a joint approach. This language signals the evolution of a joint ATM approach that could be presented to ICAO. The European Commission's press release announcing the Memorandum of Cooperation, see *supra* n. 40, explicitly acknowledges the parties' intention to support global standardization of ATM systems through ICAO.
44. See *supra* n. 41 (commenting on the FAA's role as US negotiator).
45. See *supra* n. 40 (explaining the relationship between the Memorandum and its sole extant Annex).
46. The language here is delicately ambiguous: while Art. I of the MOC Annex, *supra* n. 40, refers to 'global interoperability between [the parties'] respective ATM modernization programs', Art. IV speaks of 'global interoperability' *simpliciter*. The further reference to 'ICAO standardization' in Art. IV leaves little doubt as to the parties' grander vision.
47. For example, all three frameworks include user-preferred trajectories and reduced separation minima as short-term goals to enhance ATM efficiency and capacity.

attached to NextGEN and SESAR.[48] Nevertheless, it is unlikely that the sovereignty dimension of interoperability will remain exclusively within the FAA remit, especially given that the agency's front-line involvement up to this point has been the direct result of State Department designation rather than statutory authority.[49] Moreover, as interoperability begins to crest the policy horizon, Congressional involvement in shaping the contours of US international legal commitments will no doubt intensify.[50] At that point, the complexity of advancing the growth of a global ATM system, even at the bilateral level, is likely to increase by an order of magnitude.

Even so, the compromises of US inter-branch (or inter-agency) competition for custody of the global ATM issue would be a small price to pay for a common US/EU legal and technical architecture that would be open to other global partners. With an interoperable system in place for two of the world's biggest aviation markets, there will be little incentive for other States (or ICAO) to incur the technical and political costs of devising separate, incompatible systems.[51]

4 CONCLUSION

A deep concern for the United States is its own tardiness in rolling out NextGEN rather than the capacity of the European Union to accomplish SESAR over the next decade and a half.[52] Nevertheless, it is important as a policy matter that both parties

48. See Andy Pasztor & Daniel Michaels, *US, EU Officials to Sign Deal to Boost Cooperation on Air Traffic*, WALL ST. J., 18 Jun. 2010, <http://online.wsj.com/article/SB10001424052748703650604575312783454419138.html>.
49. See *supra* n. 41 (discussing the roles of the State Department and FAA in the global ATM process).
50. Under contemporary US foreign relations law and practice, Congress must assent, either *ex post* or *ex ante*, to any international legally binding agreement affecting US domestic law that is finalized by the Executive branch through one or more of its administrative agencies. See RESTATEMENT (THIRD) OF FOREIGN RELATIONS LAW OF THE UNITED STATES § 303(2) & comment e.
51. See JACK L. GOLDSMITH & ERIC A. POSNER, THE LIMITS OF INTERNATIONAL LAW 86–87 (2005) (applying the same logic to the development of international communications standards). The matter can also be framed in the vocabulary of 'path dependency'. Once the United States and European Union achieve interoperability between NextGEN and SESAR, other ATM modernization initiatives will become 'path dependent' on an US/EU interoperability framework that will have already attracted equipage commitments from the air transport industry's primary stakeholders (i.e., airlines). Moreover, even if a hypothetical 'better model' for ATM interoperability could be developed, States may still be reluctant to adopt that model if the trade-off is an inability to interface their ATM systems with those of the two dominant aeropolitical powers.
52. See Mouawad, *supra* n. 9. NextGEN is projected to cost an estimated USD 30 to USD 42 billion to complete. *Ibid.* Not surprisingly, funding for NextGEN is a matter of continuous debate, but bipartisan support is difficult in a political environment polarized by the US Government's record-setting debt. The Democratic-controlled Senate has been unable (or unwilling) to reconcile its version of funding legislation for NextGEN with the bill passed by House Republicans. See *ibid.* As well as funding challenges, NextGEN also faces resistance from labour unions concerned that the phasing-out of ground-based radar facilities will mean job losses for air traffic controllers. See Pasztor & Michaels, *supra* n. 48. And the US airline industry, already

have agreed to prioritize a programme to link their two evolving systems together to the mutual advantage of their commercial airlines. Certainly, US policymakers will watch the flow of cooperation closely and will expect to see tangible gains before committing additional resources to longer-term commitments. While the 2010 Memorandum and Annex, unlike the 2007 US Air Transport Agreement and its 2010 Protocol, lack any form of binding dispute settlement,[53] it is more likely that the cooperative structure now being built will avoid defections because of the rational interest of both parties in ATM interoperability.

At two levels, the demonstration effects of a successful outcome for US/EU ATM cooperation will be even more powerful than those of the economic reforms implemented in the 2007 US/EU air transport agreement. First, although the US and EU systems do not enjoy the sheer geographic coverage of the Russian and Canadian landmasses, for example, their air transport markets account for 60% of global air traffic share[54] and access to these markets is critical for air carriers seeking to assemble international networks. Globally, therefore, the industry has a strong economic incentive to encourage other governments to integrate with the US/EU ATM systems. Second, to reprise one of the principal themes of this Chapter, a seamless US/EU ATM architecture is destined to become the ICAO standard. As such, global interoperability will flow from the regional effects of US/EU cooperation. And an understanding of that fact is very much at the core of the US response to Europe's SESAR.

---

freighted with a heavy cost structure, is reluctant to commit its own resources without clearer FAA benchmarks for NextGEN's rollout. As one aviation analyst framed it, 'This is an industry that is not operationally driven. It is financially driven. And unfortunately, the airlines have learned to be very circumspect'. Mouawad, *supra* n. 9.

53. See *supra* n. 43 (discussing Art. 18 of the US/EU Agreement).
54. See *That Was Then . . . This is Now*, AIRLINE BUS. 25th ANNIVERSARY ED., December 2010, at 15.

PART III

TOWARDS A MORE PERFORMANT AIR TRAFFIC MANAGEMENT IN EUROPE

Chapter 13

Network Management

*Massimo Garbini**

1 GROWING DEMANDS FROM ATM

In a continuously evolving scenario, where the national borders are overridden to cover ever widening distances in order to build an efficient European transport network, I find it hard to identify a sector as much impacted by such ambitious objective as the air transport one. The traffic growth, due to the exponential increase[1] of customers moving throughout the European continent and beyond, makes this moment in time challenging for those who work in the Air Traffic Management (ATM) industry.

Open-minded approaches and innovative tools need to be sought in order to ensure the achievement of the new millennium objectives. From the European institutions to the operational actors, every single organization is called to embrace a brand new perspective based on the realization of a true single European sky. Nevertheless, I find it equally hard to think of a time more inspiring and ambitious than this very one.

Since decades, the ATM industry would base its business strategy on a decentralized approach, mainly related to local constraints; the cooperation with stakeholders outside the national barriers was kept at informal subsidiary level, while industries concentrated on local investments to improve their

---

* Massimo Garbini, Director General, ENAV.
1. <www.eurocontrol.int/content/single-sky-europe>.

Daniel Calleja Crespo & Pablo Mendes de Leon, *Achieving the Single European Sky: Goals and Challenges*, pp. 121–127.

individual performance. The lack of a vision focusing on the overall benefits of the network meant a high fragmentation of the airspace, inevitably leading to a scarce integration and organization among the actors of the air transport value chain, which resulted in poor delivery of functionality and reliability.

The adoption of the Single European Sky (SES) initiative by the European Commission in 2001 marks a radical change in air traffic management, which is then called to face the dramatic traffic growth foreseen at European level, implying a challenging increase of passengers and goods moving throughout the continent and beyond. The increase of traffic at local and international level became the catalyst for evolving pattern of European industries; the objective of enhancing capacity turned out to be not only a local matter but also an international business, due to the dimension and complexity of European air transport.

In order to address the consequent threat of a capacity crunch due to an inefficient ATM infrastructure, and the exponential traffic growth foreseen to be more than double by 2020, as well as the environmental issues related, European ATM configuration had to be radically reviewed, starting from a fundamental principle: the European ATM system was to be recognized as a cohesive whole – to be managed at network level.

2 THE CURRENT SITUATION

2.1 New Models of Cooperation

In line with the evolving context, ATM major actors have modified and innovated their approach at national and international level, aware that only through a network coordinated perspective – the only one capable of ensuring the synchronization of strategies and operational initiatives amongst all the stakeholders involved, the achievement of a real integrated ATM network will be possible.

If we take the case of ENAV, since the beginning of 2000's, my company has been undertaking significant efforts to engage partnerships throughout the European continent with the aim to structure robust models of cooperation; that led to set up several international projects, showing the competence to correctly interpret the changing reality and, in some case, the capability to anticipate it.

Guided by the deep belief that only a transnational coordinated approach will allow to realize an efficient and integrated network, ENAV promoted the establishment of a series of partnerships which turned out to be the successful response to the new scenario.

In 2003 ENAV and DSNA, the French Air Navigation Service Provider, launched the COFLIGHT Programme, aimed at designing and implementing a next generation Flight Data Processing System which will facilitate the integration of advanced tools in the global ATM system[2].

---

2. <www.enav.it/portal/page/portal/PortaleENAV/Home_EN/ServiziEAttivita_EN?CurrentPath=/enav/en/services/international_activities/international_projects/coflight>.

The successful technological partnership between the two Air Navigation Service Provider (ANSPs) suggested to extend such cooperation and, in 2006, DSNA and ENAV launched the 4FLIGHT Programme, which will provide a next generation ATC common system, in compliance with SES Regulation and able to pave the way to integrate the future Implementation Packages 2 and 3, defined within the Single European Sky ATM Research (SESAR).

ENAV also engaged a partnership with NATS – the UK ANSP – which envisages an operational cooperation aimed at sharing best practices and know-how of day-to-day operations, developing new training modules, and making the best use of scarce ATCO resources in SESAR Joint Undertaking (SESAR JU) activities. Similar experiences have also been launched bilaterally with AENA, DFS and LFV: respectively, AENA in the field of strategic analysis, DFS in terms of operational collaboration, and LFV in the research area.

However, the new model of cooperation was not to be limited to bilateral partnerships. On the contrary, a wider alliance would have possibly meant the highest return in terms of benefits for the network. Therefore, on occasion of the negotiating process for the admission to SESAR JU started in 2007, ENAV performed a leading role in promoting a joint action with the other five major European ANSPs involved in the very same process: AENA, DFS, DSNA, NATS and NORACON A6 Group. The A6 alliance was born.

The successful outcome of the A6, which led not only to the admission of all its members to the SESAR JU, but also to the consolidation of ANSPs position within the organization and gained the recognition of their central role in the modernization of the European ATM infrastructure, suggested to extend the cooperation to the main areas of interest which, along with the Research and Development activities performed by the SESAR JU, will ensure the achievement of a real and effective SES.

By identifying key areas of activity, the A6 aims at providing for leadership in critical operational and technical strategy areas, ensuring the needed coordination, communication and oversight to address the issues and secure the realization of a transnational integrated network. Moreover, through the setup of an A6 long-term cooperation, the participation to the international tables is of paramount importance to raise their harmonized and synchronized position at the level of the major European stakeholders, even when carried out by individual ANSPs.

For this purpose, ENAV involvement in the working groups and consultation fora of several European and global organizations – such as International Civil Aviation Organization (ICAO) for what it concerns regulations, communication, surveillance, procedures, Civil Air Navigation Services Organization (CANSO) – for the representation of ANSPs position at global level, and EUROCONTROL – as explained hereafter, represents a two-fold chance: on one hand, it is an occasion to provide a coordinate and aligned position coming from the six major European ANSPs; on the other hand, it represents an opportunity to acquire and maintain a holistic and updated oversight of the international scenario to be reported within the A6 Alliance.

2.2 The Single European Sky

The development of these new models of cooperation amongst the major ATM stakeholders have grown in parallel with the radical change of the European institutional scenario. Indeed, I believe the two paths have followed interrelated lines of evolution.

After the adoption of the Single European Sky proposal in 2001, the European Commission forwarded it to the European Parliament and Council to enable the co-decisional process to start. After a long and difficult negotiation, the SES first package (SES I) was published in 2004, delivering a new regulatory framework aimed at laying the foundations of a transnational integrated network able to cater for the foreseen traffic growth.

The SES I implementation, indeed, represented a first step towards a true European approach in the ATM system, but still not cogent enough to overcome the substantial lack of coordination amongst all the stakeholders involved. At the time, the ATM system was purely conceived and managed at local level. Consequently, the SES I regulatory framework soon turned out to be insufficient to adequately address the challenges that a true single European sky meant: a network perspective was yet to be built. However, the SES adoption encouraged the establishment of new partnerships and the reinforcement of the existing ones. In particular, the introduction of new organizational and operational policies included the concept of Functional Airspace Blocks (FABs), which translated into an official mandate the need to reduce the European airspace fragmentation.

ENAV took on the challenge and in 2006 launched the Blue Med FAB, together with the Cypriot DCAC, the Greek HCAA and the Maltese MATS. After the successful completion of the feasibility study in 2008, Blue Med is currently undergoing the definition phase, aiming at defining all necessary actions, implementation and validation processes to be performed. The Blue Med FAB represents a perfect match with the network objectives pursued at European level by involving the Mediterranean area – which is an emerging resource of the European ATM, it means not only the opportunity to maximize the use of such airspace portion, but also the chance to involve non-EU interface in order to export the benefits of a defragmented environment beyond EU borders.

Nevertheless, the FAB's experience contributed to highlight that only a synchronized and aligned commitment, with the A6 leading role performed through effective cooperation, would have speed up the implementation of SES. In this sense ENAV has been a forerunner.

In 2006, when the European Commission launched the consultation for the SES second package, the ATM industry was ready. The partnerships established, as I briefly described here with before, the incredible effort spent by the ANSPs to help the European institutions understand their pivotal role in the evolution of the European ATM system, and the network perspective finally gained led to the adoption of a far more effective and objectives-driven regulation. In 2009, the European Commission launched the SES second package, aimed at reinforcing and speeding up the implementation of the SES through the identification of five pillars (technology, safety, performance, airports and human factor) and a binding legislation. In particular, a new performance scheme was introduced,[3] which established challenging community-wide performance targets and, therefore, turned out to be a further trigger for accelerating the process of setting up an effective integrated system: in such context, the network management (NM) functions had become central for achieving the performance targets, now set at network level.

When in June 2010, the European Commission launched a consultation workshop to start gathering ideas and positions on the implementing rule to be adopted for the NM, in order to offer a legislative support to the NM functions, the ANSPs immediately realized the importance of addressing correctly its definition.

For this purpose, they not only helped identifying the main criticalities arisen so far at European level, but they also pointed out the technical-operational nature of the NM functions: that implied the major governance role of the operational actors (ANSPs, Airlines companies, Airports), to be accomplished in coordination with the Member States, the European Commission and the European Aviation Safety Agency (EASA).

When the Network Functions Implementing Rules was adopted by the States at the meeting of the Single Sky Committee in February 2011, the coordinating role of the Network Manager and the composition of the *Network Management Board* (NMB) described in the document fully reflected the needs highlighted by the ATM industry. But what about the Network Manager assignment?

2.3 EUROCONTROL Reform

Since the beginning, the Network Manager mandate to EUROCONTROL (the European Organization for the safety of the Air Navigation) has been bound to its indispensable reform. Indeed, it was evident that the original EUROCONTROL configuration could not cope with such assignment, which implied a brand new approach based on transnational integrated vision of the ATM system. Besides, the necessary review of EUROCONTROL strategic orientation had to take into consideration the impacts SES regulatory framework had on the European scenario, including the separation between regulatory and service provision activities – as envisaged in the community regulations.

Since 2009 EUROCONTROL has started a radical internal reform in order to shape its functional and institutional structure in the light of the new European challenges.

ENAV has proactively participated to the reorganization of EUROCONTROL, based on three pillars: support to SES Regulation, support to technological innovation for the synchronization of the European Research and Development

3. See Commission Regulation (EU) No. 691/2010 of 29 Jul. 2010.

plans, and indeed NM functions. In particular, in order to ensure adequate working arrangements to address this last one, EUROCONTROL set up a new directorate, with the aim to provide an effective support to ATM service provision, deliver network-wide ATM services, and monitor the network performance timely and efficiently. I believe EUROCONTROL reform is another unquestionable signal of the ever changing scenario we are not only framed in, but have to take part to.

3 FUTURE CHALLENGES

Moving from the fragmented approach the air transport industry had always had since its beginning, to a global vision of the ATM system where the network is at the core of the modernization of the ATM infrastructure, represents a significant goal to be proud of. However, defining a vision and structuring a model is not enough. Fragmentation, lack of operational synchronization – as demonstrated by the ash crisis occurred in April 2010 – and not always coordinated positions at institutional level, are still here to testify that correctly interpreting the reality doesn't mean to shape it. As rhetorical as it might sound, it is time to make it happen.

We all showed a constant and strong commitment to build up a model which enabled us to achieve the objective of a true SES. We designed and adopted the instruments to adequately address the ambitious targets set at the European level; and we all know it has frequently meant very complex organizational and operational changes.

Now we must use them. The big issue is how.

I believe that the positive results achieved by the joint initiatives that I only partially mentioned herewith on behalf of ENAV, have to be carefully taken into account when we talk about the future. The past experiences have clearly shown that individual approaches, based on local visions, cannot go very far. That means a two-fold path: on one hand the industrial partnership has to be enhanced and maximized, considering the pivotal role of the operational actors in the timely delivery of an integrated ATM system. As I stated before, only synchronized efforts and aligned strategies will lead to achieve the objectives set at the European level.

On the other hand, although tightly related to the reinforcement of cooperations, there is the ATM industry proactive participation and involvement in the development of a network management which enables centrally managed operations to guide the process vertically. In this sense, the delivery of efficient NM operational functions, attached to a new model to deploy a modernized ATM system, is of paramount importance to ensure the successful implementation of a SES.

The time is challenging and the expectations are high.

The modernization of the ATM infrastructure really represents a key enabler to accomplish important goals in Europe, in terms of economic growth, mobility, occupation and environmental benefits. On the contrary, its failure could mean a potential yearly loss to Europe of about EUR 50 billion of added value in 2020, not considering the loss related to the investments already made by the whole community.

The achievement of SES objectives literally lies in our hands. Let us prove we are capable of it.

Chapter 14

The Introduction of Military Dimension into the SES: A New Paradigm for the European Commission

Gilles Fartek and François Rivet[*]

1 INTRODUCTION

The military is an instrument to execute State's obligations in support of national policies and international agreements. Hence, sovereignty issues are a primary concern and military tasks, such as air policing and defence, and must take absolute priority over any other activities. Evolving worldwide security threats require continuous adaptation of military strategies and tactics, which in turn result in changing military airspace and airspace management requirements. To fulfil these commitments, EU Member States require keeping full capacity of action and sufficient level of preparedness for their armed forces. Providing military with a permanent access to the airspace without discrimination and sufficient airspace for sufficient airspace for adequate education and training is therefore essential. In addition of being airspace users, military are also active as air navigation service providers as well as regulators.

---

* Gilles Fartek and François Rivet, former military advisers to the Air Transport Directorate, European Commission, Single European Sky and SESAR Unit.

Daniel Calleja Crespo & Pablo Mendes de Leon, *Achieving the Single European Sky: Goals and Challenges*, pp. 129–136.

Military flights are significant in European airspace with State Aircraft Fleet in the ECAC area estimated by Eurocontrol to amount to over 1,100 large aircraft over 3,300 combat aircraft, almost 2,300 light aircraft, around 4,500 helicopters and some 400 paramilitary aircraft. The military operations in Europe are conducted from 150 main military airfields but military activities account for a small proportion of total air traffic. Whilst civil air traffic is forecasted to double every twelve years, military activities are expected to grow at a significantly lower rate.

The airspace is a common but scarce resource that must be managed flexibly to answer all airspace user's needs while balancing commercial needs and defence requirements. Currently, 32% of the upper airspace in the European core area is shared between civil and military activities, with a time sharing of 75% to civil traffic and 25% to military operations. Some military activities temporarily require a large zone of airspace. The location of some of the airbases can substantially increase the difficulties in the already existing bottlenecks in the civil air traffic. However, military needs reflect changing requirements and an increasingly global role. Military flights today carry out a more varied operational repertoire. Their airspace requirements as a result also change. This has an impact on the way in which overall airspace is organized and used.

Where segregation is essential to preserve flight safety, it is necessary to optimize the time periods in which any particular sector of airspace is allocated to military needs, especially during peak periods for civilian traffic and in high-density airspace. Whilst today much of the training is within national borders and near airbases, substantial gains for optimizing civil and military use of airspace can only be achieved through adequate direct cooperation between civil and military partners.

As a consequence, a permanent partnership between defence and transport authorities is essential to preserve a permanent access to the airspace for European defences any time and anywhere without discrimination. Also, armed forces must be provided with sufficient airspace for adequate education and training.

2 THE MILITARY INVOLVEMENT IN THE DEVELOPMENT OF THE SINGLE EUROPEAN SKY CONCEPT

In 1999, Mrs Loyola de Palacio, Vice-President of the European Commission in charge of Transport, made the reform of air traffic management in Europe one of its priority actions. The first related action was the launch of a debate about this reform in order to deliver improvements by a more integrated approach reflecting the requirements of a modern European air transport.

With the intention to move towards a single sky established under the European transport policy, in line with the approach followed for the completion of the single market and for the euro, Mrs de Palacio had the vision that the development of a common foreign and security policy within the European Union had provided opportunities for organizing the involvement of the military.

Identified at the earliest stage as a challenging but fundamental element of success, the involvement of Defence partners in the whole process has required the support of highest political authorities and the set up of new ad hoc mechanisms enabling military authorities to work closer together with their civilian counterparts outside the traditional EU structures, and in particular outside the usual intergovernmental processes of the Second Pillar.

At that specific time, the military were mostly considered as a constraining factor due to the performance of training missions in large areas preventing the access of commercial flows in large portion of airspace, especially in the so-called the 'Core Area', and being accused to try to 'retain their traditional privileged treatment in the sharing of airspace'.[1] This argument was very much used by civil aviation authorities, ANSPs and airlines to explain the important delays of commercial flights, and to hide more important problems linked to the high level of fragmentation of the ATM system. The reality is that since the mid-1990s, military authorities made important efforts to better plan their missions and to limit the booking of necessary airspace at the strict minimum, while enhancing the civil-military management of airspace through the implementation of the Flexible Use of Airspace. At the same time, the military activity had declined dramatically since the end of the Cold War ten years ago following in the reduction of defence budgets and training areas previously occupied only a few hours a day, often outside the peaks activity calendar. In the first quarter of 1999, air operations over Kosovo had a significant impact on the European ATM system which was still operated along national borders sometimes conflicting with operational requirements at European level. The closure of the airspace around the Adriatic Sea and the priority given to military operations related to traffic and transit operations in Central Europe had led to increasing delays of more than 20% of commercial flights. This event had also been seized by the civil air traffic to justify the delay and attributed largely to the military.

Deeply respectful of the military institution and convinced of the need for a strong European and national defence, Ms. de Palacio invited the Ministers of Defence to participate to the High Level Group on the in the same terms as the Minister of Transport, with the intention to assess the real impact of military operations on civil traffic, to better understand the military requirements and needs, and to find a way to build in common a single sky over Europe benefitting all airspace users without discrimination.

At the time of the High Level Group (HLG), most of the air navigation management competences were still exercised at national level, with an important role of coordination given to EUROCONTROL for organizing the development of common rules and standards but without any power of constraint regarding their implementation. The involvement of military in all the EUROCONTROL's decision-making processes was enhanced since the early implementation of some elements of the Revised Convention signed in 1997. EUROCONTROL was therefore considered as the usual and only forum where the Civil and Military worked

1. The creation of the single European Sky /* COM/99/0614 final, Annex 4 page 24.

together to deal with the airspace use, organization and management. However, the representation of civil interests was preeminent whereas the ability for military airspace users to influence decision-making process was rather limited despite a reasonable representation at all levels of consultation and decision.

Established at the beginning of 2000, the High Level Group gathered the Director General of the Civil Aviation Authorities and Departments of the then fifteen Member States of the European Community and their national military counterparts. It was able to deliver a final report within less than nine months. The full participation of military representatives to the work and their important contribution brought to the elaboration of the conclusions and recommendations, had comforted Ms. de Palacio and the civilian participants of the HLG that, far away from the initial judgments, were extremely dynamic and innovative in their approach. The studies also demonstrated clearly that military activities were only responsible for a small part of air traffic delays and that the military were really motivated to work even more closely to enhance the flexible use of airspace, even proposing the development of cross-boundary training areas to free up parts of space where civilian traffic was blocked at certain times of day and year. The possibility of relocating aerial training areas in Europe had also been examined, but was rejected due to the budgetary, social and strategic impact that would cause the relocation of air bases. The quality of these contributions confirmed the initial sense of Ms de Palacio regarding the existence of a European military community informally supporting her initiative. Finally, the decision was taken that the military interests should be fully taken into account in the development and implementation of the future EU regulations and that coordination between European military interests should be sought to develop consolidated demands and common positions.

The involvement of defence national representatives within the European Commission working structures was an important step forward, creating a new and unusual situation in the field of Common Transport Policy. The military community had some initial reluctance to see the European Commission intervening in the defence area where no competencies was delegated by States, but finally recognized that some potential benefits being directly involved at the appropriate European level. The civil-military approach was completed by the attribution of the Civil Military use of airspace sub-groups chair to French national military representative.

Until the adoption of the first Single European Sky legislative package in 2004, Ms de Palacio has been a fervent advocate of the involvement of the Second Pillar of the European Union. Unfortunately, that vision was too advanced and European Countries remained very cautious with the idea of establishing a link between the two pillars. Due to the importance of the domain and with the view to ensure the setting up of the appropriate expertise within the future Single European Unit within the Air Transport Directorate, Ms de Palacio decided to create a position for a military detached national expert, a premiere within the European Commission structures, out of the crisis management structure. The need for representation of military expertise in all future aviation development is still confirmed in the European Commission and related Agencies, as demonstrated by the recent recruitment of a permanent military adviser by the SESAR JU. More than ten years after, the idea of Ms de Palacio of putting in place the necessary institutional structures for better representing the military dimension, the European Defence Agency (EDA) created in 2004 has recently been tasked by the Ministers of Defence of its twenty-six Member States[2] to identifying possible future activities to study the safeguard of military interests in advance of and during the implementation of the SES as well as all similar initiatives currently carried out by many institutional players in the field of SES Air Traffic Management Research (SESAR), with the aim of avoiding any duplication of efforts.

3 THE INVOLVEMENT OF THE MILITARY IN SINGLE EUROPEAN SKY AND SESAR

The Single European Sky legislation is without prejudice to the sovereignty of the EU Member States and to their requirements relating to public order, public security and defence matters. However, the content, scope or carrying out of military operations and training do not fall within the sphere of competence of the European Union. The SES legislation applies fully to all movements of State aircraft including military, customs and police aircraft when these movements are flying according to General Air Traffic (GAT) rules.

The military are directly involved the in preparatory, consultative and decision-making processes on the same level as their civil aviation counterpart to preserve defence interests in all Single European Sky developments. This approach marked a new process within the European Union. Several new mechanisms have also been introduced in the SES management whereas legislative provisions favouring military interests are introduced stepwise since the adoption of the first package in 2004.

The SES legislation has established the Single Sky Committee, an important entity established to give opinions on legislative proposals, within which each EU Member State has been allocated two seats and a single vote for representing defence interests. This is an important element of consideration, the Committee playing a crucial role in the governance of the Single European Sky. The military also has an observer status in a number of other important bodies linked to SES, such as the Industry Consultation Body (ICB) and the SESAR Joint Undertaking Administrative Board where defence voice is therefore ensured.

Member States adopted in 2004 a general statement on military issues related to the single European sky, stating that Member States should, in particular, enhance civil-military cooperation and, if and to the extent deemed necessary by all Member States concerned, facilitate cooperation between their armed forces in all matters of air traffic management through appropriate channels and bodies.[3]

2. Denmark has an opt-out of the CFSP.
3. See Statement by the Member States on Military Issues Related to the Single European Sky, OJ L 96/9, 31 Mar. 2004.

The SES legislation has already favoured a civil-military dialogue at national, regional and European level and had enhanced the military-military coordination across the borders since its adoption. In addition, a special safeguard clause has been inserted in the framework Regulation 549/2004[4] pursuant to which Member States are allowed to take any measures to the extent to which these are needed to safeguard essential security or defence policy interests.[5]

A dedicated Regulation, and its associated European specifications, have been adopted in order to apply all over Europe the concept of Flexible Use of Airspace (FUA) that guarantees civil and military airspace users equal access to the airspace enabled by common management of airspace structures.[6]

An important target of the Single European Sky policy is the de-fragmentation of the organization and service provision in the European airspace. This has resulted in the development of Functional Airspace Blocs (FAB) that must be operational in 2012 with the aim to manage flows based on operational requirements rather than existing national borders.[7]

Having the responsibility to organize their participation in FABs, the Member States have identified the importance of addressing the question of sovereignty and the need for military involvement in FAB Governance structures. This process has already favoured regional civil-military dialogue, as well as military-military cooperation across the borders. In addition, each Country and FABs will be further subject to performance requirements defined by the European Commission in the field of safety, efficiency, capacity and cost of the organization of the airspace and the services delivered. A better management of the European network and the search of more direct routing and capacity shall need a strong civil-military dialogue at State and FABs level to come to results, including an appropriate application of the Flexible Use of Airspace and the proper usage of available airspace by all airspace users.

Each Member State has established a National Supervisory Authority to certify and designate service providers and to keep oversight on the performance. In several States this has lead to the increased cooperation between civil and military entities in charge of supervision, the creation of military supervisory authorities, and the choice for applying voluntarily the SES legislation in certain areas. This is particularly true for the certification of military service providers and the attribution of the European Air Traffic Control license to military controllers.

---

4. Regulation (EC) 549/2004 of the European Parliament and of the Council of 10 Mar. 2004 laying down the framework for the creation of the single European sky OJ L 96/1, 31 Mar. 2004.
5. Article 13 of Regulation 549/2004 stipulates that 'This Regulation shall not prevent the application of measures by a Member State to the extent to which these are needed to safeguard essential security or defence policy interests'.
6. Commission Regulation (EC) 2150/2005 of 23 Dec. 2005 laying down common rules for the flexible use of airspace, OJ L 342/20, 24 Dec. 2005.
7. See Regulation (EC) 1070/2009 of the European Parliament and of the Council of 21 Oct. 2009 amending Regulations (EC) 549/2004, (EC) 550/2004, (EC) 551/2004, (EC) 552/2004 in order to improve the performance and sustainability of the European aviation system, OJ L 300/34, 14 Nov. 2009.

The Single European Sky shall develop performance indicators for the European network that will permit to get a precise assessment of the quality of the use of the airspace, and develop tools and procedures to enhance the management of the airspace at national but also at regional level in order to guaranty the consistence of the design of the airspace, its management and its use.[8] This has been a trigger for many military authorities to seek more cooperation with the civil aviation authorities to also apply these requirements, where appropriate. Innovative solutions shall have to be looked at to allow the military to get maximum benefits from the expected overall improvement of the European network performance.

The Single European Sky policy also intends to regulate the interoperability of systems and procedures. Military shall also have to be closely associated with the definition of interoperable procedures, systems and information exchanges to ensure maximum interoperability and compatibility between civil and military systems. The insertion of unmanned aircraft system (UAS) in the Single European Sky shall also require common efforts from both parties to solve this new challenging issue in Europe and to offer a single regulatory solution for the whole region.

4 CONCLUSIONS

The adoption of the second SES package, together with the endorsement of the SESAR Master Plan and the evolution of the EASA competences, shall bring important changes in the civil European aviation environment, setting up a more integrated system encompassing the whole chain of safety. It will be important to ensure that all necessary efforts are made to optimally integrate the military dimension in the future European aviation developments, by making best use of existing arrangements and by strengthening the necessary partnership between Transport and Defence interests.

Beyond and in the absence of a possible unified European military representation, Ms de Palacio has supported the commitment of States to promote cooperation between armed forces to implement the most effective Single European Sky while respecting the defence requirements. This impetus has allowed the military to be involved from the start and to be present at all stages of development of this project within a community organization. This is vital for the military to guarantee that future solutions in terms of equipments and standards shall not reduce their capability of joining and applying the overall system. Future solutions developed by the ATM Master plan in terms of equipment and standards should contribute to increase their operational capability in the future system by providing

8. See Commission Regulation (EU) 691/2010 of 29 Jul. 2010 laying down a performance scheme for air navigation services and network functions and amending Regulation (EC) No. 2096/2005 laying down common requirements for the provision of air navigation services, OJ L 201/1, 3 Aug. 2010.

appropriate interoperability and compatibility between civil and military systems, while limiting the costs of onboard equipment for defence aircraft. To that end, the full participation of both the civil aerospace and defence industry in the future developments and implementation phases is important, as both sides can expect important savings and efficiency gains from such a collaborative approach.

The permanent involvement of European defence interests in all future developments shall be probably more necessary tomorrow than today. Innovative solutions shall have to be looked at to allow the military to get maximum benefits from the expected overall improvement of the European network performance. Many efforts are still required to ensure a better engagement of key defence stakeholders and to enhance civil–military cooperation so that all airspace users can benefit from the success of the Single European Sky.

The years following the departure of Ms. de Palacio demonstrated her vision of the need of military involvement in regulatory processes within the aviation sector. However, this example has not been followed by other services of the Commission that might have similar interest in such approach. The opening of direct military participation to the activities conducted within the European Commission should now be facilitated by the dilution of the 'Pillars' previously sealed before the Treaty of Lisbon. Furthermore, the greater coordination and consistency between civil and military should be favoured by the creation of a High Representative of the Union for Foreign Affairs and Security Policy, de facto merging the post of High Representative for the Common Foreign and Security Policy and European Commissioner for External Relations and European Neighborhood Policy. This new approach will certainly owe something to Mrs de Palacio who was able almost ten years ago to ensure a closer cooperation between military and civilian authorities based on the Single European Sky initiative.

Chapter 15

Performance Review: Implementation

Anne Lambert and Tim Johnson***

1 INTRODUCTION

This chapter considers what the increasing focus on performance in Single European Sky (SES) legislation means in practice for European Air Traffic Management (ATM). It is written primarily from an Air Navigation Service Provider (ANSP) perspective but it also looks at some of the implementation challenges faced by the national regulators and EU law-making authorities.

It does not purport to be a complete description of the SES legislation on performance. Rather, the aim is to describe in a general sense how the SES performance scheme has been developed, what changes implementation will entail to current practice, and what changes may occur in future. It also seeks to draw some general reflections and lessons.

The central thesis of this chapter is that implementation of the SES Performance scheme is a significant challenge for both ANSPs and their regulators. It will require a step change in the degree of commitment to improved performance by ANSPs, their regulators and owners. And implementation may have potentially

* Anne Lambert, Director of European and Government Affairs, NATS.
** Tim Johnson, Head of Strategy, NATS Services. The views set out in this chapter are those of the authors and do not necessarily represent those of NATS.

Daniel Calleja Crespo & Pablo Mendes de Leon, *Achieving the Single European Sky: Goals and Challenges*, pp. 137–146.

far – reaching implications for the way in which ANSPs are managed and governed. The success of the scheme will need to be assessed over an extended, rather than a short, period of time. Above all, all those involved in its implementation should always remember that the worthy objective of this scheme is to improve the service provided to European airspace customers, and in turn their customers, who in most cases are the travelling public.

2 THE ROAD TO THE SES PERFORMANCE SCHEME

The experience of each ANSP implementing SES and the performance scheme will inevitably vary. This is not surprising given that each of the twenty-seven EU Member States to whom it applies will have different starting points. Some States already have relatively advanced regulatory regimes in place. For example, in the UK, NATS' en route business has been subject to economic regulation by a regulator independent of government for some ten years. Other States, while not going so far as to establish independent economic regulators, have nevertheless themselves set some operational and financial performance targets for their ANSP. And in other cases, performance requirements have been less comprehensive.

These variations in national practices have occurred despite extensive performance measurement by Eurocontrol's Performance Review Commission and the overall targets for the network set by Eurocontrol's Provisional Council. However, these targets were not binding and it is fair to say that, despite the quality of Eurocontrol's measurement work, most ANSPs have not hitherto specifically planned or delivered their performance by reference to the Eurocontrol targets.

The arrival of the SES Performance Scheme, which starts in January 2012, will change this. For the first time there will be a legally defined EU-wide approach to measuring performance in the four key areas of cost, delay, environmental impact and safety. There are EU-level targets in each of these four areas.[1] And National Supervisory Authorities (NSAs) are legally required to set binding targets for performance in these four areas on the ANSPs they regulate.[2]

But before looking at implementation in detail, it is useful to re-cap the origins of the SES Performance Scheme.

3 SES I, AGREED IN 2004

The SES I Regulations contained objectives to improve performance. For example, the original SES Framework Regulation of 2004 set out the overall objectives to enhance safety, improve efficiency and minimize delays. However, while it provided for evaluation of air navigation performance by the Commission, drawing on the Eurocontrol work, SES I did not directly address performance. Rather, it

1. An EU-level safety target will not be set until the second reference period starting in 2015.
2. National targets for environment and safety are not required until the second reference period starting in 2015.

concentrated on creating a common regulatory framework and setting down some operational standards.

Some of the elements of this common framework are very relevant to performance and are, in effect, the essential underpinnings of the future performance regime. For example, it required States to establish national supervisory authorities independent of ANSPs. As a minimum the Regulation requires such separation to be functional. We suggest that legal separation is preferable – to reflect in a legally enforceable way the key principle of separation of service provision from regulation.

Other rules in the SES I package also provided relevant underpinnings for performance, most notably the common requirements for certified ANSPs as well as common principles for charging, including increased levels of transparency around ANSPs' financial performance.

In some States, these reforms required changes to their existing approach. In others, a new approach or process has been required. However, generally, whilst some effort has been required to implement these requirements, our view is that the changes required have not been very far-reaching. And nor have they led to fundamental changes to the way in which ANSPs and the EU ATM network are managed.

However, SES I did launch Functional Airspace Blocks, commonly known as FABs, 'with a view to achieving maximum capacity and efficiency' as well as 'maintaining a high standard of safety'. Potentially, these could be a springboard for significant re-organization of the ATM and ANSP landscape, either in themselves or as a catalyst for other alliances.

Yet progress in the aftermath of SES I was not as rapid as expected. Only one FAB – the UK/Ireland FAB – was set up under SES I and to date (early 2011) only one other (Denmark/Sweden) is operational. Nevertheless, some useful operational benefits to airlines in terms of better performance have been delivered. For example, it is estimated that the benefits to be realized from the UK/Ireland FAB projects which enable shorter track distances, reduced fuel burn and less $CO2$ emissions, will lead to an estimated EUR 35 million of cost savings to airline customers each year.

And plans for other FABs to cover all of European airspace are now progressing. The nature of those plans vary from the ambitious to others that are more measured in their aspiration. Unsurprisingly, given the history and nature of the subject matter, all the FAB discussions contain challenges. But it is clear that the very fact of having to establish a FAB is also prompting thinking about longer-term structures and alliances, either specifically in the FAB format or something slightly different. While it is hard to make firm predictions, it does look as if FABs could be the catalyst for greater change in the longer term, including more joint working, further alliances and, ultimately, possible merger of existing ANSPs.

4 THE RATIONALE FOR ACTIVE EU-LEVEL PERFORMANCE MANAGEMENT

As can be seen from this brief description, while SES I was a start, it did not lead to major change. Indeed, much was left unaltered. Yet, after SES I was agreed, it became clear that the challenges faced by European ATM were changing and increasing. For example, in the four years after SES I was agreed, traffic increased by some 13%. While the post-2008 recession has interrupted this growth and traffic levels are still below 2008 levels, it is forecast that demand will continue to grow in the long-term. And, as cost pressures have increased, so have demands from airlines customers for the price of ATM to be reduced.

In addition, as demand has increased, so has awareness of the environmental impact of aviation. It is notable that the SES I objectives did not include an environmental objective – an omission unthinkable under SES II. Aviation fully accepts this focus on the environment – and equally accepts that it must play its part in mitigating the environmental impact of aviation. Much work has gone into this, including by ANSPs, and good progress is being made.

So the original rationale for SES remains essentially unchanged although through SES II there are some changes to emphasis and scope, and in particular a greatly increased focus on performance. The details are described elsewhere in this book. The following section looks at what the Performance Scheme will mean for ANSPs in terms of performance, process, risks and management of their business.

But first it is worth pausing briefly to consider why it is necessary to regulate for performance. Answering this question is important for both the design of, and response to, any performance scheme. We believe that regulation is only needed where the market cannot effectively deliver what customers reasonably require or to address the management of externalities. In a contestable market, customers can choose their supplier and can negotiate on quality and price. However, for good reasons, it is hard to apply this market model to significant parts of the ATM network. The en route ATM business is a 'natural monopoly'. Indeed, this is enshrined in SES Service Provision Regulation,[3] which requires States to designate ANSPs on an exclusive basis for a particular area of airspace. But where there is no contestability, regulators can step in. Thus, the purpose of regulation is, in effect, to be a proxy for market forces.

To some extent regulation will always be a second best. Market forces are usually more likely to ensure customer requirements are met effectively. So it is important that any performance regulation does not inhibit moves towards contestability. In the UK, provision of ATM services at airports has long been contestable. In other words, airport owners/operators are free to choose who provides such services and manage the performance of the service provider through an arm's length commercial contract. NATS has no monopoly on terminal ATM service provision – and indeed only provides such services at 15 of the 90 or so UK airports where terminal ATC services is required. Indeed, we are now seeing some significant liberalization of European terminal ATM markets, driven by a desire to improve performance and demonstrate value to customers. Spain introduced legislation in 2010 to liberalize terminal ATM services and at the time of writing is expecting to start awarding contracts to new terminal ANSPs later in 2011. Sweden

3. See Art. 8 of Regulation 550/2004.

also introduced legislation in 2010 to separate ATM from airport ownership and is also currently tendering airport ATM contracts at many of its large and smaller commercial airports. Germany already commercially tenders airport ATM at a number of its smaller airports.

The existence of contestable market models as well as monopoly markets is recognized and anticipated in SES II, which allows Member States, subject to due process, not to set determined costs or cost efficiency targets where terminal air navigation services are subject to market conditions and also apply a lower level of financial transparency at certain airports. However, there is an ongoing challenge for policy makers and regulators to ensure that the SES performance scheme is implemented in a way that supports rather than undermines the long-term contestability of those markets.

5 SES II, 2009

SES II heralds a much more significant challenge for ANSPs than SES I. It is more significant not only in terms of implementation but also in terms of the risks that ANSPs will bear and how they manage their businesses for performance. It also brings increased responsibilities for both the European and national regulatory authorities.

In early 2011 we are only at the start of the SES II journey. But it is worth spending some time looking forward to what it means, what are the implementation challenges and what changes it might bring. (This chapter does not aim to give a full description of the rules of the SES II performance scheme. The detail can be found in the Regulations themselves.[4])

First, there is a greater role for both the EU and National Supervisory Authorities (NSAs). At EU level, the Commission is taking on a much more prominent role in both setting and assessing performance. It is the Commission who proposes and, after approval of the Single Sky Committee, sets the EU-wide performance targets. It is also the Commission who is ultimately responsible for approving (or not) the National (or FAB) Performance Plans. In these roles the Commission is advised by a new body, the Performance Review Body (PRB) – a role for which Eurocontrol's existing Performance Review Commission has been designated. And the NSAs are legally required to set binding national (or FAB) targets, as described below.

Second, the performance targets themselves. The reference level for the overall ambition and for the national (or FAB) targets are the EU-level targets, set by the Commission[5] in the areas of unit cost, delay, safety and environmental performance. These EU targets are not directly binding at State level. Instead the national (or FAB) targets set in States' National (or FAB) Performance Plans

4. See Commission Regulation EU 691/2010 on the Performance Scheme. Also Commission Regulation EU 1191/2010 amending the Charging Regulation 1794/2006.
5. See Commission Decision 2011/121/EU.

are binding. These targets have to be 'consistent with' and 'make an adequate contribution to' the EU targets. At national (or FAB) level, SES requires that ANSPs to will have formal targets set by their National Supervisory Authority (NSA) in the areas of costs, delay, safety and environmental performance – although formal targets for the latter two must await the second reference period, starting in 2015.

This means that from January 2012, all EU en route operations will be subject to binding targets for unit costs and delay. These targets are 'binding' in the sense that consequences follow when targets are missed and, on the other side of the coin, incentives apply when targets are met. Such penalties and incentives will be financial in the case of the unit costs target. Penalties and incentives for delay targets may be financial – or they may comprise measures such as corrective action plans. But whatever the mechanism, all en route ANSPs have to meet the targets set by their regulators – or face consequences if they do not.

Third, SES II also sets out a formal process that both ANSPs and NSAs must follow in terms of drawing up business and national performance plans and consultation with stakeholders. There must also be consultation on the elements that make up the charges – the costs allowed by the NSA for the purpose of setting the targets, the targets themselves and how these translate into the charged unit rate. And, of course, extensive ANSP operational and financial information must be available to the NSA for monitoring as well as to the Commission and PRB. There are also new requirements on airports and airlines to provide a range of operational performance information.

6 PRACTICAL IMPLICATIONS OF THE PERFORMANCE SCHEME

While the Performance Scheme is not yet up and running – it starts on 1 January 2012 – some consequences are already clear:

(i) There will be a significant increase in financial and operational transparency of ANSPs. Much more information than hitherto will be provided by NSAs, ANSPs and indeed airlines and airports. Transparency and the scrutiny that it brings – be it by peers, regulators, the PRB or informed third parties – will bring greater pressure to bear on improved performance. Public benchmarking against one's peers is always a powerful incentive, although care will be needed to ensure that this is done in a way that doesn't undermine the effective operation of contestable ATM activities, for example through excessive levels of financial transparency (which could hinder commercial negotiations) or creating conflicts between regulatory and contractual targets.

(ii) There will be much more work for regulators at both EU and national level. As described above, EU regulators set the EU-wide reference targets and also assess the National Performance Plans. National regulators have to set the determined costs and national targets as described above. Thus NSAs have to decide, in advance of each reference period, the appropriate level of costs for an efficient ANSP within their regulatory responsibility. This is not a simple exercise and will require many regulators to extend their capabilities. The NSA must have regard to the EU-level targets. Yet if an NSA is too aggressive in seeking cost cutting in the initial stages, it could be setting ANSPs up with little chance of succeeding. That will not be helpful. And indeed could perversely push up financing costs. So the regime and ANSPs should be set up to succeed and not to fail. Equally NSAs needs to be suitably ambitious – 'business as usual' is not the desired outcome. And clearly the balance of incentives and penalties must be right to ensure that improved performance is encouraged. All this require skill, knowledge, understanding and, above all, sensible judgment on the part of both NSA and European regulators. Above all, safety must remain paramount.

(iii) Each NSA has to draw up a National Performance Plan containing the national targets and setting out the regulatory approach to improving performance. This can be done at FAB level instead of national level, though for the first reference period it is expected that most Plans will be at national level.

(iv) One particular challenge for regulators will be to understand and measure on a consistent and reliable way the contribution the many different parties make to the overall performance of the European aviation network. Airports and airlines, as well as ANSPs, are very significant contributors to network performance, for example through airport scheduling activity. For the performance scheme to be effective and create meaningful incentives, ANSPs should be measured and targeted only on those aspects of performance they can genuinely control and which can be accurately measured.

(v) Given the new challenges for national regulators and EU policy-makers, there will be a natural tendency for regulatory costs to increase. To some extent, a modest increase may be justified. But a significant increase in regulatory costs, both nationally and at a EU level, would be difficult to justify and poses potential risks to the credibility of the performance scheme, particularly from airspace customers who are pressing for better overall price performance.

(vi) For ANSPs, the Performance Scheme brings some major changes:

- It means the end of the 'cost recovery' system and its replacement by the discipline of financially incentivized targets. Hitherto, for most ANSPs (NATS is an exception – its en route operation has not operated under cost recovery since 2001 and UK terminal services are provided in a contestable market) if costs exceed the level planned in the annual budget, the difference can be recouped in future years. In essence, a 'costs plus' arrangement. This will end under SES II. Instead, ANSPs will have to manage their businesses to keep within the envelope of 'determined costs' set by the regulator. There will be incentives to do so. For example, in the case of NATS (a majority private sector owned company), if the business is managed so that costs are lower than the costs set by the NSA, then profits will be higher. However, if costs exceed the level set by the NSA, profits will be lower. Different incentives may apply in other States with different ownership structures for ANSPs.

- The introduction of risk-sharing. Under the 'cost recovery' system, if actual traffic was less than forecast, then all of the difference could be passed onto customers via the unit rate in subsequent years. This will no longer be allowed under SES. Instead, the risk of traffic being lower than forecast, together with any upside arising from traffic being higher than forecast, must be shared with airlines according to a formula set down in the Regulation. This provides that up to 70% of the loss of revenue (where traffic is lower than forecast) as well as at least 70% of any additional revenue (where traffic is more than forecast) is borne by users.
- Costs risk-sharing. The Regulation also provides for some limited sharing of costs risks – for those costs which are outside the ANSP's control. In other words, there is a limited ability to pass on to customers variances in such costs from what was planned. Nevertheless, for those costs that are properly within the control of an ANSP – for example salary costs – the risk is borne by the ANSP.

We should also add, in case the reader thinks we are arguing that the new Performance Scheme is easy for NATS, that it does mean significant changes for NATS as well. NATS is of course accustomed to operating under incentivized en route performance targets and within a financial envelope set by the NSA, the UK Civil Aviation Authority (CAA). However, the SES performance rules differ in some key respects from the current UK system. And sometimes altering a well-established and detailed mechanism is more difficult than starting from a blank canvas! So implementing the SES Performance Scheme is occupying much time and effort in both NATS and the UK Civil Aviation Authority.

It is too early to assess all the impacts of the above changes. However, at least three general consequences can be inferred:

- Management by results. It is clear from the above, that ANSPs will have to manage their businesses, and the risks they now face, so to deliver the targets set by the regulator. This is likely to bring changes in management focus.
- Consequences for financing. For those ANSPs that borrow or raise funds commercially, the fact that they now bear risks, some for the first time, is of course highly relevant to financiers. Lending to risk-bearing entities will obviously require a higher cost of capital than lending to government-owned entities who do not bear risk.
- Changing risk profile for ANSP owners. As ANSPs take on a different level of financial risk, so it follows that ANSP owners – whether they be State or private sector shareholders – will also bear additional risk based on the

performance framework, and the ability of their ANSP to manage the risk associated with their performance. And States will need to recognize that the ANSP will need to be governed to manage the required results, and can no longer be managed according to political priorities – or rather these priorities need to be aligned with SES targets.

7 CONCLUSIONS

A number of general conclusions can be drawn from this brief overview:

- The new Performance Scheme poses significant challenges for industry and regulators alike. To date, relatively modest levels of time and effort has been spent implementing SES I (outside FABs). Much more will be needed for SES II.
- Both ANSPs and regulators need to ensure they are equipped for the challenge. In particular States need to ensure that Regulators have sufficient resources in terms of people and skills to undertake the tasks they have been given albeit without significantly increasing the costs administering the new regulatory framework.
- Most ANSPs also face significant challenges and changes to the way they are managed. It is important that regulators recognize the length of journey that ANSPs will have to go on to adapt to the new regime. For many, this is the first time that incentivized performance targets, akin to commercial disciplines, will be applied to ANSPs – that is, a very different culture. So whilst clearly it will be important for the credibility of the regime to demonstrate early process, the overall success of the regime should be judged over an extended as opposed to a short time frame.
- Yet it is vital for the future health of European aviation that the Performance Scheme succeeds. This points to a pragmatic approach in the early years so as to ensure credibility and confidence. The degree of change needed should be taken into account in applying the Performance Scheme during the first reference period. The Commission should focus on sensible implementation and targets, not those that are easy to argue for but which have little chance of ever being delivered.
- Looking further ahead, the increased focus on performance may well prompt more far-reaching changes as ANSPs seek to improve performance on cost and other areas. We believe it likely that a number of different models of cooperation will emerge in order to reduce costs. FABs may be one way. But cooperation and alliances short of FABs are also likely as ANSPs seek to share costs of some services with other ANSPs so to reduce overall costs. For example cooperation on provision of training and information services can be envisaged in more specific alliances or joint ventures. Some ANSPs in FABs may even decide to merge – though it will

be important to guard against a result which must mean a larger monopoly than that which exists now.

- And for those States where ANSPs are, in effect, part of government and wholly State-owned, the new risks especially in terms of costs and traffic may lead to a re-evaluation of the benefits of such ownership. Some moves towards creating the conditions for contestability are already being seen in the increasing choice of providers invited to be involved in providing terminal ATC services at airports. We can expect such moves to continue though the core 'en route' business seems likely to remain a monopoly for the foreseeable future.
- The Performance Scheme takes place against changing technology aided by the SESAR project. Indeed the two – that is, the Performance Scheme and the SESAR project – should work hand in hand. SESAR provides the enabling technologies to help the SES performance Targets to be met. Neither can succeed by itself but together they are powerful forces for change.
- Finally, we should always keep in mind the fundamental rationale for this significant new piece of legislation. And that is to improve the quality and price of the service experience of customers of European airspace, and in turn their customers, who in the main are members of the travelling public. That is indeed an entirely worthy aim, and should continue to be borne in mind by all parties as they negotiate the challenges ahead.

Chapter 16

The Regulation of Air Navigation Charges

François Huet[*]

1 PARIS 1919: THE STORY STARTS HERE

The first international reference to the concept of charging for the recovery of costs incurred for the provision of services to aerial navigation is probably to be found in the Paris Convention of 13 October 1919,[1] ('*Convention relating to the regulation of aerial navigation*'). This Convention, which entered into force on 11 July 1922, was drafted by the special Aeronautical Commission formed on 6 March 1919 under the auspices of the Paris Peace Conference. Its Article 24 provides that:

> Every aerodrome in a contracting State, which upon payment of charges is open to public use by its national aircraft, shall likewise be open to the aircraft of all the other contracting States. In every such aerodrome there shall be a single tariff or charges for landing and length of stay applicable alike to national and foreign aircraft.

---

* François Huet, EU Commission. The views expressed are purely those of the author and may not in any circumstances be regarded as stating an official position of the European Commission.

1. See e.g., <www.spacelaw.olemiss.edu/library/aviation/IntAgr/multilateral/1919_Paris_conevention.pdf> and <www.icao.int/icao/en/hist/stamps/1919_the_paris_convention.htm>.

Daniel Calleja Crespo & Pablo Mendes de Leon, *Achieving the Single European Sky: Goals and Challenges*, pp. 147–166.

This was limited to airport services and costs as, by this time, there was of course no provision of air navigation services (ANS) as we know it today. However, principles of equal access and non-discriminatory treatment were already laid down, and would remain.

The next following decades saw traffic grow due to the gradual entry into service of better aircrafts that were to become profitable airliners, the development of air mail services and, mainly for Europe, the need to ensure links with the colonies and overseas territories. In this period, air travel was blossoming largely through State support, whether in the form of equity or subsidies. 'Flag carriers' were fully State-owned. Like for other forms of transport such as road and rail, government intervention in the civil aviation industry through public funding was seen as part of a wider economic policy stimulating economic growth through improved mobility and strong links with the empire or colonies. For this reason, in spite of growing technological needs and the gradual deployment of more sophisticated air navigation services, for a long time States did not impose charges for the services that they were providing to commercial aviation. In Europe, as we shall see, the funding of ANS was fully ensured through States' budgets until 1971.

2 THE CHICAGO CONVENTION OF 1944 AND ICAO: LAYING DOWN THE KEY PRINCIPLES OF CHARGING FOR AIR NAVIGATION SERVICES

The Convention on International Civil Aviation (the Chicago Convention),[2] establishing the International Civil Aviation Organization (ICAO), laid down the basis for today's worldwide civil aviation and expressed the key principles underlying the imposition of charges both for airports and air navigation services. Building on the 1919 Paris Convention, Article 15 of the Convention on '*airport and similar charges*' set out the principles of:

(1) equal access to airports and ANS facilities;
(2) non-discrimination (charges for foreign airspace users should not be higher than charges for national and foreign airspace users);
(3) transparency (all charges 'shall be published and communicated to the ICAO' and'shall be subject to review by the Council, which shall report and make recommendations');
(4) cost-relatedness (no charge 'shall be imposed (. . .) in respect solely of the right of transit over or entry into or exit from' the territory of a contracting State. Charges must correspond to costs actually incurred).

In 1958, ICAO held a first Conference addressing specifically the issue of 'Route Facilities Charges in International Air Transportation', where the main principles

2. Doc 7300/9 <www.icao.int/icaonet/dcs/7300.html>.

'to be applied by governments wishing to charge airlines for the air navigation facilities their aircrafts use on international flights' were agreed:[3]

(1) Charges must be non-discriminatory.
(2) Charging systems should take into account both the actual cost of providing and operating the facilities and the effect of these charges on the finances of the aircraft operators. Charges should not be imposed for facilities not required or used.
(3) Charges should not be imposed in such a way as to discourage the use of facilities and services necessary for safety or the introduction of new aids and techniques.
(4) The charging system should be as simple as possible.

The Conference press release noted that 'the burden on some governments of providing these [air navigation] facilities free was becoming too great, and that user charges must be regarded as inevitable sooner or later in a number of cases', but it also acknowledged that the 'costs allocable to international civil aviation would in most cases be too large to be repaid in full in the form of user charges at the present time or in the near future without running the risk of impairing the financial position of airlines'.

Because of the heterogeneous situation of worldwide air transport and of the then seventy-two ICAO Member States, no specific method of charging was recommended and the Conference left the issue for States' discretion, provided that they adhere to the key ICAO principles. The Conference also predicted that it was '*probable that for some years they will not find it expedient to attempt to recover more than a small part of what they are entitled to recover in this way*'. And yet, five main types of charging systems were considered: With a weight factor only, with weight and distance factors, with a parameter depending on the kind of flight and nature of facilities required, with a parameter depending to the route flown, or general levies on fuel and oil provided at international airports.

Nine years later, the ICAO Conference on Charges for Airports and Route Air Navigation Facilities ('CARF') of March-April 1967 treated this time airport and air navigation charges separately. Having reiterated the key principles of 1958, the most relevant outcome of this Conference was the statement that there should be a single charge per flight (covering all air navigation services) and that, having considered the various possible methods, the recommended one should be a system based on flight distance and aircraft weight.[4]

The codification of the key ICAO principles on charges was set in 1973 in the first edition of the 'Statements by the Council to Contracting States on Charges for Airports and Route Air Navigation Facilities'.[5] As a general principle, it stated that *providers may require the users to pay their share of the related costs*, including

3. ICAO News Release 8 Apr. 1958: <www.icao.int/icao/en/nr/1958/pio195804_e.pdf>.
4. ICAO News Release 21 Mar. 1967: <www.icao.int/icao/en/nr/1967/pio196706_e.pdf>.
5. Doc 9082-C/1015, to be renamed '*ICAO's policies on charges for airports and air navigation services*' in 2001. All versions are available at <www.icao.int/icaonet/dcs/9082.html>.

interest, depreciation and administrative costs. But it also stressed that civil aviation 'should not be asked to meet costs which are not properly allocable to it'.

In a nutshell, the ICAO principles for ANS charging were, and to a large extent still are, about recovering only the costs – but all the costs – incurred for the provision of air navigation services, following transparent allocation, justification and genuine user consultation.

ICAO Document 9161, the 'Manual on Air Navigation Services Economics'[6] was subsequently developed to 'provide practical guidance material to assist those responsible for the management of ANS in improving the efficiency and finances of these services'. This Manual is now updated regularly, following the evolution of practices and thinking on charging for air navigation services. As we shall see in the following sections, the European initiatives, first stemming from EUROCONTROL and then the European Commission, were substantial for the evolution of ICAO policies, recommendations and guidance material.

3 AN INNOVATIVE MULTILATERAL APPROACH: EUROCONTROL'S ROUTE CHARGES SYSTEM

In Europe, the initiative towards charging for ANS provision started from a request by the Federal Republic of Germany in 1965, asking the EUROCONTROL Organization to carry out '*an enquiry into charges for the use of air traffic control services*' and make appropriate proposals for a joint system. As a consequence, EUROCONTROL set up a European Inter-governmental Working Group to study the practical problems related to the en route ANS costs and possible charging. The work of this Group, which also fed the proceedings of ICAO's 'CARF' Conference mentioned above, resulted in the setting up in 1970 of EUROCONTROL's multilateral route charges system, which is still in operation and growing.

A multilateral Agreement 'relating to the collection of route charges' was signed on 8 September 1970 by the then seven EUROCONTROL Member States[7] and allowed them to introduce as from 1971 route charges in their airspace. Bilateral agreements were signed by the organization and the Member States empowering EUROCONTROL to collect the route charges on their behalf. In parallel to the amendment in 1981 of the EUROCONTROL Convention, a 'Multilateral Agreement relating to route charges', replacing the instrument of 1970, was signed on 12 February 1981[8] and entered into force on 1 January 1986 for the benefit of ten Member States.

Through the implementation of this simple, collective and cost-efficient route charges system (a single charge per flight, billed in a single currency by a single collecting institution on behalf of all its contracting States), including regional decision-making and foreseeing periodical user consultation, Europe was at the

6. <www.icao.int/icaonet/dcs/9161/9161_en.pdf>.
7. <http://untreaty.un.org/unts/1_60000/24/5/00046219.pdf>.
8. <www.eurocontrol.int/crco/public/standard_page/reference_documents.html>.

forefront of innovation as compared to other regions of the world. In 2011, the EUROCONTROL system serves thirty-eight Member States, foresees to collect some 6.5 Billion Euros of route charges with a recovery rate of more than 99% and has an administrative cost of some 0.3% of the amount collected.

Following ICAO's recommendation that the recovery of costs incurred for the provision of ANS should be progressive, the EUROCONTROL route charges system started with a recovery in 1971 of only 15% of the final 1969 (n-2) costs. The recovery rate then progressed to 30% in 1973, 60% in 1975, 75% in 1978, 90% in 1979, and 100% in 1981. The final step was to change from the recovery of historical costs (the recovery in year 'n' of the final costs of year n-2, known in n-1), to a system based on the recovery of forecasted costs estimated in relation with forecasted traffic, with carry-over to the following years of the possible over or under recoveries due to a difference between forecasted and actual costs and/or traffic. This was achieved in April 1983.

The basic principles of the EUROCONTROL multilateral charging scheme, in line with ICAO recommendations, were:

(1) As from 1983, full cost recovery mechanism, with a carry over of under or over recoveries incurred in year n to year n + 2.
(2) Single charge per flight, billed in a single currency – first the US Dollar and the Euro as from 1991 (putting EUROCONTROL at the forefront of introducing Euro as a billing and settlement currency) – to be shared by States according to the partial charge required for use of the airspace within each State's competence. A monthly exchange rate adjustment mechanism protected users and Member States from currency exchange rate variations.
(3) No distinction between upper and lower airspace services.
(4) Consultation of airspace users.
(5) Non-EUROCONTROL States could by unanimous agreement of the EUROCONTROL Member States be admitted in the route charges system as contracting parties.[9]

The EUROCONTROL multilateral route charges system has always been purposely very stable. No fundamental change has to be reported since its creation, with two notable exceptions:

(1) In 1998, the switch from a 'Most Frequently Used Route' (MFUR – the statistically most frequently used route for a given city pair) system to a 'Route per State Overflown' (RSO) charging system, allowing a more accurate billing, closer to where the costs are generated and the services are used.

9. Spain became in 1971 a contracting party to the multilateral agreement for route charges, long before becoming a full EUROCONTROL Member State in 1997. Hence the creation of the terminology of *enlarged* Committee and *enlarged* Commission for route charges.

(2) The integration of a possible alternative charging regime based on independent economic regulation.[10] This major change was requested by the United Kingdom as a necessary prerequisite to the partial privatization of its air navigation service provider, the NATS, to allow private investors to drive cost-efficiency, decrease charges and generate profit. The principle of this regime was for the regulator to set for the air navigation service provider in advance for a period of five years 'conditions from which the maximum level of the unit rate shall be determined in each year of the review period'. This was the first exception to EUROCONTROL's automatic full cost-recovery mechanism.

The United Kingdom will remain the only EUROCONTROL Member State to have implemented the independent economic regulation regime until 1 January 2012 when the second Single European Sky (SES) package will generalize the principle of economic incentive. This principle, a tool to generate to encourage an efficient and effective service at the lowest possible cost for the benefit of airspace users, will then change from being an exception to being the norm, at least for those EUROCONTROL States submitted to the SES.

4 AN INTER-GOVERNMENTAL INITIATIVE: THE ECAC INSTITUTIONAL STRATEGY (INSTRAT)

The nineties were years of steady traffic growth. The national air traffic control systems were not able to cope with the demand and delays started becoming a serious matter of concern as the situation became gradually unbearable for the industry and the public opinion. In such a context, two different initiatives were launched: An inter-governmental one under the auspices of ECAC (the ECAC Institutional Strategy – Instrat) and a European Community one with the SES initiative.

On ECAC side, the Transport Ministers of all ECAC Member States approved on 14 February 1997 the '*ECAC Institutional Strategy for Air Traffic Management in Europe*', designed to promote the development of air navigation among member countries of EUROCONTROL and ECAC, mainly through ECAC's harmonization and integration programme for air navigation routes (EATCHIP), and the corresponding programme for improving air traffic services at airports (APATSI). The strategy also contained a cost-efficiency and a performance review dimension, with the idea of establishing an independent monitoring of the level of performance.

The legal instrument for the implementation of this strategy was the revision of the EUROCONTROL Convention, signed on 27 June 1997.[11] The early implementation of certain provisions of this revised Convention was decided on

10. Decision No. 52 of EUROCONTROL's enlarged Commission dated 16 Jul. 1999.
11. However, to date, this Convention has not formally entered into force because it has not been ratified by all EUROCONTROL Member States. This is why the main governing body of the organization is still a 'Provisional Council'.

9 December 1997,[12] which allowed the creation in 1998, on a provisional basis, of a Performance Review Commission composed of twelve independent senior commissioners supported by a Performance Review Unit, composed or EUROCONTROL experts. Within the next few months a Performance Review System, ensuring the collection of performance related information, the monitoring of the evolution of performance in several key performance areas in full transparency, including cost-effectiveness benchmarking and the issuing of recommendations, came to life within EUROCONTROL. Its weak point was that the recommendations were not binding and their implementation was based on States' goodwill; there was no central approach to performance and the genuine efforts of some Member States were offset by the lack of action of others.

This evolution allowed EUROCONTROL to present two interesting contributions in ICAO's Conference on the Economics of Airports and Air Navigation Services (ANSConf 2000) in June 2000:[13] One of them was an action paper on the '*Determinants of the economic regulation airports and air navigation services*' (ANSConf-WP/88), recommending the amendment of ICAO Doc 9082/5 to reflect the principles of economic regulation. The Conference welcomed this recommendation and in its report:[14]

> recommended that, in order to assist States that may wish to establish an independent mechanism for the economic regulation of airports and air navigation services, ICAO include guidelines on the establishment of such a mechanism in the Council Statements in Doc 9082 and other relevant guidance material.

The other EUROCONTROL contribution was an information paper (ANSConf-WP/66) describing the EUROCONTROL Performance Review System and its achievements, including in the domain of cost-effectiveness. The introduction of the 7th Edition of ICAO Doc 9082, published in 2004, reflected the economic Regulation principles (Paragraph 15) and also recommended the '*Development and application of performance parameters*' (Paragraph 16).

5 THE FIRST SINGLE EUROPEAN SKY PACKAGE (SES I): ESTABLISHING A GATE-TO-GATE, TRANSPARENT, LEVEL PLAYING FIELD ON AIR NAVIGATION SERVICES CHARGES

In parallel to ECAC's Institutional Strategy, the European Commission perceived the limits of the inter-governmental approaches based on consensus. The worsening saturation of the European airspace and the increase of delays led the Commission to present in 1999 a Communication on the '*creation of the Single European*

12. Decision No. 72 of EUROCONTROL's Permanent Commission.
13. <www.icao.int/icao/en/atb/meetings/2000/ansconf2000/Documentation.htm>.
14. ICAO Doc. 9764.

Sky',[15] which qualified the situation in the airspace as '*disastrous*', and expressed doubts on the ECAC initiative:

> Although the aeronautical community has developed a strategy for the years ahead – the strategy for the 2000s – it is doubtful whether this initiative, which is based on EUROCONTROL's traditional working methods and does not contain a clear plan of action for the development and implementation of new concepts and procedures of air traffic management, is the right response if major structural reforms are not made both at national and at European level.

The Communication concluded that:

> The congestion of airspace calls for measures other than technical ones in the short term in order to prevent any further crises. (. . .) Structural reforms are also needed to permit the creation of a single European sky by way of integrated management of airspace and the development of new concepts and procedures of air traffic management.

This was the starting point of the SES initiative, resulting in the first SES package, with the notable effects of creating at Community level a performance review benchmarking system '*drawing upon the expertise of Eurocontrol*' (Article 11 of the framework Regulation) and bringing competence on air navigation charges at Community level.

The legal basis for the common charging scheme established under the first SES package laid in Chapter III '*Charging schemes*' of the service provision Regulation No. 550/2004 of 10 March 2004.[16]

Article 14 set out the general principles of '*greater transparency*' of charges.

Article 15 set out the key principles fully compliant with, and going beyond, ICAO recommendations, to be applied when establishing the cost-base for charges.

Article 16 set out the measures for the necessary review of the compliance of charges with the principles and rules of the SES.

The principles set out in Article 15 were materialized and detailed in Regulation (EC) No. 1794/2006 of 6 December 2006 laying down a common charging scheme for ANS (the charging Regulation),[17] developed by the Commission with the assistance of EUROCONTROL's Central Route Charges Office (CRCO) upon Commission mandate.

According to its Recital 3, the Regulation was designed to encourage the safe, efficient and effective provision of ANS to the users that finance the system and to promote integrated service provision. According to Recital 4, it pursued the overall objective of improving cost and operational efficiency of ANS in Europe.

The common charging scheme laid down by the charging Regulation built on the EUROCONTROL multilateral system for en route costs and charges,[18]

15. COM/99/0614 final <http://eur-lex.europa.eu/LexUriServ/LexUriServ.do?uri=COM:1999:0614:FIN:EN:PDF>.
16. OJEU L 96, 31 Mar. 2004, 10.
17. OJEU L 341, 7 Dec. 2006, 3.
18. Recital 7 of the charging Regulation provides that '(. . .) the rules developed in this Regulation should be consistent with the Eurocontrol Route Charges System'.

confirming in particular EUROCONTROL's full cost recovery mechanism and formula for calculating route charges with its weight and distance factor, but it also broadened the scope and strengthened the content of this system with a view to establishing a single, fully transparent, cost-related and cost-efficient, European ANS charging scheme, covering both en route and terminal phases of flight and thus ensuring a truly gate-to-gate approach.

As a result of a long consultation process and in order to secure a qualified majority in the Single Sky Committee (SSC), the charging Regulation was the result of a number of compromises. This led some commentators to declare at the time that the newly adopted common charging scheme lacked ambition and only offered a '*prudent enhancement*'[19] to the pre-existing situation. However, time and implementation showed that the Regulation was much more substantial than this and triggered some major changes to the European charging system. It also built the necessary foundations for the second SES package.

First of all, the scheme materialized the principle of *separation between service provision and regulatory functions* set up in Article 4(2) of the framework Regulation No. 549/2004: Further to the provisions of Annex II of the Regulation, each main entity incurring costs was now requested to fill in a specific reporting table and being fully accountable for it, and provide the requested additional information. This meant that, typically, the reporting tables were to be completed separately by the air navigation service provider, the meteorological service provider and the regulator, that is, the national civil aviation authority (be it the Directorate General of Civil Aviation (DGCA), Civil Aviation Authority (CAA) or Ministry for Transport, depending on each Member State's internal organization) Beyond the costs incurred for the provision of air navigation services; the cost base also included (Article 5.2 of the Regulation) the costs incurred by the relevant national authorities, the cost of the recognized organizations and the costs stemming from international agreements (e.g., the EUROCONTROL costs). The national authority had the responsibility of collecting and aggregating the data

19. Extract from the Conclusions of the 'Mandate Workshop' of 4 Sep. 2006 organized by EUROCONTROL 'Impact of the draft Regulation on a common charging scheme':

> 5.4. A majority of participants in the workshop agreed with the CRCO's and the Chairman's assessment that stakeholders felt that the proposed text of Common ANS Charging scheme is a 'prudent enhancement'. This was in line with the European Commission's indication that the proposal was only a first step in the right direction, to be reviewed and enhanced in the light of experience.
>
> States and ANSPs generally agreed that the proposed text was a modest step in the right direction, providing a degree of flexibility which would bring additional transparency of costs and cost allocation; and would allow some interesting innovations such as incentive schemes.
>
> A minority of States/ANSPs however wondered about the interest of implementing a new system, which was likely to generate additional costs, when there were doubts about its added value.

User organisations (and in particular IATA) were in general doubtful and expressed the view that globally, the text proposed made very little change as compared to the present situation. (<www.eurocontrol.int/ses/gallery/content/public/docs/crco/Conclusions_Wksp.pdf>).

from all the national accountable entities and producing a consolidated table, thus providing the total national Air Navigation Services (ANS) cost-base chargeable to airspace users. For the terminal costs and charges, each airport above 50,000 commercial movements had to fill in a reporting table, the national authority establishing a consolidated table. This increased knowledge of the main components of the national cost base and their evolution over time brought a level of transparency that had never been reached before, allowing for example, to have a view on the relative share and the evolution of Meteorological (MET) costs or regulatory costs in the overall national cost-base.

A second major innovation was the *gate-to-gate* scope of the Regulation, encompassing not only en route, but also terminal ANS costs and rates which were submitted to the same transparency and cost-relatedness obligations. This was an important step forward as, until this Regulation, there was no European binding rule or regulation organizing the cost-relatedness and transparency of terminal ANS costs and tariffs. Not all States had established a terminal cost base and unit rate, and terminal costs were, therefore, partly or totally allocated to the en route cost base and recovered through the route charge, in contradiction with the basic ICAO principles of '*user pays*', and '*civil aviation should not be asked to meet costs which are not properly allocable to it*'. Those States which calculated terminal ANS costs and recovered them through the imposition of a terminal charge did so in a completely uncoordinated way, resulting in the coexistence in Europe of a patchwork of schemes and formulae, without any centralization of information and therefore no possibility to compare and benchmark. The charging Regulation put an end to this situation and established a transparent level playing field between all European air navigation service providers (ANSP) through the requirement to calculate costs according to the same template and apply charges using the same formula.

The Regulation achieved this major improvement to secure transparency of the entire national ANS cost bases and to ensure a clear separation between en route and terminal costs. Through this, implicitly, the Regulation forbade the existence of cross-subsidies between en route and terminal cost bases, but this was questioned and had to be made explicit in the revision of the Regulation under the SES II package. The Regulation also recognized clearly the possibility for terminal costs to be financed at least partly by 'other revenues', thus recognizing the intricacy of airport financing.

Mention should be made of the provisions of Article 1.6 and Annexes I and III allowing Member States to opt for a simpler reporting and not to calculate terminal unit rates when they can establish that the ANS at airports below 150,000 commercial movements per year are provided under market conditions. This was implemented by the United Kingdom and Luxembourg.

The diversity of pre-existing local situations and the requirement to limit the redistribution effect amongst airspace users led the Commission to propose a transitional phase before the complete application of the charging Regulation to terminal costs and charges: Article 18(2) allowed Member States to defer the obligation to calculate a terminal unit rate until 1 January 2010. All but six Member States made use of this deferral possibility. Furthermore, Paragraph 2 of Annex V of the Regulation foresaw a transitional period of five years to converge towards a unique formula with a weight factor of 0.7.

The EUROCONTROL route charges system facilitated the Commission's oversight of all but two EU Member States[20] for their en route costs and unit rates. For the terminal costs and unit rates, the Commission organized and chaired as from 2010 multilateral consultation meetings twice a year in June and November, back to back with the sessions of the EUROCONTROL enlarged Committee for route charges where multilateral consultation on en route costs and rates was taking place.

A third innovative element of the charging Regulation was the introduction of the new concept of *charging zone* (Article 4 of the charging Regulation). The initial Commission ambition was that such charging zones, with a single cost base, harmonized rules (e.g., for exemptions or incentive schemes) and a single unit rate would better match the actual organization of service provision and provide more flexibility as compared to the national FIRs. It also aimed at matching the geographical scope of Functional Airspace Blocks (FABs) created under Article 5 of Regulation (EC) No. 551/2004 (the airspace Regulation). Member States however resisted this ambition on the ground that the national practices were too dissimilar, in particular due to national law constraints (e.g., tax issues or exemption policies) and that to require the establishment of a single cost base and a single en route unit rate may be a deterrent for the establishment of FABs. The Commission accepted to temporarily abandon this obligation in the short term but expressed the intention to reassess the situation in 2008 (Recital 9 of the Regulation). The charging zone concept remained, through which it was for the first time possible to establish a charging area be based on operational requirements rather than on national boundaries. However, at the time of drafting this contribution, no cross-border charging zone has for the time being been established as a result of this Regulation, unless the pre-existing Belgium–Luxembourg zone would be considered one.[21] Even the cost-base of the Maastricht Air Traffic Control Centre, which provides services to the upper airspace of the Benelux and part of Germany, is split between the four concerned States who calculate three separate unit rates.

These charging zones extend from the ground to the upper airspace, thus bringing in Europe an end to the discussion[22] on the appropriateness of envisaging

---

20. Estonia and Latvia, which therefore had to fulfil their reporting obligations directly to the Commission. Latvia has become EUROCONTROL's 39th Member State on 1 Jan. 2011. Estonia is, therefore, now the only remaining EU Member State requiring a specific Commission oversight.
21. Through a bilateral agreement between both States, Belgium controls the en route traffic of Luxembourg. It calculates a single cost base and establishes a single unit rate for both countries.
22. Discussion held notably in 2001 within EUROCONTROL's '*Possible Pricing Mechanisms*' Task Force created to 'study the possible pricing mechanisms which may promote the best use of airspace capacity within the framework of the ATM 2000+ Strategy' and delivered a final report, containing recommendations, for the November 2001 Session of EUROCONTROL's enlarged Committee for route charges. However, these recommendations were not followed by the EUROCONTROL Member States.

differentiated charging between upper and lower airspace. This was without prejudice to the possibility for a Member State to '*establish a specific zone for a complex terminal area*' (Article 4(3)), but such a possibility was never used for the obvious reason that the charges in such areas would be extremely high.

The fourth key innovation was the possibility, offered in Article 12, to set up and apply *incentive schemes*, on ANSPs (e.g., as a result of independent economic Regulation, as was already done in the UK) or on airspace users (in the form of charges modulation e.g., to encourage equipment of aircraft that increases capacity, or to reward the choice of less congested routings). However, with the exception of the UK system, none of these possibilities were used: As it was optional and there was no binding performance target system, there was no incentive for Member States and ANSP to set up incentive schemes. This was one of the shortcomings of the first SES package.

In addition to these four key innovations, the Regulation offered other improvements to the pre-existing situation:

Consultation: Airspace user consultation was organized in Articles 8 and 15. Building on the existing EUROCONTROL multilateral route charge system, the Regulation however added the obligation to provide the relevant material (reporting tables and additional information) three weeks in advance of the consultation meeting. Non-compliance with this requirement constituted an infringement to the provisions of the Regulation. As a result, the transmission of data improved substantially in timeliness as well as in quality. Furthermore, the charging Regulation put an obligation on Member States to consult airspace users before taking strategic decision: the establishment of a charging zone (Article 4) or the setting up of incentive schemes (Article 12)

Exemptions from charges: In compliance with the ICAO 'user pays' principle, the charging Regulation requested transparency on the costs of exemptions and demonstration that these costs are not recovered from the other airspace users in conformity with paragraph 46 of ICAO Doc. No. 9082. Furthermore, the charging Regulation added two optional exemption categories to the ones already existing in the EUROCONTROL system: The humanitarian and police / custom flights (Article 9, (f) and (g)), which were often already granted but not codified.

Compliance review and enforcement: One of the main weaknesses of the EUROCONTROL route charge system was – and remains – its weak enforcement powers, beyond States' goodwill and some kind of 'peer pressure' exercised through the processes foreseen in a non-binding document known as the 'FIFU Handbook' (for 'Financial Information For Users'). In comparison, the Article 16 of the service provision Regulation No. 550/2004 implemented powerful tools: Article 16(1) entrusted the Commission with the responsibility of exercising an 'ongoing review' of the States' compliance with the rules contained in the charging Regulation, whilst Article 16(2) gave the Commission the responsibility of investigating in case of allegation of non-compliance or non-application of the principles and rules of the Regulation. The ongoing review function resulted in the Commission entrusting EUROCONTROL to analyse the cost bases of three Member States in 2009, and of two other ones in 2010. No major infringement was detected, but the process had the positive result of allowing the interpretation of certain provisions of the text and highlighting 'best practices'. The threat of the investigation tool of Article 16.2 was on its side a deterrent powerful enough to sort out a few situations of suspected misuse or abuse before needing to use it up to its conclusion.

Another ICAO Conference on the Economics of Airports and Air Navigation Services, 'CEANS'[23] (15 to 20 September 2008), happening just after a 'Worldwide Symposium on Performance of the Air Navigation System'[24] and right at the moment of assessment of the results of SES I and the preparation of SES II, gave an opportunity to Europe and the European Commission to present their progress in the performance and charging areas and drive again the evolution of ICAO recommendations: CEANS-WP/34, co-presented by EUROCONTROL and the European Commission, allowed presenting the progress made in the performance benchmarking and unveiled the intentions of the SES II package, still under preparation, to move to a system of binding performance targets with incentives. The European contributions also insisted on the economic crisis affecting the industry and the financial difficulties faced by airlines. They noted that air navigation charges amounted to more than 10% of the IATA airlines' operating costs,[25] (but up to more than 20% for the low fare operators) and called for actions with a view to improving the overall performance of the system and assisting airspace users.

The Conference recommended that:

> ICAO should amend paragraph 16 of Doc 9082 to recommend the establishment of performance management systems by service providers, and to include the major elements of a performance management system with emphasis on the selection of Key Performance Areas and related indicators, and that ICAO should establish a dialogue, where appropriate, with regional organizations on economic performance with a view to improving performance of the air navigation services system.

The revision of ICAO Documents 9082 and 9161 are now ongoing and almost completed under the auspices of the Air Navigation Services Economics Panel (ANSEP) and the Airport Economics Panel (AEP).

6 THE SES II PACKAGE: AIR NAVIGATION CHARGES AS A TOOL TO IMPROVE SUSTAINABILITY AND PERFORMANCE OF THE EUROPEAN AVIATION

The review in 2007 of the achievements of SES I, foreseen in Article 12 of the framework Regulation, was threefold: Report of 21 December 2006 from the

23. <www.icao.int/ceans/Docs.htm>.
24. <www.icao.int/icao/en/anb/meetings/perf2007/index.html>.
25. This was fluctuating depending on the variation of the price of fuel.

EUROCONTROL Performance Review Commission,[26] report from the High Level Group (HLG)[27] of July 2007 ('A framework for driving performance improvement') and Commission Communication of 20 December 2007 'First Report on the implementation of the Single Sky Legislation: achievements and the way forward'.[28] A better performance of the provision of air navigation services, including continuous improvement on safety, was acknowledged as being crucial to maintain competitivity of aviation and support economic growth. Furthermore, an overriding need to improve the efficiency of aviation for environmental reasons had also grown significantly. The focus of the SES II package under preparation was on performance and sustainability.

The several crises faced in the 2000s had also demonstrated concretely the perverse effects of the automatic full-cost recovery of air navigation charges: In periods of traffic decrease, this system generated an automatic increase of charges, thus aggravating the difficulties already faced by airlines and leading to a further decrease of demand. Conversely, additional revenue obtained through good management and cost-containment had to be returned to airspace users: the system did not offer any incentive to ANSPs to encourage good management, cost-containment and productivity increase.

The performance scheme, adopted as Regulation (EU) No. 691/2010 of 29 July 2010,[29] the amendment of the service provision Regulation by Regulation (EU) No. 1070/2009 of 21 October 2009[30] and the amendment of the charging Regulation by Regulation (EU) No. 1190/2010 on 16 December 2010[31] together achieve the quantum leap of putting an end to the paradigm of automatic full cost recovery that had prevailed in Europe since 1983 and make the charging scheme evolve into a tool for achieving performance.

Under this new regulatory environment, 'determined costs' (as opposed to the previous 'full costs')[32] are to be fixed in advance for each year of the performance reference period[33] following procedures set out in the performance and charging Regulations. The ratio with traffic forecasts allows establishing in advance 'determined unit rates' for each year of the reference period. Any variations to these predefined unit rates are subject to a risk-sharing mechanism set out in the charging

26. 'Evaluation of the impact of the SES initiative on ATM performance' <www.eurocontrol.int/prc/gallery/content/public/Docs/PRC_Evaluation_of_SES.pdf>.
27. Created in September 2006 by Vice-President Barrot
28. COM/2007/0845 final, <http://eur-lex.europa.eu/LexUriServ/LexUriServ.do?uri=CELEX:52007DC0845:EN:NOT>.
29. OJEU L 201, 3 Aug. 2010, 1.
30. OJEU L 300, 14 Nov. 2009, 34. This Regulation amends the four basic Regulations of the first package.
31. OJEU L 333, 17 Dec. 2010, 6.
32. Article 15.2(a) of the amended service provision Regulation sets out the principles of 'determined costs' defining the maximum costs to be set in advance for each year of the reference period in relation with traffic forecasted.
33. According to Art. 7 of the performance Regulation, reference periods are normally of five years, but the first reference period, being considered as a transitional one, is reduced to three years: 2012–2014.

Regulation, which is the incentive for cost-efficiency. This creates a regime close to a cost capping in a multi-annual framework.

In application of the performance scheme, performance targets at European level have been set for the first period 2012–2014 by Commission Decision No. 2011/121/EU of 21 February 2011.[34] The cost-efficiency target is a reduction in real terms of the average European Union-wide determined en route unit rate.[35] Member States (or FABs) are now required to adopt before end June 2011 their national (or FAB) performance plan with, for each year of the reference period, their 'determined unit rates'. Once the national determined unit rates will be set, the Commission will be able to visualize ex-ante the cost-efficiency efforts made by each State against the EU-wide target and, if necessary, ask for a revision of the plan.

The charging Regulation creates the incentive for reaching the cost-efficiency performance target through the setting up of a balanced sharing of the financial risk between Member States/ANSPs and airspace users. The key article of the amended charging Regulation is its new Article 11a, establishing the risk-sharing mechanisms that apply to the two parameters of the setting of unit rates, that is, traffic and costs:

6.1 Traffic Risk-Sharing

Under the previous full cost recovery system, costs remaining equal, traffic variations resulted in additional revenue or a loss carried over to the next years (typically n+2). Paragraphs 2 to 7 of Article 11.a now establish a traffic risk-sharing mechanism:

In practice, the costs submitted to traffic risk sharing are those of the ANSPs. Paragraph 2 identifies the costs that are not impacted by traffic variations and therefore are not submitted to this risk-sharing: The costs established in application of Article 5.2 (basically costs that are incurred by the regulator), the costs of meteorological service providers, and the authorized carry-overs from a previous year or period.

Paragraph 3 establishes a 'dead band' of plus/minus 2% of traffic variation over a given year as compared to the forecasted traffic, within which all additional revenue is retained by the ANSP and all loss is borne by the ANSP. This is the variation bracket within which the service provider is deemed to be able to absorb the variation with normal management tools and consequently bear the full risk or keep all the possible profit. Concretely, in case of traffic higher than expected, the service provider will use the additional revenue to provide the additional capacity needed. If traffic goes down it will absorb the loss through commensurate cost containment.

34. OJEU L 48, 23 Feb. 2011, 16.
35. Resulting from the ratio between all the European costs for providing en route ANS and the European traffic.

Paragraphs 4 to 7 establish that, for traffic variations beyond these plus / minus 2% and a limit of plus / minus 10%, the traffic risks and opportunities are shared between ANSPs and airspace users: ANSPs bear 30% of the losses or retain 30% of the additional revenue, whilst airspace users bear 70% of the losses or retain 70% of the additional revenue. In the course of discussions, this 70/30 risk allocation was deemed to reflect a reasonable proxy for the share between fixed and variable costs of the ANSPs and to provide a reasonable but meaningful incentive for ANSPs to gradually become more adaptable to context changes.

Beyond 10% of unexpected traffic growth or decrease, the full cost recovery applies again in particular in case of traffic collapse to protect the financial viability of ANSPs, safety and continuity of service. It has to be said that such unexpected traffic evolution was never attained, even in the worst years of crisis of the last decade. This threshold is in reality a risk limiter for ANSPs: in case of 10% or more of traffic decrease over the year, the maximum risk exposure for ANSP is of 100% for the first 2% of traffic decrease and 30% between 2% and 10%, resulting in a maximum total loss of 4.4% of the revenue of the year (more or less two weeks of billing).

6.2 Cost Risk-Sharing

This is developed in Paragraph 8 of Article 11a. The determined costs principle applies to all entities that have costs eligible to recovery from airspace users (ANSP, regulator, meteorological service providers). This leads to a capping of the determined costs established and adopted before the reference period: If costs are higher than planned, the loss is borne by the entity concerned. If they are lower thanks to good cost control, the additional revenue collected from charges is retained by the entity concerned: This is an incentive towards good management, economies of scale and productivity gains.

As a consequence, during the reference period, the only parameters of adjustment of the 'determined unit rates' set in advance as part of the performance plan are:

(1) Every year, further to Article 6.1, the application of the delta of inflation between forecasted and actual inflation (as measured by Eurostat).
(2) Every year, the application of traffic risk-sharing mechanism (depending on the entities).
(3) Every year, the implementation of incentive schemes (Bonuses/maluses), if any.
(4) At the beginning of each period the application of the authorized carry-overs from the previous period (including points 1 to 3 above and, for the first two reference periods, the 'legacy costs', i.e. the losses incurred under the previous full cost recovery regime).
(5) At the end of the period, a limited number of cost factors deemed to be 'uncontrollable' (Paragraph 8c of Article 11a) can be recovered through a

carry-over to the next period (or returned to airspace users in case of lower costs) if agreed by the National Supervisory Authority concerned.

This is listed in Annex IV paragraph 2 of the Regulation.

The coupling of the setting of cost-efficiency targets with the risk-sharing mechanisms allows creating a virtuous behaviour. If the targets are set at the right level, that is, reachable but ambitious enough, the ANSPs will in the short term increase the adaptability and reactivity of their service provision to context changes. I the medium term, under the oversight of their National Supervisory Authority, they will be prone to undertake structural measures to improve productivity without affecting safety, for example, in the form of collaboration, common procurement, or merger of some services within FABs. They will also be incentivized to make optimal technological choices, in line with the SESAR objectives.

For a transitional period ending on 31 December 2014, this risk-sharing mechanism may not apply to terminal costs and unit rates (Article 2 of Regulation No. 1191/2010 amending the charging Regulation). This is because the transitional period established under the first charging Regulation will only end up in 2015; there is therefore not yet a level playing field among ANSPs, no meaningful benchmarking and no historic data allowing the setting up of performance targets.

Beyond the crucial introduction of cost capping and risk-sharing mechanisms, the amended charging Regulation introduces a number of other substantial changes, as follows:

Incentive mechanisms: Article 12 has been modified. The economic Regulation is not an alternative regime anymore; as a consequence Paragraph 2 is now about the possibility, offered by the performance Regulation, to set up incentive schemes for the achievement of performance targets by the ANSPs, for example, in the performance areas of environment or capacity / delays, as provided in Article 11 of the performance Regulation. Paragraph 3, dealing with incentives on airspace users, has been expanded to now also cover the environmental benefits and the investment in SESAR-validated technologies. The performance scheme and the Regulation of charges are not only for ANSPs; they also aim at driving the behaviour of airspace users in view of improving the overall performance of the network.

Common projects: Article 5.3 creates the link between charges and SES II's technological pillar (SESAR). In conformity with Recitals 7 and 8 of Regulation (EC) No. 1070/2009 and as laid down in Article 15a of the service provision Regulation, the 'common projects' concept materializes the possibility to finance partly through charges the large, cross-border technological products arising from SESAR and the ATM Master Plan and requiring ad hoc governance and financing. It is also a tool to help Member States and ANSPs to make optimal technological choices. The Commission is currently working on proposals on the governance and financing of the deployment of SESAR, to be presented to the Council and European Parliament before the end of 2011.

Functional Airspace Blocks (FABs): Interestingly, the SES II package has moved the concept of FAB from Article 5 of the Airspace Regulation No. 551/2004[36] to a new Article 9.a in the service provision Regulation. FABs now become a true performance tool aiming at defragmenting service provision. However, experience and discussions have shown that it would be unrealistic to impose in the short term that FABs have a single charging zone with completely uniform rules (e.g., exemption policies or tax issues). The new Article 4 of the charging Regulation acknowledges this fact and now only requires that, when FABs establish a single charging zone, they should '*ensure consistency and uniformity in the application of the Regulation to the airspace concerned to the maximum possible extent*'. The Commission accepts that it will be more beneficial to the European network to have large charging zones following operational requirements but with slightly heterogeneous rules than to continue with the traditional charging zones following national borders.

Market conditions for airports below 150,000 movements: As economic incentives on ANSPs now become the norm, there could be a temptation to abuse the possibility of declaring that airports are placed under market conditions in order to benefit from simplified reporting obligations and be exempted from the obligation of calculating terminal unit rates. To avoid this, the conditions to fulfil to benefit from the conditions of Article 1.6 have been reinforced. The Commission has stronger powers to ask the State concerned to review its assessment and the validity of the demonstration is limited to the duration of the reference period.

Calculation of costs and unit rates in local currency: In the provisions of the first charging Regulations costs had to be established in local currency (Annex II), but Annex VI gave both the Euro and the local currency for the calculation of the unit rate. This resulted in some problems in case of substantial variations of exchange rates and the determination of the exchange risk and who should bear it. This has now been clarified: Articles 6 and 13 require clearly that both costs and unit rates be established in local currency. Member States are now assured to recover their national costs irrespective of possible variation of their currency against the Euro. The EUROCONTROL system, which bills charges in Euro, contains a monthly adjustment mechanism recalculating the exchange rate between the local currency and Euro and allowing Member States and airspace users to be protected against local currency appreciation or depreciation. The exchange risk of costs that may be incurred by ANSPs directly in Euro (e.g., in some States fuel, electricity, IT, etc.) is borne by the ANSP.

Consultation: Now that the cycle of setting costs and unit rates is pluri-annual, Article 8 on consultation merges and simplifies former Articles 8 and 15. Consultation is to be exhaustive and detailed before the beginning of the reference period and has to take place in the context of the general consultation on the performance scheme. On the other hand it may be more basic during the period, as most

36. OJEU L 96, 31 Mar. 2004, 20.

adjustments will be quasi automatic, resulting from the application of inflation (Article 6), possible adjustment mechanisms (Article 11a) and possible financial incentives (Article 12).

7 THE CHALLENGES AHEAD

The SES II package shows a close connection between its different elements: The charging Regulation materializes the financial aspects of the performance scheme and implements economic incentive with a risk-sharing mechanism. The FABs are now tools to defragment service provision and generate cost-efficiency gains. They are encouraged to set a single charging zone or at least a cooperative framework within which economies of scale will be easier to achieve. The deployment of technology is addressed through the integration of the concept of common project, allowing tailor-made governance and financing schemes for the large, cross-border projects affecting the performance of the network, to the overall benefit of airspace users.

2012 will be a crucial year where all elements of the SES II package shall converge and start delivering performance benefits whilst maintaining or reinforcing safety: The performance Regulation has now entered into force and Member States have communicated to the commission of their 2012–2014 performance plans, by the set deadline of June 2011, for application as from 1 January 2012. At the time of drafting this article, the commission is in the process of assessing the 28 performance plans that have been collected. The charging Regulation has entered into force and shall apply as from the 2012 en route costs and unit rates, in full synchronization with the performance scheme. The proposals on SESAR deployment governance and financing are expected before the end of 2011 and should be put in place in 2012. FABs must all be established by 4 December 2012 at the latest.

This will be combined with the implementation as from March 2011 of the Directive 2009/12/EC of 11 March 2009 on airport charges[37] and the start of discussions on a comprehensive ‘airport package’ currently being prepared by the European Commission with a high level of priority and aiming *inter alia* at enhancing the airport dimension of the SES II package.

The support and expectations expressed by all stakeholders in the high-level conferences of Madrid (February 2010) and Bruges (October 2010) as well as the political support reiterated in several transport councils give assurance that the aviation world is committed to the success of the SES. The commitment of staff will also be an essential element, and this is why the human factor pillar is also referred to as the ‘overarching pillar’ of the SES II initiative.

The next key year will then be 2015, with the start of the second performance reference period, which will this time be of five years and encompass all four Key Performance Areas (safety, environment, capacity and cost-efficiency) both for en route and terminal air navigation services. In the cost-efficiency area in particular,

37. OJEU L 70, 14 Mar. 2009, 11.

the costs and unit rates of terminal ANS will also be submitted to performance target-setting. The performance scheme will be more complex to manage with more indicators to balance and weigh against each other (safety remaining the overriding objective) and maybe more incentive mechanisms, but it will also build on three years of experience.

After three years of test and experience learning, 2015 will be the age of maturity for the performance scheme of the SES II package, including its cost-efficiency dimension.

Chapter 17

SES Environmental and Efficiency Benefits: Reduction of Emissions

Paul Steele[*]

1 INTRODUCTION

It is estimated that there will be 15.9 million flights in European airspace by 2020, a 50% increase from 2011. If urgent action isn't taken, 20% of those flights will be delayed, and 1.5 million of them will be grounded because there will be no available airspace for them. At the same time, airlines are pursuing aggressive targets to improve fuel efficiency by 1.5% per year and to achieve carbon neutral growth from 2020.

To meet these challenges, the European ATM Master Plan – which was endorsed by the European Council in March 2009 – set a number of targets for the operational and technical pillar of the Single European Sky (known as SESAR) to meet by the year 2020. These targets are (1) to increase safety by a factor of 10, (2) reduce ATM costs by 50%, and (3) provide a three-fold increase in ATM capacity to meet future demand. Perhaps most important of all, the Single European Sky has the vital task of delivering (4) a 10% reduction in CO_2 emissions per flight.

When considering the environmental aims of SES it is important to understand the context of the environmental challenge facing aviation at global level, as air transport seeks to grow in a carbon-constrained world. What is the environmental

* Paul Steele, Director Environment, IATA.

Daniel Calleja Crespo & Pablo Mendes de Leon, *Achieving the Single European Sky: Goals and Challenges*, pp. 167–178.

efficiency of European ATM today and why is SES so important for meeting our climate change targets? What lessons can be drawn from the development of the industry's own carbon targets and its successful track-record of reducing emissions over the past fifty years? It is essential that these points are understood by everyone engaged with the Single European Sky, for although the capacity, safety and cost efficiency benefits of the project are much needed and very welcome, it is the environmental benefits, through greater route efficiency, which will deliver a vital contribution to combating climate change.

IATA and its members have a considerable vested interest in seeing a successful SES. We have strong views on what needs to be done to deliver change, as well as on the future benefits of harmonizing the airspace beyond Europe's borders. SES is attempting to achieve great things, not least in the environmental sphere, and it makes sense to take stock and see what lessons we can learn from the process, to ensure SES delivers its promises for a cleaner, more efficient future for European aviation.

2 WHY AVIATION MUST BE PART OF THE CLIMATE CHANGE SOLUTION

The focus on aviation's contribution to climate change has been so intense in recent years that we have forgotten that for most of the period of commercial jet transport, it was reductions in *noise* that regulators, the public, and politicians wanted to see.

How things have changed! While noise is still an important issue for people living near an airport, it has become secondary compared to the overwhelming interest in greenhouse gas emissions that has developed in the last ten years. Historically the aviation industry was probably a bit too comfortable with its position in this debate. Contributing only 2% to man-made carbon emissions according to the Intergovernmental Panel on Climate Change (IPCC), airlines and manufacturers assumed that a combination of a good track-record, plus the undoubted economic benefits of air transport, would make aviation an unlikely target for climate activism.

But we were wrong. We underestimated the extent to which aviation has become a symbol of economic development, and of globalization. Aviation brings people, goods, and ideas together. It stimulates technological and economic development, and makes no apology for seeking to expand its role in doing so. This is anathema to certain people whose values are different: those willing to sacrifice economic development for the sake of ecology. Such views have always existed, but what became different in the 1990s was that these views made common cause with local anti-airport campaigns.

3 HOW THE INDUSTRY DEVELOPED ITS ENVIRONMENTAL TARGETS FOR THE FUTURE

So a sea-change in thinking was required. Rather than just rely on our track-record, we had to show that we were serious in our approach to climate change.

Furthermore, we needed to take the same approach across the whole industry, working as one towards tough targets on climate change. Ultimately, we succeeded in this to the extent that the industry is actually ahead of the politicians at global level.

In 2007 IATA set down some challenges for the industry. We posed the possibility of a carbon-free future, with measurable milestones along the way. In 2008 this vision was confirmed when the major players from all the key sectors – airlines, airports, air navigation service providers, and manufacturers – signed a declaration committing themselves to concerted action on climate change. This was closely followed by the articulation of a clear set of targets. We agreed to:

- increase fuel efficiency by 1.5% per year to 2020;
- to cap net emissions from 2020 through carbon-neutral growth;
- and to reduce net emissions by 50% by 2050, compared to a baseline year of 2005.

These targets are without question the toughest and most rigorous of any global industry. For a slow-growing business to cut its emissions by 50% would be impressive – for an industry growing by around 5% a year on average, it is a very tall order. The industry cannot achieve these targets entirely by itself – it needs the close collaboration of industry and governments. However, the industry is committed to doing its bit and aviation has met every challenge placed in its way in the past. Since 2004 alone, IATA's Green Teams have helped the industry cut emissions by some 76.7 million tonnes of CO_2. Equally importantly, our four pillar strategy offers a detailed plan for bringing our emissions down. No other business has backed up its climate change commitments with such a comprehensive plan.

The four-pillar strategy aims to reduce emissions via a combination of four separate but interconnected tracks:

(1) Technology
(2) Operations
(3) Infrastructure
(4) Positive Economic Measures.

The technology pillar is mostly focused on delivering fuel efficient aircraft into the fleet. Innovations such as new air frame engine, designs and lighter materials, will continue the trend which sees each new generation of plane achieve a saving of around 20% on its predecessor. The development of sustainable biofuels offers the potential for net carbon savings of up to 80%, and will be a crucial element in the industry's carbon reduction plans.

Operations refers to finding emissions savings in the way aircraft are flown. An example is CDO (Continuous Descent Operations) which enables an arriving aircraft descends continuously, to the greatest possible extent, by employing minimum engine thrust. Other examples embrace the use of ground power at airports (rather than relying on engines) and taxiing on one engine.

While keeping safety as paramount, the infrastructure pillar is aimed at increasing the efficiency and capacity available at airports (to remove delays and holding) and more importantly, a fundamental reform of air traffic management, enabling aircraft to make the most of on-board technology, and seeking to do away with the archaic procedures of a national-border-based ATM system.

Finally, the industry agrees that positive economic measures will be necessary as a temporary measure, to help incentivize the development of more innovative fuels and technology. Some form of carbon offsetting may also be required in order for aviation to meet its 2020 aim of carbon-neutral growth.

The endorsement of the four-pillar strategy by both the aviation industry and ICAO marks a further step – along with the 2020 and 2050 targets – towards a comprehensive solution for aviation carbon emissions.

4 EUROPEAN ATM TODAY

How does the four-pillar strategy translate to the situation in Europe today, and more specifically, to the role of air traffic management?

ATM is a major source of wasted emissions, through inefficient use of airspace. Exactly how much fuel is wasted is difficult to ascertain, as there are conflicting statistics available. In 1999, the Intergovernmental Panel on Climate Change suggested that global airspace was on average about 12% inefficient. A 2008 study by CANSO (the Civil Air Navigation Services Organisation) put the figure at around 6%–8%, reflecting improvements over the first half-decade of the twenty-first century, most notably the introduction of Reduced Vertical Separation Minima (RVSM). But crucially, this improvement was not noticeable in Europe. CANSO members estimated that European airspace remained some 11% inefficient – leaving huge room for improvement.

The European Performance Review Commission (PRC) claims European airspace is 94% efficient. The European Commission has said that ATM is responsible for some 16 million tonnes of avoidable CO_2 emissions. One of the lessons which European ATM can draw from the aviation industry work on environment is the importance of coming up with consistent statistics. But what is beyond doubt is that considerable inefficiency persists, and that it is worse in Europe than in any other region.

Why is European airspace less efficient than, for example, the US? Fragmentation is the principle answer. Europe's thirty-seven air navigation service providers (ANSPs) operate around sixty-five Area Control Centers (ACCs) each duplicating the task of its neighbour. By contrast, over an area roughly the same size, the US FAA has twenty ACCs. Russia's plans are even more impressive; over an even larger area it is consolidating its centres from 118 to 13. The duplication of resources is irritating enough to the airlines that have to pay for all of this infrastructure, but the wider implications are far more damaging: such a system institutionalizes airspace fragmentation on a massive scale within Europe. During an era when the majority of Europe has abolished their own currencies to form monetary union and removed land borders to facilitate the free movement of people and trade, not a single airspace border has changed, or the numbers of ACCs been reduced.

5 A SOLUTION: THE ESTABLISHMENT OF FABs

Fragmentation means that aircraft fly longer routes because it leads to increased pockets of restricted airspace. It makes traffic flow management more complex, makes civil-military cooperation more difficult, and leads to delays, lack of capacity, increased costs, and eventually, if demand continues to rise, will have safety implications. The overall economic cost of fragmentation is estimated at EUR 1 billion per year. This figure is on top of the EUR 3 billion per year wasted through avoidable delays and 429 million unnecessary flight kilometres.

A key step towards reducing fragmentation in European airspace has been the creation of nine Functional Airspace Blocks (FABs), grouping ANSPs together to improve airspace coordination, and introduce efficiencies. According to a European PRC 'Evaluation of Functional Airspace Blocks' report in 2008, the relative inefficiency of European airspace can be characterized as follows:

- 64% of en route deviations attributable to routing within each State;
- 11% of en route extensions attributable to the interfaces between States within each FAB;
- 25% of en route extensions attributable to the interfaces between FABs (thus requiring action at European level).

Not all of this inefficiency is recoverable, due to trade-offs between shortest mileage, optimization of vertical movements, or reduction of conflict in dense airspace to the benefit of safety and capacity. Nevertheless, the opportunities to reduce emissions through reducing these route extensions are clear. Some 203,000 tonnes of CO_2 are wasted every year as a result of the route extensions created by the interfaces between the States in FAB EC alone (France, Germany, Switzerland, the Netherlands, Belgium and Luxembourg). And a staggering 723,000 tonnes of CO_2 could be recovered annually by optimizing the interfaces between the nine FABs.

6 THE BENEFITS OF SES AND SESAR

So, the need for reform in Europe's skies is obvious. But it might not be immediately obvious that a Single European Sky is the only way forward. Perhaps it is only right that we revisit first principles and remind ourselves why SES is so important. After all, if most of the problems are within the states, perhaps the states themselves can fix the problems faster? In reality, the PRC report makes it clear that the FABs have already contributed to solving national airspace issues, through an increased pressure to achieve 'quick wins' and a larger geographical area of airspace being available to find solutions to problems which would be difficult to solve at national level.

Therefore, it is clear that while national ANSPs can make some efficiencies, and technology can achieve a great many things, it is only through meaningful, fundamental reform of European airspace that the full benefit of the emissions savings that we know are possible will be made.

The European Air Traffic Management Master Plan's goal for a 10% reduction in CO_2 emissions per flight is challenging, especially when the inefficiency of European airspace is estimated to be between around 89% in 2006 (CANSO and ICAO figures). This means that SES and its SESAR component need to make European airspace around 99% efficient by 2020. Given inevitable constraints such as aircraft separation minima, noise restrictions, and lack of runway capacity, 99% seems unrealistic. Yet, practical trials in European airspace are showing that improvements of this magnitude are not only possible – they are achievable with current techniques and technology.

7 THE TARGETS OF UK NATS

NATS, the UK ANSP, set its own independent 10% emissions saving target in 2008 (for 2020, with a baseline of 2006). It has characterized the 'perfect flight' in which all possible inefficiencies are eliminated:

- A seamless taxi on the ground, with no delay, and using as little engine thrust as possible.
- A continuous climb departure, leading to a continuous cruise climb, enabling the aircraft to reach its optimum cruising altitude as efficiently as possible.
- An optimum route, as short as possible to the destination, or taking advantage of weather conditions to reduce track mileage or fuel burn, and using optimum cruising speed.
- A continuous approach and descent, eliminating holding.

NATS itself, with partners BAA and British Airways, tested the perfect flight on a London-Edinburgh shuttle in 2010. The result was a saving of 350 kg of fuel – almost one tonne of CO_2, representing a saving of more than 10%. The challenge for NATS is now to roll out the perfect flight across its entire network. This it anticipates achieving in three stages: (1) improved flight planning and route availability; (2) better procedures using new technology, reducing holding and improving ground operations; and (3) airspace redesign to enable aircraft to achieve continuous climb and descent, and optimum routes.

The achievements of the NATS perfect flight show what can be done at national level. And similar projects are taking place across not just in European airspace, but at global level, such as the US NextGen programme, or the ASPIRE (Asia-Pacific Initiative to Reduce Emissions) project in the Pacific.

8 IATA'S EFFORTS PERTAINING TO EFFICIENCY

IATA too has been heavily involved in airspace efficiency programmes. In Europe it has partnered with Eurocontrol, CANSO and ACI Europe to deliver the European Flight Efficiency Plan (FEP). Launched in 2009, the FEP aims to save 1.5 million tonnes of CO_2 per year, through five streams:

(1) Enhancing en route airspace design to optimize distances flown. (Reducing distance flown by 0.1% could save around EUR 20 million per year.)
(2) Improving airspace utilization with enhanced civil-military cooperation and better coordination of flight planning. This could reduce distance flown by 0.7%.
(3) Improving terminal areas procedures including Continuous Descent Approaches (CDA).
(4) Improving airport operations, particularly reducing tax times.
(5) Improving awareness of best practices to save fuel.

In 2009 in line with stream 3, a CDA Action Plan was agreed, to roll out CDA at 100 European airports by 2013, saving 500,000 tonnes of CO_2 a year.

The work on finding efficiencies by flight phase (clearly illustrated by the NATS trial and the FEP) is continuing with a number of SESAR projects, conducted in partnership with IATA member airlines. One of the most ambitious projects has been the Atlantic Interoperability initiative to Reduce Emissions (AIRE), which began trials in 2009, and seeks to reduce noise and fuel burn through all phases of flight, gate-to-gate. More than 1000 separate trials of different 'green' operational procedures have been conducted under the auspices of AIRE in Europe, including two complete gate-to-gate flights from Paris to Miami.

The work was divided into three phases: surface, terminal, and oceanic. Three hundred and fifty-three surface trials were conducted at Paris Charles De Gaulle. These included taxiing on half engines, minimizing taxi time, and reducing waiting time at the runway threshold. Three different sets of trials were held in the terminal area: at Paris (CDG and Orly), Stockholm Arlanda, and Madrid. These trials – more than 700 in total – looked at the application of Required Navigation Performance (RNP), CDAs, and Continuous Climb Departures (CCD). Some of the results are startling. For example, the CDA trials at Madrid (Barajas) showed fuel savings of 25% during descent, compared with a non-CDA flight.

Two projects investigated the optimization of flight profiles in oceanic airspace. In the NATCLM project several Air France and TAP Portugal flights to the Caribbean and Americas, controlled by NAV Portugal and the FAA, trialled cruise climb techniques. These tested both vertical and lateral optimization, making use of up-to-date meteorological information to calculate a better flight plan en route. In Iceland the Oceanic-Nat ADSB project looked at thirty-eight flights on the Keflavik-Seattle route, evaluating optimized cruise climb, direct routing, and variable speeds. CO_2 savings of these various techniques ranged from 90 kg to over 1 tonne.

Finally, two fully optimized gate-to-gate flights, from Paris to Miami, were conducted by Air France and American Airlines on 6 and 7 April 2010. During the nine-hour flight, the enhanced procedures were applied at each flight stage and coordinated among all the project participants. As a result of these trials, Air France estimated that if they were applied to all their long-haul flights to and from North America, it would result in CO_2 savings of 135,000 tonnes per year.

IATA is also bringing the industry together to make airspace improvements. In 2010 IATA launched the IATA Flexible Routing programme (iFlex) which will allow airlines to reduce carbon emissions and fuel burn by up to 2% on certain long-haul flights. ATC providers across the globe are being challenged by new city-pairs, ultra-long haul aircraft, increasing traffic and the constraints being imposed by traditional airspace structures. The iFlex programme concentrates on long-haul routes through low-density airspace in regions where maximum benefit can be achieved through a more flexible airspace structure. The South Atlantic and Africa are the initial focus concentrating on the Johannesburg – Atlanta and Dubai – Sao Paolo routes. IATA is currently working with airlines, ICAO, air navigation service providers and governments on proof-of-concept work which will include data analysis and route simulation using modern flight planning tools. Early modelling of the iFlex programme suggests that airlines operating a ten-hour intercontinental flight can cut flight time by six minutes, reduce fuel burn by as much as 2% and save 3,000 kilograms of CO_2.

These projects show that the environmental benefits of delivering ATM operational efficiency improvements under the Single European Sky are numerous, but how are these benefits to be delivered? What needs to happen over the next decade to make meaningful progress, and how can IATA help? Perhaps there are lessons to be learned from the success of airlines and aircraft manufacturers in reducing fuel burn over the last five decades.

9 ACHIEVEMENT OF THE AVIATION INDUSTRY INCLUDING MANUFACTURERS AND AIRLINES WITH RESPECT TO EMISSIONS REDUCTIONS

Since the 1960s tremendous technological advances in engines and aircraft have allowed a plane to take a passenger 70% further on the same litre of fuel. Each new class of airplane has been some 20% more fuel-efficient than its predecessor. And similar gains are on the horizon, continuing to help aviation reduce its emissions. How have the manufacturers succeeded in doing this, while at the same time reducing noise and building safer, more luxurious and much larger planes? And can any lessons be drawn which are of relevance to the air traffic control sector?

Firstly and most obviously, the engines have changed. The major engine manufacturers have continually improved their engines in ways unimaginable to the early jet pioneers. These companies were forced to innovate because of two simple factors: *demand* and *competition*.

The demand for improved efficiency came from the customers. In the face of oil price volatility it was obvious to airlines that fuel was going to be a significant factor in overall running costs (today it is 29% and rising). Fuel efficiency would help to cut costs and would create a competitive advantage in the market place. And it was the element of competition that was crucial to the rapid pace of improvement. Without demand, there is no incentive to improve at all. But if the demand is being serviced by a monopoly supplier, it is very difficult to force the supplier to improve. If there had been no competition between engine suppliers, it is inconceivable that the jet engine would have developed as it has.

A similar story can be seen when one considers the airframe manufacturers. Although their efforts were perhaps more focused on safety, comfort and space, as production became more sophisticated, aerodynamics to reduce fuel burn, and innovative materials to reduce weight, have become key selling-points. Again, these advances are a result of demand and competition.

So does this story contain any lessons for the future of air traffic management? It is IATA's belief that the concepts of demand and competition can produce results in almost any setting. Air Traffic Control should be no exception. With the issue of engine development, one has to acknowledge that the military was perhaps the major agent of change in the past (no less subject to the laws of demand and competition). But this is not the case today, and it is clear that the engine manufacturers are innovating just as strongly for their civilian customers as for their military customers of old. On the other hand, the drive for change has not come from air traffic control's military users, but from its civilian customers.

So it is not for lack of demand that progress has stalled. We don't use an engine design from the 1960s on our aircraft, because airlines long ago demanded something better. We are still using an air traffic control system conceived in the 1950s, even though we have demanded better. So what is the problem?

It is the lack of competition that has been crucial to the lack of development in air traffic control. It is lack of competition which has prevented the development of truly innovative solutions, has kept costs high, and has prevented drastic improvements in airspace efficiency.

10 THE IMPORTANCE OF LEADERSHIP

What does the history of aviation's environmental achievements and future plans tell us about the delivery of complex ideas and difficult targets? It tells us that the crucial element is leadership. It was leadership which brought collective agreement on our industry climate targets. It was leadership that led to the development of revolutionary new aircraft and engines, whether it was the vision of an innovative airline boss – a Juan Tripp, or a Gerhard Holtje – to ask for an entirely new kind of plane, or an innovative engineer like Joe Sutter or Bernard Zeigler.

In Europe, there have been some innovative leaders of the Single European Sky, such as Loyola de Palacio. I also applaud the focus brought by Transport Commissioner and Commission Vice President Siim Kallas, and Air Transport Commission Director Daniel Calleja to the implementation of SES Package II. But while the leadership of the Commission is essential, it is leadership from individual European governments, and from industry players, which has the potential to unblock reform. Where has been the visionary speech by a senior government figure? Where has been the national airspace strategy published that incorporates SES in its thinking? Technological innovation, stimulated by demand and competition, can deliver continued incremental improvement. But SES needs the step-change in capability which only inspirational visionary leadership can deliver.

11 APPLYING THE LESSONS OF HISTORY TO EUROPEAN ATM TODAY

The elements of demand, competition and leadership are essential pre-requisites for change. Some are easier to encourage than others, and with ATM in particular, competition is a politically fraught issue.

But we have seen progress. Last year, even the most closed shop of all, Spain, opened up its ATM towers to competition. The insistent calls for efficiency improvements are bringing the long monopoly of the state to an end. But introducing a competitive framework for aviation within the borders of the country should be only the first step. The bigger prize is cross-border consolidation.

Through discussions at both EU and ICAO level, it has long been accepted that it is possible for a nation to 'sublet' its national airspace to a neighbouring provider, without incurring a loss of 'sovereignty'. 'Airspace sovereignty' in this understanding is not exercised through the actual process of aircraft navigation, but through the exercise of choosing which provider to allow to manage aircraft over your country. In this sense the process is a little different to the underlying concept of the Functional Airspace Blocks.

In October 2010 a European Aviation Summit chaired by the Belgian Presidency of the EU released 'The Bruges Declaration' which stated that FABs should correspond to 'operational requirements and the needs of airlines, rather than national borders'. It also called for 'ambitious binding performance targets' for air navigation services to be set. These performance targets were debated throughout the second half of 2010, following an initial consultation released in August, which proposed targets across a wide range of ATM metrics.

However in October, as a result of national negotiations, the original proposed targets were watered down. IATA's press release at the time summed this up as two steps forward and one step back. Even as progress towards Functional Airspace Blocks was being made, the targets that would help them become more effective were being rendered almost meaningless.

Another condition that has been more successfully carried out is the reform of Eurocontrol. This was mandated by the December 2009 Eurocontrol Council, and under the leadership of David McMillan, real changes have been made to the organization. Detailed design work on new structures, work programmes and objectives is under way. In addition to SESAR, other elements of the SES – the network manager, the safety oversight harmonization – are underway, to various levels of progress. The establishment of the network manager role is of particular importance, as the extent of the NM competence to strategically direct European air traffic flows will be crucial to the level of integration and efficiency that SES achieves.

12 BENEFITS FOR TRAVELLERS IN 2021

In tackling such a complex subject as SES, it is easy to lose sight of how the achievement of the SESAR targets will actually benefit the airline passenger of tomorrow. So let us look ahead to what European aviation will be like ten years from now. Let us imagine that the Single European Sky is a functioning reality, performing as we would expect. As the twenty-first century celebrates its twenty-first birthday, how will the flying experience be different for the millions of passengers that will rely on aviation every day?

Firstly, they will have a dim recollection that there always used to be irritating delays to their journey. These disappeared when the airspace improvements of SES, coupled with advances in Airport Collaborative Decision-Making, enabled planes to depart on schedule every time. Only incredibly severe weather can now disrupt seamless on-time air travel.

Secondly, passengers will be aware that their journeys will be shorter. Thanks to SES eliminating minutes of wasted flight time from every flight, planes now fly much straighter routes. Better civil military cooperation has removed pockets of restricted airspace and freed up more capacity.

Thirdly, although passengers might not realize it, SES has meant they are paying less for their flight. By reducing track mileage and delay, SES has reduced the tonnes carbon airlines would otherwise have to offset. This in turn has lowered what might otherwise have proved to be (depending on the price of carbon) a significant additional charge on a ticket.

Of course, environmental savings are so much more important than just the effect on ticket price. The very ability of aviation to grow in Europe at all is tied up with the successful achievement of its environmental goals. If SES were able to save 10% of the emissions of aviation, that would be enough, alongside our own technological achievements and the adoption of biofuels, for us to reach our goal of carbon-neutral growth from 2020. So it is not just travellers that stand to benefit from SES; potentially, it is the whole planet.

13 CONCLUSION

There are two alternative narratives at work to describe the Single European Sky. The first, subscribed to by many of my airline colleagues, is that it is late, expensive, politically hamstrung, and isn't delivering what it promised. It is mired in confusion, riven by special interest groups, and has lost sight of why it exists in the first place. The second view, held by many who have worked hard to deliver it over the past few years, is that SES is ground-breaking, unprecedentedly complex, requires unheard-of political and industry cooperation, and is attempting to harness some of the most advanced technology in the world. In that context, it is making remarkable progress and remains on track.

Which of these two scenarios is closest to the truth? It is a vital question because it goes to the heart of the environmental targets which aviation is striving to reach. The answer is that it is a mixture of the above. It *is* ground-breaking and complex; it *is* political and expensive.

The question from an environmental point of view is 'will it deliver what it promises?' Can the tough environmental targets it has set itself be reached? From an airline perspective, there is unfortunately some doubt. The watering down of the performance targets and the rate of efficiency improvements give us concerns that the full benefits of SES will be realized. This is frustrating because as we have seen, individual trials of optimized flights show that the SESAR targets are possible.

So how do we bridge the gap? In this chapter I have attempted to explain how the industry developed its global emissions targets, and why it is confident it can reach them, based on its successful track record in the past. This track record was delivered not just through setting demanding targets, but through competition, and visionary leadership. Applying these principles more thoroughly to SES would, in the opinion of the airlines, drive greater improvements in the longer term. We believe the onus is on European governments to take the necessary steps to reform, and that a review of progress in 2013 will help to decide whether a more top-down approach to the design, use, and management of European airspace is required.

The stakes are high. The restrictions legislators are introducing on carbon emissions will limit the demand for air transport if we continue along the same path. There is a small but vocal group of people who will rejoice at that – but there is a much larger silent majority who would not want to see that happen. And the future of European economic competitiveness depends on more, not less, connectivity. So the environmental aims of SES simply have to work. There is no other option.

Chapter 18

The Coordinator for the Functional Airspace Blocks System: The Task and the Report

Georg Jarzembowski[*]

1 INTRODUCTION

As air traffic management is the backbone of civil aviation, both for passengers and freight as well as for military aviation, a more efficient functioning of the air traffic control systems is an important component for the establishment of an effective Single European Sky in the European Union (EU). Towards that purpose, the air traffic management of the 27 Member States shall no longer be organized according to national airspaces, but in cross-border airspace blocks, regardless of State borders: the so called Functional Airspace Blocks (FABs) to be completed by 4 December 2012. A Coordinator of the European Commission for the Functional Airspace Blocks System has been appointed to assist in the establishment of the FABs. This article shall describe the Functional Airspace Blocks and the task of the FAB Coordinator, and shall report on the progress of

* Georg Jarzembowski, Attorney-at-law in Hamburg; since 2010 The Coordinator of the European Commission for the Functional Airspace Blocks System; 1991 until 2009 Member of the European Parliament. The views are those of the author and not necessarily those of the European Commission.

Daniel Calleja Crespo & Pablo Mendes de Leon, *Achieving the Single European Sky: Goals and Challenges*, pp. 179–187.

the establishment of the Functional Airspace Blocks, based on the situation as of 1 July 2011.

2 THE FUNCTIONAL AIRSPACE BLOCKS

The Functional Airspace Blocks are based on the original Single European Sky Legislative Package of 2004 – now called SES I – with its four basic regulations, the Framework Regulation,[1] the Service Provision Regulation,[2] the Airspace Regulation,[3] the Interoperability Regulation,[4] and on the Single European Sky II Legislative Package of 2009 – the SES II – with its two further regulations, the Regulation amending the four basic regulations and the Regulation on aerodromes, air traffic management and air navigation services as well as on the European Aviation Safety Agency (EASA).[5]

The common objective of the European Legislation for the Single European Sky is to achieve a harmonized regulatory framework for the effective creation of the Single European Sky – with high air traffic safety standards, optimized capacities, an efficient, also cost-efficient air transport system, and less environmental impact in favour of our citizens, our aviation community, our economy, and our environment.

The detailed rules on the Functional Airspace Blocks (FABs)[6] were part of the SES II Legislation introduced as an important tool for assisting the establishment of the Single European Sky. A Functional Airspace Block shall be 'an airspace block based on operational requirements and established regardless of State boundaries, where the provision of air navigation services and related functions are performance-driven and optimized with a view to introducing, in each functional airspace block, enhanced cooperation among air navigation service providers or,

1. Regulation (EC) No. 549/2004 of the European Parliament and of the Council of 10 Mar. 2004 laying down the framework for the creation of the single European sky (the framework Regulation), OJ L 96, 31 Mar. 2004, 1
2. Regulation (EC) No. 550/2004 of the European Parliament and of the Council of 10 Mar. 2004 on the provision of air navigation services in the single European sky (the service provision Regulation), OJ L 96, 31 Mar. 2004, 10.
3. Regulation (EC) No. 551/2004 of the European Parliament and of the Council of 10 Mar. 2004 on the organization and use of the airspace in the single European sky (the airspace Regulation), OJ L 96, 31.3.2004, 20.
4. Regulation (EC) No. 552/2004 of the European Parliament and of the Council of 10 Mar. 2004 on the interoperability of the European Air Traffic Management network (the interoperability Regulation), OJ L 96, 31 Mar. 2004, 26.
5. Regulation (EC) No. 1070/2009 of the European Parliament and the Council of 21 Oct. 2009 amending Regulation (EC) No. 549/2004, (EC) No. 550/2004, (EC) No. 551/2004 and (EC) No. 552/2004 in order to improve the performance and sustainability of the European aviation system, OJ L 300, 14 Nov. 2009, 34 and Regulation (EC) No. 1108/2009 of the European Parliament and of the Council of 21 Oct. 2009 on amending Regulation (EC) No. 216/2008 in the filed of aerodromes, air traffic management and air navigation services and repealing Directive 2006/23/EC, OJ L 309, 24 Nov. 2009, 51
6. See especially Art. 9 a of the Service Provision Regulation.

where appropriate, an integrated provider'.[7] Thus, air traffic management would no longer be rendered according to the boundaries of Member States, but according to a number of operationally useful and performance-driven air zones, that together as a system shall cover the whole airspace of the European Union, and where appropriate, also the airspace of neighbouring countries.

The neighbouring Third States that are generally committed to implement the Single European Sky through Membership in the European Economic Area, by a special bi-lateral treaty, by an Euro-Mediterranean Aviation Agreement, or by an agreement establishing the European Common Aviation Area (ECAA), are Iceland, Norway, Switzerland, Morocco, Bosnia & Herzegovina, Croatia, as well as the Former Yugoslav Republic of Macedonia, Montenegro, Serbia, and the United Interim Administration Mission in Kosovo. Furthermore, the associate partners are Albania, Egypt, and Tunisia, while observers are the Kingdom of Jordan and Lebanon.

During the preparation and the legislative process of the SES II Package, some officials in the European Commission (EC) and some Members of the European Parliament pursed the idea that – having the definition of an FAB in mind – the optimal solution for defining the individual Functional Airspace Blocks on operational grounds was to decide on the airspace regions of the FABs in a single and separate process on the European level ('Top-down approach'). Yet the Member States were in no way willing to share their individual national powers with each other and with the European Parliament. As the European Commission and the European Parliament wanted at least some progress for the Single European Sky, the Top-down approach was neither proposed nor introduced in this legislative procedure. The SES II Legislation on the FABs was based and adopted on the 'Bottom-up approach' – meaning that the Member States are responsible to define and set up the Functional Airspace Blocks by the mutual agreement of two or more Member States.

On the other hand, the Council and the European Parliament agreed in the FAB provision of the Service Provision Regulation that the Member States are obliged to inform the Commission and the other Member States about their plans and to give them an opportunity for observations, as well as to implement the Functional Airspace Blocks by 4 December 2012. Moreover, in the Transport Council Meeting of 4 May 2010, the Council – motivated by the Volcanic Ash Cloud Crisis – called on the European Institutions and the Member States to accelerate the implementation of the Functional Airspace Blocks.

Meanwhile, the European Commission has, with the consent of the Single Sky Committee,[8] enacted the Regulation (EU) No. 176/2011 on the information to be provided by the Member States before the establishment and the modification of an

7. See already Number 25 of Art. 2 of the Framework Regulation.
8. The Single Sky Committee (SSC), composed by Member States' representatives, with observers from third countries and Eurocontrol, and headed by the Aviation Director of DG MOVE, was established in 2010 to support the European Commission in the SES implementation. The SSC is asked to give its agreement on the draft implementing rules and community specifications before the Commission adopts these.

FAB,[9] and has drafted guidance materials for the establishment and modification of Functional Airspace Blocks,[10] that are finally to be issued in Summer 2011.

Furthermore, the European Commission has already established EU-wide performance targets for the provision of air navigation services for the first parts of the years 2012 to 2014.[11] The decision of the EC serves to define targets on environment, capacity, and cost-efficiency for 2014, but no safety targets will be made for the first period. The targets are very technically determined, look insignificant, and are hardly understandable, but are quite demanding, as the resistance by the Member States against them in the defining stage has proven. The environment target – improvement by 0.75 % in route extension – shall, especially due to a much more efficient routing of the airplanes, lead to huge reductions in CO2 emissions and to big savings in flight time and fuel consumption. The capacity target – improvement in delay times by 0.5 minutes – shall, especially by better planning of the capacity usage of air routes and airport operations, lead to further savings in flight time and fuel consumption. The cost-efficiency target – reduction of the determined unit rate for air navigation services from EUR 59.97 in 2011 down to EUR 53.92 in 2014 – shall, especially by reducing the support costs in the air navigation service administration/organizations, lead to large savings for the airlines and also to higher efficiency in the whole system. Awaiting a nominal air traffic growth of 3 % under normal circumstances, these improvements would also permit a carbon-neutral growth of aviation and a capping of the real costs for the air traffic management.

In order to achieve these EU-wide targets, the Members States have to take the respective actions in the fields of their responsibilities, such as the air navigation service providers and the airport capacity planning. In preparation for this, they are, according to Article 11 of the Framework Regulation, now obliged, either at the national level or together with other Member States, for the level of the Functional Airspace Blocks to determine their performance targets on the environment, capacity, and cost-efficiency. These targets that were meanwhile submitted may differ in detail from the EU-wide targets, but have in all come to the same effects and we have to be consistent with them. These consistencies of the national/FAB performance targets with EU-wide performance targets have to be assessed by the European Commission that can, if necessary, demand corrective measures.

Despite the primary responsibility of the Member States for establishing the Functional Airspace Blocks it is the responsibility of the EC, as the Guardian of the European Treaties, to assess and to judge if and how the Member States fulfil their obligations to establish the FABs in the correct factual way and on time. The Commission will carefully observe the developments and, if the necessary steps are not taken by the Member States in 2011 and 2012, should certainly use its

---

9. See Commission Regulation of 24 Feb. 2011, OJ L 51, 25 Feb. 2011, 2 – see also para. 9 of Art. 9 a of the Service Provision Regulation.
10. See para. 8 of Art. 9 a of the Service Provision Regulation.
11. See Commission Decision of 21 Feb. 2011, OJ L 48, 23 Feb. 2011, 16.

political and legal powers and tools to motivate the Member States to fulfil their obligations according to the Single European Sky Legislation.

3 THE TASK OF THE FAB COORDINATOR

The SES II Legislation also introduced the office of a Functional Airspace Blocks System Coordinator (FAB Coordinator) 'in order to facilitate the establishment of the Functional Airspace Blocks'.[12] The Commission that was authorized to designate – with the consent of the Single Sky Committee – a natural impartial person on a part-time honorary basis, appointed the author of this article, a former long-standing Member of the Transport Committee of the European Parliament, to this office.[13]

To fulfil his generally described tasks, the FAB Coordinator of the European Commission meets the individual Transport Ministers/State Secretaries to inquire on the state of progress with the establishment of FAB, can, upon the request of the concerned Member States, help overcoming difficulties in the negotiation process among them and shall motivate the Member States to speed up the process. He shall also bear in mind that the Functional Airspace Blocks need to cooperate among themselves and that only an effective interconnectivity of the FABs will lead to an efficient System of Functional Airspace Blocks. In that sense, the FAB Coordinator also has regular meetings with the Transport Commissioner and DG MOVE, with the European Parliament, as well as with the aviation stakeholders.

By his obligatory reporting to the Commission, the Single Sky Committee, and the Transport Committee of the European Parliament, on the state of the FAB establishment progress, basically every three months, the FAB Coordinator keeps the European Institutions, the aviation stakeholders, and the public, aware of the progress or non-progress of the FAB establishment.

4 THE FAB COORDINATOR'S PROGRESS CRITERIA

In order to assess and to report on the progress of the establishment of the Functional Airspace Blocks, the FAB Coordinator developed the following, so-called Focal FAB Progress Criteria.

(1) The state of affairs: in this category, the progress or non-progress, from the beginning of the negotiations between the Member States of an FAB via the signing of the State agreement between the FAB Member States to the official notification thereof, to the European Commission, is documented in detail.

12. See Art. 9 b of the Service Provision Regulation.
13. See Commission Decision of 12 Aug. 2010, COM(2010) 5110 final.

(2) The FAB safety case: here, the development of common rules and procedures for enhanced safety within an FAB shall be adopted and followed.
(3) The enhanced cooperation of the National Supervisory Authorities or (optionally) a joint FAB Supervisory Authority: the more cooperative or integrated supervision of the Air Navigation Services by the NSAs within the FAB shall be noted.
(4) The enhanced cooperation of the Air Navigation Service Providers or (optionally) an Integrated Air Navigation Service Provider: as the better cooperation or even integration of the ANSPs is the key for the improvement in efficiency of the air traffic management, this development shall carefully be looked at.
(5) The cooperation or (optionally) integration of the civil and military air traffic controls: the flexible use of airspace between the civil and military aviation – at best by joint air traffic controls – is another key point to be examined.
(6) The performance plan, as per FAB or as per the Member States, and their consistency with the EU-wide targets: a performance plan – either as per a Member State or preferably, as per FAB – as a decisive tool for establishing the chief priorities of the operations, is charted.
(7) The added value of the FAB based on cost-benefit analyses: The Member States should – before/during taking any action – analyze the steps and costs necessary to achieve ideal efficiency towards the results of their evaluations on the foreseen added value as an important administrative tool.
(8) The cooperation with the Network Manager: the cooperation of the FAB Member States with the Network Manager, towards the improvement of airspace use, is another key element for the improved efficiency of air traffic management, and should thus be looked at.
(9) (Optionally) agreements on common principles regarding charging policy: as the amounts charged towards air navigation service fees – besides being an important factor on cost-efficiency of the air traffic management systems – are an important element in the cooperation/integration process for the ANSPs agreements, agreement on the principles of the charging policy among the Member States, per the FAB, would be a rather useful and noteworthy first step.
(10) (Optionally) additional agreements, for example, on combing and/or sharing technical support, such as air traffic controllers' training and mobility, on equipment planning and deployment related to the SESAR program, and on the incorporation of the airport dimension: Positive steps taken towards an enhanced cooperation would be most helpful towards the efficiency of an FAB; for example, in the support area for ANSPs, such as the ATCO training; in the common planning and implementation of new air traffic control hardware and software (see the SESAR projects); as well as in the relationship between the ANSPs, the

airplanes, and the airports – the latter being very important, as the Single European Sky concept is based on the 'gate-to gate' concept for aviation.

5 THE INDIVIDUAL FUNCTIONAL AIRSPACE BLOCKS

Based on the Bottom-up approach, the Member States have so far been employing Functional Airspace Blocks, including some Third countries,[14] whereby the configurations of the individual FABs are not always totally comprehensible from a Top-down approach. As it is so far not possible to assess the effective progress in the FAB establishments, the following State Agreements or other important developments should be studied in order to get a preliminary understanding of the FABs:

(1) The United Kingdom – Ireland FAB
This FAB was the earliest FAB – already established before the SES II Legislation was defined and adopted, and that by a Memorandum of Understanding between the Government of the United Kingdom of Great Britain and Northern Ireland and the Government of Ireland (a State Agreement) – signed on 12 June 2008, and in force since 14 July 2008. Memoranda of Understanding between the British and the Irish Aviation Authorities and between the British and the Irish Air Navigation Service Providers were signed on 12 June 2008. Closer cooperation between the two ANSPs to enable full exploitation of potential benefits was not considered at that point in time. Yet, a new and important development is that, according to a Memorandum of Understanding of 8 March 2011, the British, the Irish, the Danish, and the Swedish ANSPs will intensify their cooperation and intent to prepare a proposal for their Governments, for a merger of the UK-Ireland FAB and the Danish-Swedish FAB.

(2) The Danish – Swedish FAB
This FAB was the second FAB to be established – established by a State Agreement between the Government of the Kingdom of Sweden and the Government of the Kingdom of Denmark – signed on 17 December 2009 and in force since 1 July 2010. The Danish and the Swedish National Supervisory Authorities also signed a Cooperation Agreement in 2010. The two Air Navigation Service Providers have meanwhile formed a common Holding Company that has, from its inception, already taken up some activities for the two ANSPs of the FAB (also see here the Memorandum of Understanding between the British, the Irish, the Danish, and the Swedish ANSPs).

(3) The North European FAB (NEFAB)
The participants of this FAB are Estonia, Finland, *Iceland*, Latvia and *Norway*. The planning for this FAB was based on a Joint Statement by the Ministers responsible

14. The (so far) participating Third States are indicated by italic letters.

for Transport on 22 September 2010. Denmark and Sweden withdrew from this initiative in February 2011.

(4) The FAB of Europe Central (FABEC)
This FAB was the third FAB with a State Agreement, signed on 2 December 2010, and consists of the Federal Republic of Germany, the Kingdom of Belgium, the French Republic, The Grand Duchy of Luxembourg, the Kingdom of the Netherlands, and *the Swiss Confederation*. A Cooperation Agreement between the six National Supervisory Authorities was signed on 27 January 2011.

(5) The Baltic FAB
The participants in this FAB are Lithuania and Poland. The planning is based on a Letter of Intent dated 29 July 2010. The Signing of a Baltic FAB State Agreement is foreseen for the second half of 2011.

(6) The FAB of Central Europe (FAB CE)
The participants in this FAB are Austria, *Bosnia & Herzegovina*, *Croatia*, Czech Republic, Hungary, Slovak Republic, and Slovenia. The planning is based on a Draft FAB CE State Agreement of 22 June 2010. The signing of the FAB CE State Agreement took place on May 2011.

(7) The Danube FAB
The participants in this FAB are Bulgaria and Romania. The planning was based on a Memorandum of Understanding at state level, signed 26 February 2010. The Signing of the Danube FAB State Agreement was scheduled for June 2011.

(8) The South West FAB
The participants in this FAB are Portugal and Spain. The Planning is based on an Agreement between the National Supervisory Authorities, signed in February 2010. The signing of a draft State Agreement was scheduled for June 2011.

(9) The FAB Blue MED
The participants in this FAB are Cyprus, Greece, Italy, and Malta – with *Albania*, *Egypt* and *Tunisia* as associate partners, as well as the *Kingdom of Jordan* and *Lebanon* as observers. The planning was based on a cooperation agreement between the principal ANSPs of Cyprus, Greece, Italy, and Malta, signed on 29 March 2010.

As this list already indicates, the implementation of the Functional Airspace Blocks varies very much in substance and time. As the FABs shall be completely established and functional by 4 December 2012 at latest, it is necessary that all the State Agreements be signed and – if necessary – ratified and in force as soon as possible, since the implementation, , for example, on the ANSP level, will need further time.

6 THE PERSPECTIVE FOR THE FUNCTIONAL AIRSPACE BLOCKS

The Functional Airspace Block will end up being a decisive, successful and efficient component for the establishment of the Single European Sky only when

- all the Functional Airspace Blocks are established in a timely manner;
- all the Functional Airspace Blocks work effectively together – what is called an effective interconnectivity – especially for the airspace design with regards to routing; and
- the nine Functional Airspace Blocks will, over time – probably starting with some FABs merging into bigger FABs – merge into one European Airspace Block, somewhat comparable with the Single Sky of the United States of America, that has even more varied basic conditions.

Taking into account the perseverance of the Member States with maintaining their national sovereignties and powers, and the different priorities of the aviation stakeholders, this perspective might need some time for realization; yet, in the interests of safety, capacity, cost-efficiency, and environmental friendliness, this perspective is worthwhile to fight for the sake of our citizens, our aviation community, our economy, and our environment.

7 CONCLUSIONS

As one decisive tool for the establishment of the Single European Sky over the European Union, the establishment of effective Functional Airspace Blocks requires especially an enhanced cooperation and integration of the Air Navigation Service Providers, and for civil and military aviation, respectively. According to the Bottom-up approach of the SES II Legislation, the Member States are obliged to organize Functional Airspace Blocks that shall improve the safety, capacity, cost-efficiency, and environmental friendliness of the air traffic management systems of the 27 Member States and the participating Third Countries. The European Institutions and the aviation stakeholders should whole-heartedly support and, if necessary, using all political and legal tools, encourage the Member States to apply their utmost commitment for establishing performance-driven Functional Airspace Blocks, effectively, and before the given time-limit.

Chapter 19

Crisis Management and the Single European Sky

*Joe Sultana**

1 INTRODUCTION

In aviation terms, crisis situations have been associated with unforeseen events which have resulted in major disruptions in the use of European airspace and/or number of major airports. This chapter on crisis management is not aimed at presenting theoretical/academic models for aviation crisis management. Rather it describes how crisis management in Europe has evolved in the last 15 years while outlining prospects for the future.

2 EUROCONTROL'S INVOLVEMENT

2.1 The Role of the CFMU

Before the establishment of the Central Flow Management Unit (CFMU) in 1995, European States used the European Office of ICAO and the EUROCONTROL Committee of Management as fora to coordinate national actions in times of crisis.

---

* Joe Sultana, Eurocontrol.

Daniel Calleja Crespo & Pablo Mendes de Leon, *Achieving the Single European Sky: Goals and Challenges*, pp. 189–200.

The decision to set up a central unit for flow management was decided by the EUROCONTROL Permanent Commission in 1989. The CFMU started its operation in 1995.

The CFMU became the tool to coordinate operations during any airspace disruptions. This operational tool however needed a structure which would bring together senior operational representatives from Air Navigation Service Providers (ANSPs) and airspace users associations.

The EUROCONTROL Committee of Management at its 178th Session in 1995, established the Crisis Management Group (CMG) as an ad hoc operational structure working in cooperation with the CFMU, in which national ATC administrations and aircraft operators establish contact to try to resolve crises. The objectives of the CMG were:

(a) To keep the members informed, through the Chairman, of events likely to lead to a crisis situation so that precautionary planning can be started in due time.
(b) To support the detailed Air Traffic Flow Management (ATFM) crisis planning carried out by the CFMU in conjunction with national experts and make all possible arrangements to:
  (i) remove the cause of the crisis; or, if that is not possible,
  (ii) increase ATC capacity to alleviate the effects of the crisis;
  (iii) ensure that the arrangements made by the experts and agreed by the CMG are supported by their administrations and are implemented;
  (iv) ensure that priority rules established for use in crises are applied and implemented.

A crisis was defined as the occurrence, or a high probability of the occurrence, of an unexpected event that seriously disturbs traffic flows and/or seriously reduces ATC capacity. The interpretation of what constitutes a crisis in each particular case was left to the discretion of the pertinent Director of Air Navigation who could then, in close coordination with the Director of CFMU, request the CMG to consider the issue.

The rationale for the establishment of the CMG was the need for efficient cooperation of the ATFM and ATC authorities at all levels in a crisis. The CFMU, with experts from States, would prepare a detailed flow management plan to cope with the crisis. The efficiency of that plan could be improved if it was possible for States to provide extra capacity. Therefore, members of the crisis management structure had to have the authority to decide on and implement measures which would help in handling the crisis and which could involve the rapid redeployment of national resources.

It was also expected that the crisis management structure should also act as an intelligence network. Members should regularly inform each other of any events that might lead to a crisis situation, particularly the possibility of industrial action. This would allow better preparation and enable members to provide correct information to senior management and to aircraft operators. Membership of the CMG was open to all ECAC States and to the aircraft operator associations.

With the CMG and the EUROCONTROL CFMU operational structure fully in place by 1998, Europe seemed ready to manage any crisis which affected European airspace. Surprisingly however, the two major crisis situations impacting Europe in the next three years did not really make use of the crisis management body, the CMG.

2.2 The Balkan War (1999)

The Balkan war in 1999 was a major crisis for European aviation. The airspace and airports of Croatia, Bosnia, FRY (Federal Republic of Yugoslavia), FYROM (Former Yugoslav Republic of Macedonia) and Albania were completely closed to all traffic. The airspaces of Hungary, Slovenia, Romania, and Bulgaria were partially affected. The airspace over the Adriatic Sea was also closed.

Conducting a war in central Europe, whilst maintaining safe and normal operation around the airspace impacted by military operations, was an unprecedented challenge. The crisis involved the movement of large numbers of military aircraft with consequent implications for civil traffic and the air traffic management services Traffic which normally would be flying over the war affected area now presented itself in the adjacent airspaces causing high demand capacity imbalances. As a result, alternative routes had to be designed and implemented at short notice.

The efforts of the CFMU were, in a way, too successful. Operational solutions were found which gave the impression that the war was a minor disruption and airspace users complained because delays in 1999 were 30% higher than expected. The aftermath of the war in 2000 and the increase in traffic across Europe aggravated the network delay situation. The crisis was perceived, managed and assessed as if it was some sort of network inefficiency rather than a major European airspace disruption which required political and institutional coordination and direction.

The CMG did not play any significant role in the Balkan crisis. Its limited membership and the designated representatives were not appropriate for the political dimension of the crisis. It however was a good operational forum to find solutions to the ongoing closures of parts of the Balkan airspace in the following months. In 2000, in order to get more senior representative participation able to address also non-operational aspects of European crisis, EUROCONTROL proposed a review of its membership. There were not many changes.

2.3 The September 11 Attacks

The September 11 attacks in the US quickly became the next unforeseen crisis affecting European aviation. On 11 September 2001, the CFMU Operations Room Team Leader was informed by a member of staff that there seemed to be a major terrorist attack in New York. He immediately called his counterpart in the US, the FAA Air Traffic Control & Systems Command Centre Supervisor in Washington.

FAA confirmed the information and advised that they were closing all US airspace with immediate effect. This meant that a significant amount of air traffic over the Atlantic heading for US was going to have to turn back over mid-ocean and divert back to European airports. In order not to worsen the impact on the European airspace, the CFMU Team Leader took the decision to ground all flights still on ground in Europe with destination US for that day.

The CFMU system identified every flight that should be grounded and sent individual messages to all affected ATC Towers and airline operators informing them that the flight was not allowed to take off due to US airspace being closed after terrorist attack. These individual messages arrived at the affected ATC Towers and Airline Operators, flight by flight, within four minutes from when the CFMU TL was first informed that there had been a terrorist attack in US.

2.4 The Establishment of a 'Crisis Management Cell' in 2001

Having dealt with the immediate crisis, coordination links were established between the FAA civil and military representatives in Brussels and EUROCONTROL CFMU. Within an hour, the FAA agreed to establish a presence in the CFMU OPS Room to help facilitate coordination. This enabled European access to restricted FAA teleconferences. Initial urgent problems surrounded the whereabouts of a number of flights which were considered to pose a potential threat by the US National Security Agency.

The CFMU, FAA, military and civil representatives and the Aircraft Operator Liaison Cell implemented an operational 'crisis cell'. All pertinent information for Air Traffic Service Providers, Airspace Management Cells, Aircraft Operators and other aviation entities (e.g., airports, ground handling agents) gathered by the cell was disseminated immediately.

CFMU came under immediate pressure from some aircraft operators and the military, to permit certain flights to proceed to the US. After contacts between the cell and the US Department of Defence in Washington and the US Air Force in Europe (USAFE) in Ramstein Germany, a procedure was quickly established for obtaining military flight approval. The operation crisis cell was kept open until the 14 September, relaying information on how/when the airspace would re-open and who would be permitted to use it when it did. The cell was also obtaining individual approvals to be able to release a small number of special flights. When US and Canadian airspace was eventually re-opened, CFMU managed the gradual return to normal operations. The cell was de-activated at around 1900 on Friday 14 September 2001.

The CFMU management of the consequences of the events of September 11 was a normal use of its expertise and systems in dramatic circumstances. The flow of information inbound and outbound was immediate and according to the CFMU customers, informative and understandable. All of the necessary telephone numbers and operational contacts were available in the CFMU Operations room and were used to good effect. The need for a specific office space located in the

Operations room for the ops crisis manager was identified. The lack of a visual display of the complete air situation was a big shortcoming and was flagged for priority action.

Following these major events affecting European traffic, EUROCONTROL and ANSPs debated the future role of the Crisis Management Cell. Given the focus of the operational experts to mitigate against disruptions and to find solutions for the airspace users, it was felt that what was needed were practical arrangements to coordinate at senior operational level whenever current operational procedures and practices are not sufficient. It was also felt that these senior operational representatives needed to meet regularly to assess any looming network disruption, e.g. industrial action, and together prepare an operational plan should the situation turn into a crisis. Given the sensitivity of these events, these meetings became informal meetings called by the Director CFMU with invited Directors of Operations. These twice yearly meetings became known as the informal DOP meetings.

During the subsequent years there were no comparable major crises affecting European aviation. The Crisis Management Cell was not convened and was de facto replaced by the DOP meetings. Minor airspace disruptions were managed at operational level between the ANSP concerned supported by the CFMU. With some ANSPs becoming more proficient in ATFCM, they took a more prominent role in finding solutions affecting their airspace.

3 THE ERUPTION OF THE ICELANDIC VOLCANO (2010)

3.1 The First Eruption

Then we had Eyjafjallajökull. On 14 April 2010, Iceland Meteorological Watch Office informed London Volcanic Ash Advisory Centre (VAAC) about the Eyjafjallajökull eruption and provided the initial input needed for the ash dispersion model used by London VAAC. At the same time, London VAAC informed EUROCONTROL's CFMU which activated its volcanic ash procedure.

To facilitate the information exchange, CFMU started organizing teleconferences where the forecasts published by London VAAC as well as the decisions taken by the individual state authorities were presented and their impact explained. There were up to 400 participants at CFMU volcanic ash teleconferences.

Based on the information received on the ash propagation on 14 April 2010, ACCs and States concerned applied zero rate/airspace closures for parts of UK and Scandinavian airspace. As the eruption continued and the ash cloud was pushed by jet streams towards continental Europe, zero rate/airspace closures (of different duration) were issued for several other airspaces. Forecasted area of ash cloud grew daily, and with it, the extent of impacted airspaces. The weekend of 17 and 18 April 2010 saw the highest number of ACCs under zero rate/airspace closures. These measures, decided independently by each affected country and applied by EUROCONTROL/CFMU caused complete chaos to European aviation and the teleconferences became complex exercises in putting some sort of order and coherence to the availability of the airspace.

An important observation to be made is that in the period from 14 April to 19 April, the cloud dispersion forecasts that London VAAC was issuing covered only the area and flight levels in accordance with ICAO Annex 3, that is, without the mention of different ash particle concentrations. At the time, the information on the hazardous thresholds of ash concentration was not available. Therefore, States concerned considered the whole zone of the predicted cloud movement as hazardous for the safety of flight operations.

Airlines started complaining about the closures, comparing the European eruption to past eruptions in Alaska and SE Asia and the different procedures applied there which in their view would have not be so disruptive. The frustrations at not being allowed to operate were fuelled by the volcanologists' prognosis, reported in the news that the possibility existed for an extended eruption of Eyjafjallajökull. Moreover, it was stated that the eruption of Katla, a bigger, neighbouring volcano was a possibility. A few airlines (e.g., KLM, Lufthansa, etc.) flew ferry flights to verify the extent of forecasted ash cloud and to see, if found, what impact the particles would have on engines. Some research institutions performed special flights with aircraft equipped with instruments for measurement of various parameters of the volcanic ash.

The prospect of widespread airspace closures was discussed at EUROCONTROL Director General level on both 15 and 16 April 2010. A teleconference of the Provisional Council was tentatively planned for 19 April. Also on the 15 and 16 April, the European Commission requested updates of the situation and on the afternoon of 16 April requested a meeting at EUROCONTROL to be fully briefed.

3.2 The Establishment of the 'ad hoc' Crisis Cell

Friday 16 April in the afternoon was the start of a full Crisis Cell operation, which was to be continuously in session until the 21 April. This ad hoc crisis cell included senior members of the European Commission, AEA, ACI, and EUROCONTROL. From an operational perspective, there was a huge task to manage the closure of airspace as the ash cloud forecasts showed possible ash in an ever increasing part of European airspace. Aircraft operators were in an impossible position of having to plan flights around airspace closures.

The ad hoc Crisis Cell had the right level of membership and also the direct link to the decision-making level of the States, Directors General of Civil Aviation and Ministers of Transport. It had the task of finding a way to reopen European airspace without jeopardizing safety of flight. The crisis cell role was not to manage the operational situation, that was the task of the CFMU network operations, but was to get continuous updates.

The crisis cell focused on how to unlock the paralysis of the European network in a situation where the potential risk to flight caused by the ash could not be accurately assessed. It was aware of the huge impact the closure was having on the aviation industry, the European economy and millions of stranded travellers. The spotlight of the world media was on EUROCONTROL and the Crisis Cell. The Crisis Cell asked EUROCONTROL to come with possible options overnight.

EUROCONTROL used all its contacts with the national authorities, FAA, airlines with experience in volcanic areas, Met Offices and other scientific entities to come up with options for the Crisis Cell. Some national authorities were in parallel looking at the risk in their own airspace and making individual decisions on how to permit flights within their respective airspace.

On 18 April EUROCONTROL proposed three options for consideration by the Crisis Cell. The Cell agreed to present all three to the teleconference of the EUROCONTROL Provisional Council and the European Commission presented the outcome of this teleconference to the EU Transport Council on 19 April. At both meetings the option that stipulated that States may allow flight operations in the areas contaminated by the lower levels of ash concentration was adopted. Flights would still not be permitted in the zones of higher ash concentration (i.e., no fly zone). In addition, EUROCONTROL was mandated to start producing charts with a buffer that would assist States in determining the no fly zone. These charts were based on the ash concentration data provided by the UK Met Office.

The crisis began to unlock after the decisions taken at these meetings were implemented on the morning of 20 April. Within forty-eight hours traffic flows in Europe were back to normal and the Crisis Cell went into a monitoring standby role.

3.3 The Second Eruption of Eyjafjallajökull

A second eruption phase materialized on 1 May and the volcanic procedures in Europe resumed on 3 May. This resulted in closures in UK and Ireland, then Portugal, Spain, Italy, and Morocco. Refinements of the option adopted were coordinated by the Crisis Cell (which now included the European Aviation Safety Agency, EASA) and on 18 May the UK Met Office started issuing new charts with three distinct zones:

(i) Black zone 'Predicted area of ash concentrations that exceed acceptable engine manufacturer tolerance levels, >0.004 mg/m^3'.
(ii) Grey zone 'Predicted area of ash concentrations in which flights are permitted with an appropriate safety case and agreement from engine and airframe manufacturers, >0.002 mg/m^3'.
(iii) Red zone 'Predicted area where volcanic ash may be encountered, <0.002 mg/m^3'.

This approach was supported by an European Aviation Safety Agency (EASA) safety bulletin describing the improved approach for volcanic ash measures, based on new UK Met Office charts.

During the entire crisis there were no incidents due to the volcanic ash. Safety was the first concern in the decision-making process and, using the available information on the amount of ash in the atmosphere and ICAO guidance material applicable at the time, the resulting airspace restrictions while rather conservative were unavoidable.

Airspace closure or application of zero rates in the period of 14 to 21 April resulted in many cancelled flights, which in turn caused many stranded passengers, heavy economic impact on airlines and an impact on European businesses that has yet to be quantified. There were more than 100,000 flights cancelled. IATA estimates that the cancellations due to volcanic ash procedures cost airlines USD 1.7 billion in lost revenue. At its peak, the crisis impacted 29% of global aviation and affected 1.2 million passengers a day. One of the reasons the impact of the crisis was of this order of magnitude is the fact that the ash cloud, pushed by high-altitude winds, dispersed over areas of very dense traffic flows, like south UK, France, Benelux, and Germany.

4 ADAPTING CRISIS MANAGEMENT STRUCTURES

4.1 The Need for International Coordination

Much has been done to be better prepared for any return of volcanic eruptions in Europe. ICAO has agreed to amendments to the ICAO EUR and NAT Volcanic Ash Contingency Plan. Another ICAO initiative resulted in an establishment of the ICAO International Volcanic Ash Task Forced (IVATF) to examine the problem of the volcanic ash at the global level. The objective of the IVATF was to develop a global safety risk management framework that will make it possible to determine the safe levels of operation in airspace contaminated by volcanic ash.

The amended ICAO EUR/NAT Volcanic Ash Contingency Plan was a significant step forward. However, the flexibility left to States in deciding in which areas of ash concentration they may declare Danger Areas allows for different approaches in the EUR and NAT regions. In particular there is a risk of creating a discontinuity at the interface between adjacent FIRs when one has a Danger Area based on Areas of High Contamination and the other established Danger Areas based on Areas of Medium and Areas of High Contamination. There are also indications that different States would use different criteria for operations in their airspace.

4.2 The Establishment of the EACCC

On 19 May 2010 the European Aviation Crisis Coordination Cell (EACCC) was established to facilitate management of any crises affecting aviation in Europe. The EACCC is co-chaired by the European Commission and EUROCONTROL and is composed of EASA as well as representatives of aircraft operators, regulators, ANSPs, airports, aircraft manufacturers, military and ICAO. Depending on the nature of the crisis, representatives of other organizations may be invited to join.

The EACCC was built on the experience from the Eyjafjallajökull 2010 crisis. It becomes activated when circumstances beyond normal environment of operations are evident and operational procedures are not sufficient to normalize the situation. EACCC has dedicated follow-up meetings to coordinate efforts to resolve the risk in a harmonized response. As a result, the EACCC decided to take a leading role in the ICAO VOLCEX 11/01 exercise.

The objective of the exercise was to test updated national and European region procedures described in the revised and agreed ICAO EUR/NAT Volcanic Ash Contingency Plan and in addition to simulate with airspace users a scenario which includes the use of a safety risk assessment methodology under consideration by ICAO and EASA and national authorities.

The exercise was based on the same assumptions of estimated amount and concentration of ash produced into the air and did not include validation of the dispersion model and forecast concentrations. There was no impact on actual traffic flying in Europe in the two days of the exercise 13 and 14 April 2011).

Overall the exercise showed that, using the revised ICAO procedures, progress has been made since last year. It also showed that the simulated scenario delivered better results in terms of operations across the European network. However, there are still national differences in the application of these procedures. This requires further efforts at European level to harmonize national responses.

The EACCC participated in the exercise as coordinator of a European ATM response. The exercise was an opportunity for the EACCC to apply its procedures and take initiatives enabling it to monitor an ongoing crisis situation and develop appropriate responses to crisis situations.

Airline representatives supported the management of the network operation and twice daily teleconferences with the EACCC full membership (European Commission, EASA, EUROCONTROL, Member States and air transport stakeholders) developed responses to ensure the best possible response to this potentially disruptive event to European aviation.

Aircraft operators were able to flight plan around areas declared as danger areas by the different States affected by the ash using a new tool developed by EUROCONTROL – the European Crisis Visualization Interactive Tool for AFTCM (EVITA). This tool provides a visual representation of volcanic ash concentration data, planned routes and the danger areas declared by national aviation authorities, allowing for improved decision-making and use of airspace.

The exercise also looked at a scenario which assumed that all conditions (including airworthiness and accurate data requirements) were in place for safety risk assessments to be the basis for a decision by airspace users to operate.

Although a few States were not in a position to apply this scenario, initial feedback confirms the EACCC view that this is the approach best suited for the European network.

5 CONCLUSIONS

5.1 Two Level Management

Following on from the exercise, there will be a detailed analysis of lessons learnt and elaboration of recommendations for further actions. The EACCC will report to the Director Generals of EUROCONTROL and European Commission DG MOVE. The European Commission will report back to the Transport Ministers, and if necessary will recommend further action to be taken.

The ash crisis has confirmed the view that crisis management needs to be managed at two distinct levels: operational and strategic/political with a strong coordination link between the two. Having either one without the other has not proved sufficient in leading all involved towards the best possible response to major crisis in Europe.

The operational level has to be a collaborative effort by EUROCONTROL's operational services/management, senior operational management of ANSPs and the directly impacted operational entities in particular airspace users and airport operators. This, in a way, is not too different than the normal process to manage and operate the European ATM network. However, in a crisis the timescales for coordination, decision and implementation are normally much shorter and the network function will inevitably play the dominant role in such crisis events. This operational crisis coordination entity has in the past been mistaken as the full crisis cell. It should change its name to the critical operations coordination cell and be clear and consistent as to its operational role and focus.

There has to be also a separate aviation crisis coordination cell at a more political level. This body needs to have quick access to the decision makers including Ministers of Transport, European Commissioner for Transport, Directors General of Civil Aviation of all European States and top management of responsible military and national security entities. Its members have to include top management from the European Commission, EASA and EUROCONTROL. It requires an effective relationship with the operational crisis coordination entity, driving the strategy and direction to resolve each particular crisis.

5.2 Regulatory Initiatives: Establishment of the Network Manager Function

A major step in this direction is the establishment of the European Aviation Crisis Coordination Cell within the framework of the Single European Sky II regulation. A Commission Regulation establishing the Network Manager Functions has been adopted and is expected to be published in the Official Journal by June 2011. The Network Manager Implementing Rule provides a formal basis for the European Aviation Crisis Coordination Cell and will replace the ad hoc EACCC established after the ash crisis.

The regulation defines a 'network crisis' as the inability to provide air navigation service at the required level resulting in a major loss of network capacity or a major imbalance between network capacity and demand or a major failure in the information flow in one or several parts of the network following an unusual and unforeseen situation.

The Network Manager shall activate and deactivate the EACCC. The EACCC will support the Network Manager in coordinating the management of the response and support the activation and coordination of contingency plans at national level. Significantly the Network Manager is charged to elaborate mitigation measures at network level to respond to a crisis and ensure continued and safe network operations.

The regulation prescribes the permanent members of the new EACCC, with one representative each from the EU Presidency, Commission, EASA, EUROCONTROL, military, ANSPs, airports and airspace users. It allows for experts to be coopted on a case-by-case basis depending on the nature of the specific event. EACCC will work closely with National Focal Points, it remains to be seen how such a composition will work in a future crisis.

5.3 The Role of Communication and Information

Communication and information management are critical elements in any crisis situation. The consolidation and timely dissemination of information on the status of the airspace, the functioning of the network and the extent of the network disruption is essential to aircraft operators, airports and ANSPs. The communication means can become overloaded quite quickly as the crisis unfolds and the impact becomes significant. The CFMU Network Operations Portal (NOP) received more than 13.5 million hits in one day during the ash crisis.

The media have discovered that EUROCONTROL is uniquely placed to provide information about the European airspace network situation and the flights within it. The Social Media were also used extensively as a quick and effective means of providing the latest information on a crisis. Real-time coordination between the European Commission, EASA and EUROCONTROL on media briefings is essential.

Having this single source of information is important for consistency of message. However, it also introduces a single point of failure for this vital communication channel and also places huge demands on scarce resources trying to find the right response to the crisis. This potential intense media interest in any event called a 'crisis' has been a factor in waiting before declaring 'minor' European network disruptions, for instance, natural disasters in Japan in March 2011, as a crisis; to the media, a 'crisis' means that you have lost control. In such cases, it is the critical operations coordination cell which has been activated while the EACCC has been put on standby.

5.4 Prospects

Experience will tell if this two level structure, centred on the Network Manager will bring an added value to the handling of major crisis affecting European aviation. It is possible that this structure is too limiting in its aviation focus and will not be in a position to engage and take initiatives using other modes of transport when major disruptions to the air transport industry cannot be solved by this industry. There is as yet no inter-modal contingency plan against a prolonged shutdown of air transport in Europe nor are we prepared for the consequences of a lengthy shutdown of European airspace.

Crisis management of aviation disruptions has come a long way since the nineties. Lessons have been learnt and improvements put in place at operational, institutional and political level. The Single European Sky regulation has been the key enabler for such progress. The effective collaboration of the different Air Traffic Management entities in crisis situations has helped minimize the impact and accelerate the resumption of operations. Crisis Management is being given the priority it deserves.

Chapter 20

Key Points and Proposals for a SWIM Regulatory Framework: The Way Ahead

Anna Masutti[*]

1 INTRODUCTION

The SES (Single European Sky) is an ambitious initiative, launched by the European Commission in 1999, to reform the architecture of European air traffic management (ATM). It puts forward a legislative approach to meet future capacity and safety needs at a European rather than at a local level.

Key objectives of this initiative are: (a) to restructure European airspace (through the Functional Air Blocks – FAB) as a function of air traffic flows; (b) to create additional capacity; (c) to increase the overall efficiency of the European air traffic management system.

The SESAR project (Single European Sky ATM Research) is the European air traffic control infrastructure modernization programme. SESAR aims at developing the new generation air traffic management system capable of ensuring the safety and fluidity of air transport worldwide over the next thirty years.

---

* Anna Masutti, Professor of Air Law at the University of Bologna. My thanks to Selex-Sistemi Integrati and its staff involved in SWIM-SUIT project for their invaluable explanations regarding the complex architecture of SWIM and for their most useful opinions regarding the governance of the system.

Daniel Calleja Crespo & Pablo Mendes de Leon, *Achieving the Single European Sky: Goals and Challenges*, pp. 201–219.

The first phase of SESAR, called the definition phase, which ended in 2008, delivered an ATM Master Plan defining the contents, the development and deployment plans of the next generation of ATM systems.

The development phase (2007–2013) will produce the required new generation of technological systems and components as outlined in the definition phase. The deployment phase (2013–2020) will seek to build the new infrastructure at a broader scale both in Europe and in partner countries. This will be carried out under the responsibility of the industry without further public funding.

In addition to the two founding members (EUROCONTROL and the European Commission), fifteen organizations have signed a membership agreement with the SESAR Joint Undertaking (SESAR JU). The programme may profit from the expertise of airport operators, air navigation service providers (ANSPs), ground and aerospace manufacturing industry, aircraft manufacturers, and airborne equipment manufacturers.

SWIM (System Wide Information Management) is a key part of SESAR and will be further described in details. The SWIM's main objective is to improve the information management and supply chain to improve the airspace management flow and capacity. SWIM has been recognized as an essential enabler of ATM applications. The ATM system can be seen as a complex, distributed real-time information processing community, populated by a large number of people and automated systems in the role of sensors, information providers, information users and decision-makers, all collaborating to ensure a safe, expeditious and efficient flow of air traffic.

SWIM, as any other system created to provide a public service, needs a regulatory framework for its functioning, including the identification of responsibilities and liabilities of the parties involved in the programme.

The design of such regulatory framework is not an easy exercise, considering the technological complexity of the system that is part of the wider project creating the future European ATM, which includes the analysis of basic principles like the sovereignty principle in order to guarantee a seamless functioning of the system. Moreover, the present regulatory framework for ATM has no proper provisions to regulate the different situations arising form the implementation of the SWIM system.

The aim of this article is to offer a comprehensive description of SWIM programme, its possible governance and the main elements for designing a regulatory framework. The future of the aeronautical information and data necessary for the safety, regularity and efficiency of air navigation is no more provided by ANSP only, as also other parties (air carriers, airports, etc.) will contribute to it. The first step of this analysis shall be the comprehension of the project and of its technical architecture, which permits to understand the functionality of the entire system and, therefore, allows us to identify the legal requirements necessary to manage it efficiently.

2 SWIM'S ROLE IN THE FUTURE ATM SYSTEM

The air transport community is becoming increasingly dependant upon the timely availability of quality information with regard to its operations and of the collaborative processes, which facilitate the overall performance of the network.

The ATM community has identified interoperability needs, which involve transforming the ATM system from an essentially distributed network of independent units to an efficient network of integrated co-operators able to cope efficiently and effectively with two-third times the current volume of traffic.

The early introduction of SWIM capability is necessary to facilitate this cooperation. Although the importance of introducing a SWIM capability-facilitating cooperation among stakeholders is now generally recognized, there is still no definitive indication on how to implement this capability and, in particular, which technologies would enable its successful operations.

As a consequence, there is a need to identify different options and demonstrate the feasibility of realizing SWIM in all its aspects and to assess the consequences on information models, information management processes, system architectures, information access and security mechanisms, as well as organizational, legal and financial implications.

For the realization of SWIM, the European Union has promoted the SWIM-SUIT project,[1] which will largely contribute to this need for technological assessment by developing a SWIM prototype providing the basis for assessment of the technological solutions adopted. It is important to stress that SWIM is a key element of the SESAR project. SWIM's main objective is to improve the information management and supply chain to increase the efficiency of the airspace management flow and capacity, that is, the ATM target.[2]

3 A BRIEF DESCRIPTION OF THE SWIM PROGRAMME

SWIM will ensure a more efficient planning and flight execution using the concepts of 'flight object' and of 'flight trajectory',[3] increasing the efficiency of air transport and its safety standards, improving the environment.

---

1. SWIM-SWIT is a research project supported by the European Commission Directorate General 'Transport and Energy' within the 6th Framework Programme. Within the SWIM-SUIT project the following activities will be performed: specification of the requirements for the SWIM implementation, not limited to the identification of the information to be managed but including the analysis of the Quality of Service (QoS) policies to be addressed as well as safety and security aspects; design and Development of a SWIM test platform (SWIM Prototype) supporting the validation of the SWIM concepts; upon this test platform a number of legacy test applications belonging to different domains of the ATM context (e.g. ATC, Airports, Aircraft Operators, etc.) will be integrated; validation of the technologies identified as enablers of the SWIM concept by means of a test campaign performed on the developed test-bed; assessment of the organizational, legal and financial implications including an analysis of the possible impact they may have on the SWIM implementation and, thus, to the associated enabling technologies. The complete SWIM-SUIT project spans three years and includes twenty partners as well as a user group which will provide inputs in terms of requirements and review of the related deliverables. See <www.swim-suit.aero/swimsuit/>
2. SWIM has been recognized as an essential enabler of ATM applications. The ATM system can be seen as a complex, distributed real-time information processing community populated by a large number of people and automated systems in the role of sensors, information providers, information users and decision-makers, all collaborating to ensure a safe, expeditious and efficient flow of air traffic.
3. Flight Object is a concept to support the flight data interoperability between all stakeholders. Its purpose is to ensure that all systems have a consistent view of the flight shared information, and

SWIM aims at integrating the ATM information network migration from a one-to-one message exchange concept to the many-to-many information distribution model.[4] The ICAO definition[5] does not differ substantially from the SESAR definition which does not focus on the producer of information, but on information itself, enabling users to create thereon applications which best suit their needs.

In essence, SWIM is developing aeronautical information management architecture for the distribution of air traffic management data, which is similar to the Internet having the same feature of the 'many-to-many' distribution of information system. It will manage surveillance, weather and flight data, as well as aeronautical and airspace status information, and will provide it securely and seamlessly to airspace users and managers. When fully implemented it could dramatically improve the capabilities of existing systems, air transport safety, reduce capital and operating costs, improve productivity, and offer flexible network system expansion.

SWIM will change radically the present system of Air Traffic Service (ATS) exchange of information, decoupling the producer of information from the consumer of information, as in SWIM every participant can be a producer as well as a consumer of information. It is important that the producer of information agrees on a level of interoperability that permits other ATM stakeholders to contribute to the distribution of information.[6]

SWIM participants have to share a few key elements: a reference data and service model, as well as roles and responsibilities that they will assume as managers, contributors and users.

---

that data is widely and easily available, subject to appropriate access controls. Trajectory is a piece of information contained in the Flight Object regarding the flight intent from gate-to-gate. The trajectory is calculated by the current manager.

4. ATM Data for a 2020 SESAR/SWIM environment are: aeronautical data, surveillance data, flight data, ATFCM scenario data, capacity and demand data, meteo data. The flight data domain is all connected to the Flight Object that is a concept to support the flight data interoperability between all stakeholders. The Flight Object will be continuously monitored in its trajectory from gate-to-gate. Its purpose is to ensure that all systems have a consistent view of the flight share information (gate-to gate), and that data is widely and easily available. A Flight Object is formed by a set of information that can be separated in particular subset and managed independently. The partition of the Flight Object can be made in respect of the stakeholders interested or no partition can be made of the Flight Object.
5. 36th Session of the Assembly of the International Civil Aviation Organisation (ICAO) Montréal, 18 to 28 Sep. 2007 – TECHNICAL COMMISSION – Agenda Item 31: Continued evolution of a performance-based global air traffic management (ATM) system.
6. Within the SES High Level Group formed in 2000 there was a military committee that contributed to the definition of the future ATM policy then translated into the EU Regulations. Therefore, even now for SESAR and SWIM a role of the military organizations should be considered. Since the airspace is a limited resource, cooperation and coordination at all levels between the civil and the military authorities and parties are necessary to enable aviation operations to be carried out safely. As recognized by SESAR, global interoperability is a key issue in respect of the future ATM/CNS infrastructure. In this context, civil-military interoperability requirements should be developed enabling military capabilities to be integrated as much as possible and allowing the information sharing supporting the operations of all parties involved.

SWIM is part of the first regulatory roadmap related to European ATM Master Plan, implementing rules, defining roles and responsibilities, licensing aspects, security issues, liabilities and ownership.[7] Such a situation will raise problems of sovereignty, State immunity, liability, applicable law and jurisdiction.

4 SWIM'S TECHNICAL ARCHITECTURE

For designing a legal framework it is important to understand the architecture and functionality of the SWIM programme. SWIM can be considered to be a multi-faceted and multi-disciplinary subject, consisting of the following constituents (in order to achieve the goal of a fully integrated, seamless European ATM System – EATMS): a physical SWIM network layer, including the essential technical IP (Internet Protocol), building blocks (e.g. transport protocols, firewalls), a SWIM infrastructure consisting of common and standardized IT services, an EATMS – wide enterprise architecture model that defines a common view on ATM business processes as recommended in the SESAR definition phase. Considering the role of SWIM for an efficient and a safe air transport, the protection of the system from external interference is vitally important. A rich security framework including authentication, authorization, confidentiality, data integrity, non-repudiation, accountability, resource management and fine-grained access control mechanisms will assure this.[8]

Different recording functions will be implemented to archive the exchanged information that may require replay, post-flight analysis or processing (e.g. replay analysis, flight-billing calculation, statistical processing, simulations, etc). Automated tools that assure uninterrupted and unattended recording will support these functions. Information collected will not form a database, but will be used to establish source of information and their eventual wrong use. This information will be used for determining obligations, liabilities and application of sanctions.

The principles established for security enable a correct distribution of information, the authorization process, and the implementation of the system.

---

7. The realization of the SES is based on a few main objectives including, *inter alia*, the creation and integration of air navigation services in Functional Airspace Blocks (FABs) (Art. 9a, Regulation 550/2004/EC).
8. In details, the security features of SWIM are: authentication: ability to verify the digital identity of the sender of a communication such as a request to log-in; authorization: determines if a previously authenticated user is permitted to perform a given operation (e.g. access SWIM data, publish SWIM data, invoke a SWIM service); confidentiality: protects messages or documents so that they cannot be made available to unauthorized parties; data integrity: provides protection against unauthorized alteration of messages during transit; non-repudiation: ensures that a sender cannot deny a message already sent, and a receiver cannot deny a message already received (non-repudiation is especially important in monetary transactions and security auditing); accountability: provides secure logging and auditing (supports non-repudiation); traceability: assures the identification of a publisher or contributor or user; resource management: ability to monitor and manage communication resources (protocols, ports, IP addresses, etc.).

It is important that the information exchanged within SWIM have the above characteristics; if not, and the information appears misleading, the publisher could be liable for damages caused by such misleading information. Another important characteristic of SWIM information is timing. Important information published late could be one of the elements that have caused an air accident. Therefore, negligence for late publication of SWIM information should be sanctioned. Sanctions can be applied even if no damage is caused by the misleading information.

5 PARTIES INVOLVED IN THE SWIM PROGRAMME AND THEIR ROLES

The SWIM programme is based on the actions of the following figures: the publisher, who is responsible for distributing a partition[9] of the Flight Object, as created by the manager who is responsible for maintaining the consistency of a particular partition. It receives from the contributors update information on the Flight Object and does the necessary processing to ensure that a coherent and consistent partition is maintained and made available to the publisher; the user, who subscribes to a partition and receives updates from the publisher; the contributor, who sets the value for a subset of a partition and makes it available to the manager for consolidation into the Flight Object.

6 PRELIMINARY CONSIDERATIONS FOR A SWIM REGULATORY FRAMEWORK

The previous paragraphs have illustrated the technical part of the project and its functionality. Such a description is essential to understand the legal aspect pertaining to a system that will play a key role in the future Single European Sky and SESAR programmes, hence for the European air transport safety.

As described before, SWIM is based on a group of independent parties (airlines, airports, air navigation service providers, etc.), private and public entities, which will exchange aeronautical information ensuring the functionality of the system for the benefit of the air traffic activities. It should also be considered that any single party of the system could be a publisher or a user of the aeronautical information operating independently one from the other. As a matter of fact there is no hierarchical relationship between the various SWIM parties.

In addition, it should also be taken into consideration that the parties are established and operate in different countries, subject to different national legislations and administrative norms. Another important issue concerns the nature, public or private, of the parties involved.

9. Partition is a particular subset of the Flight Object that is of interest to one set of stakeholders and divides the Flight Object into separate pieces that may be managed independently.

The functionality of the system is assured by a set of technical procedures that could be the basis for designing a governance structure ensuring the compliance with a regulatory framework establishing a proactive relationship among the SWIM parties.

Naturally, the relationship among the various parties of the system should be clearly defined in order to assign responsibilities and liabilities in case of damages caused by an air accident.

All parties should be subject to the same strict rules for the information supply to guarantee the air navigation safety. Similarly, they should be subject to a uniform liability system. Such a solution could raise problems especially in respect of the air navigation service providers subject to, as far as liability is concerned, their national law that differs from one country to another.[10] In other words, should the air navigation service provider be responsible for damage, it should be identified as liable for compensation, and it can, therefore, be compelled to fulfil its obligations.

The implementation of the SES foresees the creation of FABs, each of them comprising more then one country. Therefore, one FAB will provide cross border ANS.

Regarding the identification of the liable party, in the case of cross-border services, two are the most common approaches: one assigns to the States the primary liability for damages arising from the failure of ATS (doctrine of the 'primary liability of the State' that is prevailing in Europe) and normally the State will retain a right of recourse against the designated air navigation service provider to obtain the reimbursement of any compensation paid. The other approach assigns to the service provider entity the liability for damages ('effective service provide' doctrine). Should the services provider not be located in the designated State, the latter should ensure that in case of damages caused by the service provider, its citizens may have the right of access to their domestic courts and to have their cases decided under the regime of the territorial State, regardless of the nationality and location of the effective service provider.[11]

Regarding the second aspect, that is, the possibility to force the liable party to compensate damages, the sovereign nature of air navigation services[12] and the

10. For a complete view of the liability of air navigation service providers, see F. Schubert, *Legal Aspects of Cross-Border Service Provision in the Single European Sky*, in *Air & Space Law*, vol. xxxv/2 (April 2010), page 113.
11. See Schubert, page 133.
12. The matter of Air Navigation Services (ANS) is ruled at international level by Art. 28 and Annex 11 of the Chicago Convention. Annex 11 of the Convention, which is specifically dedicated to Air Traffic Services, including Air Traffic Control Service, Flight Information Service and Alerting Service, establishes the corresponding standards and practices. It contains an important requirement for States to implement systematic and appropriate air traffic services (ATS) safety management programmes. Similarly, Annex 10 of the Chicago Convention (Aeronautical telecommunications), which deals with Standards and Recommended Practices (SARP's) on radio navigation aids used by planes is also to be underlined. Therefore, according with the above provisions of the Chicago Convention, States are the ultimate guarantors of the integrity, operational performance and reliability of their national ATS systems.

status of the service provider could raise the problem of immunity of jurisdiction. However, applying this principle could strongly affect the rights of injured parties when States are involved in service provision.[13]

The State immunity rules were recently codified by the International Law Commission in a Convention adopted by the UN General Assembly on 2 December 2004. Under this Convention, which tends to reflect the *communis opinio* of different countries, only actions that can be defined as commercial transactions may be excluded from judicial immunity. As regards SWIM services, the State immunity rules imply that damage deriving from commercial services may be subject to claims for compensation whereas damage caused by sovereign acts would benefit from procedural immunity according to Article 28 of the 1944 Chicago Convention.

The previous reasoning entails that all parties involved in SWIM must be subject to a common regulatory framework. A first step could be the identification of the correct regulation source that could be, considering similar sectors, contractual or authoritative source, the latter being national or supranational. In further details the regulatory sources suitable for a European project like SWIM could refer to community law, or auto-regulation (code of conduct). These sources should not be considered necessarily alternative as they can interact in a continuous dialogue as legal instruments to discipline the SWIM services.

To come to an effective discipline for SWIM it may be helpful to examine similar worldwide information networks like Internet and identify solutions that can be taken into consideration for our purposes.

7 INTERNET GOVERNANCE AND A CODE OF CONDUCT: POSSIBLE SIMILARITIES WITH SWIM

Undoubtedly, the analysis of SWIM architecture shows quite a number of similarities with the Internet (*Interconnected Networks*). Therefore, to define possible SWIM governance it can be useful to examine what happened and what is going to happen for the Internet.[14]

The traditional Internet model of access and distribution of information was based on the paradigm of access through browser (client web) to the information available on numerous servers distributed in the web (web sites). In such a model there was a clear distinction between the role of publisher of information and user of information. In the new paradigm of the web, called web 2.0,[15] every publisher can be a user and vice-versa and this does not happen because of the large number

13. See P. Manzini & A. Masutti, *An International Civil Liability Regime for the Galileo Services: A Proposal*, *Air & Space Law*, Vol. XXXIII/2 (April 2008), 114.
14. The Internet has become a ubiquitous tool for commerce, education, social services and everyday social interaction. Human-to-human interactions are now increasingly supplemented by machine-to-machine interactions—the so-called '*Internet of things*'—that underpin important activities even when we may be unaware that the Internet is involved.
15. The Internet 2.0 is more and more a network of independent networks inter connected in a world-wide dimension based on a family of protocols (Internet Protocols – IP).

of instruments available for the creation and publication of contents (web-authoring), but just with the creation of new models of widespread contribution (socialization among users).[16] We are moving from a one-to-one message exchange concept to the many-to-many information distribution model. The web is so considered as the new world *agora* where information is exchanged. All this represents a real revolution for ICT and software industry as the new applications and services will be web-centric.[17]

All these elements are common to the future SWIM structure. Another common element is represented by the impossibility, for Internet or for SWIM, to apply the traditional juridical instruments to tie a particular case to a place and its applicable rules.

Internet regulation has been the subject of international discussions since the mid-1990s, with the EU being an 'early mover' in terms of identifying key public policy issues to be discussed between EU Member States and with international partner countries.[18]

Since then, governance of the Internet continues to be a crucial public policy priority given the way in which the Internet has transformed the lives and working environments of millions of citizen.[19] In the vast concept of Internet regulation its governance was defined by the Working Group on Internet Governance as '*the development and application by Governments, the private sector and civil society, in their respective roles, of shared principles, norms, rules, decision-making procedures, and programmes that shape the evolution and use of the Internet*'.[20] Policies and mechanisms for Internet governance have been topics of heated debate between many different Internet stakeholders, some of whom have very different visions for how and indeed whether the Internet should facilitate the free communication and flow of ideas and information ensuring the stability of the system.[21]

---

16. This new paradigm is quite well represented by social networks like Facebook and Twitter which are fed by multimedia contents called *User Generated Contents (UGC).* A new word has now been coined: *Prosumer* which identifies the user that is also producer of information.
17. A good example is represented by VoIP (Voice on Internet Protocol), the new very cheap way of telephone communication.
18. Communication of the Commission to the European Parliament, The Council, the Economic and Social Committee and the Committee of Regions on '*Future Networks and the Internet*' – SEC (2008) 2516.
19. For the purpose of establishing governance principles for Internet, the Internet Corporation for Assigned Names and Numbers (ICANN), was set up in 1998 and was created as a unique experiment in self-governance with an ambitious agenda to bring together all the relevant stakeholders to cooperate on the coordination of these resources. In September 2009 ICANN has completed its first ten years of agreement with the US Government. During the last meeting in 2009 it was requested that ICANN refers not only to the US Government but to the entire Internet community. Another international organization is the *Internet Governance Forum* (IGF). Its purpose is to support the United Nations Secretary General in carrying out the mandate from the World Summit on the Information Society (WSIS) with regard to convening a new forum for multi-stakeholder policy dialogue.
20. Report of the Working Group on Internet Governance – Chateau de Bossey – June 2005.
21. In many occasions it has been stressed the need to guarantee security and stability of the global Internet, the respect for human rights, freedom of expression, privacy, protection of personal data and the promotion of cultural and linguistic diversity.

Before presenting the governance systems proposed for Internet, a key difference between Internet and SWIM must be highlighted: both Internet and SWIM users will publish or receive information, but SWIM users will be only the members of the restricted air transport community, able to enter the system through access codes and identification procedures. On the contrary, the access to Internet does not require any formalities except the identification of the access point.

However, the differences between the two systems do not prevent us from analysing the international debate on the governance of the Internet that may be useful to identify some results or suggestions for designing a governance for SWIM.

The conclusions of different debates have led to establish the principles that for every organization where many parties operate with a certain degree of freedom, it is advisable to set up a 'code of conduct'. The code of conduct is a tool that enables the creation of a set of technical rules (whose technical specification and nature cannot be neglected being important for the functionality of the system) that need to be codified to give them a legal strength.

The idea to have a 'code of conduct' ruling an environment having technical features like SWIM is not new. At international level valuable examples offered by the Internet and air and space activity experiences may be found. Especially for Internet many similarities with SWIM support the idea to follow an analogue path.

In theory, a set of technical rules can be implemented through a private law instrument, for example a private agreement, or a framework agreement between the parties involved and the authority entitled to enforce such framework agreement. However, the reason why a code of conduct should be envisaged for SWIM – on the basis of examples offered by other fields – is that it seems the best way to establish basic rules binding for a large number of parties involved who have to implement technical activities.

Every organization, whether it is a company, or a private entity, has expectations of how its members should act among each other and with those outside of the organization. The set of principles that govern these expectations is referred to as a code of conduct. Organizations may impose penalties for breaking their codes of conduct.

A code of conduct creates a set of rules for specified circumstances that becomes a standard for all who participate in the group and represent themselves outside of the group. There are various definitions of 'code of conduct' in relation to the matter subject to a 'soft regulation' for different activities.

For example, Article 2, f) of the Directive 29/2005/EC[22] on 'Unfair business-to-consumer commercial practices in the internal market' defines the 'code of conduct' as:

> an agreement or set of rules not imposed by law, regulation or administrative provision of a Member State which defines the behaviour of traders who

22. Directive No. 2005/29/EC of 11 May 2005 concerning unfair business-to-consumer commercial practices in the internal market.

undertake to be bound by the code in relation to one or more particular commercial practices or business sectors.

In more general terms a 'code of conduct' can be defined as a set of rules outlining the responsibilities of or proper practices for an individual or for an organization. Related concepts include ethical codes and honour codes or a code outlining the responsibilities of or best practice for an individual or organization, such as a set of principles of good corporate behaviour adopted by a business.

The Internet Society (ISOC)[23] has developed some principles regarding the code of conduct in a handbook for 'Site security policy'[24] that is a proposed guide to setting computer security policies and procedures for sites that have systems on the Internet.

The principles contained in the proposed guide refer to the policies for access to computing resources (hardware, software, information) and what happens when such policies are violated.

A key part of creating policies refers to some kind of risk assessment to decide what really needs to be protected and the level of resources that should be applied to protect them. Once policies are in place, procedures to prevent future security problems should be established. Actions to be taken when unauthorized activity is suspected should also be established as well as types of procedures to prevent security problems.

The code of conduct examines the decisions that have to be taken on the spot as the incident occurs, and suggests that issues can be discussed in advance; the occurrence of an accident is an opportunity to improve security policies. At very last, the ISOC document suggests the definition of responsibilities and sanctions for security violation.

However, despite international forums and discussions, statement by many countries on the necessity to have worldwide Internet governance, concrete results have not been achieved until now on this important issue. In any case, the efforts described here above show a wide spread need to have a governance for Internet. This is the lesson learned: as anticipated, the first instrument from Internet that could be considered for a SWIM governance is a code of conduct that helps to identify the main principles for a correct functioning of SWIM.

Many other fields have adopted a code of conduct to regulate their functioning. Only two cases that could be considered near to SWIM will be described: the code of conduct for the outer space activities and the Computer Reservation System (CRS) for the air transport.

---

23. The Internet Society (ISOC) is a non-profits organization founded in 1992 to provide leadership in Internet related standards, education, and policy. With offices in Washington DC, USA, and Geneva, Switzerland, it is dedicated to ensuring the open development, evolution and use of the Internet for the benefit of people throughout the world.
24. Network Working Group, July 1991 – This handbook is a combined effort of the Security Area and User Services Area of the Internet Engineering Task Force (IETF). It is a guide to setting computer security policies and procedures for sites that have systems on the Internet; it lists issues and factors for site operators to consider when setting their own policies.

8 THE CODE OF CONDUCT FOR OUTER SPACE ACTIVITIES

Even the European Union is interested in the application of codes of conduct. The following, relating to space, is an interesting example. On 17 December 2008, the Council of the European Union approved the text of the draft Code of Conduct for outer space activities, which will serve as a basis for consultations with third countries.[25] The Council considered that strengthening the security of activities in outer space is an important goal in the context of the expanding space activities that contribute to the development and security of States. The code should be applicable to all outer space activities conducted by a subscribing State or jointly with other States or by non-governmental entities under the jurisdiction of a subscribing State, including those activities within the framework of international intergovernmental organizations.

The code, in codifying new best practices, contributes to transparency and confidence-building measures and is complementary to the existing framework regulating outer space activities. It states the freedom of access to, exploration and use of outer space and exploitation of space objects for peaceful purposes without interference, fully respecting the security, safety and integrity of space objects in orbit, the inherent right of individual or collective self-defence in accordance with the United Nations Charter. It establishes also the responsibility of States to take all the appropriate measures and cooperate in good faith to prevent harmful interference in outer space activities.

The code defines the responsibility of States, in the conduct of scientific, commercial and military activities, to promote the peaceful exploration and use of outer space and take all the adequate measures to prevent outer space from becoming an area of conflict. Finally, it states the compliance with existing regulations and international treaties, measures on space operations and debris control and mitigation, registration of space objects and a consultation mechanism.

9 THE CODE OF CONDUCT FOR THE COMPUTERIZED RESERVATION SYSTEM (CRS)

It has been mentioned before that a system which involves so many parties may be regulated by a code of conduct containing professional obligations of fair behaviour (the so-called soft law). However, in some cases the regulation of a system requires a legal instrument, outlining best practices and responsibilities, issued by an authoritative source, which incorporates the code of conduct into a binding regulation ('hard law').

25. Council conclusions and draft Code of Conduct for outer space activities PESC 1595 CODUN 59 – 3 Dec. 2008.

As an example, it may be useful to mention the regulation of a sector through a code of conduct whose behaviour rules have been incorporated into an EU Regulation. The Regulation (EC) No. 80/2009 of the European Parliament and of the Council of 14 January 2009 (repealing Council Regulation (EEC) No. 2299/89) designs the code of conduct for computerized reservation systems.

Computerized Reservation Systems (CRSs) are systems that centralize fares of participating air and rail carriers and enable subscribing travel agents to provide instantaneous information on fares and availability to customers, to confirm customers' bookings and issue tickets. The CRS code of conduct aims at guaranteeing that CRS operate in a transparent and non-discriminatory way, preventing distortions of competition in the air transport supply chain for air and rail transport. CRSs must provide information on fares and availability in a neutral manner without bias. The CRS code of conduct prohibits carriers that can have decisive influence on a CRS from discriminating against other CRSs. The regulation under exam introduces a set of behaviour rules that have to be adopted by system vendors and by providers of transport services. These rules prevent the system vendors to fix unfair clauses in the contract to be signed with the adhering members, or impose transparency or publicity norms by the participants to the system (Article 3) or rigorous behaviours ensuring the functioning of the system without adopting discriminatory attitudes towards competitors (Article 10). Article 15 establishes fines that the European Commission may inflict in case of infringement of the regulation (Article 13). Since a long time the air transport sector has adopted rules of conduct for its operators, intending to associate for the development and exploitation of new technologies enabling to supply better services to the customers. The operators accept these rules that, in case under examination, are set up by an EU regulation that includes a fine scheme to ensure a correct functioning of the system.

10 CONSIDERATION FOR A CODE OF CONDUCT FOR SWIM

Previous considerations on Internet, outer space and CRS have described organizations based on work performed by independent parties having no hierarchical relationship between them. The functionality of SWIM described in the first part clearly shows that all these activities have many similar aspects in common. Therefore even for SWIM a code of conduct could represent a first step ahead.

10.1 SWIM Technical Features: A Basis for a Code of Conduct

A code of conduct for SWIM can certainly be created taking into consideration the examples described here above regarding the Internet, the CRS and the activities in outer space.

SWIM already contains many principles and rules regarding the security of data like, for example, authentication, authorization, confidentiality, non-repudiation, standardized language and service interoperability.

Regarding the technical principles, the functionality foreseen by the development of the technical programme is based on technical features and rules. For example, the SWIM 'security service' shall offer functionality for authentication and authorization. It includes a control mechanism for access; the authentication that is the ability to verify the digital identity of a sender of a communication or request of log-in; the authorization for access and publish SWIM data; the access control criteria based on assigned roles, dynamic characteristic of the data being accessed like geographical location or time; the identification of users through a precise definition of user and associated attributes, their classification into groups, roles and organizations; the access privileges.

The authorization process has two objectives: to allow access to authorized subscribers only and to guarantee the security of the system.

In order to guarantee the compliance with the technical principles for the safety of air transport, the code of conduct should be characterized by the following features: complete and precise description of the technical principles, which ensure the stability and security of the system and the traceability system which allows the identification of eventual responsibilities; identify the legal instrument to make the technical principles and rules compulsory for all parties involved; a system of administrative sanctions for infringement of the above rules;[26] in case an infringement causes damage to third parties and/or their properties, a third party liability regime should be set up.

Regarding legal instruments, technical principles and rules should become compulsory for all parties involved. In other words a legal framework allowing full functionality of SWIM in the European ATM System foreseen by the SES regulations should be set up.

All these technical features should be translated into a set of compulsory rules for the SWIM users, assuring in such a way the correct functioning of the system within a complete legal framework. Such rules establishing a compulsory behaviour of the parties involved must be collected in a 'code' that becomes, therefore, a code of conduct. The code of conduct can be the first instrument allowing the functionality of SWIM. Considering the importance for a safe ATS in Europe the provisions of the 'code of conduct' should be compulsory for the SWIM users: this target could be reached through a European regulation establishing statutory instruments, relating in particular to safety and security matters and leaving to the private parties to regulate their commercial relationship. In drafting the regulation it should also be considered the European provisions against the dominant position in the marketplace. Indeed, the SWIM operator must be prevented from abusing of a dominant position characterizing the monopolistic situation existing in the past in various sectors like energy, telecommunications or transports. Article 102 of the TFEU Treaty is aimed at preventing undertakings that hold a dominant position in a market from abusing that position to the detriment of consumers.

26. The sanctions for non-compliance with the code of conduct rules are normally represented by fines.

10.2 SWIM Services: Commercial Relationships and Contractual Provisions

It is reasonable to assume that the SWIM system will be operated by the European Commission or most probably by an entity delegated by the European Commission to operate and commercially exploit the system. It may also be assumed that to receive the SWIM services an annual subscription fee should be paid and finally that the annual subscription of SWIM services paid by the major parties of air transport (airlines, airports, ANSP, etc.) be mandatory. Such conclusion comes from the consideration that presently commercial flights cannot be provided without using existing ATS.

This raises the question on how to regulate the relationship between the operator and the SWIM users.

In the last few decades, a large number, if not the majority, of modern commercial contracts for activities implying a large number of customers are made on terms established by one party and offered to another party on the 'take it or leave it' basis. These contracts are often known as 'contracts of adhesion', written in a standard form. Familiar examples of adhesion contracts are contracts for transportation or service concluded with public carriers and utilities and contracts of large corporations with their suppliers, dealers and customers, or with banks or insurance companies. In such circumstances a contract becomes a kind of private legislation, in the sense that the stronger party unilaterally fixes the terms of the contract rather than through a process of bargaining. Enforcement of such standard contracts can be justified on the ground that they are economically necessary to today's transactions.[27]

Considering the different situations in which this kind of contract has been used, also in SWIM case the adhesion contract appears to be one of the suitable framework agreements to regulate the bilateral relationships between the parties involved in the SWIM programme.

Here above it has been foreseen that an operator will provide and offer SWIM services. It will certainly be one party of the contract. The other party is represented by a multitude of SWIM users (independently from their role of manager, publisher and contributor, as in any case they are SWIM users).

It is evident that the operator cannot bargain with each SWIM user any clause of the contract and it is the interest of users to start using SWIM services as soon as possible, avoiding long and time-consuming negotiations with the service provider.

In this situation, it seems that a standard framework agreement set up by the operator, which the users can undersign (adhere to) to purchase SWIM services, be the most suitable instrument to regulate such a relationship.

27. A common adhesion contract that we can consider in our analysis is the adhesion contract with a financial entity issuing credit cards. This contract foresees a repeated use of services rendered by such financial entity for a large but limited number of subscribers of its services. The subscribers undersign an adhesion contract which sets up the main rules for the use of the credit card, but also other rules to avoid a misuse of the same credit card. All these rules permit a correct functioning of the credit card system.

Therefore, when a user intends to buy SWIM services he will simply finalize the standard framework agreement by adhesion, accepting all its clauses that might have been already agreed by its association.

Considering the peculiar terms of the contract of adhesion, the European regulations concerning the consumer's protection, regulations that have been approved for similar contractual situations where one party has a stronger position than the other party, should not be disregarded.

The European Union and the single Member States, regulating an open and liberalized market, had one major objective: the consumer's protection also through the prevention of dominant positions in the marketplace. With particular reference to the commercial transactions (goods or services), the legislations of nearly all countries have adopted regulations that prevent an adhesion contract from containing unfair contract terms.

These principles for the EU Member States are contained in the Unfair Contract Terms Directive (1993/13/EC), which introduces a notion of 'good faith' in order to prevent significant imbalances in the rights and obligations of consumers on the one hand and sellers and suppliers on the other hand. This general requirement is supplemented by a list of examples of terms that may be regarded as unfair. Terms that are found unfair under the Directive are not binding for consumers. The Directive also requires contract terms to be drafted in plain and intelligible language and states that ambiguities will be interpreted in favour of consumers. Member States must make sure that effective means exist under national law to enforce these rights and that such terms are no longer used by businesses.

Nevertheless, the purpose of Directive 13/1993/EC is to harmonize the laws, regulations and administrative provisions of the Member States relating to unfair terms in contracts concluded between a seller or supplier and a consumer. The Directive offers also the definition of 'consumer', which refers to '*any natural person who, in contracts covered by this Directive, is acting for purposes which are outside his trade, business or profession*'.

It may also be assumed that SWIM services will be offered by the owner or by the operator of the system to natural or legal persons which will act for purposes which are inside his trade, business or profession and therefore can not be identified as a 'consumer'. Hence, the provisions of the EU Directive and its adoption by the European Member States are not applicable to the adhesion contract envisaged for SWIM services.

The main elements of the adhesion contract applicable to the SWIM transactions could be the following. Regarding the parties of the SWIM adhesion contract, it may be assumed that every party (manager, publisher, user and contributor) will sign the adhesion contract as one party. The other party should be the owner or the operator (technical and/or commercial) of the system (contractor). The contract shall start defining the scope and general provisions. The main scope of the framework contract will be to procure uninterrupted and secure SWIM services by the contractor in favour of users. The contractor shall supply SWIM services as certified to ensure a safety and seamless ATM. The contract shall describe the different services offered by SWIM, their features and their performance standards. The safety of the system is based on the compliance of services with the performance indicators.

For each service a fee system shall be established as well as the corresponding payment method, which will comprise provisions in case of late, or lack of payment and eventual sanctions for interrupted services. The future organization of SWIM could imply the existence of subcontractors like for example the ANSPs signing a contract with a European operator of SWIM. This opportunity should be carefully examined in respect of the level of liability and the corresponding insurance coverage.

10.3 General Principles Regarding Liability

While remembering that we are moving in the field of the contractual liability, the framework agreement shall comprise two different provisions in case of wrong or misleading or incomplete information not causing or causing damage. In the first case, the contract shall foresee that, in case wrong or misleading or incomplete information published in the system has not originated problems or even incidents, but was potentially a cause of incidents, a sanction should be established. In this case the (administrative) sanction acts as a deterrent. The contract shall designate who is in charge of such evaluation and of imposing sanctions. Sanctions will be progressive and proportional in respect of the gravity of the mistake up to the notice and termination of the contract. Such a sanction system will be developed in two directions: the first one against the contractor when fails to maintain the performance standards of the system; in the second case against the users, when misleading information is supplied, violating the contract obligations or code of conduct. In the second case, when damage is caused to the user by wrong or incomplete information, a liability system including a compensation system for damage of properties and personal injury to the victims should be designed. Normally, principles of private law quite common to Member States for compensation of damage comprise the loss of profit and accruing damage, and these principles will be taken into due consideration.

Let us consider a first example: wrong information regarding a 'flight object' is disseminated by an ANSP. This information causes considerable delay only. The framework contract shall provide that in case airlines claim for damages to the SWIM operator, the latter will be guaranteed by the ANSP that disseminated the wrong information on the basis of the private law principle. This example gives us also the opportunity to consider that the framework contract could establish also limitation of compensation, when the amount of damage could be quite high. However, it should be foreseen the case that wrong or misleading or incomplete information causes an accident and huge damage to third parties.

Let us consider a second concrete case: wrong information regarding a 'flight object' is disseminated by an ANSP (user). This information is received through SWIM system by an aircraft that crashes because of wrong information creating huge damage to persons and properties. Also in this case the framework contract shall provide that in case airlines claim for damages to the SWIM operator (contractor), the latter will be guaranteed by the ANSP.

The difference of this case is that it may cause enormous damages that should require a dedicated regulation. Certainly, in order to limit the risk of compensating consistent damage caused by the malfunctioning of the SWIM system, the operator and the subcontractors may provide for an insurance coverage according to the market conditions and limits.

As any other contract, the applicable law, the jurisdiction and, eventually, an arbitration clause shall be part of the contract. As far as applicable law and jurisdiction are concerned, the situation may be complicated by the fact that SWIM users reside in different countries, with different legislations and by the fact that the European Commission could be the owner and/or the operator of the system; in case of claims filed against the European Commission, the European Court of Justice would be the competent court.

11 CONCLUSIONS

SWIM – as part of SESAR – represents a revolution of the present ATS information system, decoupling the information producer from information user, designing a system where many independent players operate with a certain degree of freedom, all capable to assume different roles: publisher, manager, user, and so forth.

Such a new situation raises problems for the creation of a regulatory framework including a governance structure and a liability system, ensuring the efficient functionality of the system. These problems arise, for example, from the fact that the future SES is based on functional air blocks (FABs) comprising more than one sovereign country and offering cross-border ATC services, which makes it difficult to identify the liable party in the event of an air accident.

As far as governance is concerned, deep analysis of the solutions to similar problems concerning the Internet could provide a model for the first step in setting up a SWIM code of conduct. In addition, other governance possibilities are those for outer space and the airlines' CRS. Such a code of conduct should be based on SWIM technical features, which include a rich security framework capable of ensuring the stability and security of the system as well as the traceability of the information source and identification of eventual responsibility and liability.

The second step would be to translate the provisions of the code of conduct into a compulsory set of rules, such as a European regulation. Given the huge investment in this project in terms of both money and wide ranging expertise, it would be reckless not to establish all elements necessary for its success. No product is marketable in the absence of a clear regulatory framework, which must include a liability system permitting fair compensation for damage caused by the misuse of the product; in our case by misleading or incorrect aeronautical information disseminated through SWIM. The establishment of the governance system should involve the input and cooperation of the insurance industry as it will be fundamental to the practical success of any adopted system.

There are several possible SWIM scenarios, involving different market conditions and rules, as the system could be operated by the European Commission or by an EU agency or by a private operator. Regardless of which scenario becomes reality, there will be the need for a clear governance system which will guarantee the functionality and efficiency of SWIM.

Given the crucial economic importance of air transport and the complex environment it operates in, the European Commission and the SESAR JU should make it a matter of priority to design the future organization of the SES and its governance in such a way as to make sure it achieves all objectives; namely, to meet significantly increased future air traffic demand, reduce delay and improve the safety and security of the European air transport system.

PART IV
TECHNOLOGY

Chapter 21
Next Generation Manufacturing Technologies

*François Gayet**

1 INTRODUCTION

The Next Generation Manufacturing Technologies (NGMT) is an initiative for industries aiming at the development of manufacturing technologies, to strengthen their industrial basis and improve their competitiveness.[1]

The Next Generation Manufacturing Technologies is a new approach on funding using a systematic methodology to select technologies and creating new synergies and leverage opportunities with high potential value to the nation. With manufacturing cost rising higher than the average of developing countries for similar capabilities, the Industry should redefine the competitive basis by application of new emerging technologies and enabling tools: technology drives innovation, innovation drives wealth creation, wealth creates jobs and technology is the engine of economic growth.

The Next Generation Manufacturing Technologies strategy is a three-part process. First, it requires a technology roadmap made of combination of research

* François Gayet, Secretary General, Aerospace and Defence Industries Association of Europe.

1. It reflects initiatives of partnership between the Department of Defense (DoD) and industries to strengthen the defence industrial basis and improve the competitiveness of US manufacturer.

Daniel Calleja Crespo & Pablo Mendes de Leon, *Achieving the Single European Sky: Goals and Challenges*, pp. 223–238.

and participant industries' inputs. Then, on a regular basis, a Forum of stakeholders will be held to execute and to reorient the roadmap for implementation. The ultimate phase is the transition towards the maturation and quick implementation of new technologies according to the plan and a widespread deployment to provide an advance manufacturing technology.

The roadmap for the Next Generation Manufacturing Technologies will focus on a *Model-Based Enterprise (MBE).* It will generate digital description with electronic representation of all attributes of the product. Moreover, it will be dynamic representation of interactions and results based on changes in parameters and modelling how it responds to various inputs.

The model assembles collections of related models into a 'metamodel' that shows results of complex interactions across products and processes and add tremendous value. It also implements radically new business processes and reengineers corporate cultures to accurately predict the results and enable enterprise-wide process management.

1.1 Model-Based Enterprise (MBE) Vision

The digital era has strongly impacted the conception of future enterprises. The knowledge of an enterprise will be captured and translated into digital information to feed efficiently all the functions from innovation to delivery of any enterprise. A knowledge-rich base makes external and internal factors available throughout the life cycle, throughout the supply chain using support tools within an integrate system and in real time.

An all-digital system is flexible: parameters and operations can be modulated to quickly evaluate alternatives and accurate the response of executives with a real-time awareness. The *Model-Based Enterprise* (MBE) facilitates the unity of all enterprise functions and particularly at the decision-making process by generating visualization tools. It also disseminates the good information in due time at the most relevant person to 'turn ideas into money'.

M&S[2] tools can quickly create a virtual representation of the best product and the most efficient process design. With resources characteristics, scaleable models, safety requirements and other specifications, it will be possible to simulate the impact of those choices on costs, performance, supply – and other factor – through accurate 3D models and virtual simulations. The role of the model is to connect and control the qualified process across. A continuous representation linked to all technical and business information provides relevant inputs to help executives to make best decisions.

One support objective of MBE is to develop open business architecture. With well-defined standards, all individual resources will be plugged together and, within appropriate security, most inefficiency inherent to complex supply chain relationships will be overcome. An organization of core elements into accurate models runs multiple scenarios and detects performance issues in order to submit autonomously the best response and the corresponding implementation plan.

---

2. Modelling & Simulation.

The main strategic impact of MBE is the integration of bottom-up/top-down process into a 'unity model'. The enterprise is seen as a whole, the MBE eliminates disconnections and aligns strategy at all levels. The integrated system coordinates information flows to the right level; implication of decisions reflected in all affected units provides feedbacks to optimize results; master model architecture accurate analysis and helps to manoeuvre. Moreover, all levels participate to the strategic responsibility and not only executives.

This open framework digests daily quantity of data on internal operations and external conditions and events to provide flexible representation schemes and analytical tools. All those information can be gathered on an interface point like a 'management cockpit' shared by users. This management cockpit will present scenarios based on best information available and all concerned users will be able to respond collaboratively to challenges.

2 SCOPE

2.1 The Next Generation Manufacturing Technologies

Support to product realization is about creating a core of manufacturing to generate value chain. The Next Generation Manufacturing Technologies distinguishes four elements which relates to other function that triggers a value chain:

(i) Innovation & Conceptualization
(ii) Product & process development
(iii) Manufacturing Execution
(iv) Life-Cycle Support.

In addition, the product life-cycle management (PLM) approach focuses on: access and control of product definition information; maintaining integrity of the product definition and related information throughout the life of the product; managing the business process; and managing and disseminating the information.

Model-based product, design and manufacturing are widely used in industry to enable rapid development, eliminating costs and time of physical prototyping. Leading companies invested in M&S[3] tools but development of a multi-disciplinary optimization of product in a model-based environment remains the key.

Modelling with complete real environment is not yet possible without specific training and a deeper level of precision in models. Present tools are complex to use and limited to normal operations by the level of detail available and the incapacity to adapt as the product ages. Moreover, the limited capability to 'plugged together' with other functions (cost modelling, design, allowance, etc.) is a barrier to multiple function optimizations and planning.

3. Modelling & Simulation.

2.2 Current State

Today, it is not possible to generate automatically a model of product from user's specifications even if more and more integrated into the process. The process is based on the requirement of management tools: it creates a database of requirements but does not generate information directly usable into an executable process.

The computing power available today can perform, in a few hours, analyses with an acceptable level of details for evaluation. Additionally, visualization technologies exist today and are used in best practice application, justifying a significant investment.

Current M&S tools generate models to design top-down manufacturing flows or to help diagnose a problem at a detailed level. The cost and the time-consuming characteristic of M&S tools limit applications to products with high return on investment and are not used as a standard practice. To develop the use of such capabilities, manufacturers should focus on long-term profits and invest largely in tool and model developments for validation and verification. Even public investments are lacking to support the needed software development, especially considering the success encountered in areas such as forging and spinning.

For instance, model-based product simulations are widely used in product certification to avoid physical destructive testing for gas turbine engines. These capabilities suffer a lack of accurate predictive capabilities and are not able to integrate uncertainties, necessary for confident validation. The little knowledge of the underlying physical and non-physical factors limit the reuse of the knowledge on one product. Modelling such physical representation demands large capabilities to capture, transform, translate and exchange knowledge and data, so it requests a larger investment.

The next major challenge is the interoperability between units to ensure the continuity of information. Engineering material and processes are not well integrated with product visualization tools; geometric representations are neither mathematically complete nor precise enough to be directly useable. In fact, the interoperability of data is still requiring a human intervention to correct the results but they started to be helped by existing transition tools. Under the interoperability lies the lack of standardization. Without data exchange, standard representations of products and processes, scalability from micro to macro level, it is difficult to reach the next stage of cost effectiveness and high performance simulation. This highlights the lack of strategic collaboration between industries throughout a supply chain.

'Virtual Manufacturing is a key to rapid final assembly for new commercial system and aircraft.' The manufacturing process uses detailed plans and raw materials to create deliverable products. In many cases the product will be humanly refined and tailored to conform more closely to the stakeholders' needs than it was originally designed. Then, the key question is how effective is a process in converting materials and design information into the right product that meet all stakeholders.

Traditional manufacturing process requires a lot of experimentation early in their life cycle. Models are made to control the process or to monitor the production rate. To overcome barriers for a wider use of model-based technologies, industry needs a better understanding of processes and materials to improve the ability to create effective models. With the adequate definition of product and process, information generated by humans will be progressively supported by modelling and visualization tools. Instead of using CAD[4] tools and mock-ups, manufacturers should convert the assembling, testing, packaging into process and distribute to shop supervisors along with instructions and training for the production staff to automate tasks like what is done for manufacturing process plans.

The application of these technologies to support the other phases of the product life cycle is still limited. The training has been undervalued in the equation because it traditionally comes after starting development. However, advances in modelling with 3D CAD and VR[5] tools has improved the quality and safety of training while reducing the cost of developing and maintaining training materials. The other barrier to a wider use is also due to a lack of budget and a cultural resistance to change when the first objective is to have the work done.

Usually, investments in 3D CAD tools are made for reliable and easy-to-maintain products. However, the no centralized recordkeeping shows how it is difficult to develop the rich database needed to understand maintenance, repair history and the costs related. Manufacturers often lose visibility on what happens to the product after delivery and cannot elaborate accurate models.

2.3 Future State Vision

The next step in product realization is to achieve a model that generates the best balanced product at the end of the chain. Moreover, the future model is also to capture and share all the data to continuously improve all processes from design to life-cycle support.

The key point of product realization process is the future ability to move back and forth between the *virtual* representation and the *physical reality* in real time, accessible to all value chain members within a comprehensive product model. This led to the creation of a comprehensive library of validated characterized models and simulations, best processes, best equipments. The standardized library of 3D representations coupled with mathematically accurate environment and material characteristics ensure the integration in plug-and-play fashion of equipment and tooling manufacturer with business and technical data.

Future M&S tools enable a better management of complex system of systems. They not only develop new products, they also build a capability to continuously optimize manufactured products considering all other products with which they interact. Some capabilities still remain to be developed in computing speed and generation of model outputs such as complex visualizations.

4. Computer-Aided Design.
5. Virtual Reality.

3 VISION AND GOALS

3.1 Goals for Product Realization

A flexible representation of complex models is a key factor to create a comprehensive computer-based modelling accessible to different type of users. The flexibility enables the user to focus on his concerned point of view in real time and configures the tool to accommodate new rules, new customer requirements and new technologies. The collaborative modelling & simulation environment is the standard-based and easy-to-use collaborative environment. This plug & play organization optimizes the value chain using inexpensive integration of new and complex models. Establishing a shared library creates a wide historic of the entire validated elements and can support all models and optimization processes.

Future tools should provide an integrated system-of-systems modelling capabilities to respond to the needs of decision-makers. An intelligent modelling capability should be developed to reduce the human intervention and accelerate the modelling at any stage of the production.

Those complex systems will provide also a cost modelling system that will consider all external and internal data to provide the most accurate analysis on costs, profitability and financial risks. A model-based process should provide the capability to follow a product in each step of its life cycle, integrate the data collected and disseminate them to the proper business function.

3.2 Innovation and Conceptualization

The future concept is built on interactions between the product and the manufacturer to translate problems into opportunities and pass the requirement on the baseline product to modify the manufacturing order. Outputted scenarios will show the best balance of technical and business attributes.

To achieve the vision, interactive visualizations and analytical tools should quickly guide the exploration over alternative products to help the choice of participant along the enterprise value chain.

Integrated M&S tools provide feedbacks on all technical and business options for the customer and the repercussions on performance, costs and other attributes. The comprehensive factor makes available for customer and manufacturers all internal and external parameters beyond their immediate visibility.

3.3 Product and Process Development

The linkage of all information into production cycle allows manipulating models in a new way. The initial conceptual model will be upgraded into a high fidelity representation considering the best balance of issues and automatically optimized. Self-analytical functions of smart models will help models to understand their own behaviour and validate themselves automatically. Those models will be able to alert the user to problems and offer alternatives, even predict how a product will behave and react to external environment and events.

Accurate advisory tools will guide managers to reduce the time and the cost of moving from concept to production. Physical validation will be only required for specific validation like safety certification.

To achieve the vision, processes should be defined in detail with a comprehensive approach to link all related specifications, analysis and other pertinent information. Those modelling should be able to scale properties and behaviour from micro to macro levels to reflect the influence of real world factors.

In addition, automatically generated process plans capability should be provided by new tools. To be more accurate tools will model risk management, uncertainty to help managers. Methodologies and standards should also be developed to help future tools to replace physical tests by virtual testing methods, except for mandatory tests.

3.4 Manufacturing Execution

Future system will be built around systems plugged together to interact as a single process and provide models to plan, visualize, implement, monitor and control the execution. With an automatic adapting ability to real-time changes, it will increase the efficiency and responsiveness while reducing all form of waste with minimal human intervention.

In future manufacture all the information will be downloaded directly from the rich model-based and used to drive, control and monitor all manufacturing processes. Moreover, analytical applications will provide deep insight into process performance and enable fast response to problems. In addition, quality information will be as continuously available as production flows on an up-to-date basis. This unlocks proactive capabilities to perform just-in-time maintenance actions and verification at each stage of life cycle.

The capability for manufacturing control system to execute manufacturing plans derived from the product model should be provided. An intelligent process control should be developed to sense material properties and adapt parameters to assure the production of certifiably correct product.

Means to match feedbacks from physical processes and models will provide alerts and requests regarding the initial requirements. With a science-based process control model, it will be possible to integrate certifications and in the mean time eliminate the need for post-process inspections.

A milestone in future manufacturing execution is to provide an intelligent model able to self-organizing models and integrating all tools around to provide a logical representation of what is needed to satisfy all requirements. This intelligent model should also monitor execution and adapt to changes in initial requirements. The other milestone is to provide rapid reconfigurable production lines to quickly adapt to changing products and processes.

3.5 Life-Cycle Support

All the models produced will collaborate to support users and personals into a synthetic operational environment simulating real-world performance. The Enterprise Knowledge Base will capture the genealogy of the product and will provide all desired types and levels of details and also be able to flag potential problems for the attention.

The model-based process for life-cycle management will update permanently the history of any product. This is particularly relevant for long-life products because it enables engineers to look back to any point.

Future model-base monitoring of product will create a total visibility of performance. Embedded sensors will monitor the system and, by comparing prognostics and diagnostics, will adjust the model for optimum performance. This 'tracking system' will allow enterprises to act early in the life cycle, monitor feedbacks of customers for design issues and opportunities for improvement and also accurate identification and analysis of trends.

Customers usually receive only basic documentation on their product. A true model-based life cycle support will make all information about product available in digital form in ways that can be openly shared across the entire supply chain. Moreover, the maintenance staff will be able to use the master product model directly available on portable interface. Maintenance will be eased by the ability to call up the product on desktop and, combined with analytical tools, they will receive instruction to troubleshoot complex problem anywhere in the world in real time.

A model-based for training will provide the basic for all training activities and will also support specific needs. In fact, highly realistic virtual hands-on training will be available simply by clicking on the applicable piece.

The life cycle simulation using model-based processes will be highly improved by capturing and applying information directly from a traceable product. Indeed, the process to acquire and translate information from users' feedbacks will enrich the fidelity and depth of product life cycle as well as training simulations. Those training tools will be declined for all different kinds of product and readily adaptable for all types and level of users. By working closer with the prime manufacturer and vendor communities, sharing methods and product detail information (with appropriate protection of sensitive information) will dramatically improve the model-based life-cycle support.

4 STRATEGY

4.1 Enterprise Resource Management

The Resource Management (RM) is the process of integrating the activities of the enterprise to ensure that the right people and the right process have the right resource at the right time to fulfil their functions.

4.2 The Current State of Resource Management

Despite the wealth of financial modelling tools, most of them are not affordable for small manufacturers or do not justify the investments. In many cases, tools are not responsive to change and vital data is trapped in legacy systems. Changing model structure formulas is a manual process and indeed makes it problematic. Fortunately the upcoming generation of financial modelling tools is tackling these issues. However, poor ability to model the cost impact of technical decisions continues to be a significant problem in the defence and aerospace sector.

An excellent range of capabilities is available from commercial application, but the high cost of acquiring and implementing such applications makes them unaffordable for many manufacturers. Creation and updating of operations models requires a significant investment in time as well in training subject-matter expertise.

Managing suppliers has always been a key to business success and the supply chain is evolving as well. Modelling of supply chain is a well-developed capability – more than 495 software applications. Today, the major challenge is to integrate real-time data with tools to enable partners to access appropriate detail while protecting sensitive data of multiple suppliers who compete with each other.

The Internet gives companies 'storefronts' opened 24/7 capable to serve hundreds of customers simultaneously anywhere in the world. The pressure is migrating on distribution systems that should be prepared to deal with robust distribution planning and accurate analysis capabilities. The main barriers come from the cost, the complexity of tools and the difficulty to model uncertainties.

Modelling is routine in the workforce management area. Salary structures and job categories are well modelled but with limited flexibility. However, many workforce management decisions are based on business reality instead of modelled scenarios. The current trend towards flexible job assignments and short-term employment is not being handled gracefully by many organizations. Ability to model these issues is lagging today; added to an outsourcing decision, purely on the basis of near-term cost and profit factors, makes companies gambling with their future as long as inability to model the long-term impact remains.

Capital asset tracking models are mature and tools such as the Balance Scoreboard Method are widely used. There is a growing need for open, fully integrated solutions capable of examining asset performance and comparing it to performance models and drawing accurate conclusions from the disparate data.

Few efforts are made to document knowledge in reusable forms despite the tremendous emphasis on knowledge management. 3D CAD product models generated by designers are now being ported directly into training media, eliminating much of the cost and time of creating documentation. These tools enable to keep the knowledge that resides in the head of key personnel at all levels of the organization.

R&D funding for technology is highly subjective, few tools exists to model the technology investment process to support specific business decisions. In this area, modelling and simulation are used to explore concepts of products. Moreover, prime contractor relying their R&T on their supply chain to act as 'system integrators' and shift the innovative burden of development and risk to smaller companies.

4.3 Vision and Goals for Resource Management

A model-based architecture will help to manage all resources across all components of the manufacturing enterprise and will allow interconnectivity with systems of different enterprises.

Future decision makers will be able to quickly predict financial implications of all decisions. The systems and models will capture financial data with precise accuracy to provide continuous view on parameters and fine-tune financial strategies.

Operation functions will be supported by clear models and simulations in real-time control and scheduling, performance monitoring, maintenance and day-to-day problem solving.

The supply chain is already supported by the widespread of model-based and management tools. They will be able to support a highly dynamic and competitive market place. Modelling and simulation tools will enable future enterprises to manage their capital assets and inventories with extreme precision and efficiency. This will drastically reduce the need for maintaining excess capacity and inventory to meet requirements. Model-based system will revolutionize manufacturing enterprise productivity and effectiveness by drawing on totally interconnected information resources to ensure that the right knowledge is available as needed to the right people and process. Future planning and decision processes will apply tools to provide technology direction and visibility of emerging technologies with significant impact.

4.4 Strategic Management

There are five distinct elements within Strategic Management: the technology portfolio management; the financial and capital assets management; the knowledge management and applications; the strategic planning and execution; and the strategic operations management. The current state and vision of Strategic Management is that one of the biggest problems is achieving a strong and responsive corporate culture because most companies are managed from the top down and operated from the bottom up.

The technology portfolio is the technical know-how and the skills of its staff. Globalization pressures have forced companies to take hard look at their technological investments and strategies. In leading companies, cost/benefit modelling and return on investment analyses are mainstream tools for making technology investments. The qualitative human decision needs to be augmented by quantitative knowledge provided from within the company and through external data mining.

Road mapping is an increasingly popular and powerful tool for guiding technology evolution but are not sufficient to assure wise investment. Systems are needed to manage the technology maturation process. Concerning acquisition, protection or exploitation of technology, models are not strong enough to link sources of accurate data to allow executives to project the outcome. Individual decision remains based on intuition as much as hard numbers and the only real source of intellectual property is the human thought process.

A major challenge for every company is a lack of standards for financial information exchange and a lack of interoperability of financial management systems. Modelling tools provide a wealth of data but the access is restraint and do not provide a full understanding of all factors. Manufactures were originally designed for large-production and limited-change marketplace. The consequence is the limited agility to incorporate new technologies and processes. Future models will provide a greatly improved prognostic accuracy.

Knowledge management is a relatively new field. It is an inseparable component of a model-based enterprise – knowledge about customers and product technologies, product data trends, etc. Companies are starting to use competency modelling to create models that harvest the skill sets, values and behaviour of their top-performing employees. They turn knowledge into useable information. In the current state, strategic planning is mostly the purview of the executives. It may be dynamic if appropriately implemented but it is not a real-time process except when 'activated' to respond to a crisis.

A master enterprise model is specific to the enterprise. A model-based intelligent advisor will guide the management team through a 'strategic management cockpit' for achieving corporate objectives and responding to challenges and opportunities. A System Wide Information Management (SWIM) is a dynamic structure that learns from inside and outside the organization. It integrates the top floor with the bottom floor and in between. The cockpit will be tailor supported by the master enterprise model which will integrate knowledge and modelling tools into an open and modular way considering their proper needs and environment.

5 WAY FORWARD: MBE[6] PROJECT PLANNING

5.1 Information Delivery to Point of Use

The project aims to develop and demonstrate model-based technologies that deliver information to end user at the point of use, wherever that user might be. Graphical views of information, within flexible and affordable systems, will be provided for heads-up, hands-free operations. Model-based tools are used since many years and the human-system interface is getting critically important. To respond to the high degree of autonomy envisioned, systems need to provide

6. Model-Based Enterprise.

integrated model-based systems capable to very complex inputs, arbitrate conflicting data to accept and store valid information before acting.

The first challenge is the ability to deepen and extend those capabilities to all functions of the enterprise. A huge existing barrier is that much valuable information is contained in legacy system because there are not readily convertible to open digital formats or isolated in external companies. Critical challenge is also establishing model-based planning to determine how processes need to operate to accommodate human-machine interface and what information needs to be communicated and to whom. Once the problem tackled, it still exist a lack in data storage. In fact, facing the huge amount of data the storage capacity will be strategic assets to provide information across different industries. Moreover, connectivity between enterprises leads to a need of safety, security and durability especially in manufacturing or military environment.

5.2 Product-Driven Product and Process Design

The project will produce product model to automatically drive downstream applications. Collaborative interactions between product and process models require a highly skilled translation of information from 'product design' (what is to be made) to 'process design' (how it will be produced). Product processes are highly dependent with other functions. Despite the widespread of computer-aided design (CAD) tools, process models are created at high level to design flows or at detail level to help diagnostic and rarely use as a standard tool to optimize processes. The use is restricted to critical applications with a clear return on investment.

Material manufacturing process designs are currently not well integrated and virtual representations are not mathematically complete or precise enough. While electronic product data exchange is common, it often requires human intervention to ensure accuracy of results. Interoperability of simulation tools is sorely lacking, as well as standards and collaboration strategies at large scale across international supply chains to achieve to coordinate efforts as a whole.

5.3 Flexible Representation of Complex Models

The objective of the project is to develop the capability to create rich product model able to support all the steps of the product life cycle with flexibility and the power to provide quickly the exact visualization of the model.

Design and manufacturing are more and more computing-intensive activities. Models are used for visual depiction but the complexity of tools and the high costs required still stop a wider use. Moreover, the tools are not integrated with downstream production or associated functions even if 80% of the costs are generated in the first 20% of the development phase.

Three main challenges are addressed to the topic. Product model must be interoperable to support the input requirements of all the applications that interact with it to provide information automatically, without manual translation. To achieve this goal, Neutral-format product definition should be provided coupled with standardized 'plug-and-play' model-based applications.

Flexible representation of complex models implies the ability to generate all needed models from a 'master' product model. If the product model enables capturing and representation of all product attributes via a single interface, then custom views for specific users can be easily produced. The clear visibility needed can be supported by achieving multi-domain support interfacing with all enterprise functions.

5.4 Intelligent Models

Intelligent models will be able to understand, seek out, acquire and act on the information they need to execute their functions. The linkage between the physical modelling realm and the logical models that provide intelligence to product will radically improve the ability of manufacturers to manage their business processes.

Physical models provide an awareness of expected response but they lack of interoperability to interpret that response and to correct in an optimizing way. 'Self-learning' models will interface with all relevant functions and will monitor input data sources and update changes.

5.5 Configuration Management for the Model-Based Enterprise

The objective is to develop an integrated system that ensures association and traceability of the right information throughout its life cycle. Configuration management of processes includes documented definition and certification of manufacturing processes, maintaining an accurate baseline of maintenance, training and other processes and structure that support the product.

In a broader business context, management of configuration data is important especially without commercial tools available.

Future tools will be able to capture the total genealogy of a product into an enterprise-wide system and compare data collected with business environment inputs to avoid unpleasant surprises such as government regulation or new standardization.

5.6 System-of-Systems Modelling for the Model-Based Enterprise

The project will develop and demonstrate capabilities and tools for integrated multi-level, multi-system modelling of products, processes and life-cycle functions in a selected manufacturing sector.

'System of systems' in the military environment refers to the ability of weapons to work together as an integrated system in-theatre and on the battlefield to accomplish individual and collective objectives. In the non-defence world, the same approach is needed in sector where a vast array of products and technologies must work all together as a single complex system.

Much work must be accomplished to turn 'system of systems' from a principle into tools and application for manufacturing enterprises. Modelling and simulation is a critical enabler of the transformation with a specific effort to providing real-time integration of 'live' assets.

New capabilities will develop and demonstrate how complex models can be quickly assembled at multi-level through an open structure and 'plug-and-play' principles.

5.7 Enterprise-Wide Cost Modelling

Cost modelling is a mature discipline. The project will establish and manage a comprehensive approach providing highly precise total product cost models that reflect not only traditional materials and direct production costs but also time-discount design and other costs such as regulatory compliance costs, overhead burden. Those data will evolve into a dynamic environment continuously updated with accurate views.

Cost modelling is a tremendous challenge for economic competitiveness to eliminate waste, reduce uncertainties and other non-value-added costs. The current generation of tools is providing greatly improved abilities to model production costs. However, hard barriers remain on rapid response capabilities of tools to changes because data are disconnected to their underlying sources and make model accuracy problematic. Future financial models will be configured to be integrated with the rest of the enterprise to provide a continuous and clear view of performance.

5.8 Model-Based Distribution

The project will develop enabling technologies and conduct proof-of-principle demonstrations of models able to deal with complex distribution requirements within a generic framework. Tremendous pressure due to higher customer expectations is lying on manufacturers' distribution systems. These systems are very responsive, distribution modelling tools enable rapid re-planning considering system upsets or weather events.

Distribution is closely tied to inventory management due to the high cost of carrying products and materials. Consequently, distribution systems adopted just-in-time practices that minimize in-process inventory but need a complex organization.

Future model-based will deliver products using the most efficient means. Indeed, the ability to accurately model the ebb and flow of demand based on seasonal patterns will enable lean strategies and reduce inventory carrying while preserving the ability to quickly surge to meet upswings in demand. Those tools will analyse different distribution approaches to quickly respond to changes in the environment and will enable modelling of complex related financial factors such as duties, taxes, tariffs, etc.

The widespread use of RFID sensors and cellular communications will provide managers with a real-time visibility of assets anywhere in the distribution network. More efficient planning will be connected to marketing, sales, etc. to predict coming requirements, quickly evaluate pros and cons and implications in order to meet the day-to-day challenges.

6 CONCLUSION: MULTI-ENTERPRISE COLLABORATION

The project aims to provide an initial set of methods and standards required for seamless interaction process among supply chain members.

The widespread of models at every level of the supply chain coupled with technical and management tools enable future manufacturers of all size to manage efficiency all the complexity of designing, producing supplying within a highly dynamic marketplace.

Model-based processes will drive the evolution of agile supply chain to quickly identify and respond to opportunities and problems. This requirement needs to quickly evaluate the ability of a supplier to support prime demand singly or with other suppliers. To do so, shared repositories accessible by authorized users are compulsory and worth the optimization at the end of the process. The future challenges to tackle are to provide ways for partners to integrate their technical and business system instead of reengineering them to support specific requirements.

Chapter 22

SESAR: The Technological Arm of the Single European Sky

*Patrick Ky**

1 TECHNOLOGICAL CHALLENGES IN ATM

Technologies in Air Traffic Management (ATM) have always been a difficult subject. It is quite amazing to look at technological progress in comparable fields, such as Information and Communication Technologies, software science or automation and compare it with what the ATM industry has been able to come up with so far.

Indeed, where telecommunications for the general public have made tremendous progress in the last twenty years, communications in ATM are still relying exclusively on usage of VHF-radio, a technique which was invented in the 1930s.

Where Command and Control systems for the military, space, urban transport or banking industries have gradually evolved to merge, analyse and synthesize enormous amounts of data in order to allow human operators to take time-critical decisions, Air Traffic Controllers still perform their tasks on a manual mode.

A number of reasons have been given to try and explain this situation. The most common excuse for the lack of automation is that one cannot automate safety critical functions, which should be under the full control of a human operator. The degree of automation reached in other sectors, such as the defence industry, or even

---

* Patrick Ky, Executive Director, SESAR Joint Undertaking.

Daniel Calleja Crespo & Pablo Mendes de Leon, *Achieving the Single European Sky: Goals and Challenges*, pp. 239–244.

the aircraft cockpit, shows that this argument is largely rhetorical. We believe that difficulties in the introduction of new technologies are coming from the size of the market itself, which does not allow for a large amount of risk to be taken by industry to innovate. Thus, the number of ATM en route systems around the world can be counted in a few hundreds, with less than ten industry suppliers competing for the market. Moreover, the constant increase of air traffic worldwide has forced ATM operators to look for short-term solutions, implementable with minimal investment and risk. Hence, it is interesting to see that air traffic controller recruitments in Europe have been proportional to traffic increase for the last twenty years. Instead of investing in new technologies, Air Traffic Control operators have, all around the world, divided the airspace in smaller control sectors, in order to make sure that human operators would deal with manageable numbers of flights. ATM has also modelled the route structure in order to organize the traffic so that problems would be easier to locate and organize for controllers, and at the same time solutions would be easier to implement. In effect, this trend has further increased difficulties to automate and bring in new decision support tools, whilst it has also increased the complexity of air traffic controllers' work and the time they need to be trained on a given portion of the airspace.

We are now faced with a situation where dividing airspace further is not possible anymore: VHF frequencies become a scarce resource, and individual control sectors have reached a size which cannot be further diminished. Moreover, old technologies which have never been replaced start to become problematic: VHF radio, which is the only communication channel between controllers and pilots, has a very limited quality of service. We will soon look at interesting situations in which the passengers surf on the web and phone their office, whereas pilots have no other communication means than antiquated VHF radio!

ATM modernization has become inevitable. The next question is: 'how can we change something which has remained essentially the same for the last 20 years?'

2 THE INFANCY OF SESAR

Individual Air Navigation Service Providers have done the maximum of what they could do individually: they invested into new generations of information displays, into tools which helped organize traffic flows, into more precise radars and navigation aids. This was very good, it helped create a better working environment for controllers, but it did not solve the fundamental issue in air traffic control, which is the interconnection of the aircraft and ground systems. Without this, Air Traffic Control systems function in an open loop: a controller cannot be certain that his/her instructions are being followed until he gets evidence on his radar screen that the aircraft is effectively doing what it is supposed to do. And an open loop system is impossible to automate.

This means in particular that any attempt to seriously modernize ATM needs to start with the replacement of VHF radio by digital communications. The ATM community does not have the right tools to find rapid solutions on this topic: most of the decisions are taken on a unanimity basis; in particular in ICAO, this results in lengthy bureaucratic processes, which always aim for the greatest common denominator, which is rarely optimal. Moreover, the ATM community does not have the mechanisms to incentivize or enforce common standards; hence, the Aeronautical Telecommunication Network, the ICAO standard for digital telecommunications, was developed in the 1990s and is still not implemented to date. Market forces, which could substitute for difficult institutional decision making, are not sufficiently strong, given the size of the market (a few hundred systems, a dozen of industrial actors).

Boeing was the first company to try and propose solutions. They launched Boeing ATM in 2000, had an aggressive plan which would replace ATM systems by aircraft-centric, satellite-based technologics. Boeing's vision of the new ATM system was that of a global system: they established 'working together teams' in the USA, Europe, and Asia, in which they were gathering input from stakeholders in order to consolidate a unique, global ATM Concept.

European industry reacted in 2002 by creating the Air Traffic Alliance, a joint venture between Thales, EADS and Airbus, which would pursue similar goals. Boeing and the Air Traffic Alliance signed a cooperation agreement in 2003, through which they would work together on the subject of ATM modernization.

On the US side, with changes taking place in the White House, the Boeing initiative gradually lost political support and momentum, the Boeing ATM division being eventually dissolved to become part of Boeing's R&D branch (Phantom Works).

On the European side, the Air Traffic Alliance convinced Mrs de Palacio, European Commissioner for Transport and Energy, that her flagship initiative, the Single European Sky, needed to be accompanied by an ambitious technological deployment roadmap; DEPLOY, which became SESAME, which became SESAR, was born.

3 THE SESAR DEFINITION PHASE

Mrs de Palacio accepted to provide funding under the Trans-European Network scheme for a large industry effort to be conducted in order to define the ATM modernization roadmap. An agreement was reached with Eurocontrol, the European Air Navigation Safety Agency, in order to use the technical resources of Eurocontrol, in complement to a EUR 30 million contract that would be signed with an industry consortium which would provide the necessary expertise and leadership for the work. Eurocontrol organized a public call for tender, stipulating that the successful bidders would need to ensure appropriate buy-in from all relevant stakeholders. A proposal was submitted by the Air Traffic Alliance, leading a consortium of thirty-five companies, including Air Navigation Service Providers, Industry, Airlines, Military, etc.

The SESAR consortium delivered in 2008 the result of its work, the European ATM Master Plan, which was endorsed in 2009 by the EU ministers of Transport.

The Definition phase succeeded in bringing all actors together to decide in record time on technological choices which would have otherwise necessitated lengthy and possibly inconclusive discussions in ICAO or Eurocontrol. It is however fair to say that the definition phase, on the one hand benefited from the work performed in particular in Eurocontrol EATCHIP and ATM 2000 strategies; on the other hand, the Master Plan did not necessarily conclude on a number of subjects which were and remain contentious.

4 THE SESAR DEVELOPMENT PHASE

The next question was then 'what to do with the Master Plan?' Was the step made in the SESAR definition phase sufficient for the ATM community to actually start developing the technologies and tools to modernize the domain?

In the meantime, the Single European Sky legislation was adopted, the comitology procedures in place and first implementing rules were starting to be issued. Wouldn't the modernization be ensured through technical standards enforced by the Single European Sky?

In fact, the Commission realized that standards could only be promulgated on sufficiently mature technologies, and therefore that a substantial amount of Research and Development was needed in order to reach the right level of technological maturity.

Jacques Barrot, Commissioner for Transport, decided to launch the SESAR development phase, which would develop the tools, technologies, and operational procedures which would become standards that would be promulgated through the Single European Sky legislation.

M. Barrot decided to propose to the Institutions to set up a specific structure, using Article 171 of the European Union Treaty, following the example of Galileo: a 'joint undertaking' is a strange body, a private company in which majority shareholders are public (in the case of Galileo, it was the EC and the European Space Agency, in the case of SESAR, it is the EC and Eurocontrol), and minority shareholders are industry.

Whereas in Galileo, the Joint Undertaking ended up being a 'Public-Public' partnership, in which the industry never found incentives to participate, the SESAR Joint Undertaking is a true Public-Private partnership, in which the three pillars EC-Eurocontrol-Industry contribute equally 700 Million EUR each to the funding of the programme. Sealing this partnership revealed to be quite an interesting endeavour; indeed, out of the fifteen industry members who are SESAR partners, a good portion of them are actual fierce competitors on ATM markets worldwide. Nevertheless, under the guidance of Daniel Calleja, Chairman of the SESAR Administrative Board which was overseeing all the negotiations, a well-balanced agreement was reached between public and private players; under this agreement, the different work packages and projects composing the SESAR work programme are lead by one of the SESAR partners, and the foundations for true technical and operational cooperation were laid down, in particular facilitating the emergence of stakeholder groups coordination (A6, for instance, is the coordination group for all ANSPs in SESAR, I3 is the equivalent for ground manufacturing industry), and subsidiarity principles (there is no need to do the same work in all ANSPs, we just need two main lines of products in Europe, etc.).

An interesting institutional problem almost blocked the entire programme. Indeed, at the end of the negotiations, and before the formal signature of partnership agreements, the institutional partners had to formally consult their mandating authorities to get their endorsement. The European Commission therefore consulted the Single Sky Committee, using a comitology procedure as established in the SESAR Regulation. Eurocontrol consulted their Provisional Council. In this instance, some non-EU members of Eurocontrol refused to approve the results of negotiations; since Eurocontrol decisions of this type are taken on the basis of unanimity, the entire process was blocked. We were in a situation where all EU member states, which fund 90% of Eurocontrol's budget, a significant part of European industry, could not go forward on an EU programme because of one or two non-EU countries. Fortunately, diplomacy found a solution to the crisis and everything settled down, with about six months of delay.

This incident was certainly the most spectacular difficulty encountered so far in the development phase of SESAR, but there are a lot of obstacles on the way to success for SESAR; in particular, obstacles due to the sheer size of the programme: 300 projects, each one depending upon five others, around 2000 persons working on the programme (in 2011) in twenty-three countries make it one of the most complex programmes ever launched by the European Union. It is as much a question of cooperation as it is of technological development. After three years of life, the SESAR development programme is still on track and will deliver its first results in the course of 2011.

5 FROM DEVELOPMENT TO DEPLOYMENT

But the best technologies are useless if they are not actually implemented in operations. The next challenge that the European Commission will face soon is the deployment of products of the development phase. The Single Sky legislation will play a major role in setting the deadlines for installation of new SESAR standards on board aircraft or on the ground. These implementing rules, promulgated through a comitology regulatory procedure, will nevertheless provide the industry with time limits, which tend to create 'last mover's advantage': it is better to target the time limit rather than anticipate on the installation of such technologies, because, given the size of the market, the technical and financial risks of an early implementation are far higher.

On the other hand, the partnership and sense of common endeavour which was created in the Definition and Development phases created a momentum within the industry which should not be lost for the deployment. It is therefore important that the European Institutions find the right governance and management model for the SESAR deployment, finding again the right balance between preservation of public interest, increased efficiency, safety and environmental impact in the sector, and competitiveness for the European industry.

Indeed, ATM modernization is not only a European issue: the USA have launched their NEXTGEN programme, the Japanese CARATS, the Chinese NCAS, etc. Aviation is a global market, the first countries or industries who come up with the right standards for new ATM equipments are likely to transform them into global standards and therefore get a competitive advantage. SESAR is therefore not only necessary for the sustainable growth of aviation in Europe, it is also crucial for European industry to continue to play a leading role on the worldwide aeronautical and air transport scene. There is no choice other than success!

Chapter 23

The European Air Traffic Master Plan: The Path So Far and the Road to Take

Ilona Crommentuyn[*]

1 INTRODUCTION

In the process of harmonizing the aviation regime within the European Union, a wide range of legislation has been produced in Brussels to establish the Single European Sky (SES). The European aviation *acquis* will be developed along the lines of the principles of the internal market, including giving more responsibilities to the industry. Consequently, the decision-making process highly depends on consultation of the stakeholders in order to align the activities of all actors involved with the needs of an evolving market. In doing so, the European aviation programme intends to bring about the most overall performing aviation infrastructure within

* Ilona Crommentuyn employed as Corporate Legal Counsel Aviation at Amsterdam Airport Schiphol (Schiphol) and is involved in Single European Sky (SES) affairs since 2007. Ilona is member of the legal team to the SESAR European Airports Consortium (SEAC), SES Coordinator for Schiphol, and vice chair of the ACI-Europe SES Steering Group. Schiphol is via the SEAC partnership a member of the SESAR Joint Undertaking and as an airport a member of the SESAR Consortium. Special thanks are attributed to Yoeri Mochtar, formerly employed at Schiphol as a trainee with the legal department. Yoeri holds an LL.M. from the University of Amsterdam and an M.Sc. from the London School of Economics.

Daniel Calleja Crespo & Pablo Mendes de Leon, *Achieving the Single European Sky: Goals and Challenges*, pp. 245–252.

Europe and beyond. The common legislative framework regulates four main domains, which are performance, safety, airport integration, and technology. This article focuses on the latter. The technology pillar of the Single European Sky programme has come a long way since its first development and is worth paying attention in the scope of this book.

On the initiative of the Council of Ministers, a Joint Undertaking was established in 2007 and is mandated to ensure the modernization of the European air traffic management (ATM) system.[1] The Consortium, established through a collaborative, contractual agreement joining the forces and expertise from all relevant stakeholders, carries out the integrated, coordinated research and development activities. The regulation endorsing a European ATM Master Plan, adopted on 30 March 2009, constitutes the technological roadmap in the process towards reaching some crosscutting challenges for aviation in Europe, which include enabling growth (or tackling the capacity crunch), reducing environmental impact, improving safety, and stimulating cost-efficiency (also enhancing Europe's competitiveness).[2] The SES ATM Research, or SESAR, Master Plan is thus at the heart in defining, developing, and deploying new technology for an advanced, harmonized European aviation system. The SESAR Master plan captures the efforts of the European aviation stakeholders, including its founding partners, so far, and is an exquisite example of the high level development of aviation technology in Europe in the last decade. For that reason, this article describes the path that has been taken in Europe in order to create the SESAR ATM Master plan and what needs to be done to reach completion of this evolving document in the Single European Sky Programme. What is the road to take and who will take that road?

First of all it is the Commission who is the gatekeeper. The Commission, on a regular basis, provides the Council of Ministers and the European Parliament with reports on the progress of the SESAR Joint Undertaking is making.[3] Furthermore, the Commission monitors consistency with the ICAO Global Implementation Plan. In 2005, the Commission set specific targets for the common aviation programme to overcome the crosscutting challenges generally and Europe's capacity restraints specifically. The targets can be summarized as follows: a roughly threefold increase in capacity (compared to 2004 levels); an improvement of safety despite the ongoing growth of air traffic; a reduction of 10% per flight in environmental impact (compared to 2005 levels); and, halving the costs per flight (compared to 2004 levels).[4] In the light of the previous, this article therefore outlines to how the SESAR Master Plan accommodates the benchmarks set in Brussels. More specifically, as this article aims to give an overview of the existence and future of the

1. Council Regulation 219/2007 of 27 Feb. 2007 (and Council Regulation 1361/2008 of 16 Dec. 2008 subsequently), Council Regulation xxx/2007 of 8 Jun. 2007.
2. *Communication from the Commission to the Council and the European Parliament*, Air Traffic Management Master Plan, 14 Nov. 2008, 4–5.
3. Article 3 of Council Regulation 219/2007 of 27 Feb. 2007.
4. *Communication from the Commission to the Council and the European Parliament*, Air Traffic Management Master Plan, 14 Nov. 2008, 4. SESAR D5, SESAR Master Plan (DLM-0710-001-02-00), April 2008, para. 2.1.

SESAR Master Plan, it will (1) outline the Master Plan's position within the larger discourse of aviation integration; (2) examine the features as defined by the Master Plan; and (3) account for possible risks to the successful implementation of the Master Plan.

The results achieved in both the definition and development phase of the SESAR Master Plan by all stakeholders has proven so far to be consistent and durable. The year of 2011 is the challenge for SESAR. In 2011, the Single European Sky programme requires an effective SESAR deployment for its successful implementation.[5] SESAR requires a solid governance, that is coupled with sufficient funding and financing mechanisms and focused on ensuring performance. In 2011, SESAR starts delivering; the future is now.[6] In order to reach the future, let us review the past first.

2 SESAR AND EUROPE'S SINGLE SKY

The SESAR Master Plan, also known as 'deliverable five', was realized after a series of extensive studies on Europe's aviation regime since 2004 which uniquely took into account the input from a wide range of industry stakeholders, such as air navigation service providers (ANSPs), airport operators, the international supply industry, and the founding members of the Joint Undertaking, the Commission and EUROCONTROL. The results from that study are to be further validated and consolidated during the coming implementation phases, thus well before the stakeholders involved are required to undertake action accordingly. The deliberative decision-making process remains an integral part of the path towards further aviation integration in Europe.[7]

The study resulting in the Master Plan was also part of a wider range of industry explorations on the current air transport network (ATN), performance targets for the ATN, defining future ATM targets, and, developing best deployment scenarios.[8] Consequently, the Master Plan builds upon and is inextricably linked to other features constructing Europe's single sky. This means that the roadmaps of these so-called deliverables encompass the lifecycle between the feasibility and deployment, that takes into account the beneficiary, funding, and financial components.[9]

Furthermore, the SESAR Master Plan is divided into three categories: the High Level Overview, the Planning Area, and the Agreed and Committed Implementation Activities. The deliverable 5 study is considered as an expression of the High Level Overview, agreed by the SESAR Consortium's strategic guideline.

5. *SESAR Joint Undertaking*, From development to deployment speech by Mathew Baldwin, 9 Mar. 2011, 6.
6. *SESAR Joint Undertaking*, In 2011, we start delivering!, Patrick Ky at the SESAR Forum, March 2011, 2.
7. SESAR Master Plan D5 (2008), 6 (Preface).
8. D5 is to be followed by D6 (Work Programme for 2008–2013).
9. SESAR Master Plan D5 (2008), 7 (Executive Summary).

The working material that accompanies the High Level Overview serves as the Planning Area, which produces necessary research, development and implementation activities, again agreed upon by the stakeholders involved. The outcome of this process, delivering common implementation actions required to improve the European ATM network, is considered the third element of the Master Plan, the Agreed and Committed Implementation Activities.[10] The latter refers to the completed and renewed ECIP/LCIP.[11] The ECIP/LCIP mechanism is a powerful means for the European Aviation Community to harmonize implementation, establish common differences, increase visibility of plans of the different stakeholders and support the provision of a single repository of all ATM-related regional/local implementation data.[12]

The Master Plan consists of a comprehensive regulatory roadmap extending beyond national boundaries, thus linking all SESAR undertakings at a transnational level. Globalization, hence integration, is key. International aviation regimes will be increasingly embedded in process of industry harmonization.[13] SESAR is Europe's share in integrating global air traffic structures, yet Europe does not stand alone in the global ATM context. Interoperability is thus essential to ensure comprehensive international solutions that contribute at many different levels.[14] SESAR is therefore automatically connected to other ATM systems. For example, ICAO announced it is spending USD 120 billion over the next ten years to achieve more global integration, while subsequently it aims to set the framework for achieving worldwide interoperability.[15] During the Eleventh ICAO Air Navigation Conference, it approved the Global Air Navigation Plan and the Operational Concept.

In addition, the Air Navigation Conference of 2012 provides the opportunity to agree to so-called Aviation Global System Block Upgrades. Another step in the direction of integrated aviation regimes is the understanding that SESAR and the U.S. sponsored NextGen do not mutually exclude one another as these initiatives may deliver Global Aviation System Block Upgrades in the future.[16] SESAR needs to fit in. The future of aviation depends on the gradual harmonization of the world's airspace. In this context, Europe is taking a leading role by taking into account the interests of all stakeholders while progressing to an ever closer aviation regime. The SESAR Master Plan is an indispensable element of the broader Single European Sky programme which will need to, in order to reach global harmonization in aviation, link globally. So, what makes that the SESAR Master Plan is up to that?

---

10. SESAR Master Plan D5 (2008), 11.
11. ECIP means European Convergence and Implementation Plan. LCIP: Local Convergence and Implementation Plan.
12. ICAO Information Paper, Montreal September 2007, HLM-AFI-IP/2, 3.
13. *SESAR Joint Undertaking*, Global Interoperability Symposium March 2011, speech delivered by Nancy Graham of ICAO, 3.
14. *SESAR Joint Undertaking*, 'SESAR: bridging Europe with the world' speech by David Bowen, 9 Mar. 2011, 9.
15. Nancy Graham (2011), 3.
16. *Ibid.*, 3.

3 SOME KEY FEATURES OF THE SESAR MASTER PLAN

The SESAR Joint Undertaking is in charge of implementing the Master Plan.[17] The SESAR Consortium, which consists of representatives of all sectors in the aviation industry, co-financed by the European Commission and EUROCONTROL, executes the definition phase since it connects Europe's expertise in the field of ATM at large.[18] The Master Plan is at the heart of integrating performance improvements (including certain ATM target concepts, costs analysis, and the roadmap for the implementation of the operational improvements) into a coherent work programme.[19] In order the take the Master Plan from the 'definition phase' to the 'development phase' one must take into account the plan's evolving, or living, operational character and its projected contribution to reaching overall Single European Sky policy objectives.

Consequently, the key features of the SESAR Master Plan are inextricably linked to the regulatory domains of the common aviation framework.[20] The first feature is to move away from 'airspace' to 'trajectory' based operations, so that each aircraft achieves its preferred (a more direct) route and time of arrival. The second feature comprises collaborative planning. All actors involved in ATM, from departure to arrival at the gate, will plan their activities based on 'system based performance', also known as System Wide Information Management (or SWIM). The third aspect envisages dynamic airspace management through enhanced coordination between civil and military authorities. Fourthly, new technologies must provide more accurate airborne navigation and optimize spacing between aircraft to optimize airspace and airport capacity. New technologies will be embedded into a harmonized and interoperable technical architecture, while taking into consideration the needs of all European regions. In addition, a more central role for the human individual also means to develop more technically advanced equipment to work safely and without undue pressure.[21]

Furthermore, the SESAR Master Plan will also contribute to achieve Europe's societal goals in the context of aviation.[22] Firstly, it will enable a threefold increase in capacity which will also reduce delays, both on the ground and in the air; i.e. 73% increase in capacity from 2004. Secondly, it will improve the safety performance by a factor of ten, i.e. the total of ATM-induced accidents and serious or risk bearing incidents will not increase despite traffic growth. Thirdly, it will enable a 10% reduction in the effects flights have on the environment; i.e. a 10% reduction per flight in environmental impact compared to 2005. Fourth, and lastly, it will

17. Article 1(5) Council Regulation 219/2007 of 27 Feb. 2007 and Art. 9 of Council Resolution xxx of 9 Oct. 2008.
18. Air Traffic Management Master Plan (2008), 2.
19. *Ibid.*, 3.
20. *Ibid.*
21. *Ibid.*, x.
22. *Ibid.*, 4–5.

provide ATM services to the airspace users at a cost of at least 50% less; i.e. a 50% reduction in cost per flight compared to 2004 levels.

As a consequence of the aforementioned, it is the author's opinion that the SESAR Master Plan seems fit for the new role of the future: to make effective deployment of the Single European Sky programme possible and to link globally. Nevertheless, there are risks that need to be accounted for when it comes to the implementation of SESAR.

4 IMPLEMENTING SESAR, OVERCOMING POSSIBLE RISKS

The SESAR Master Plan is comprised of three separate but related 'implementation packages', each of which are made of two so-called 'service levels'. The deployment of the 'implementation packages' is linked to the existing European legal framework, i.e. implementing rules and specifications (such as Network Management and ETSI). Thus the regulatory roadmap must take into consideration the execution of the Master Plan. When implementing the Master Plan one must continuously assess operational risks. The Master Plan, however, provides such risk management mechanism through an early identification of the high level risks and associated mitigation risks.

During the writing of the SESAR Master Plan, the high level risks with respect to service delivery were indicated as follows:[23]

(1) the lack of homogeneity when deploying 'Implementation Package' 1 (IP1);[24]
(2) the lack of governance in the deployment phase leading to unsuccessful deployment of 'Implementation Packages' 2 and 3 (IP2 and IP3);[25]
(3) the lack of investment into SESAR by the key stakeholders;
(4) failure and/or delays to develop or validate the advanced technologies required to support the new ATM concept; and
(5) failure and/or delays to implement the SWIM.

Similarly, the high risks with respect to institutional and management issues are as follows:[26]

(1) the insufficient support from the regulatory framework to the deployment process;

---

23. *Ibid.*, 6.
24. IP1 (2008–2013) represents the foundation of the ATM Deployment Sequence on which the following IPs are built.
25. IP2 (2013–2020) will deliver a wider information-sharing environment, which aims at improving efficiency of the ATM network at large and implementing the ATM system in 2020.
    IP3 (2020 onwards) will address the activities necessary for further enhancing performance of the overall ATM system beyond 2020 (i.e., to fully realize the so-called ATM Target Concept).
26. Air Traffic Management Master Plan (2008), 7.

(2) the failure to manage human resources in time of changes; and
(3) the absence or late defragmentation on the European airspace.

Risks to the SESAR Master Plan may be defined as undesired events or a series of events, which reduce confidence in the Master Plan as such, thus representing a potential obstacle towards delivering 'target concept'. Risks are treated through mitigation action plans to reduce the likelihood of the event materializing, thus increasing confidence and encouraging decision making.[27] The process of capturing and analysing the risks exists of identifying, analysing, and treating the event.[28] In order to address and minimize the aforementioned risks it is necessary to accompany each update of the SESAR Master Plan with a review of the high priority risks and associated mitigation risks.

For example, the Commission attributed importance to a continuous review of IP1. For that reason a so-called IP1 Steering Group has been formed. This Steering Group (including a team of experts consisting of representatives of all stakeholders) reports to the Single Sky Committee, on the progress of IP1. The Steering Group identifies the relevant measures with regard to enhancing airside capacity methods and best practices (based on EUROCONTROL's capacity and efficiency implementation manual). This represents a key feature to mitigate IP1 deployment risks.[29]

The objective of the Master Plan is to meet the performance targets and to deliver the expected benefits to the ATM stakeholders. In order to achieve the anticipated results, seven requirements have been identified as critical for the successful implementation of the SESAR ATM Master Plan:[30]

(1) Establishing a common European legislative framework, although regulation should only be used where necessary in accordance with 'better regulation' principles to reach agreements and to support enforcement of commitments across the diversity of Member States and stakeholders interests.
(2) A performance driven approach, which means that the European-wide system for setting, agreeing, and maintaining performance targets will need to be developed within the regulatory framework as anticipated by the European Commission to reach the required improvements in safety, efficiency, capacity, environmental sustainability and cost-effectiveness. The whole approach needs to be supported by a comprehensive monitoring and reporting system.
(3) Clear ownership and endorsement of the SESAR Master Plan at all levels: political, regulatory and industry.
(4) Definition of clear governance and leadership structure for the deployment activities covering all phases is vital.

---

27. SESAR Master Plan D5 (2008), 90.
28. *Ibid.*, 91.
29. Single Sky Committee of 6–7 Apr. 2011, *SSC 11/41/15* (Agenda Item 10.1), 30 Mar. 2011, 1.
30. SESAR Master Plan D5 (2008), 102.

(5) The establishment of a single system design function. This function needs to be formed as referenced in SESAR Deliverable D1 for the design of the technical architecture of the future ATM system.
(6) To ensure interoperability of SESAR results at regional and global level, it is necessary to link the system design activities with the existing standardization processes including the military and the respective regulatory structures.
(7) It is up to the industry to balance costs and benefits.

As a result of the foregoing, it is the author's conclusion that the aforementioned seven requirements must be met, but may be difficult to meet, given its high standard character.

5 CONCLUSION: THE FUTURE IS NOW: WHAT ROAD TO TAKE?

The future is now. In 2011, SESAR will need to start to deliver and the global harmonization has taken its first steps, through, inter alia, the Memorandum of Understanding between Europe and the United States. 2011 is also the year for the deployment of the Single European Sky programme.

The SESAR Master Plan is, as explained, a critical factor for that. The SESAR Master Plan came into existence through joint efforts of public and private partnership in the 'definition phase' and that partnership has successfully executed the tasks set out in work packages, which resulted in the objectives set out in the SESAR Master Plan. At the time of writing, the SESAR Joint Undertaking consists of (associate) members from twenty-three countries, while there are 2,000 employees staffed on 300 projects, which all operate under the umbrella of the SESAR Master Plan. Collaborative decision-making remains the key feature of SESAR's operational structure.

The outlook for 2011–2012 is that the first projects will be delivered in 2011 and that the Master Plan will be updated accordingly, in order to accommodate the changing environment in aviation industry. SESAR will be implemented between 2011 and 2014. The change of the European ATM regime will lead to achieve railway precision in the sky, a network for ATM-data (SWIM), and operations in which human operators concentrate on high value-added tasks.

Again, the aforementioned is possible as long as the stakeholders (such as the ANSPs, airports, airliners, and other industry partners) continue to be included in the process of fundamentally changing aviation in Europe. If jointly committed, SESAR, along the lines of the Master Plan, can deliver results. If so, using the words of the Executive Director of the SESAR Joint Undertaking Patrick Ky, Europe's aviation industry will start delivering in 2011.[31] That is the road to take for the SESAR Masterplan, its creators and stakeholders: to remain a joint undertaking!

31. *SESAR Joint Undertaking*, Patrick Ky [executive director] at a SESAR Forum, March 2011, 3.

Chapter 24

The Unmanned Aerial Systems Enhancing Security

*Alfredo Roma**

1 INTRODUCTION

Since 1989 the Transport Ministers of the European Civil Aviation Conference (ECAC) decided on an Air Traffic Management (ATM) strategy for the 1990s in response to the air traffic crisis of the late 1980s. This strategy was taken forward under the guidance of the ECAC Directors General of Civil Aviation. In view of the expected doubling of air traffic over the subsequent fifteen years, the Ministers realized that without major new initiatives European ATM systems would not be able to keep up with the traffic.

The ATM Strategy for the years 2000 onwards, to cater for the forecast increase in European air traffic, was launched at the MATSE/6 meeting on 28 January 2000 in Brussels. It was suggested to plan and organize the European ATM on a pan-European basis in order to cope with the ever-increasing demand for its services, while respecting the States' prerogatives for the provision of air

---

* Prof. Alfredo Roma is member of the Advisory Council of the European Space Policy Institute (ESPI) of Vienna and consultant for the aerospace sector. He has been President of the Italian Civil Aviation Authority (ENAC), President of the European Civil Aviation Conference (ECAC) and National Coordinator for the Galileo GNSS Programme on the Cabinet of the Italian Prime Minister.

Daniel Calleja Crespo & Pablo Mendes de Leon, *Achieving the Single European Sky: Goals and Challenges*, pp. 253–263.

traffic services over their own territories and the requirements of sovereignty and defence.

In December 1999,[1] a High Level Group (HLG) was established by the Commission to investigate and report on the underlying issues. The HLG's recommendations were accepted by Member States of the EU and resulted in four legislative measures, which came into effect in April 2004.[2] The objectives of the initial project were to reform the architecture of European ATM, meet future capacity through the creation of Functional Airspace Blocks (FABs), and improve safety and security standards of the European air transport system.

In 2007, the Commission concluded that the desired results were not being realized fast enough and that further actions were needed. This led to the publication of a communication entitled 'Single Sky II – Towards a more sustainable and better performing aviation' which formed the basis of the Commission's SES II package. The Single European Sky (SES) II package consists of five main pillars: performance, safety, technology, airport capacity and the human factor. The SES II Regulation amending the four high-level SES regulations was published in the Official Journal of the EU on 14 November and came into force on 4 December 2009.[3]

Delivering the SES is of the utmost importance for the future of European aviation. The Iceland volcanic ash crisis and other events prove how fundamental and urgent it is to have a better-integrated EU airspace through the SES initiative. A key enabler for accelerating the full implementation of the SES is the deployment of new ATM technologies and procedures.

In 2009, the European ATM system controlled about 10 million flights. On some very busy days, more than 33,000 flights have been controlled. In 2020, the number of yearly controlled flights should reach 17 million, with peaks of about 50,000 flights per day. The current European ATM system is organized on the basis of more than 60 controlled sectors and brings together national networks of air routes without any European optimization. As a result, each flight is in average 50 km longer than needed, inducing needless fuel consumption, gas emission of about 5 million tons of CO_2 and an additional cost of one billion Euros per year. The total cost of the current fragmentation is estimated to be four billion Euros per year. This shows the urgency of realizing the SES programme.

Single European Sky ATM Research (SESAR) project is the European air traffic control infrastructure modernization programme, designed to realize the SES. It aims at developing the new generation air traffic management system capable of ensuring the safety and fluidity of the European air transport over the next twenty years.

The SESAR Programme is now in its development phase managed by the SESAR Joint Undertaking (SJU), the first ATM public-private partnership set up as an EU body. The SJU's mission is designed to ensure the modernization of the

1. COM (1999) – 614.
2. Regulations No. 549, 559, 551, 552/2004/EC
3. Regulations No. 1070/2009/EC and No. 1108/2009/EC

European ATM system by coordinating and concentrating all the relevant research and development efforts in the EU. The SJU will develop and validate the new generation of ATM technologies and procedures that will constitute the SES technologies and procedures. Its founding members are the EU and EUROCONTROL. It has fifteen industrial members and several other associated partners.

The SESAR Master Plan includes a chapter regarding the future integration of Unmanned Aerial System (UAS) in the civil airspace. EUROCONTROL is working on a two-stream programme for UAS airspace integration: the near-term objective is to enable UAS integration into today's ATM systems, but for the future there must be research into UAS capabilities that will enable the machines to integrate into the SES's advanced ATM systems beyond 2020 in the context of SESAR.

2 THE ROLE OF UAS IN THE REALIZATION OF SES AND THEIR MARKET

A key element that has been considered in the realization of SES is the role of the UAS. Actually, the definition of Unmanned Aerial Vehicle (UAV) or Unmanned Aerial System (UAS) is a misnomer as the aerial vehicle is not unmanned but rather remotely piloted. Accordingly, the International Civil Aviation Organization (ICAO) Circular No. 328 of October 2010[4] has proposed the more correct wording of Remotely Piloted Aircraft (RPA) or Remotely Piloted Aircraft System (RPAS) the latter comprising the air vehicle, data link system and the ground station that plays a vital role for the RPA control and communication with ATM or other entities ensuring a certain level of safety and security. These acronyms will be used in the following parts of this article.

RPAS range from extremely simple, short-range vehicles to multi-million dollar aircraft with almost global reach. Large airframes RPAS – sometimes equipped with jet engines – offer the possibility of complex missions, especially those related to civil protection or civil defence, requiring the RPAS to fly at medium or high altitude and in difficult meteorological conditions. Light RPAS normally fly at low altitude and for local or short-range missions. For both classes of RPAS, the mission depends on the payload and the ground station capacities to collect, process and disseminate data for the mission's purposes, RPAS piloting and the ATM information system. Simple RPAS generally carry little more than a video camera and sensors that send images and data over limited distances to a ground station that has limited links to other units. Larger RPAS can carry sophisticated types of camera and sensors, while signal intelligence systems (ELINT/COMINT) and ground-surveillance radars are also becoming common, those systems can be associated to RPAS missions. The ground stations are linked to a larger and faster network. In a near future the satellites will play a key role for the RPA

4. Circular 328 AN 190 – Unmanned Aircraft Systems (UAS) Unedited advance edition, subject to further official publication.

piloting and communications, and hence for their reliability. While in the military domain RPAS are already widely used under specific conditions and in segregated airspaces, RPAS developments for civil use are still in the early stages. However, recent studies confirm that a civil market with a growing number of potential civil applications is emerging. The idea of deploying RPAS for security purposes found a growing support among civil and military authorities.

Large RPAS are seen as useful for SAR (Search And Rescue), surveillance of large areas, for instance forests or fishing grounds and State borders also for prevent illegal immigration, geographic and geological survey, forest fire fighting, climate monitoring, protection of critical infrastructures and disaster recovery.

In Europe, the market for light RPAS under 150 kg already exists since local aviation authorities have regulated this sector in accordance with the provisions of Regulations 1592/2002/EC, 216/2008/EC and 1108/2009/EC.[5] The use of light RPAS is significant for civil security operations, in particular for supporting the fight against building fires, post fire investigations, nuclear power stations monitoring, motorway road traffic collision monitoring. RPAS greatly improve the pre-intervention situational awareness of the authorities, which can be of prime importance in case of dangerous environments like collapsed buildings caused by earthquakes, chemical clouds, floods, and so forth. Light RPAS are also widely used for the wildlife and nature observation whereas they reveal excellent capabilities in supporting the meteorological domain. Other applications concern atmospheric and climate research, land monitoring and ocean monitoring. Light RPAS are also capable to efficiently complement satellites, offering an excellent reactivity and a more permanent availability to the relevant authorities when ground infrastructures are out of use. In addition, light RPAS are easy to transport, relatively simple to deploy, easy to launch and recover and permit a high degree of controllability.

The vast number of applications of RPAS, which have partly been mentioned above show their role for enhancing security. The use of RPAS for security purposes has received high attention from many governments, especially the United States of America. In particular, the benefits of using RPAS in border surveillance by improving coverage along remote sections of the national borders have been stressed. Electro-Optical (EO) sensors (cameras) can identify an object the size of an iPad from an altitude of 60,000 feet. RPAS also can provide precise and real-time imagery to a ground control operator who would disseminate that information so that motivated decisions regarding the deployment of border patrol agents can be taken quickly. Additionally, an RPA used along the borders can

---

5. Regulation (EC) No. 1592/2002 of the European Parliament and of the Council of 15 Jul. 2002 on common rules in the field of civil aviation and establishing a European Aviation Safety Agency.

Regulation (EC) No. 216/2008 of the European Parliament and of the Council of 20 Feb. 2008 on common rules in the field of civil aviation and establishing a European Aviation Safety Agency, and repealing Council Directive 91/670/EC, Regulation (EC) No. 1592/2002 And Directive 2004/36/EC.

Regulation (EC) No. 1108/2009 of the European Parliament and of the Council of 21 Oct. 2009 amending Regulation (EC) No. 216/2008 in the field of aerodromes, air traffic management and air navigation services and repealing Directive 2006/23/EC.

fly for more than thirty hours without having to refuel, compared with a helicopter's average flight time of just over two hours. The capability of RPAS to fly for prolonged periods of time has important operational advantages over manned aircraft. Therefore, the range of RPAS is a significant asset when compared to border agents on patrol or stationery surveillance equipment. In addition, RPAS accidents do not risk the lives of pilots as do the helicopters.[6]

For many years Southern Europe has been facing the problem of illegal immigration. Recently this problem has become dramatic after the revolt against the authoritarian regimes in the North African countries. A proper use of RPAS could help to prevent shipwrecks, increase security and provide suitable means to face the problem posed by mass migrations.

Besides the uses mentioned above, we expect many other situations in which the deployment of RPAS could prevent damages to persons and properties. The monitoring of sensitive sites such as airports, ports, railways stations and energy power plants may prevent terrorist attacks, natural disasters or serious accidents in the air or on the sea.

3 THE EUROPEAN HIGH-LEVEL CONFERENCE ON RPAS

The European Commission (EC) and the European Defence Agency (EDA) co-organized on July 1, 2010 in Brussels a high-level conference dedicated to RPAS. Over 450 senior government officials and industry representatives attended the conference and discussed the potential of RPAS for European users, their economic, technological and industrial impact, as well as a common European way forward. Presentations by senior representatives of European stakeholders' group outlined the enormous advantages that RPAS could offer to the citizens for their security, the financial savings and environmental benefits through reduced fuel consumption as well as CO2 emissions. Some presentations focused on civil applications like civil protection, costal surveillance, fire fighting and flights in volcanic or nuclear clouds. Regarding civil defence, the dual use of RPAS was also outlined. The conclusions of the conference show the intention of the European Commission to form a HLG having the task to deliver in one year time a report for the integration of RPAS in the common airspace.

4 THE RPAS OPERATIONS WITHIN THE FUTURE EUROPEAN AIR TRAFFIC MANAGEMENT

SESAR brings a new dimension to the European ATM, which has a wide effect on all airspace users including RPAS. The SESAR Concept of Operations (CONOPS)

6. Cristofer Bolkom: Homeland security: Unmanned Aerial Vehicles and Border Surveillance. Report for Congress. Congress Research Service – Library of Congress – 28 Jun. 2004 – RS 21698.

for 2020 fully recognizes RPAS. It expects increasing numbers of RPAS starting with military missions and extending to many types of civilian tasks, with machines ranging from very light to heavy. The basic assumption is that, when an RPA enters non-segregated airspace, the provision of an Air Traffic Service (ATS) to the RPA must be transparent to Air Traffic Control (ATC) and other airspace users. For instance, controllers should not be expected to do anything different than they would do for other aircraft under their control, nor should they have to apply different rules or work to different criteria. An RPA should be able to comply with 4D Trajectory Management processes and/or ATC instructions and have equipment and capabilities applicable to the airspace within which they intend to operate. Conversely, it has been stressed many times that RPAS should not be penalized by stricter rules than those applied to manned aircraft.[7]

ATM procedures as well as technical and operational requirements need to be taken into account for the future integration of RPAS in a mixed traffic scenario where manned and unmanned aircraft will coexist in non-segregated airspace. The INOUI project[8] is a response to the challenge of integrating RPAS as new airspace users besides commercial aviation, business aviation, general aviation and military aviation into the future ATM system.

The operations of RPAS itself have to comply with the existing and future regulations and procedures of manned aviation as feasible. A general concept of RPAS integration is that RPAS shall pose no greater risk than manned aviation. Consequently, RPAS and their operations shall show equivalence to manned aircraft to the highest degree. RPAS are only accepted as another class of airspace user that, subject to conformance to appropriate regulations, are allowed to operate in non-segregated airspace.

The future ATM systems will evolve towards a more strategic trajectory based system, with increased levels of automation and integration, in both air and ground segments.[9] All the ATM actors will require exchanging information regarding any aspect of the operation. Special attention should be paid to the trajectory related information, that is, predicted trajectories and air to ground synchronization. The

7. See: Anna Masutti: Proposals for the Regulation of Unmanned Air Vehicle Use in Common Airspace, Air & Space Law 2009.
8. In alignment with the regulatory framework provided by EASA, EUROCONTROL and others, INOUI defines an operational concept, proposes operational procedures and assess the technologies to support them in order to facilitate the integration of the UAS in the airspace and airport paradigm foreseen by 2020 and beyond. The overall objective of INOUI is to assess different domains of the ATM system of today and 2020 to develop proposals for UAS integration into the operational concept for the future. This activity will complement the activities of the SESAR definition phase, filling the gaps with regard to the particularities of UAS. The project is related to the Research Domain 4.g 'Innovative Air Traffic Management Research' of the FP6-2005-AERO-4, Research Area 'Open Upstream Research'.
9. The SESAR project is bases on two basic concepts: the trajectory and the flying object. Trajectory is information contained in the Flight Object regarding the flight intent from gate-to-gate. Flight Object is a concept to support the flight data interoperability between all stakeholders. Its purpose is to ensure that all systems have a consistent view of the flight shared information, and that data is widely and easily available, subject to appropriate access controls.

future system of exchange of information is contained in the System Wide Information Management (SWIM) project. SWIM represents a key element of SESAR. SWIM will assure a more efficient planning and flight execution using the concept of 'flight trajectory', increasing the efficiency of air transport and its safety standards, improving the environment. SWIM is part of the first regulatory roadmap related to European ATM Master Plan, implementing rules, defining roles and responsibilities, licensing aspects, security issues, liabilities and ownership.[10]

RPAS will need to have the same interoperability capabilities of manned aircraft and future airborne systems, in order to allow a seamless integration into the future ATM system designed by SESAR, including the SWIM information system.

5 THE EXISTING LEGAL FRAMEWORK

The ICAO Convention in its Article 8, first sentence, establishes that 'no aircraft may be flown without a pilot', that is without a pilot onboard 'over the territory of a contracting State without special authorization by that State and in accordance with the terms of such authorization'. ICAO has also established that RPAS must meet at least the same level of safety and operational standards as manned aircraft. Thus, RPAS operations must be as safe as manned aircraft insofar as they must not present or create a greater hazard to persons, property, vehicles or vessels, whilst in the air or on the ground, than that attributable to the operations of manned aircraft. The equivalent risk objective is that RPAS operations shall not increase the risk to other airspace users or third parties. Any detrimental change in aviation safety or levels of risk would be contrary to the prime objective of civil aviation authorities. The ICAO Global Aviation Safety Plan (GASP), introduced with Resolution A33-16, should be applicable to RPAS operations.

However, the potentiality of RPAS cannot be proven until they are allowed to fly in the segregated area only and if appropriate legislation and regulatory measures are not established and come into force. Necessity to have quickly a full set of common European rules on RPAS airworthiness and integration of RPAS within the non-segregated airspace has become an urgent matter. Lack of this regulation framework prevents the industry to build pertinent business plans and to launch the developments required to answer civil customer's needs. In addition, it should be considered that the major European industries but also the SME have already invested consistent capital in this sector. It is time they start receiving a reasonable return on investment through a sales perspective.

10. SWIM is developing aeronautical information management architecture with an Internet approach for the distribution of air traffic management data. It will manage surveillance, weather and flight data, as well as aeronautical and airspace status information, and will provide it securely and seamlessly to airspace users and managers. When fully implemented, it will dramatically improve the capabilities of existing systems, the air transport safety, reduce capital and operating costs, improve productivity and offer flexible network system expansion.

The European legislation has divided the RPAS in two major groups, which is each regulated by different authorities:

(i) RPAS with a maximum take-off mass of more than 150 kg; these systems are regulated by the European Aviation Safety Agency (EASA);
(ii) RPAS with a maximum take-off mass of less than 150 kg commonly designated as light RPAS whose regulation is left to the national civil aviation authorities.[11]

The separation of RPAS according to their weight derives from a correct interpretation of rules established by the above-mentioned Regulations 1592/2002/EC, 216/2008/EC and 1108/2009/EC. Article 3 of Regulation 216/08 appears to be broad enough to include RPAS.[12]

For instance, the United Kingdom developed a set of rules governing the operation of military and civil aircraft. A civil aircraft registered in the United Kingdom, which is exempted from the EASA Regulation, must have a certificate of airworthiness and a permit to fly issued by the UK civil aviation authority, pursuant to the terms of Air Navigation Order of 2000.[13] The CAA has published guidance regarding airworthiness and the requirements for small RPAS in CAP 722 since 2001. CAP 722 divides RPAS in four categories: below 7 kg, more than 7 to 20 kg, more than 20 to 150 kg, more than 150 kg.

Such a distinction, based on the weight of RPAS, has raised a vast debate on its pros and cons. For example, it has been argued that leaving the regulation of light RPAS to the national CAAs it would create a number of regulatory frameworks that do not necessarily match.[14] Another objection concerns the fact that an accident caused by an RPA of 145 kg or 155 kg could generate very similar damages, while different regulations would be applicable to the two very similar RPAS. It would be much more sensible to distinguish the RPAS with respect to their kinetic energy (KE). That is why, in August 2009 EASA has published a 'policy' providing guidance to industry on the application for airworthiness certification of their respective RPAS products. Said policy is based on the principle that the risk for third parties on the ground is broadly proportional to the KE of the aircraft at the moment when it will hit the surface. In turn the KE is proportional to the mass of the RPA and to the square power of its speed. Other aviation authorities in the world, for instance the FAA in the USA, Transport Canada and the Australian CAA, share the principle of airworthiness risk driven by KE.

RPAS weighting more than 150 kg can fly in segregated airspace only, as no EU regulation exists to allow them to fly in the civil airspace. The above-mentioned Regulations 1592/2002, 216/2008 and 1108/2009/EC establish that EASA is responsible for the certification of RPAS weighing more than 150 kg.

---

11. See note 3 here above.
12. See Anna Masutti *ibid.*
13. See for instance Arts 87 and 129; see also: the Rules of the Air Regulations of 1996.
14. Pablo Mendes de Leon: European Regulation for UAS below 150 kg. ESPI – Vienna, November 2010.

Safety is represented for manned aircraft by a consolidated system of rules regarding design, manufacture, maintenance and operation of aircraft, ATM/ANS procedures, systems and services, personnel licensing, and aerodrome operations. Within these rules is the concept of a global safety level made of target numbers expressed in terms of acceptable probabilities for accident: these rules have to be applied to RPAS on the basis of the equivalence principle.

In creating the criteria for the certification of RPAS, some basic principles should be taken into consideration. First of all, as mentioned above, RPAS should not be penalized with more requirements than those for manned aircraft. The principle of impartiality or fairness should also be applied to avoid creating regulations exclusively tailored to RPAS. Therefore, RPAS must also comply with the regulations in force for manned aircraft and applied by ATC servicc providers.

Similarly, the principle of equivalence, that is equivalent risk and equivalent operation should be applied. It refers to the need to maintain a safety standard at least equivalent to the one required for manned aircraft; RPAS should not have to comply with higher standards even if they are technologically possible.

Finally, a civil liability system should be designed for damages caused to persons or property deriving from RPAS use as a result of accidents. This requires a number of issues to be resolved, such as the identification of the applicable law(s) and of the liable party.[15]

6 TECHNOLOGIES ENHANCING SAFETY OF RPAS

In order to ensure the same level of safety of manned aircraft, a key role can be played by technologies permitting RPAS to detect, sense, and avoid other aircraft; addressing communications and physical security vulnerabilities; improving RPAS reliability; and improving human factors considerations in RPAS design.

Some existing technologies can already enable an aircraft to avoid collisions with other flying objects. Here is a brief description of some equipment:

- Airborne Collision Avoidance System (ACAS), an airborne safety net, whose purpose is to avoid mid-air collisions. ACAS detects and displays nearby transponder equipped traffic and, when necessary, computes appropriate manoeuvres either to be avoided or to be manually followed by the pilot flying.
- Traffic Collision Avoidance System (TCAS II) is a technical implementation of ACAS.
- Airborne Separation Assistance System (ASAS), whose purpose is to assist the flight crew in ensuring separation from other aircraft. ASAS, in addition to present TCAS logic, shall permit the exchange of trajectories and resolution proposals between aircraft and ATC or directly between conflicting aircraft.
- Automatic Dependent Surveillance – Broadcast (ADS-B), which allows pilots to 'see' other aircraft, as position and other aircraft parameters, such

15. See Anna Masutti, *ibid.*

> as speed, heading, altitude and trajectory are simultaneously broadcast to other ADS-B capable aircraft and to ATC. ADS-B is now based on the GPS signal whose availability is not guaranteed by the US military authority. ADS-B will become an excellent collision avoidance system when operating with the European Global Navigation Satellite System Galileo.
>
> Regarding telecommunications, RPAS need a dedicated spectrum of frequencies free from interferences, jamming or spoofing ensuring continuity and integrity for their seamless operations.

There is no doubt that RPAS technology has reached a high level of sophistication and reliability. However, Research and Development continue through programmes such as MIDCAS,[16]) which will hopefully permit RPAS to fully comply with the ICAO requirement to offer equivalent safety standard of manned aircraft, without compromising existing aviation safety levels or increasing risk to third parties in the air. In the last two decades, automation solutions for manned aircraft have more and more reduced the pilot workload and interventions, even in emergency situations, increasing safety standard. Hence, the manned aircraft increasingly operate like remotely piloted aircraft.

We conclude that the safety standards of manned and unmanned aircraft are now very close. However, technologies like 'Sense & Avoid' equipments for RPAS are developing and improving, while new TLC satellite systems may offer a high degree of reliability, continuity and integrity for ensuring a safe remote piloting and telecommunications.

7 CONCLUSIONS

The purpose of the recent ICAO Circular 328 AN 190 of October 2010 is to apprise States of the emerging ICAO perspective on the integration of RPAS into non-segregated airspace and at aerodromes. The Circular recognizes the important and potential of RPAS for civil use, especially for security applications. However, it states that:

> Current UA are unable to integrate safely and seamlessly with other airspace users, the basis for which is twofold – the inability to comply with critical rules of the air, and the lack of SARPs[17] specific to UA and their supporting systems.

16. The MIDCAS (Mid-Air Collision Avoidance System) project is directly related to Unmanned Air Systems Air Traffic Insertion. One of the main issues that need to be solved is the requirement for traffic separation and mid-air collision avoidance in non-segregated air space, also related to as 'Sense and Avoid'. Sense & Avoid (S&A) is defined as the process of determining the presence of potential mid-air collision threats and manoeuvring clear of them. Participants to the project are: European Defence Agency, France, Germany, Italy, Spain and Sweden.
17. SARP – Standards and Recommended Practices are developed by ICAO and cover all technical and operational aspects of international civil aviation, such as safety, personnel licensing, operation of aircraft, aerodromes, air traffic services, accident investigation and the environment.

This last sentence appears to be excessively prudent as today's technology already permits these capabilities. The real problem is the lack of a regulatory framework, including, *inter alia*, airworthiness certificate, licensing and a civil liability system. However, it follows from this circular that also ICAO is determined to design a regulatory framework permitting the RPAS to fly in the common airspace.

In Europe there are many initiatives under way. EASA published the Advanced Notice of Proposed Amendment (ANPA) in 2005, followed by its Comment Response Document (CRD) on 6 December 2007. The main findings are now explained in sufficient detail in a 'policy document' published in 2009 and discussed with stakeholders, including EUROCAE WG-73. The objectives of this 'policy' are to facilitate RPAS applications and to ensure a level of safety/environmental protection at least equivalent to comparable manned aircraft.

Besides INOUI, described here above, JARUS is a project developed by some European National Authorities under leadership of The Netherlands and EASA regarding operational and technical regulations for RPAS. EUROCAE WG 73 is developing a requirements framework that would enable unmanned aircraft to operate within the constraints of the existing ATM environment in airspace without segregation from other airspace users.

The EU is, therefore, in the position to take the lead of this project supporting the study for designing a regulatory framework able to accommodate the RPAS in the common airspace. This will develop the market of RPAS for civil use and their applications enhancing security.

PART V

THE HUMAN FACTOR

Chapter 25

The Human Factor in the Single European Sky

*François Ballestero**

1 INTRODUCTION

The European Transport Workers' Federation (ETF) has always assessed the role of the human factor in Air Traffic Management (ATM) as critical. If only one reason had to be put forward to justify this insistence, the interdependence between air safety and human performance would be this overriding argument.

The reliance of air safety on human performance has always been a major concern in the industry. However, not until the 1970s had this issue been analysed in an innovative way which has enabled significant progress to be made. The Tenerife airport accident (1977) is very often quoted as the triggering factor that led to increasing research and development in this area.

In the last three decades, ATM has made huge steps in technical innovation, automation, developing new systems and procedures to improve the capacity and flight efficiency in order to accommodate the users' requests. The ATM industry is now in a process to accelerate this automation. The Single European Sky ATM Research (SESAR) program, which is the technological pillar of Single European Sky (SES), is contributing to this acceleration, but even with enhanced technology, human performance remains a key contributor to air safety and, moreover, the

* François Ballestero, European Transport Workers' Federation.

Daniel Calleja Crespo & Pablo Mendes de Leon, *Achieving the Single European Sky: Goals and Challenges*, pp. 267–280.

human factor is seen as essential for the development of the air traffic control future tools.

The ETF is proud to have been the organization which advocated the development of a fifth pillar dedicated to the human factor when the SES II legislation was being discussed. In the end, the European Commission understood the value of our request and arguments and took it on board with a Commission statement annexed to the legislation.[1]

The ETF is also delighted to have been the co-organizer with EUROCONTROL of a conference dedicated to safety and human performance in ATM.[2] With an audience of some 180 participants, this conference held in early February 2010 was a real success. The momentum and the conclusions of the conference need to be pursued.[3]

Since its creation in the ATM sector, the ETF has also been with the employers' organization, Civil Air Navigation Services Organisation CANSO the promoter of the European Social Dialogue which is an essential component of a good human performance. A lot of meetings and conferences, and notably some dedicated to 'Just Culture', have shown the way towards employers-employees joint initiatives in the human factor area.

The ETF contribution which follows this introduction articulates a number of items which show how and why the fifth pillar is relevant for implementation of the SES legislation, also for meeting ATM objectives and above all for air safety. Many ETF colleagues who are ATM professionals (ATCOs and ATSEPs) have contributed to this text.

2 FABs: COOPERATION IS THE KEYWORD

2.1 The Introduction of FABs

The FAB concept is a key component of the SES initiative. It has been introduced by the European Commission to overcome the natural fragmentation of service provision and seeks to disregard the geographical boundaries that define current arrangements. Having foreseen the importance of FAB implementation and the possible structural consequences it could have on Air Navigation Service Providers (ANSPs), and therefore the resultant social consequences on their staff, the ETF has been highly involved in the debate, trying to promote solutions that are able to improve the system whilst respecting the social interests of ATM workers.

The ETF has strongly advocated the bottom-up approach as the only realistic means to establish FABs. It is the only one that permits an efficient consultation process with all stakeholders including social partners. On the contrary, if a top-

1. Council of the European Union Single Sky Package 25 Mar. 2009, Brussels.
2. EUROCONTROL & ETF Joint Conference: Safety and Human Performance, 2–3 Feb. 2010.
3. EUROCONTROL & ETF Safety and Human Performance: Conclusion and Actions, 2–3 Feb. 2010.

down approach is adopted, it will be much more difficult to achieve an efficient consultation process. The two SES legislative packages, in 2004 and 2009, confirmed the bottom-up approach as the appropriate way to implement FABs; for the ETF this is a success.[4]

Some stakeholders see FABs as a vehicle to promote consolidation of service provision with important industrial consequences like closure of ACCs, disappearance of current ANSPs, privatization and competition on support services and so forth. The ETF does not accept this strategy. *First*, because of the social consequences: if FABs lead to social dumping and reductions in the number of jobs, FAB developments will not be supported by staff whereas there will be legitimate and strong reactions from the national trade unions to protect the interests of their members, withdrawing support to SES. *Second*, because the ultimate goal of FABs, as clearly expressed in the SES legislation, is to enhance the level of service provision in terms of safety, capacity, costs and environmental impact. It is not the objective to implement forced consolidation of service provision within FABs.

This illustrates why the ETF tried to feed the debate around FABs with concrete proposals taking into account not only the improvement of the service but also the social dimension. The Palermo conference, jointly organized in October 2004 by the ETF and CANSO,[5] was a beginning of a fruitful piece of work within the framework of the European ATM Social Dialogue, to achieve a better understanding of the social partners on FABs. The Palermo conference principles[6] are still used as references for consultation processes at European, FAB and national level.

2.2 ETF Vision on FABs: Co-op Model

The major contribution of the ETF to the establishment of FABs is the Co-op Model, published in 2008.[7] This document gathers all the political principles supported by ETF members for FAB establishment. Therefore, the Co-op Model promotes cooperation between ANSPs instead of competition or consolidation of service provision and outlines the public service role of air navigation services. It also advocates the need for a proper social dialogue process in each FAB project. It gives proactive guidelines for the implementation of cooperation on specific and important issues such as governance, National Supervisory Authorities (NSAs), central functions and technical developments.

The ETF members used the content of the Co-op Model to influence the debate in their own FABs in different countries. For instance, in FABEC, the ETF national unions have produced a definition of the Co-op Model applied to FABEC (Co-op

4. See Annex.
5. Joint CANSO-ETF Conference, Functional Airspace Blocks (Palermo 2004).
6. Joint CANSO-ETF Conference, Functional Airspace Blocks; Joint Statement from the Palermo Conference (Palermo 2004).
7. ETF–ATM Committee Co Op Model <www.etf-atm.org/co-op-model-for-fabs.html> (2011).

Model for FABEC). Their proposals were taken into account as a real alternate scenario to consolidation of services and were supported by the majority of the ATM workers of the six countries involved. The Co-op Model for FABEC proposes the creation of a governance structure. This structure should be public, should have its own legal entity and should be based on two levels: one for the States involved (Council of States) to take strategic decisions, to deal with the sovereignty aspects, to draft FAB performance plans and to organize the supervisory activity. A second level of governance should also be set up at ANSP level to organize the cooperation on service provision and to deal with the central functions of the FAB such as flow management, AIM, training etc. This two-level governance structure, with a decision-making process based on consensus between stakeholders, is a way to implement an integrated airspace for cooperation.

The Co-op Model for FABEC also makes specific proposals for social dialogue implementation. The ETF believes that sufficient access should be granted to national trade unions to a FAB Social Dialogue body.

A clear distinction has to be made between the social dialogue at FAB level and the national social dialogue. For the ETF, FAB Social Dialogue has to be used as a tool to pave the way for national negotiations, as each FAB decision, that could have social consequences, has to be first endorsed by the national trade unions. The civil aviation world agrees that the involvement of workers is a key element for FABs implementation. However, six years after the first SES regulations have been published, the majority of FABs still have problems with the social dialogue implementation at FAB level.

The ETF policy on FABs relies on the capacity to make concrete proposals to influence the process in a positive way, not only on being able to provide positive effects on users and on ANSPs, but also on the capacity to defend the workers' interest. The ETF philosophy on FAB is not to act in place of its national members but to provide guidance and support when requested.

3 SESAR: STAFF INVOLVEMENT KEY TO SUCCESS

3.1 Objectives

The SESAR program reflecting the technical pillar of SES II aims for the replacement of the current ATM infrastructure throughout Europe, with a new system that will be able to cope with the huge increase of air traffic, foreseen for the next decades.

With the introduction of the newest industrial technologies as well as by the implementation of rational and new procedures, and by applying a common all-over well- coordinated approach too, EU Member States want to provide a more efficient, more punctual, truly ecological and much safer Air Traffic Service, carried out within the geographical dimensions defined, for the upcoming mid-term future.

The SESAR project had been divided in three phases: the definition phase, the development phase and the deployment phase.[8]

3.2 Definition Phase: ETF Achievements

The ETF decided to invest and engage in SESAR from the early beginning, at a time when the program was still called SESAME, back in 2004. The principles of staff involvement and its importance were not yet clearly understood by all the stakeholders involved.

Therefore, the ETF showed a strong determination in order to bring proactive guidelines into the entire SESAR project. Our organization put all its professional efforts and free capacities into the project, getting its experts (ATCOs, ATSEP, FDAs and AIS-Staff) directly involved in different relevant working packages, such as human factors, social factors, training, concept of operations and system architecture.

Despite the fact that many external and internal organizational constraints occurred during that period, the ETF successfully contributed by achieving a lot of important results, especially in the fields of the social, human and system domains.

In the European ATM Master Plan, produced at the end of the definition phase (2006-2008), it has been clearly stated:[9]

(1) The staff involvement in the wide-spread European projects as a key of success, particularly if adequate participation had been granted from the early stages of the various project life cycles.

(2) The necessity to address all human factor aspects, keeping always the human element in the loop, especially referred to a future fully automated where operators will have to face up an increased traffic capacity in a very complex environment. The human flexibility will remain one of the last 'tools' able to manage contingencies, degraded modes of operation and non-nominal situations for instance, bad weather conditions, failure of equipment, priority and emergency situations, accidents, terror attacks.

Hundreds of technical issues raised by the ETF concerning the Concepts of Operations (CONOPs) feasibility are still open. The development phase is the right stage to reassess them within the real environment.

---

8. See Ch. 22 of this book.
9. SESAR Consortium, SESAR master plan D5, <www.sesarju.eu/sites/default/files/documents/reports/DLM-0710-001-02-00-D5.pdf> (2008).

3.3 Social Dialogue in SESAR

The definition phase also identified the need for a broad and comprehensive linkage to the social partners as a risk reduction measure:

- to ensure proper attention to and linkage of social issues arising from the SJU activities;
- to identify and promote best practices/guidelines on social issues and change management through the developmental and implementation stages;
- to disseminate and review SJU output from a social factor point of view;
- to stimulate communication of the social aspects within the European Aviation Community.

The establishment of a long-term, reliable and stable partnership to enable negotiations to take place in an atmosphere of trust is important, for:

- exchanging views and searching for common ground;
- adopting joint positions in text and where appropriate preparing proposals for consideration and where agreed, prepare proposals for legislation;
- cooperating on the social issues of any structural change within the social dialogue.

One of the main goals for the ETF participation in the SESAR implementation is to address and secure the social consequences of SESAR, along with SES II and the numerous FABs throughout Europe.

3.4 Development Phase, ETF Achievements

The ETF, understanding the tremendous impact of SESAR towards fundamental global changes in ATM, set up its action plan for the development phase in different levels:

(1) Technical contribution: organizing a bigger group of experts, that is thirty workers among ATCOs, ATSEPs, Meteorological and Flight Data Operators, involving also ground handling operators and pilots in the various SESAR Projects. Performing 'Validation and Verification' activities as kind of an 'International Validation Team';
(2) ETF coordination: three coordinators for SESAR, to plan the work of the thirty experts and creating a direct link with the ETF Steering Committee;
(3) Social dialogue contribution: building a political strategy to address all SESAR social consequences, sharing points of view with the employers and making joint declarations, agreements, guidelines and so forth.
(4) Governance: within the SESAR-JU Administration Board.[10]

---

10. SESAR Board meeting, ADB (M) 016, 14. Dec. 2010, < www.sesarju.eu/sites/default/files/documents/adb/ADBM016.pdf> (2011).

To keep these domains separated ensures avoidance of any conflicts of interests of the ETF experts within the technical working packages improving their credibility in the eyes of all stakeholders.

4 THE PERFORMANCE SCHEME AND ITS SOCIAL IMPLICATIONS

A correct consultation process involving all relevant stakeholders gains better commitment of all actors to the targets of the SES II Regulation. Consultation was considered as a key enabler for success in establishing a SES. Very sensitive core issues, such as the Performance Regulation,[11] require deep involvement and full commitment of directly affected groups like ANSP staff. The ETF is committed to the objectives of performance improvement, promoting the bottom-up approach and a good consultation of staff representatives.

Increased time pressure has led to a poor preparation of the mainly written consultation process. Insufficient time for this process and the lack of adequate consultation bodies led to frustration amongst staff and staff representatives, and finally to low commitment of this group.

The establishment of a staff consultation body called the 'Expert Group on Social Aspects'[12] came too late to contribute to relevant decisions like the performance scheme, charging regulation[13] and the European target setting.[14] Therefore, reasonable concerns and constructive remarks were not taken on board during the drafting phase of these decisions. As a result, the endorsement of the European performance targets had to be postponed several times before their final adoption in the Single Sky Committee.

Operational and social concerns raised by the ETF were not taken into account. Consequently, the above set of regulations has negative social implications throughout Europe. During the target setting process, the ETF has continuously warned that the existing socio-economic differences throughout Europe make the setting of uniform performance targets an unfeasible approach, and this remains our opinion. The ETF is concerned about the unbalanced trade-offs in favour of cost reductions to the disadvantage of safety, the environment and capacity. This is the result of over-ambitious performance targets creating extreme cost pressures on ANSPs.

---

11. Commission Regulation (EU) 691/2010 of 29 Jul. 2010 laying down a performance scheme for air navigation services and network functions and amending Regulation (EC) No. 2096/2005 laying down common requirements for the provision of air navigation services, OJ of the European Union L201/1 of 3 Aug. 2010.
12. European Commission, Decision 2010/9016/EU of 20 Dec. 2010 on the establishment of the consultative expert group on the social dimension of the Single European Sky.
13. Commission Regulation (EC) 1794/2006 of 6 Dec. 2006 laying down a common charging scheme for air navigation services, OJ of the European Union L341/3 of 7 Dec. 2006.
14. European Commission Decision 2011/121/EU of 21 Feb. 2011 setting the European Union-wide performance targets and alert thresholds for the provision of air navigation services for the years 2012 to 2014, OJ of the EU L48/16 of 23 Feb. 2011.

As a consequence, many providers have launched different kinds of cost-cutting measures. Both the cost-reduction approach and the impossibility of convergence of the ANSPs' labour costs can result in social tensions. Due to the fact that around 70% of the costs of ANSPs are labour costs, the staff is strongly and directly affected by these measures. Recent developments supported by various examples show severe negative social implications on ANS employees. Cuts in training, language proficiency and safety budgets compromise safety and labour standards. Early retirement has been shown to be an effective tool for reducing staff costs. Reduction of resources invested in pension schemes will have a contrary effect in the long term perspective.

The ETF and its affiliates have observed collective agreements being terminated ex parte. We see attempts to cut pension schemes or cancel negotiations concerning their creation. We are facing requests to re-negotiate collective agreements, reduce salaries and reduce investments in employees' health and recreation programs as well as reductions of budgets for personnel development.

Discussions about the flexible deployment of staff, called 'mobility', have just been started. The ETF is urging that the social costs of such models shall be considered adequately in a cost analysis. The ETF is strongly concerned about the tendency of outsourcing labour. This will lead to a downward spiral of falling salaries, a downgrade of social standards, reduced quality and flexibility of service and finally risks the European ANS reliability and stability.

The ETF has collected evidence that the over-emphasis on the Cost Key Performance Area[15] is leading to strong negative social implications. Disproportionate reductions of staff numbers or inability to attract new workforce may lead to unsustainable business and a destabilized service provision of ANS.

Central European Air Traffic Services (CEATS), a FAB prototype launched before the SES, failed because it promoted consolidation, closure of facilities, mergers of ANSPs and put the highest emphasis on cutting costs. The political impediments, a lack of consultation with all stakeholders, unknown social consequences and costs of industrial disputes which were not considered in any CBA lead CEATS on the washout way. The lack of the support of the staff and the associated social action has been recognized as one of the main reasons for the decline of the project.

5 JUST CULTURE

5.1 FRAMEWORK

Up until today there is not yet a single and universally recognized definition of Just Culture. We can describe it as an atmosphere having as first objective the safety improvement through a no-blame approach that will increase the number of

15. EUROCONTROL, SES II Performance Scheme: Proposed EU-Wide Performance Targets for the Period 2012–2014 (EUROCONTROL Brussels 2010).

reports, discovering the hidden failures of the system. Just Culture is a warranty for safety, citizens and workers.

Making culture means to spread the value of proactive and preventive safety of Just Culture which, through the increase of reports, helps to analyse the inoffensive and occasional mistake finding the appropriate standard to avoid catastrophic accidents. We can state that Just Culture is based on the communication of occurrences by operators who are not prosecuted if their actions, omissions or decisions taken are not a consequence of painful behaviour or gross mistake. An efficient reporting system must be created.

The approach to errors and occurrences can happen in two fundamentally different ways: focus on the individual or focus on the system. In the first case we talk of a blame approach and in the second case of a functional approach.

The ETF considers that the functional approach has better results for the safety of the air industry. Indeed, its aims are to understand the reason behind the error asking two main questions: How and why did the system defence fail? What can we do to drastically reduce the repeat of the same errors?

Just Culture in one word – Prevention! It is a parachute of the whole system.

5.2 Legislative and Cultural Obstacles

European Regulations and Directives[16] contain a list of occurrences for which a report is mandatory or voluntary. A fundamental element is the protection of the operator who is not required to disclose his/her name in order to increase reports.

Reality is different. In many EU countries there is no legal protection for operators reporting occurrences. Moreover, the high specialization of these jobs for instance, Medic, ATCOs and Pilot represents a hurdle in many EU States in law courts for the full acknowledgement of competencies, responsibilities and risks. In these cases the blaming attitude aligned with the above-mentioned individual approach has a strong role.

Just Culture is also a cultural issue based on trust, perceived commitment on safety and relationships. A good atmosphere of trust among management and front-line operators will increase the flow of safety reports. On the other side, blaming or punishing those who choose to share their own mistakes causes a fearful atmosphere restraining occurrence reports. Trust can only be achieved through a continuous dialogue among staff and management to understand the mutual problems and positions.

To avoid misunderstandings we wish to be clear that Just Culture does not mean impunity. It shall not protect individuals acting wilfully or with gross negligence. But in all the other situations caused by a human being, taking into account that error is part of the human nature, or by wrong procedure, the criminal investigation, the prosecution and the imposition of sanctions will not prevent the

16. Council Directive 94/56/EC of 21 Nov. 1994 establishing the fundamental principles governing the investigation of civil aviation accidents and incidents, OJ of the EU L 319/14 of 12 Dec. 1994.

repetition of errors but will have negative consequences on the reporting, functional analysis, necessary to improve the whole system.

A blaming approach has strongly negative effect on safety.

5.3 Social Dialogue WG on Just Culture: Charter and Guidelines

In 2004 the ATM Social Partners, the ETF and CANSO established the Just Culture Working Group (WG) in the EU Social Dialogue framework, to create guidelines to support and accelerate the implementation of the Just Culture principles in Europe. In October 2006 the WG extended its activity to the civil aviation sector involving other Civil Aviation stakeholders such as ACI (Airports Council International), AEA (Association of European Airlines), ERA (European Regions Airlines) and ECA (European Cockpit Association).

The WG adopted a 'Charter'[17] to spread among public opinion and authorities leading a political scope, and 'Guidelines'[18] with concrete steps and proposals to implement Just Culture in any company.

The ETF played a very significant role in leading the discussion on both documents. Disciplinary action should be contemplated only in case of reckless action, or omission to take action, in a wilful and intentional way that is not in keeping with training, responsibilities and experience. Management should take favourable account of the fact that a member of staff has complied with his/her responsibilities to cooperate and to report the circumstances of the incident. All managers should understand that they can directly affect the attitudes of staff towards both the company and safety. Neglecting this fact can lead to an environment where wilful acts of misconduct occur. Managers and staff have a joint responsibility to discuss areas where there are barriers to improve the incident reports. These very important topics contained in the 'Guidelines' were and are the first steps towards a modern, new concept of efficient and effective system, based on proactivity, tolerance and a non-punitive attitude.

The process is still long. The ETF will continue to push to reach its ambitious objective to improve safety through a real safety culture that supports Just Culture and promotes incident reporting. It is hoped that Europe will be able to demonstrate the strength of its history and civilization.

6 ATSEP, THE COMPETENCY PILLAR

The ETF defends and promotes the ATM staff part of the safety chain. And since the origins of the SES, the ETF advocated that the safety and efficiency of ATM relies on the competence of ATM professionals, ATCO, ATSEP, or FDA.

---

17. Charter for just culture in Aviation: European Civil Aviation Social Partners Charter for Continuous Improvement in Aviation Safety. 31 Mar. 2009.
18. Company Guidelines on Just Culture, 31 Mar. 2009.

The Air Traffic Safety Electronics Personnel (ATSEP) are the ATM professionals in charge of ATM and CNS safety-critical systems. Their role is to install, maintain and manage those legacy and future systems which allow their ATCO colleagues to freely and safely manage the sky. The SESAR definition phase recognized their key role, and the impact of new technologies, like SWIM, 4D FDPS (Flight Data Processing Systems), DataLink, which will drive important competence challenges.

6.1 From Licensing to Competency

The ETF with IFATSEA – the ATSEP's international professional association – claimed and promoted a licensing scheme for ATSEP for SES I. The outcome was an impact assessment at the request of the European Parliament. Although deferring the need of a formal licensing scheme, it recognized the need of a common training and competence scheme for ATSEP, on the ground of safety and SESAR future challenges.

Within the ATM Social Dialogue framework,[19] the social partners, the ETF and CANSO jointly with the Commission agreed to put forward an ATSEP Training Scheme and produce, through a mandate to EUROCONTROL, new competence requirement regulations. A comprehensive EUROCONTROL Task Force, the ATM Technical Staff Task Force,[20] worked for two years and produced an ATSEP Common Core Content Initial Training manual. This remarkable effort marked also the first active involvement of ETF experts in a EUROCONTROL drafting group.

6.2 Enter EASA

With the extension of EASA scope to ATM, the Commission, under its 5th pillar initiative, mandated EASA to draft ATSEP competence regulations.[21] Again, the ETF was able to demonstrate its expertise and involvement[22] to help EASA create a dedicated ATSEP Working Group and draft an ATSEP Implementing Rule which will provide a consistent training and competence scheme for European ANSPs.[23] Noteworthy, in parallel, ICAO is drafting similar competence and scoping materials for ATSEPs.

---

19. Observatoire social européen (2010) fiches sur le dialoque social sectorel Européen. Projet coordonné par Christophe Degryse.
20. EUROCONTROL Specification for air traffic safety Electronics Personnel Common core content initial training (ed 1) (EUROCONTROL Brussels 2009).
21. European Aviation Safety Agency, terms of reference, AM.001(a) & (b).2010.
22. Calleja D. letter commission: Air Traffic Management Regulation in EASA. 16 Jun. 2010.
23. EUROCONTROL Specification for Air Traffic Safety Electronics Personnel Common Care Content Initial Training (ed. 1), (EUROCONTROL Brussels 2009).

6.3 Conclusion

The ETF commitment and expertise has led to ATSEP recognition. The Competency Regulation under development is also a success of the ATM Social Dialogue which overcame many difficulties and conflicting positions to come together eventually on the 5th pillar and human performance principles. This undertaking also highlighted the need to coordinate the different bodies and organizations, principally EU, SJU, EUROCONTROL, Social Partners and EASA, helped to pave the way for the next increments of the 5th pillar.

7 SOCIAL DIALOGUE AND CONSULTATION ON THE IMPLEMENTATION OF THE SES

For years the ETF has been involved in the Air Traffic Management Social Dialogue (ATM SD) together with CANSO. This structure has employed a variety of tools, agreements, statements, joint projects, pursuant to which appropriate joint recommendations have been made to the European institutions and to the social partners' national members and defined priorities included in their work programs.

For the ETF, this ATM SD must contribute to and promote growth, quality jobs, social Europe and sustainable ATM policies. The ETF sees these work programs as means of further reinforcing the social partners' autonomy. Nevertheless for the ETF, the legislative approach and the negotiating approach are complementary; both are needed in order to develop social rights. For this, it is necessary that the European ATM policies integrate the social dimension inside of the legislation.

The ETF is aware that the development of European Social Dialogue presupposes strong involvement of European and national employers and trade unions' representatives. In this respect, the ETF highlights the crucial importance of social dialogue in building trust and good faith between trade unions and employers and in finding balanced solutions to social questions.

During the process of adoption of the Single European Sky Package II, the ETF considered that the ATM Social Dialogue should enter into a new phase, one that will improve the capacity of social dialogue to negotiate and to be officially consulted by the Commission on its policies regarding the implementation of the SES. For the ETF, it was a way to seek a more active involvement of the social partners through a mature practice of dialogue in the spirit of a win-win approach. The ETF wishes to impose a qualitative leap forward in sectoral social dialogue throughout Europe, notably in ensuring a better inter-relation of the latter with social dialogue at European, FAB and national levels in Europe.

The ETF had strived for the adequate official consultation of the ATM Social Dialogue by the European Commission on all matters and proposals linked with the social implications of the SES. Thanks to its pressure, the Commission decided to set up a 'SES Social Aspects Expert Group' with the aim to advise the Commission with respect to the implementation and development of the single European sky regarding all measures having significant social implications.[24]

A new era is beginning. It is up to the social partners together with the Commission to put in place the right mechanisms that give a good future for the ATM industry and for the ATM employees. This is only possible if SD and consultation becomes a reality at all levels, including at the FAB level.

8 CONCLUSION

FABs, SESAR, performance schemes and Just Culture are important aspects which show how the SES implementation may be impacted positively or negatively depending on the integration or the non-integration of the 5th pillar as a guiding principle.

Cooperation is the way forward. We cannot accept a European ATM market based only on business targets, cost reductions and competition. In a moment of crisis, it is important to understand and support the efficiency of the sector, in order to help the recovery of the global economy. But the first ATM target has to remain safety without any trade-off. And safety is a cost, a cost requesting investments, time, involvement and will.

Early staff involvement has a key role in the SES implementation. FABs, SESAR, Just Culture and licensing cannot be implemented without the involvement of the trade unions representing the staff. Employees will have to deal with all the SES novelty; only with their commitment, support and acceptance SES may become a real success.

Keeping the human being in the core of the system will guarantee the required flexibility to comply with the passenger's requests. New tools will improve the system performance supporting ATCOs to manage the increase of traffic and workload. But human beings are the only assets able to manage and react to, for instance contingencies, degraded modes, terror attacks and emergencies, that will continue to be part of the European air transport sector.

Other SES items may have been evoked. Actually all the implementation areas of SES are concerned. The human factor is never absent: either considered as a simple economic parameter which can be modulated for a desired economic output, or being integrated as an asset to be developed for the common ATM goal which is enhancing safety and gaining efficiency; giving priority to the one or to the other makes a huge difference to the output.

As mentioned above, an efficient social dialogue is the pivotal tool in this respect. Quite obviously it has to be effective at each relevant level: national, regional (FAB) and European and it requires time and resources but, in the end, it delivers an optimized output far less expensive and less time consuming.

The SES is planning for the future. All the ETF affiliates also turn their eyes to the future. Together, they want to make the ATM industry safer, they strive to bring

24. See *supra* note 12.

more capacity to the users, they care for the environment, and they do not forget that resources have to be optimized.

Let us give workers the opportunity to be actors of their industry future!

François Ballestero, Riccardo Rubini, Olivier Joffrin, Norbert Payr, Jean-Pierre Etienne, Janos Lakatos, Frédéric Liorzou, Rudolf Fisher, Lucio Antoniani and Luigi D'iddio (and *Andy Mooney* for the English language).

Chapter 26

Just Culture

*Marc Baumgartner**, *Martin Chalk*** *and Jez Pidgen****

1 DEFINING THE CONCEPT

The political goals of Single European Sky do outline the need to improve safety by a factor of 10. This is one of the biggest challenges in the complex socio-technical environment like aviation. In order to push safety further, while increasing capacity and reducing delays at the same time, a greater set of data than that is available today is required. Some of the barriers identified, which make gathering of data difficult nowadays, mention the fact that the reporting culture can only follow the principle of open or 'just' culture reporting. Therefore, the Just Culture approach becomes an essential element to improve the current European and global aviation system.[1] Moving towards a more automated system, with a multitude of sub-systems composing a high complexity/high reliability or high risk system, there is a need to have a Just Culture approach. Thankfully, the accident rate is very low in aviation compared to the distance travelled per passenger. On the other hand, with this low accident rate, aviation will not learn enough from accidents and will

* Marc Baumgartner, former President of the International Federation of Air Traffic Controllers Associations (IFATCA).

** Martin Chalk, Former President of the European Cockpit Association – ECA.

*** Jez Pidgen, Chairman of the Professional and Legal Committee of IFATCA.

1. European Commission, Flightpath 2050, 16, March 2011.

Daniel Calleja Crespo & Pablo Mendes de Leon, *Achieving the Single European Sky: Goals and Challenges*, pp. 281–297.

therefore need to learn more from incidents. In order to make the operators report the incidents without fear of judicial actions (unwanted outcome of the actions), there is an absolute need to have a 'Just Culture' approach.

A Just Culture supports learning from unsafe acts. Any event related to safety, especially human or organizational error, must be first considered as a valuable opportunity to improve operations through experience, feedback and lessons learnt.

The commonly agreed definition is:

> 'Just Culture' means a culture in which front line operators or others are not punished for actions, omissions or decisions taken by them that are commensurate with their experience and training, but where gross negligence, wilful violations and destructive acts are not tolerated.[2]

When talking about Just Culture, many efforts have to be carried out to explain that it is not a 'cheque blanc' for the human operator, but that it is part of the essentials with regard to improve safety of a complex socio-technical system. As Schubert (2004)[3] highlights, there are legal barriers to improve the safety culture in aviation and that one of the possible ways to remove these barriers is the introduction of Just Culture on a conceptual basis. These barriers have to be defined and explained by the aviation community to the judicial world. As Van Dam (2009)[4] outlines, the concept of Just Culture has become better understood and accepted by aviation personnel.

However, the need for a 'Just Culture' is generally not understood and reconciled with the judicial system and legislators and the situation is likely to get worse if adequate measures are not taken. The removal of identified obstacles against the establishment of a Just Culture in ANS does not necessarily require the creation of additional regulations at international/regional level, but should concentrate firstly on appropriate implementation actions at domestic levels. Research shows why Just Culture is an essential or basic requirement for the future of the Safety Culture which becomes a must if the political goals of SES (ten-fold increase in safety) should be achieved. The IFATCA's[5] professional and legal committee has proposed a structured review of this literature and introduces the notion of guidance material.

2 DEFINING LEGITIMATE AND ILLEGITIMATE BEHAVIOUR[6]

2.1 Types of Behaviour

Reducing incidents in Air Traffic Control and other high risk organizations is both desirable and feasible, while eliminating them is desirable but not feasible:

2. European Commission, Regulation 691/2010 Art. 2 k) and IFATCA policy IFATCA manual 4.4.A-1.
3. F. Schubert, Legal barriers to safety culture in aviation, 2004.
4. Van Dam Roderick, Preserving Safety in Aviation : 'Just Culture' and the Administration of Justice in Air and Space Law vol. 22, number 2, 2009.
5. IFATCA Professional and Legal Committee, Just Culture; Guidance for MAs conference Paper, 2011.
6. This chapter uses a common law approach; in states where Roman law applies, negligence is defined differently.

> No system can completely avoid errors. Any discussion of reliability must start with that as axiomatic.[7]

Just Culture does not equate to a lack of accountability. A no-accountability culture is neither feasible nor desirable; wilful violations, gross negligence or reckless/destructive acts are not acceptable within ATC.

In order to correctly apply Just Culture, it is important to be able to determine what constitutes 'gross negligence, wilful violations and destructive acts'. By defining what is legitimate and illegitimate behaviour one can start to determine the degree of culpability.

A good starting point in determining what type of behaviour has occurred is the four types of behaviour identified by David Marx which might result in unsafe acts. It should be stressed that not all of these behaviours necessarily warrant disciplinary sanction. The section explaining about the behaviour explores this issue further:

> *Human error* – an inadvertent action; inadvertently doing other than what should have been done; slips, lapse mistake.
>
> *Negligent conduct* (or at-risk behaviour) – behavioural choice that increases risk where risk is not recognized or is mistakenly believed to be justified. This will be examined further in section 'Construction of Risk'.
>
> *Reckless conduct (or gross negligence)* – behavioural choice to consciously disregard a substantial and unjustifiable risk.
>
> *Intentional 'wilful' violations* – when a person knew or foresaw the result of the action, but went ahead and did it anyway.[8]

Identifying the difference between negligence and gross negligence is quite straight forward. To be grossly negligent, the risk has to be one that would have been obvious to a reasonable person. In both civil and criminal liability contexts it involves a person taking a conscious unjustified risk, knowing that there is a risk that harm would probably result from the conduct, and foreseeing the harm, they nevertheless took the risk.

Negligence can be defined as:

> Conduct that falls below the standard required as normal in the community. It applies to a person who fails to use the reasonable level of skill expected by a person engaged in that particular activity, whether by omitting to do something a prudent and reasonable person would do in the circumstances, or by doing something that no prudent or reasonable person would have done in the circumstances. To raise a question of negligence, there needs to be a duty of care, and harm must be caused by the negligent action. In other words,

7. Karl Weick, *Organizational Culture as a Source of High Reliability (California Management Review)* (University of California Press, 1987).
8. David Marx, *Patient Safety and the Just Culture: A Primer for Health Care Executives* (Columbia University, 2001).

> where there is a duty to exercise care, reasonable care must be taken to avoid acts or omissions which can reasonably be foreseen to be likely to cause harm to persons or property. If, as a result of a failure to act in this reasonably skilled way, harm/ injury/ damage is caused to a person/ property, the person whose action caused the harm is negligent.[9]

Gross negligence differs from negligence. Where negligence is the failure to recognize a risk that should have been recognized, and gross negligence is a *conscious* disregard of an obvious risk, and *knowing that harm would probably result*. Gross negligence is more culpable than negligence.

Determining what constitutes negligence is a more complex issue. Although there would appear to be a clear explanation, a closer look at this definition actually just shows how complicated the issue is, and how difficult it can be to clearly define what negligent behaviour is.

Examining the definition leads to the following questions:

> *What is 'normal'* versus *'negligence' in a community?*
>
> Or, what is a *'reasonable level of skill'* versus *'recklessness' in a particular activity?*

Unfortunately, the answers to such questions are infinitely negotiable. Furthermore, if the person asking this question has little or no expertise in the area, there is more chance of an unfair or inappropriate response.

Various tools have been developed to help answer the question of culpability. One of those is the so-called Decision Tree, as described by James Reason in the Culpability Decision-Tree (see Appendix A). When using this tool, the assumption is that the actions under scrutiny have contributed to an accident or to a serious incident. There are likely to be a number of different unsafe acts that contributed to the accident or incident. Reason believes that the Decision Tree should be applied separately to each of them.[10]

The Decision Tree is used to examine individual unsafe acts committed by either a single person or by different people at various points of the event sequence. The tree is a simple flow chart, starting from the top left segment *Were the actions intended,* and includes five distinct stages:

(1) *Intended act*: The first question in the Decision Tree relates to intention if both actions and consequences were intended, then it is possibly criminal behaviour (such as sabotage or malevolent damage).
(2) Under the influence of alcohol or drugs known to impair performance at the time that the error was committed. A distinction is made between substance abuse with and without 'reasonable purpose' (or mitigation).
(3) Deliberate violation of the rules and did the system promote the violation or discourage the violation; had the behaviour become automatic or part of

9. Sidney Dekker, *Just Culture: Balancing Safety and Accountability* (Ashgate, 2007).
10. James Reason, *Managing the Risk of Organizational Accidents* (Ashgate Publishing Limited, 1997).

the 'local working practices'. This will be examined more closely later in this chapter.

(4) *Substitution test*: Could a different person have made the same error under similar circumstances (determined by their peers).
(5) *Repetitive errors*: The final question asks whether the person has committed unsafe acts in the past. This does not necessarily presume culpability, but it may imply that additional training or counselling is required.

However, Decision Trees are also open to individual interpretation; for example the question:

> *'Were there deficiencies in training or selection?'* – Who decides what is deficient?
>
> James Reason refers to the substitution test put forward by Neil Johnston in the Decision Tree:
>
> > If the unsafe acts of a person are implicated in an incident then the following test should be applied. Substitute the individual concerned for someone else coming from the same area of work and having comparable experience and qualifications. Then ask the question: 'In the light of how events unfolded and were perceived by those involved in real time, is it likely that this new individual would have behaved any differently?' If the answer is 'probably not' then apportioning blame has no material role to play.

He adds that this test can be expanded upon by asking the individual's peers:

> Given the circumstances that prevailed at the time, could you be sure that you would not have committed the same or similar type of unsafe act?' If the answer again is 'probably not', then blame is inappropriate.[11]

3 THE INFLUENCE OF OUTCOME

The outcome of an event will alter the degree to which people feel there is a need for accountability:

> If the outcome of a mistake is really bad, we are actually more likely to see that mistake as more culpable than if the outcome is positive.[12]

Two similar errors may result in two different outcomes. If the outcome from the error is severe, that is, an accident, this will negatively influence how the behaviour that led up to it is viewed. The more severe the outcome, the more likely it is that mistakes are seen, and more things are discovered which people have to be accountable for. Conversely if the same error occurred, but there was no resultant incident, the call for accountability will be significantly less.

---

11. *Ibid.*
12. Dekker, *supra* n. 9.

Just Culture, however, should not be about matching consequences with outcome. With knowledge of outcome, it becomes almost impossible to go back and understand the decisions and actions made by somebody who did not yet have that knowledge of outcome.

4 THE INFLUENCE OF HINDSIGHT

4.1 Definition of Hindsight

People's judgment of human behaviour can become significantly affected by the effects of hindsight:

> There is almost no human action or decision that cannot be made to look flawed and less sensible in the misleading light of hindsight.[13]

Sidney Dekker describes the dangers of hindsight when examining an incident:

> Hindsight means that we oversimplify causality (this led to that) because we can start from the outcome and reason backwards to presumed or 'plausible' causes.
>
> Over estimate the likelihood of the outcome (and people's ability to foresee it), because we already have the outcome in our hands.
>
> Over rate the role of rule or procedure 'violations'. While there is always a gap between guidance and actual practice (and this almost never leads to trouble), that gap takes on causal significance once we have a bad outcome to look at and reason back from.
>
> Misjudge the prominence or relevance of data presented to people at the time.
>
> Match outcome with the actions that went before it.
>
> With hindsight, it is easy to see exactly the kind of harm that people should have foreseen and prevented. That harm, after all, has already occurred. This makes it easier for behaviour to reach the standard of 'negligence'.[14]

When making an assessment of the culpability of a person's actions or behaviours, it should only look at whether they made sense given the situation at that time, not with the benefit of hindsight.

4.2 Drift to Failure

Drift to failure can be defined as 'the slow, steady uncoupling of local practice from written procedure.'[15]

---

13. Lord Anthony Hidden, *Investigation* into the *Clapham Junction Railway* Accident (HMSO, 1989).
14. Dekker, *supra* n. 9, 2007.
15. Scott Snook, *Friendly Fire; The Accidental Shootdown of U.S. Black Hawks over Northern Iraq* (Princeton University Press, 2000).

When a new set of procedures are first implemented, these new rules are usually closely followed. During this initial period, people assume that the procedures are there for good reason, and that they meet the operational requirement. At this point, the uncertainty regarding the consequences of failing to follow the procedures is high.[16] As time passes and experience levels grow, individuals and groups begin to find what they consider to be better ways of operating.[17] Individuals adjust their behaviour to better align with their perception of the current demands; as a result, actions develop which drift away from the established procedures.

These practices gain legitimacy if they are repeated without any negative side effects. If they survive for long enough without affecting global interests and if local procedures are successfully repeated without consequence, they stand a good chance of becoming an accepted practice.

4.3 Detection of Drift

This drift is a gradual, often imperceptible movement. These changes by themselves appear insignificant. However, over time, and in combination, they can create an unacceptably high risk.

Constant demands for local efficiency dictate further drift, moving incrementally further away from the original start point. This demand may come from within the subgroup or may be perceived or actual pressure from an outside source, for example, unit management. This drift may in turn meet no resistance, and the practices become accepted within each subgroup. Drift will vary between individuals and subgroups (e.g., different watches/units). Each subgroup follows its own unique path, developing its own local practice, angling ever further from the baseline of the original start point.

Individuals in different subgroups act based on the assumption that people outside that are behaving in accordance with the original set of established rules (Figure 26.1):

> We naturally, and rightfully, assume that when we interact, others will conform to standard rules of engagement. And, we do this knowing full well that we ourselves rarely act in accordance with such formal norms in the absence of others. Problems occur when either party miscodes the situation or fails to act in accordance with shared rules- either because they are unaware of the others presence or personally ignorant of the applicable behavioural rule.[18]

16. *Ibid.*
17. *Ibid.*
18. *Ibid.*

Figure 26.1 Different Sub-groups Act Differently to the Original Set of Established Rules

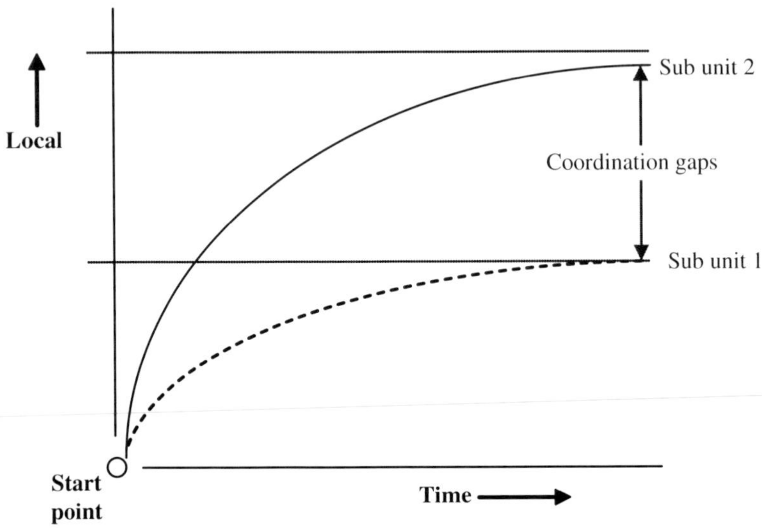

This problem often becomes apparent when subgroups that do not normally interact (this relationship is known as loose coupling) are required to interact more closely (tight coupling). Previously undetected coordination gaps, created by differing degrees of drift, are brought to light. When physical interdependence of subgroups climbs, the gap between the local practices actually being followed in the subgroups and the practice that they assume others are following constitutes a set of conditions that increases the likelihood of coordination failures.

Drift is notoriously difficult to detect, particularly while there is no obvious adverse effect; i.e., an incident. However, just because the system is not broken, it does not necessarily mean that it is not breaking. The stable outcome of normal operations (reliability) can prevent observers from recognizing the steadily increasing disconnect between originally designed mechanisms and evolving organizational reality:

> As is often the case with such tragedies . . . the warning signs were there; however at the time, no one recognized them for what they were. Only in hindsight do they grab our attention as important indicators of a breaking system.[19]

It is often only because an incident occurs as a result of such an action that drift is detected. If in this situation we were to apply the substitution test described in above, and ask a peer of the individual involved:

> Given the circumstances that prevailed at the time, could you be sure that you would not have committed the same or similar type of unsafe act?,

it is likely, given the nature of drift, that the answer would be *'probably not'*.

---

19. *Ibid.*

When we look at previous events and question the actions and decisions made, we have the advantage of *hindsight*. Because we know the outcome, the decisions made at the time of the incident look unreasonable to us. However, the people who made them at the time thought they were perfectly normal. The fact that they had carried out the same action many times before without incident convinced them that it was safe.

5 NORMALIZATION OF DEVIATION

There are certain similarities between 'drift to failure' and 'normalization of deviation' as both deal with a variation over time from previously established rules or procedures. With 'normalization of deviation', there is an official act of acceptance of that variation, and an acceptance of the risk involved in it. The dictionary definition of deviance is 'Differing from a norm or from the accepted standards of a society.'

Normalization of deviation can be explained as:

> a long term phenomenon in which individuals or teams repeatedly accept a lower standard of performance until that lower standard becomes the 'norm'. Usually, the acceptance of the lower standard occurs because the individual/team is under pressure (budget, schedule, etc.).... However, by 'getting away' with the deviation, it is likely they will do the same thing when the same stressful circumstances arise again. Over time, the individual/team fails to see their actions as deviant.[20]

An example of normalization of deviation might start with a piece of equipment functioning at a lower standard than first designed; this deviance from the norm is highlighted, but then deemed acceptable for continued use:

> Behaviour the group first identified as technical deviation was subsequently reinterpreted as within the norm for acceptable performance, then finally officially labelled an acceptable risk. They redefined evidence that deviated from an acceptable standard so that it became the standard.[21]

In a similar way to 'drift to failure', detecting deviation is difficult. Every time no-adverse reaction to the deviation is observed, this serves to reinforce the view that the new standard is an acceptable risk, and thus this becomes the new norm. Furthermore, this cycle will often repeat, and further deviation will become normalized:

> Repetition, seemingly small choices and the banality of daily decisions in organizational life-can camouflage from the participants a cumulative directionality that too often is discernible only in hindsight.

---

20. Mike Mullane, <www.mikemullane.com>.
21. Diane Vaughan, *Challenger Launch Decision: Risky Technology, Culture and Deviance at NASA* (Chicago University Press, 1996).

Hence, if subsequently the reduced capability of the equipment is a causal factor in an incident, the decision to accept or 'normalize' that deviation is often open for criticism as negligent/at-risk behaviour.

Again when the decisions made are questioned, we do so with the benefit of hindsight. Given the information that they had available at the time, it is most likely that people would not have viewed acceptance of the deviation as excessively risky behaviour.

6 RULE BREAKING

With time, people adapt their behaviour to match their perception of the operational requirement. This may take the form of adapting existing rules or disregarding them completely.

The characteristics of rules will affect the extent to which they are followed:

Recency: the date of origin may affect the legitimacy of a rule or procedure or knowledge of its existence.

Relevance: the degree to which a rule or procedure is defined as relevant to a particular task or to organizational goals.

Complexity: a rule or procedure having many interrelated parts may be difficult to interpret, generating mistake out of misunderstanding.

Vagueness: when a rule is stated in general or indefinite terms or unclearly expressed, mistake can happen.

Rule breaking can be broken down into the following categories:

Unintentional (understanding): people do not know how to apply the procedures.

Unintentional (awareness): people act as if there is no procedure.

Situational (cannot do it): it is impossible to get the job done by following the rules strictly.

Optimizing (I can do better): it is possible to get the job done better or faster by not adhering to the rules. This category can be further sub-divided into personal or organizational optimizing, dependant on whether the benefit is to the individual or the organization.

Organizational optimizing is where a person does not adhere to a rule intentionally, but does so with good intentions, the outcome however was not as intended.

Personal optimizing is considered more culpable than organizational. As before, the rule is intentionally broken, and the outcome was unintended; but with personal optimizing a person does this for personal gain; i.e., to be able to leave work early.

Exceptional (e.g., an emergency): people have to disregard a rule to solve an exceptional problem.

Routine violations: rules are broken because it is felt that they are irrelevant, or people do not understand the consequences.

Reckless violations: a rule was violated without thinking or caring about the consequences.

Figure 26.2 shows how the different types of rule breaking fit within a Just Culture environment. Here, the differentiation between human error/at-risk behaviour and reckless conduct is the line between legitimate and illegitimate behaviour.

If a person makes a conscious decision to break a rule, but believes the risk in doing so was justified, or breaks a rule unintentionally, this choice may be widely viewed as negligent (at-risk) behaviour.

If however a person breaks a rule, knowing that there is a risk that harm would probably result from doing so, and foreseeing the harm, they nevertheless broke that rule, this is classified as a wilful/reckless violation or gross negligence. This applies also to those who intentionally break a rule but with unintended consequences for personal gain.

Figure 26.2 Different Possible Rule Breaking

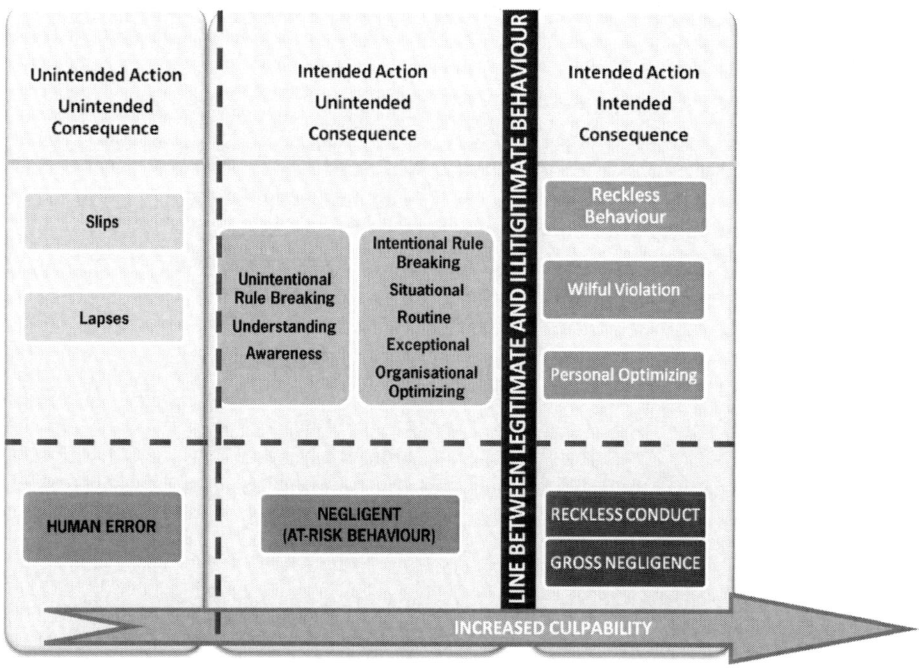

7 CONSTRUCTION OF RISK

If we want to look at how people, in executing their work, decide what the difference is between legitimate and illegitimate behaviour, we have to look at how people assess what constitutes 'risk':

> Each person occupies a different position in the world, which leads to a unique set of experiences, assumptions and expectations about the situations and objects he or she encounters. From integrated sets of assumptions, expectations and experience, individuals construct a worldview, or frame of reference, that shapes their interpretations of objects and experiences. Risk is not a fixed attribute of some object, but constructed by individuals from past experience and present circumstances and conferred upon the subject or situation. Individuals assess risk as they assess everything else-through the filtering lens of individual worldview.
>
> Risk is in the eye of the beholder; it can be present or absent in the same situation or object, or, if present, present to a greater or lesser extent. The framework becomes self-confirming because, whenever they can, people tend to impose it on experiences and events creating incidents and relationships that confirm to it.
>
> Because worldview affects the social construction of risk, a particular object or situation with a readily ascertainable capacity for harm (e.g. a knife) can be interpreted differently by different people. When risk is no longer an immediately knowable attribute of the object and the possible harm associated with it depends on other, less knowable factors we move into the realm of uncertainty and probabilities.[22]

This is where the degree of culpability and hence negligence of a person's behaviour becomes difficult to assess; as each person has a different worldview, and therefore understanding of the risk involved in any act.

In most work situations, individuals are faced with freedom in respect to how they carry out normally successful procedures. The flexibility and speed of professional expertise evolve through a process of adaptation to the peculiarities of the local environment. Perception of the quality of the work is immediate, and the benefit of the adaptation can be seen. In contrast, the effect of these adapted actions on the wider situation may not be seen for some time and only then if coincident to many other factors.

Judging whether a person made a justified behavioural choice that increased risk, or took an unjustifiable risk is strongly influenced by both outcome and hindsight. Successful repetition of at-risk behaviour by a person will serve to confirm the validity of their behaviour, and that the choice is justified; it is only when the behaviour is followed by a failure that their personal worldview is altered, and their actions become questionable:

> The challenge if we really want to know whether people anticipated risks correctly is to see the world through their eyes, without knowledge of

22. *Ibid.*

outcome, without knowing exactly which piece of data will turn out critical afterward.[23]

8 TECHNICAL AND NORMATIVE ERRORS

Charles Bosk[24] highlighted a difference between the way errors are perceived after the event (but not the actual error itself):

- *Technical errors* are those that are described as commensurate with a person's level of experience and training.
- *Normative errors* include negligence and wilful violations, but are also concerned with a level of 'professionalism'.

When someone makes a technical mistake, they are performing their role relative to their level of training and experience, but their present skills fall short of what the task requires. For an error to be considered technical, it has to meet two conditions:

- The frequency or seriousness of errors should decrease as experience goes up, for example, if a person keeps making the same mistakes over and over, it may be difficult to keep seeing them as purely technical.
- The other condition for a technical error is that it should be disclosed as an opportunity for learning and improvement. Not reporting can turn a technical error into a normative one.

Normative errors are errors which question the professionalism of those involved. Normative errors are about professionals not discharging their roles diligently.

The distinction between normative and technical errors is broadly similar to the difference between legitimate and illegitimate behaviour described in the Just Culture definition. The important difference is that an error may be a legitimate mistake, commensurate with experience and training, but it may be viewed subsequently as illegitimate, if, for example, the individual fails to report an incident. Not disclosing often means that a mistake will no longer be seen as honest.

9 MANAGING BEHAVIOUR

As we have seen, behaviour can be broken down into three types: normal errors, negligent/at-risk behaviour, and reckless conduct (gross negligence)/wilful violations. What is an appropriate way to manage these behaviours?

Normal errors are inadvertent actions. Therefore, disciplinary action is considered inappropriate for this behaviour, but it can be managed through changes in

23. Dekker, *supra* n. 9, 2000.
24. Charles Bosk, *Forgive and Remember – Managing Medical Failure* (University of Chicago Press, 2003).

the immediate'system'; for example, changes in procedures or airspace design to make the situation which led to the error less likely or further training for individuals or teams to improve performance.

Negligent or at-risk behaviour. Behaviour where risk is either not recognized or mistakenly believed to be justified. This behaviour can be mitigated by understanding what at-risk behaviours exist, removing incentives for such behaviour and increasing awareness of the increased risk of such behaviour. Incentives should be created to promote a change in behaviour; for example, encouraging staff to highlight unworkable procedures rather than create unofficial work-arounds. Again, disciplinary action is considered inappropriate for this behaviour.

Reckless conduct (gross negligence) and wilful violations can be grouped together as one type when considering how to manage behaviour. This is the type of behaviour where disciplinary action can be considered appropriate. As previously highlighted, a Just Culture does not tolerate '*gross negligence, wilful violations and destructive acts*'.

There is much debate as to how people calculate the costs and benefits of their actions; for example, not adhering to a rule, or taking a justified risk. Included within this is the probability of getting caught and being punished, and whether that is a real deterrent.

There is also the question as to whether disciplinary action is suitable for managing normal errors and negligent/at-risk behaviour. Clearly where an action is either unintended, or the action is intended but is followed by an unintended consequence, the use of punishment as a deterrent is likely to be ineffective:

> a person acts 'recklessly' with respect to a result if s/he consciously disregards a substantial risk and acts only 'negligently' if s/he is unaware of a substantial risk s/he should have perceived. The narrow distinction lies in the actor's awareness of risk. The person acting negligently is unaware of harmful consequences and therefore is arguably neither blameworthy nor deterrable.[25]

Conversely, the opinion is voiced that by having a disciplinary option, reckless behaviour will be discouraged:

> when people have knowledge that conviction and sentence (and punishment) may follow conduct that inadvertently creates improper risk, they are supplied with an additional motive to take care before acting, to use their facilities and draw on their experience in gauging the potentialities of contemplated conduct. To some extent, at least, this motive may promote awareness and thus be effective as a measure of control.[26]

---

25. Robinson & Grall, *Element Analysis in Defining Criminal Liability: The Model Penal Code and Beyond* (1983).
26. American Law Institute Model Penal Code, Article 2. General Principles of Liability, Explanatory Note 2.02, 1962.

In sum, it would appear that simply knowing whether a mistake was legitimate or illegitimate was sufficient to determine whether an individual was considered culpable. What however is more important is *who* gets to decide where the line between legitimate and illegitimate sits, and what rules, values, traditions, language and legitimacy this person uses when they do so:

> Almost any act can be constructed into a wilful disregard or negligence. Rather than a prosecutor saying 'You have nothing to fear if you've done nothing wrong', a more accurate portrayal would be 'if I decide you have done nothing wrong, you have nothing to fear.[27]

In many instances, the decision as to whether the line has been crossed will be taken by someone with little or no domain expertise. In the case of judicial proceedings it is likely that neither the judge nor jury will have any relevant expertise either.

The greater the role of domain expertise in the process, the less chance there is of unfair or inappropriate disciplinary or judicial proceedings. Domain experts have an easier time forming an understanding of the situation as it looked to the person at the time, for the following reasons:

- They probably know such situations from their own experience.
- It is easier for them to understand where somebody's attention was directed.
- It is probably easier for them to understand the various goals that the person in question was pursuing at the time, and whether these were reasonable given the circumstances.
- It is also easier for them to assess whether any unwritten rules or norms may have played a role in people's behaviour.

Accountability is often only retrospective and tries to find somebody to blame. It feeds the demands of the press, politicians or other parties, who may be eagerly awaiting signs that something is being done about the problem.

Normally the ATC system is better served not by blaming people, but by getting people actively involved in the creation of a better system to work in. An inappropriate disciplinary response to an incident will be more likely to lead to secrecy and under reporting, than a safer working environment:

> Accountability that is backward-looking tries to find a scapegoat, to blame and shame an individual for messing up. But accountability is about looking ahead. Not only should accountability acknowledge the mistake and the harm resulting from it. It should lay out the opportunities for making changes so that the probability of such harm happening again goes down.[28]

---

27. Dekker, *supra* n. 9, 2000.
28. Dekker, *supra* n. 9, 2000.

11 CONCLUSION AND WAY FORWARD

Recent works to on domain expertise and bridging the gap with judiciary have seen the light and Schubert (2010)[29] describes a possible way ahead. The EU directive (691/2010) on Performance review will need to further establish guidance material for the States and ANSPs in order that legal impediments are reduced to bridge the gap.

11.1 Domain Expertise

The proposed expert pool[30] should consist of a mix of individuals selected from the aviation industry and from the legal profession. Those with a legal background would receive a substantial additional training in aviation, whereas those coming from the aeronautical business would be given a solid legal education.

The mandate given to these experts would be to evaluate safety occurrences from an operational, technical and legal point of view. To become credible, the task should not be entrusted to a single individual, but to a small college of people with various skills, to ensure a comprehensive and balanced evaluation of each case. Some promoters of the idea suggest that the mandate given to these experts should be to act as a filter and to decide upstream from the judicial system, which cases should be subject to a criminal investigation, and which cases should not be considered by the judicial system. Whereas the proposal is tempting, it would be extremely difficult to implement in practice in the light of the changes that States would need to make to their legal systems to accommodate such a function, that would formally substitute to the criminal investigators. The history of the measures undertaken to implement a Just Culture in aviation indicates that most States show a great reluctance to modify their national laws. The most immediate and promising steps should be imagined within the existing legal framework. A more realistic mandate would be to entrust these experts with the responsibility to produce an opinion on the opportunity or need to prosecute a given case. The decision to do so would formally remain with the judicial instances but, provided the programme is conducted with rigor, the opinion would carry a strong authoritative value.

11.2 Bridging the Gap

The Just Culture model policy[31] of the Global Just Culture Taskforce (Eurocontrol coordinated global multi-disciplinary taskforce) gives as well avenues for States to open the dialogue between the aviation domain and the judicial world. This Model Policy is further an assistance for establishing a level playing field in Europe, this is needed as with the EU regulation (216/2010) on performance, Just Culture will be measured and all the States and Service Providers will have to comply with it.

29. F. Schubert *Resolving the Just Culture Deadlock* (Skyguide, 2010).
30. Eurocontrol-IFATCA initiative Aviation Expert Training 2011.
31. Just culture taskforce, Just Culture Model Policy 2010.

Appendix A

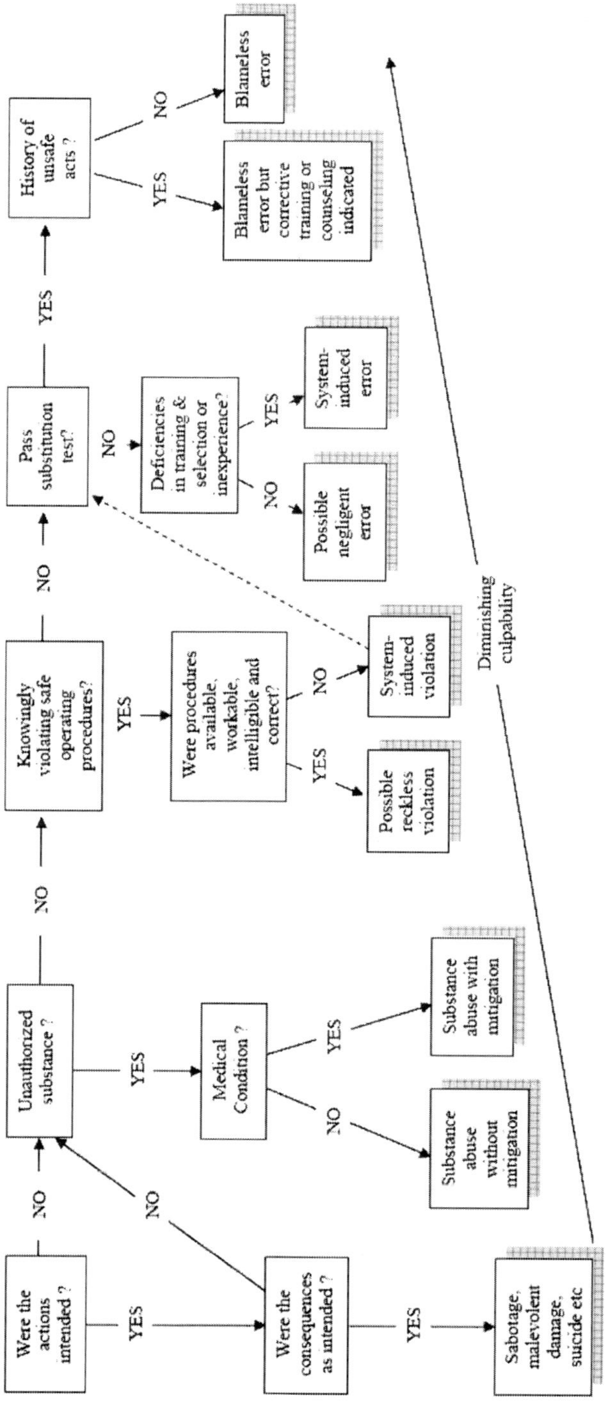
Were the actions intended ?
YES
NO
Were the consequences as intended ?
YES
NO
Sabotage, malevolent damage, suicide etc
Unauthorized substance ?
YES
NO
Medical Condition ?
NO
YES
Substance abuse without mitigation
Substance abuse with mitigation
Knowingly violating safe operating procedures?
YES
NO
Were procedures available, workable, intelligible and correct?
YES
NO
Possible reckless violation
System-induced violation
Pass substitution test?
NO
YES
Deficiencies in training & selection or inexperience?
NO
YES
Possible negligent error
System-induced error
History of unsafe acts ?
YES
NO
Blameless error but corrective training or counseling indicated
Blameless error
Diminishing culpability

Chapter 27
The Role for the Human Being in Single European Sky

*Marc Baumgartner**

1 'ESTABLISHMENT OF A ROAD MAP FOR THE HUMAN OPERATOR'

More than a decade has passed since the Vice-President of the European Commission, the late Ms de Palacio, has invited the European Staff representative organization to the first of many meetings in her office, to discuss the human implications in what soon would become the Single European sky initiative. From the very beginning Mme de Palacio said 'we have to take the bull by the horns'.[1] She explained that the staff in the Air Traffic Management (ATM) sector and in particular the air traffic controllers had to be associated with the creation of the Single European Sky. Classical, social and labour issues come to the mind of many politicians and the greater public as the sector, and in particular the profession of air traffic controllers has a reputation of always being on strike. Unlike many other professions, the air traffic controllers' profession has been prone over the last fifty years to a cyclic incidence of uphill battles, which have impacted on countries, governments and economies. In the 1970s up to the mid 1980s the battles

---

* Marc Baumgartner, former President of the International Federation of Air Traffic Controllers' Associations (IFATCA).

1. Madame de Palacio – addressing Annual IFATCA Conference in 2001, Geneva.

Daniel Calleja Crespo & Pablo Mendes de Leon, *Achieving the Single European Sky: Goals and Challenges*, pp. 299–313.

for recognition led to some of the most spectacular ripples in the post-World War II shaping of society, just to quote a few Germany (1973), France (1979) and the huge crisis in 1981 when the US President Ronald Reagan fired 11000 air traffic controllers. This continued over the fifty years of existence of the International Federation of Air Traffic Controllers' Associations as the unique declaration of the state of alert (a form of martial law) against a profession was pronounced recently in Spain (2010).

Air Traffic Control (ATC)[2] is one of the world's youngest professions. Like many modern professions, it has developed from the humblest beginnings into a highly sophisticated and technology dependant occupation. With ATC, there was no 'big bang'. It was not discovered or invented but it has evolved gradually, driven by demand. Circumstances have dictated that it developed slightly differently from region to region, from country to country and even from city to city. The basic principles remain the same, however, whether one is using highly sophisticated synthetic radar displays and employing satellite communications, or making do with antiquated, procedural control methods – with World War II vintage High Frequency radio equipment. ATC is the Science, some say the Art, of maintaining safety by keeping air traffic separated, whilst at the same time ensuring expedition and efficiency. At times, these concepts do not lend themselves to complementary action and it is then that a controller is tested and his or her skills come to the fore.

Once man became airborne in a heavier-than-air machine, his ingenuity and parallel developing technologies have permitted him to continually fly higher and faster. Much the same may be said of ATC. To safeguard the aviation scene, ATC has also employed developing technologies to manage the traffic. Unfortunately, the terrestrial developments have never kept pace with the airborne improvements. It has been in the area of this technology gap that the national air traffic control systems have been tested, often found wanting and frequently from whence the protests and controller disputes have derived.

Even today, many people are unaware of the role of the air traffic controller. Few comprehend what is involved in keeping aircraft apart and, sometimes, getting them closer together. On the other hand, for those of us who do, it is all too easy to sit back and take for granted the modern air traffic control systems where they exist, the sophisticated aircraft that use them and the myriad components and facilities required to handle them safely and efficiently.

Air traffic control or air traffic management[3] forms an important part of the transport infrastructure in all countries around the globe. The missions of air traffic control are, according to the International Civil Aviation Organization (ICAO) Chicago Convention (Art. 44), to:

– ensure the safe and orderly growth of civil aviation throughout the world;

2. Vidler Neil, 'Under control – The Story of the International Federation of Air Traffic Controllers Association's', IFATCA, 2001.
3. ATM includes all the services related to air navigation services; that is: Air Traffic Services (ATS), Air Space Management (ASM), Air Traffic Flow Management (ATFM). Air Traffic Control is part of Air Traffic Services according to ICAO.

- meet the needs of the people of the world for safe, regular, efficient and economical air transport;
- promote safety of flight in international aviation.

The 190 signatory states of the Chicago Convention who are also members of ICAO are requested to set up the legal and organizational structure in order to comply with the above requirements. In most European countries this has been carried out by splitting oversight including regulation and service provision. For the so-called Air Traffic Services providers the ICAO mantra creates a challenging triangle between safety – cost – and capacity (Figure 27.1).[4]

The global air transport of 2010 deals with 2.4 billion passengers, 43 million tonnes of cargo, 32 million jobs, just one accident for every 1.4 million flights, 2% of global carbon emissions and USD 545 billion in revenue[5]. An enormous system that has evolved over more than 100 years starting with the first flight to a global Air Transport System with thousands of aircraft .

Despite the worst economic recession in eighty years the sector still faces continuous growth. This is primarily due to the fact that the world population will experience continuing growth, mostly in developing and emerging countries. By 2050, the world population is expected to reach 9 to 10 billion people.

Creating the proper balance between people-planet-profit (economical) has been a challenge for aviation industry since decades and will remain its major challenge for the decades to come.

In the mean time the world faces serious crises: in the beginning of the twenty-first century in terms of economy, climate and in terms of the people that use the transportation system, those that live in the vicinity of airports and those that work in the aviation industry their variable and diverse needs.

Through this chaos the world develops a sustainable but liberalized air transport system in a well organized manner. Sustainable in the sense that the need for

Figure 27.1

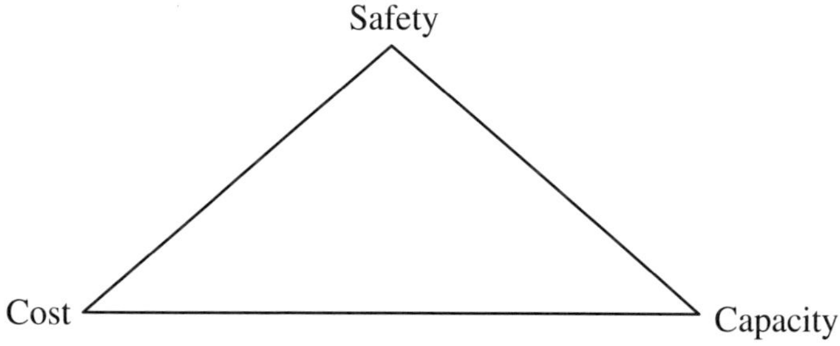

4. ACARE LTIR, not published report on the future of Aeronautics research, 2011.
5. <www.iata.org/pressroom/speeches/Pages/2010-06-07-01.aspx>.

passenger travel will remain and even increase as a consequence of globalization, as a result of the innovation that has led to the change of business models (Southwest, Ryanair). Sustainable also in terms of environmentally friendly or green air transport to mitigate the impact on climate change.

The aviation industry has a mathematical safety tolerance of $1x10^{-7}$ or, expressed differently, a disastrous accident is managed to 1 in 10,000,000.[6] Like other ultra-safe macro-technical systems such as the nuclear industry or the European railroad system. The safety of these systems becomes asymptotic around a mythical frontier placed somewhere around $5x10^{-7}$ risk of a disastrous accident[7] per safety unit.[8] Science also talks about high risk industries, where the accidents are rare but potentially disastrous and where safety is strongly related to the human actor involved in creating, maintaining the system safe. As such high risk industries are among the most complex socio-technological living systems, the role and the importance of the role of the human operator should not be underestimated and needs to be included right from the beginning of the design and regulatory point of view. Therefore, the political will of Commissioner de Palacio, to have representatives of the professional staff organization associated from the very beginning in this huge European change process can only be applauded. Through associating the representative organizations of the air traffic controllers, the pilots and the air traffic safety engineers (ATSEP), a major enabler of the future system has become a part of the change process. However, it took more than ten years to create a political framework to SES. That framework was achieved through the so-called Madrid declaration (Figure 27.2).[9]

The declaration created the so-called fifth pillar outlining that *Acknowledging the human factor as the overriding enabler of change.* The social partners are a key contributing factor to the achievement of the single European sky and need to be effectively associated. The participants to the Conference acknowledge the necessity to:

(1) promote the involvement of staff representatives in the implementation of the Single European Sky at all levels;
(2) ensure the adequate level of competence and training of the professionals in charge of delivering safety;
(3) build the performance scheme on a genuine safety culture, integrating effective incident reporting and 'just culture' as the basis for safety performance.

6. R. Amalberti, The paradoxes of almost totally safe transport systems, in safety science 37 (2001) 109–126.
7. A 'disastrous accident' is an accident causing human death, and/or loss of property, and/or important consequences on the environment or on the system's economic viability.
8. Safety units vary according to industry or transportation mode (running time, passenger/km, number of airport movements, etc.).
9. European Commission, <http://ec.europa.eu/transport/air/single_european_sky/doc/2010_02_26_madrid_declaration.pdf>.

Figure 27.2

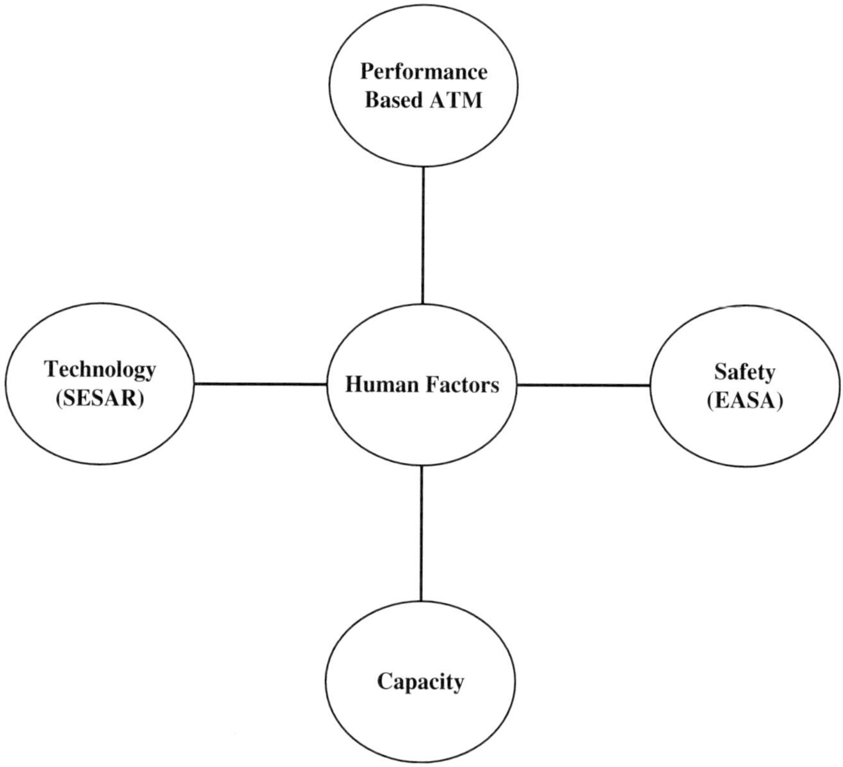

2 SEMANTIC FIRST

Although politically speaking, this declaration is a recognition of the need to involve the human being into the change process, there is certainly a need to be more consistent with definitions and words. The involvement of the human being in the change process is an overriding success factor for any changes, in particular in a socio-technological environment like ATM. Unfortunately, the Madrid declaration and other documents refer to the Human Factor, which in aviation research and science terms means something different than most probably was meant by the decision makers in Madrid.

The human factor science talks about the involvement of the human (operator) in the socio-technological system and the impact of several influencing factors. This will be discussed in more detail below. The human element in the change process is something which is broader than the human factor and involves elements like exchange of practices, experience on mobility and training, change management, understaffing and better allocation of human resources. Human factor and new generation of professional and performance within FAB,[10] the Commission in a presentation to the ICAO Council in February 2011 stated its expectation for the fifth pillar: develop competencies in training and development, promote an open reporting and ensure effective involvement of social partners.[11]

3 HUMAN FACTOR

The importance of Human Factors to flight safety was officially recognized by the International Civil Aviation Organization (ICAO) in 1986 when the 26th Assembly adopted Resolution A26-9. As a follow-on to the Assembly Resolution, the Air Navigation Commission formulated the mission of the Flight Safety and Human Factors Programme as follows:

> To improve safety in aviation by making States more aware and responsive to the importance of Human Factors in civil aviation operations through the provision of practical Human Factors material and measures, developed on the basis of experience in States, and by developing and recommending appropriate amendments to existing material in Annexes and other documents with regard to the role of Human Factors in the present and future operational environments. Special emphasis will be directed to the Human Factors issues that may influence the design, transition and in-service use of the future ICAO CNS/ATM systems.

The Human Factor digest number 8 gives a further high level definition of the Human Factor.[12]

The aviation professionals referred to in the Madrid declaration are air traffic controllers, pilots and air traffic safety electronics personnel. This chapter principally examines the air traffic controllers. However, the other staff in ATM should be kept in mind when Human Factors generally are addressed.

Most Human Factors issues in ATC are not new but derive from fundamental human capabilities and limitations. For instance, Paul Fitts[13] in 1951 had a first formal look at human factors in the provision of ANS.

Yet the Human Factors element has to respond to changes that originate elsewhere, for example in increased air traffic demands or technological advancements. The achievement of the full expected benefits of these advancements requires the successful matching of human and machine, so that humans do not impede technical progress because they have been given tasks beyond their

10. SES deployment strategy, Commission draft paper SEC (1580/2010).
11. Tytgat Luc, presentation ICAO Council February 2011.
12. ICAO Circular 241.
13. Human engineering for an effective air-navigation and traffic-control system by Paul M. Fitts, editor. A report prepared for the Air Navigation Development Board, under the auspices of the NRC Committee on Aviation Psychology.
    Published 1951 by National Research Council, Division of Anthropology and Psychology, Committee on Aviation Psychology in Washington.

capabilities. The aim of Human Factors in ATC is to match human capabilities and limitations with the specifications and design of the ATC system. This matching of human and system is an active process, the achievement of which may imply changes to either or both. Successful matching requires the correct application of the extensive Human Factors data available.

The Human Factor element applies knowledge of how human beings perceive, sense, learn, understand, interpret, process, remember and use information, and also applies knowledge of how to measure human performance and its effects within a functioning system. Human Factors examines the many ways in which the controller and the system can affect each other, and helps to reveal whether the main influence on events is the structure of the ATC system or the actions of individual controllers. Human Factors knowledge is applied to ATC to understand and quantify the interactions between the system and the human. It is used to guide how each should adapt to the other and to suggest how human and system requirements that may appear to differ can nevertheless all be met so that ATC efficiency and safety are optimized without harm to the controllers performance.

Thus, Human Factors knowledge is applied both to effects of the human on the system and to effects of the system on the human.

The emphasis on Human Factors in ATC are in constant change as human factors (science) itself has changed. At one point the emphasis was on function allocation, particular in the era of Artificial Intelligence and automation. Prior to this the emphasis was on, workload; this changed to task load as human factors as a science evolved, and the understanding of workload changed. At one stage, interface design was an important emphasis as was situational awareness. Only for the emphasis to return to one or more of these facets of Human factors.

4 HUMAN ELEMENT

IFATCA in its global statement on the future of ATM highlights the importance of the Human elements in two chapters. [14]

4.1 Humans Together with Technology

The ATM system is comprised of humans and technology acting via procedures on information. Clearly there is a need for the technology, for without technology for flight there would be no ATM system. However, the need for humans at operational levels is under discussion. The 'flight engineer' is no longer a standard member of the flight crew. Unmanned Aerial Vehicles (UAVs) are rapidly increasing in number and sophistication. Are air traffic controllers becoming redundant? What will be the future actors in the ATM systems? Elements like Collaborative

14. IFATCA, global statement on the future of ATM, 2007.

Decision Making or sense and avoid do pose these questions with regard to having more actors (airline operators, pilots, UAV operators etc.) being part of the various elements of provision of ATM.

Humans will be necessary in the operational areas, including air traffic controllers, for many years – but as the technology and systems evolve, the role and the function of humans will evolve. The need for humans is because of the strength of the human in managing systems in a rational and flexible way that is based on sensible thinking and judgment not programming, especially when handling unforeseen events.

The problem has been 'that to err is human' and many ATM system 'errors' have been assigned to human error. This has led to the belief that the human being is the cause of the problem and that removing the human will improve safety. First world societies have however a need for an explanation and needs to link an accident to a human wrong doing. Science talks about Judeo-Christian original sin. However, 'to act unreasonably and inflexibly' at times seems to be the attribute of technology, especially when unanticipated events are encountered. Human operators have become very frustrated at being blamed for 'errors' and yet receive no recognition that in fact humans who have made the automation work, for example by doing tasks that automation was supposed to handle, but does not do so correctly. What is needed is a recognition that the strengths of the human and the strengths of the automation are both required – and that both have limitations that must be mitigated. Dekker (2002) speaks about the need to allow failure to succeed in the future. [15]

With extended development and use, technology can replace certain human activities. There has been much learned in progressive development of flight deck systems that makes UAVs feasible for some operations today. There is no such equivalent yet in the development of systems that would replace air traffic controllers – but this is not to say that future systems may replace some air traffic control functions. The 'assistant' to the executive controller, whether a controller or support staff, is in the not too distant future going to find himself/herself compared to the flight engineer.

It is difficult to talk of technology on a 'global scale' in relation to ATM systems. In a so-called 'advanced technology' industry such as air traffic control, it would be expected that electronic display systems would be the norm – if only because electronic displays support the sharing of data much more efficiently than information on paper. It is not only third world situations where such displays do not exist – but even a busy environment such as the North Atlantic is only now getting electronic air traffic control displays for the entire route! It is an indictment to ATM that some airline operating companies can display updated aircraft positions for their fleet around the globe but the ATM system cannot. However, assuming that the collaborative global approach to ATM will first identify and address the most pressing needs, the rest of this Chapter will address what is the next step from basic electronic display of traffic and basic electronic sharing of ATM data.

15. S. Dekker, The bad apple theory.

4.2 Humans and Automation

In order to meet the increasing safety and other performance targets of ATM, an increasing level of automation will be required; however, the human being shall at all times remain the manager of and not the servant of the automation. In basic terms this means that the human being will choose what is to be done, delegate the execution of the task(s) to the automation and be able to intervene if required, which could be qualified as such as a paradox and a huge challenge for the future automation process.

The automation support of the human roles within ATM must be developed and implemented in a way that fosters trust and confidence by the human in the automation functions. A new layer will be created in future ATM systems where the function of the human and the system need to be a collaborative system where the mutually dependent operation still remains safe. Good and bad experiences regarding the successful implementation of automation in the cockpit will be used in designing automation in other areas of ATM, especially for air traffic controllers. High reliability systems such as fly-by-wire, full automatic landing, etc. have been implemented in aircraft and a similar rigour is required in the development of ground-based automation, especially when the automation function (or failure) will have consequences for multiple aircraft at a time.

The tasks and nature of human roles within ATM will evolve with automation. For air traffic controllers, this will involve changes such as reduction/removal of 'house-keeping' tasks such as frequency changes, the delegation of specific tasks or responsibilities to other agents (both human and automation), adjustments in work-style to support a more strategic trajectory management traffic flow. Changes to the staffing required at positions, and the changes on how the human will be able to use the capacity when mundane tasks or part of will be automated. It is important to make sure that the job satisfaction and professionalism remains high and the overall human experience in the future system, while different, will not be any less attractive or important than it is today.

The humans' role in the system will be by design, and not become a residual task such as 'the human does whatever the automation can't complete'. The ATM system design approach will ensure that the strengths of the human and of the automation are both maximized while the weakness of the human and the automation are both minimized. Degraded and Recovery modes of automation will especially ensure that the human is never overloaded or expected to do more than is humanly possible.

System error – that is not just 'human error' but the deficiency of human and/or automation – will be monitored and lessons learnt. Particular care will have to be taken in the system design, to avoid traps for the human operator or work around becoming necessary because of an inadequate design process.

The human being will not be responsible for automation that is not within the ATM system design or capacity of the human to monitor and manage. The human operator of automation will not be responsible for automation behaviour that is not within operator's ability to influence. The human will not be responsible for information supplied by automation that the human is unable to verify. The human will not be solely to blame for failure to use the automation correctly if the actions of the human were not grossly negligent as a deficiency in the automation's interface to the human is also indicated. When the human has to change work practice as a work-around to a task that automation is supposed to do but does not, then this will be treated as a system error that should be promptly corrected.

The changes in humans' role within ATM will affect staff selection, training, competency requirements especially for 'emergencies' involving degraded automation and possibly even ratings and endorsements. Representatives of the humans who will 'operate' the automation will be involved throughout the design, simulation, implementation and review of its introduction. Though the next generation of aviation professionals might still be currently in pre-school age, special care will have to be taken for those who are starting their thirty-year professional career now, with regard to the changes in working environment and their career evolution.

5 THE NEED FOR A SOLID ROADMAP TO ESTABLISH WHAT THE ROLE SHOULD BE FOR THE HUMAN IN THE SINGLE EUROPEAN SKY

The inclusion of the human operator as one of the pillars in the SES II is a significant and essential step to involve the whole spectrum of the human dimension in this important undertaking. Recent examples have shown that the operators are crucial to a sustainable growth of the aviation sector.

The fifth pillar is an essential de-risk exercise and needs to be carefully planned and executed; otherwise, there exists the possibility that all the technological and regulatory improvement projects will not deliver the expected benefits. All the actors shall work together to identify the current baseline and propose some possible actions to assist this huge change management programme. Representatives of the human being have made a declaration on the need to have a roadmap established which looks in particular at the crucial role the human will play in the future Single European Sky.[16]

IFATCA's contribution is highlighting a few key issues which are not limited to Europe identified and are proposed in a roadmap in order to capture in a structured way the identified challenges.

In particular for the SESAR deployment phase and the next steps of SES, which will be performance driven, a Roadmap outlining priorities for the integration of the human operator in the change process should be elaborated serving as guiding principles for the integration of the human operator. From an air traffic controller's controller point of view the following elements will have to be part of such a human operator/element roadmap.

16. ECA, IFATCA press release 2 Mar. 2011.

The key issues which should be covered by such a roadmap for ATCOs are the following:

- the current system is understaffed – 15% to up to 50% in some countries;
- air traffic controllers are eligible for retirement 10% over the next two years;
- transition phase needs more ATCOs (15% more than optimum) – to cope with innovation and new technology validation;
- increased mobility will assist to cope with staff shortage – not as long as service provision is not standardized (currently up to twelve months to retrain);
- retain and recruit sufficient air traffic controllers which is a difficult challenge as the sector is not anymore attractive enough;
- the Human Pillar is crucial for success of the future ATM system;
- it must be recognized that the future system will only work if it is working with the human being at the centre and not working against the human being;
- industrial relations in ATM – tension due to a new commercialized approach;
- a need for Just Culture approach in order to improve safety.

The air traffic controllers[17] will be a key enabler for the future innovation in the sector. There is however a need to involve the air traffic controller from the outset in the development, design, validation and deployment for new and innovative technology and create in a sustainable manner in order to achieve a well staffed working environment.

5.1 The Current System Is Understaffed

IFATCA data indicates that there is a staff shortage globally of an average of 15% (going up to 50% in certain countries). IFATCA recently conducted a survey of its Member Associations (MA). The results revealed a significant disparity about the perceptions of staffing levels between the MA and the Air Navigation Service Provider. Most MAs reported that the staffing numbers and/or principals reported by their ANSP are insufficient or incorrect. Traffic in most cases is increasing at double the rate compared to the staffing increases for last year. Some ANSPs are opting not to replace retiring staff at this stage.

Planning for staff by ANSPs is lacking. It is only realized that there is a critical shortage when it is too late.

It seems like accurate preplanning is lacking and ANSPs do not like acknowledging to the public and users that there is a staff shortage and keep it hidden up to the last possible moment. Last minute drastic measures are implemented to try and correct the staff shortage and most of the time it involves the remaining ATCOs to help save the day. This situation adds more pressure to the current system and can lead to tiredness and potential sickness due to a lack of adequate rest periods.

17. IFATCA, briefing for the international transport forum 2010, internal.

Generally speaking this is the ANSP cyclic dilemma when in an economic downturn finances are squeezed with the first to be limited is recruitment followed by an upturn then a controller shortage and increased training.

5.2 Air Traffic Controllers Eligible for Retirement

The shortage of air traffic controllers will be exacerbated as approximately 10% of the world controllers are eligible to retire in the next two years. The standard response to this shortage by many ANSPs is to resort to overtime and to unilaterally increase the retirement age. Both of these practices reduce the safety of the aviation system. Where early retirement schemes are available, a trend is noted that many ATCOs do retire to plan at the earliest possible moment.

5.3 Transition Phase Needs More ATCOs

New research and development and modernization programmes such as SESAR in Europe and NEXTGEN in the US need during the development and validation phase approximately 15% more staff than the optimum staffing levels.

5.4 Increased Mobility Will Assist to Cope with Staff Shortage

Due to the fragmentation of the air navigation service provision and a non-existing standardization in working environment, compared to for instance a cockpit, the mobility of the air traffic controller is not even in the short term alleviating the shortage of air traffic controllers.

Mobility of air traffic controllers has existed for the past forty years, experience has shown that it takes approximately between three to twelve months to re-train a so-called *conversion* ATCO, in tower and approach units and nine to sixteen months in ACC environment (a qualified ATCO from country/location A, getting training in a country/location B).[18] Influencing factors are:

- Complexity of the airspace and procedures
- Working tools
- Training habits
- Cultural issues.

One important aspect of the duration of the re-training or conversion period is the dependency on the level of automation in the new facility versus the age and experience of an ATCO. In controller conversion training, it is inversely proportional to experience and age. The older and experienced you are in a facility, the longer it will take to re-train in another. This is different from pilots.

18. IFATCA, The controller 3/2009.

5.5 Retain and Recruit Sufficient Air Traffic Controllers

The ICAO conference on Next Generation Aviation Professional[19] has highlighted the need for aviation to take due consideration the 'growing unattractiveness of aviation as a possible career choice' compared to the past. In light of the future challenges of innovation and modernization in the sector, first thoughts and work has started at ICAO level to look at the 'new' profile and competence skills needed.

IFATCA together with CANSO[20] have published a brochure on Next Generation Aviation Professionals,[21] outlining the challenges and needs for the future, when it comes to ATM.

Recruitment thus ongoing lacks the challenges of traffic growth and the transition requirements, throughout the world.

5.6 The Human Factor in the Next Generation ATM System

As we are in a transition phase from a skill or craft of air traffic control to a science of ATM, there is a need to have the human factor addressed in a very prominent way during the research and development phase.

6 THE HUMAN PILLAR AS SUCCESS FOR THE FUTURE

Recognizing the crucial need that the future system will only work if it is working with the human at the centre and not working against the human, the European Commission in its Madrid declaration has introduced the so-called Human Pillar as an essential element for the success of the Single European Sky.

Nextgen recognizes the need that the human element is taken into account. However, it does not necessarily place as much importance on this element as SESAR.

7 THE HUMAN FACTORS CASE: AN ESSENTIAL REQUIREMENT FOR ANY FUTURE SYSTEMS

In order to build the future system with the Human element integrated from the start there is a need to have a conceptual approach.[22] This is outlined in a method

19. Montreal, 18–20 May 2011; see: <www2.icao.int/en/TRAINAIRPLUS/Lists/Calendar/DispForm.aspx?ID=1>.
20. CANSO – Civil Air Navigation Service Organization <www.canso.org>.
21. CANSO/IFATCA – joint publication, Next Generation Aviation professional, Montreal 2010.
22. Eurocontrol, The Human Factors Case: Guidance for Human Factors Integration, Brussels 2007.

called the human factor case. Designing a complex, automated ATM system requires the designers to address a wide range of engineering issues that relate to hardware, software and the operational environment.

However, the human aspects of jobs, tasks and procedures must also be designed. The basic HF question to consider is 'How can the hardware, software, and the work environment be optimally designed for effective and efficient use by trained operational personnel?'

It is important to understand that there is not a simple answer to this question. This concept is best depicted by the Human Factor pie (Figure 27.3).

7.1 Industrial Relations in ATM

The ATM sector is in constant evolution and transition from government 'public service' to more commercialized operations. This has particularly affected the relations between employer and employees. This might be a hindrance or a barrier

Figure 27.3. HF Pie

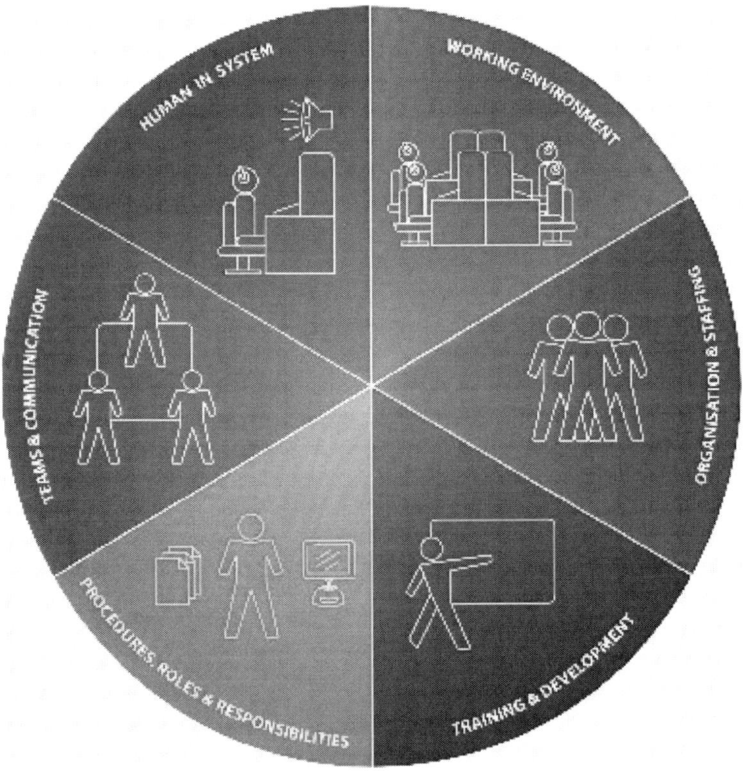

for innovation in some countries. In the first decade of the twenty-first century, some of the problems stemming from this trend are that, as the government and the air navigation service providers go along with being more commercialized in their approach, some of the elements affecting the working conditions such as pension, retirement funds and sufficient staffing, become points of dispute between the social partners.

8 CONCLUSIONS AND WAY FORWARD

The human being and in particular the air traffic controller will be a key enabler for the future innovation in the sector. There is however a need to involve the air traffic controller from the outset in the development, design, validation and deployment work for new and innovative technology while creating a sustainable, well staffed working environment in order to achieve this.

Cooperation between all members of the ATM community is he best way to address the problems being experienced in ATM. That cooperation is a serious working together requiring pragmatism and compromise by all involved. This involves collaborative decision making that requires involvement in the process and in the consequences. It requires commitment to change and a will to act at all levels including at state level. This approach of cooperation and commitment to act is more important than the final technology or procedures that will be implemented.

PART VI

ANNEXES

Annex 1
Article Ms Loyola de Palacio

Loyola de Palacio on the Single European Sky

Vice-President of the European Commission and Commissioner for Transport

The Single European Sky regulations have been adopted. What are now the priorities for the European Commission as regards their implementation?

It is indeed with great satisfaction that we are now able to note that the regulations have been adopted by both the European Parliament and the Council of Ministers of the European Union. This marks the end of several years of hard work, but also the start of new developments and challenges.

The Single European Sky is needed now just as much as when we started work four years ago. The downturn in traffic has given us some breathing space, but we have to be prepared for traffic to double by 2020. The downturn also shows that it is important to have robust financial arrangements in order to ensure the sustainability of air traffic management. It is now clear that there is considerable scope for improving the efficiency of European air traffic management. We should also keep in mind that since 2000 there have been two major accidents. We cannot merely continue with existing programmes – we need to establish clear priorities and pursue concrete improvements quickly. Finally, new technologies – including satellite navigation and data link communication – are being developed which will allow us to improve the efficiency and safety of the system, provided we are able to decide what to do with these technologies.

The regulations provide us with the appropriate instruments and political framework for addressing these problems.

Our first priority is to establish the necessary structures and arrangements for future work. This applies especially to measures designed to ensure the involvement of the Member States and all the stakeholders in the process, through the creation of a Single Sky Committee and Industry Consultation Body and by means of the cooperation arrangements with EUROCONTROL.

Practical work has already commenced on several priority areas. We have proposed several mandates to be given to EUROCONTROL for the technical drafting of implementing rules on airspace design, new charging systems, Flexible Use of Airspace and Functional Airspace Blocks. The new regulations also require us to act quickly as regards the issuing of a draft regulation on the licensing of air traffic controllers.

But it is not only the European Commission that has to proceed without delay, as the Member States themselves are required by the regulations to set up properly staffed national supervisory authorities at arm's length from their service providers. These authorities have to issue certificates to service providers, a necessary condition for the development of cross-border service provision.

What is the prime role of the European Commission as regards the SES regulations?

This is not just a European Commission project – it also needs to bring the various stakeholders, regulators and service providers on board. Through the combined efforts of all these parties and with the help of EUROCONTROL, we need to seize the opportunities for improvement.

Nevertheless, it also has to be acknowledged that under the SES regulations, the Member States have delegated considerable regulatory and implementation powers to the European Commission. It is our responsibility not only to initiate new rules and standards, but to oversee their implementation, to keep things moving when inevitable difficulties arise and to assess the process and propose further work.

What are the main challenges which lie ahead?

The regulations were adopted unanimously by the Council of Ministers and by an overwhelming majority in the European Parliament. This shows that there is widespread understanding and agreement that the problems of safety, capacity and efficiency are ones that can no longer be resolved solely by national measures, but demand a broader European perspective and common action by all of the European Community. Therefore, we do not envisage major political problems.

The main challenge will be to make sure that all stakeholders vigorously pursue the opportunities created by the regulations. We need to see rapid progress towards functional airspace blocks and cooperation between service providers.

What are the main opportunities which lie ahead?

The Single European Sky will create unified rules for all Member States on how to use common airspace. These rules will enforce the adaptation of the air traffic management system to the needs of the users. Air traffic control will increasingly reflect traffic flows rather than national borders. Cross-border functional airspace blocks will be created and the Single European Sky will provide the framework for the Member States to implement these functional blocks.

The Single Sky initiative will provide the necessary regulatory backing to bridge the capacity and productivity gaps that have been so strongly highlighted by the recent reports of EUROCONTROL's Performance Review Commission. SES will lead to more transparency, improved communication through technical interoperability and more efficient flow and capacity management. This will benefit both the service providers and the airspace users through lower investment and operating costs as well as a more efficient utilisation of resources. Reducing fragmentation in technical systems and harmonisation of controller licensing will lead to lower costs both in investment and in the flexible use of the workforce for the service providers and ultimately to a safer environment for airspace users and controllers alike.

What will be the role of the European Community within EUROCONTROL?

An important role will be played by the European Community-EUROCONTROL relationship in developing the Single European Sky and handling wider ATM-related matters. In most cases the common view of the European Community will be represented by the European Commission.

Our role in EUROCONTROL will be two-fold:

- First of all, we will act as a normal Member of the EUROCONTROL Organisation, representing the 15 (soon to be 25) EU Member States on issues of Community competence. This includes all the obligations and rights of the contracting parties. Therefore, we expect to participate actively in the valuable work and discussions in EUROCONTROL working groups and the Provisional Council, whilst reflecting the common objectives of EU States and ensuring that the political EU agenda is supported by and consistent with work on technical and operational issues.
- Secondly, there will be a special relationship with the European Commission whereby use will be made of EUROCONTROL's expertise in creating the Single European Sky. This will entail the issuing of mandates to EUROCONTROL and involvement in their implementation at EUROCONTROL.

How will the two organisations cooperate?

We expect the cooperation of the two organisations to be very active and to take place on various levels, from technical working groups at EUROCONTROL to coordinated action in international fora. This cooperation will be covered partly by the European Community's membership of EUROCONTROL and partly through expansion into other areas. This does not mean that we will be taking work away from EUROCONTROL, but that the work performed in the two organisations will generate significant synergies if coordinated wisely.

It is clear that EUROCONTROL will continue to play a major role in its own right in ATM. The Single European Sky regulations have created a balanced way of developing synergies between the two entities, and allow each organisation to concentrate on what it does best. We have no intention of duplicating the technical expertise that has been built up over the years at EUROCONTROL, and I believe that EUROCONTROL welcomes the benefits of the EU's binding regulatory powers and proven decision-making structures in this field of work.

The potential synergies are also reflected in arrangements that align the work of the two organisations. In parallel with the European Community's membership of EUROCONTROL, the European Commission and EUROCONTROL signed a Memorandum of Cooperation in December. This will provide the necessary framework for EUROCONTROL's contribution to the Single European Sky initiative. In the course of this year, we will develop a comprehensive set of programmes to share work between us and to organise the details of EUROCONTROL's technical input into future legislation. The system of "mandates" that I mentioned earlier will define the objectives and timetables of these rules. By accepting these mandates, EUROCONTROL has committed to drafting a technical proposal, conducting an extensive consultation process and delivering the results to the European Commission for adoption by the Single Sky Committee. This approach will make it possible to proceed in a structured manner and to ensure the convergence of the political agenda and the technical activities.

Additional areas of cooperation will extend beyond the Single European Sky as such to research and development, statistical information, GNSS and international cooperation. In the international arenas, Europe will need to become more visible and actively explain the initiatives we are taking in fields such as Galileo and EGNOS. Furthermore, we should increasingly assume an active role in international organisations, establish a close working relationship with our main international partners and assist other parts of the world with improving the performance of their own air traffic management systems. In all this work, it is essential that we work together and in agreement with EUROCONTROL. The positive results of this kind of European cooperation in international fora were evident in the work of the 11th Air Navigation Conference in Montreal, and we expect the same fruitful cooperation to continue in the future. ■

Annex 2
Consolidated SES Regulations

SINGLE
EUROPEAN
SKY

SES I and II consolidated

The 4 Regulations creating the Single European Sky
Internal working document

February 2010

Disclaimer: *This is an internal working document of the Commission. Consolidation is unofficial. Only the legal acts published in the Official Journal are authentic.*

SES I and II consolidated

This document tries to consolidate for working purposes the four Regulations creating the Single European Sky on the basis of the changes introduced by SES II, i.e. Regulation (EC) No 1070/2009 which entered into force 4 December

2009. Article 6(2) and (6) of Regulation (EC) No 551/2004, as amended, shall apply from the date specified in their respective implementing rules but no later than 4 December 2012.

To identify the changes, text stemming from Regulation (EC) No 1070/2009 is in blue. Please report errors or mistakes to the Commission/F.2: tren-singlesky@ec.europa.eu

- **Regulation (EC) No 549/2004 of the European Parliament and of the Council of 10 March 2004 laying down the framework for the creation of the single European sky (the framework Regulation)**[1]
- **Regulation (EC) No 550/2004 of the European Parliament and of the Council of 10 March 2004 on the provision of air navigation services in the single European sky (the service provision Regulation)**[2]
- **Regulation (EC) No 551/2004 of the European Parliament and of the Council of 10 March 2004 on the organisation and use of the airspace in the single European sky (the airspace Regulation)**[3]
- **Regulation (EC) No 552/2004 of the European Parliament and of the Council of 10 March 2004 on the interoperability of the European Air Traffic Management network (the interoperability Regulation)**[4]
  - **Amended by Regulation (EC) No 1070/2009 of the European Parliament and of the Council of 21 October 2009 amending Regulations (EC) No 549/2004, (EC) No 550/2004, (EC) No 551/2004 and (EC) No 552/2004 in order to improve the performance and sustainability of the European aviation system**[5]

THE EUROPEAN PARLIAMENT AND THE COUNCIL OF THE EUROPEAN UNION,

Having regard to the Treaty establishing the European Community, and in particular

Article 80(2) thereof,

Having regard to the proposal from the Commission,

Having regard to the opinion of the European Economic and Social Committee,
Having regard to the opinion of the Committee of the Regions,

Acting in accordance with the procedure laid down in Article 251 of the Treaty,

Whereas:

(1) Implementation of the common transport policy requires an efficient air transport system allowing the safe, regular and sustainable operation of air transport

1. OJ L 96, 31.3.2004, p. 1
2. OJ L 96, 31.3.2004, p. 10
3. OJ L 96, 31.3.2004, p. 20
4. OJ L 96, 31.3.2004, p. 26
5. OJ L 300, 14.11.2009, p. 34

services, optimising capacity and facilitating the free movement of goods, persons and services.

(2) The adoption by the European Parliament and the Council of the first package of the single European sky legislation, namely, Regulation (EC) No 549/2004 of 10 March 2004 laying down the framework for the creation of the single European sky (the framework Regulation), Regulation (EC) No 550/2004 of 10 March 2004 on the provision of air navigation services in the single European sky (the service provision Regulation), Regulation (EC) No 551/2004 of 10 March 2004 on the organisation and use of the airspace in the single European sky (the airspace Regulation), and Regulation (EC) No 552/2004 of 10 March 2004 on the interoperability of the European air traffic management network (the interoperability Regulation) laid down a firm legal basis for a seamless, interoperable and safe air traffic management (ATM) system.

(3) In response to strong demand from industry, Member States and other stakeholders to simplify and increase the effectiveness of the regulatory framework for aviation in Europe, a high level group on the future of the European aviation regulatory framework (the High Level Group) was established in November 2006. The High Level Group, made up of representatives of the majority of stakeholders, submitted a report in July 2007 containing recommendations on how to improve the performance and governance of the European aviation system. The High Level Group recommended according the environment the same importance as safety and efficiency in the aviation system and insisted that industry and regulators should work together to ensure that ATM contributes as much as possible to sustainability.

(4) At its meeting of 7 April 2008 the Council invited the Commission to develop, in accordance with the recommendations of the High Level Group, an overall system approach in line with the gate-to-gate concept to enhance safety, improve ATM and to increase cost efficiency.

(5) In order to complete the creation of the single European sky, it is necessary to adopt additional measures at Community level, in particular, to improve the performance of the European aviation system in key areas such as the environment, capacity and cost-efficiency, all having regard to the overriding safety objectives. It is also necessary to adapt the single European sky legislation to technical progress.

(6) Council Regulation (EC) No 219/2007 of 27 February 2007 on the establishment of a Joint Undertaking to develop the new generation European air traffic management system (SESAR) calls for the development and implementation of an ATM Master Plan. The implementation of the ATM Master Plan requires regulatory measures to support the development, introduction and financing of new concepts and technologies. It should result in a system composed of fully harmonised and interoperable components, which guarantee high performance air transport activities in Europe. The schedule for implementation of the single European sky should take into consideration the timescale foreseen for the development and

deployment phases of the SESAR programme as a part of the single European sky. Both processes should be closely coordinated.

(7) The concept of common projects, aimed at assisting airspace users and/or air navigation service providers to improve collective air navigation infrastructure, the provision of air navigation services and the use of airspace, in particular those that may be required for the implementation of the ATM Master Plan, should not prejudice pre-existing projects decided by one or several Member States with similar objectives. The provisions on financing of the deployment of common projects should not prejudge the manner in which these common projects are set up. The Commission may propose that funding, such as Trans-European Network or European Investment Bank funding, may be used in support of common projects, in particular to speed up the deployment of the SESAR programme, within the multiannual financial framework. Without prejudice to access to that funding, Member States should be free to decide how revenues generated by the auctioning of aviation sector allowances under the Emissions Trading Scheme are to be used and to consider in this context whether a share of such revenues might be used to finance common projects at the level of functional airspace blocks.

(8) In particular where common projects are deployed, care should be taken, inter alia, through the application of comprehensive and transparent accounting, to ensure that airspace users are not double-charged. Common projects should be deployed to the benefit of all stakeholders and should ensure equal treatment thereof.

(9) To ensure the consistent and sound oversight of service provision across Europe, the national supervisory authorities should be guaranteed sufficient independence and resources. This independence should not prevent those authorities from exercising their tasks within an administrative framework.

(10) National supervisory authorities have a key role to play in the implementation of the single European sky and the Commission should therefore facilitate cooperation among them in order to enable the exchange of best practices and to develop a common approach, including through enhanced cooperation at regional level. This cooperation should take place on a regular basis.

(11) The social partners should be better informed and consulted on all measures having significant social implications. At Community level, the Sectoral Dialogue Committee set up under Commission Decision 98/500/EC should also be consulted.

(12) To drive improved performance of ATM and air navigation services (ANS), it is necessary to establish a framework for the definition, implementation and enforcement of binding performance targets in key performance areas in line with the policies of the International Civil Aviation Organisation (ICAO). An indispensable feature of such a framework should be an appropriate mechanism for reporting, examining, evaluating and disseminating performance data of ATM and ANS along with a relevant incentive scheme to encourage achievement of the targets.

(13) National supervisory authorities should have the flexibility to reflect specific national or regional circumstances when formulating their national and regional plans. When approving or adopting national plans, Member States should be entitled to make appropriate modifications.

(14) When establishing charges for air navigation services the Commission and Member States should endeavour to use common forecasts. Some flexibility should be permitted in those cases where traffic diverges significantly from forecasts, in particular by using appropriate alert mechanisms.

(15) The costs determined by the Member States at national level or at the level of a functional airspace block which are intended to be shared among airspace users should take account of performance targets.

(16) For the cross-border provision of services, Member States should ensure that the designation of an air traffic service provider is not prohibited by any national legal system on the grounds that it is established in another Member State or is owned by nationals of that Member State.

(17) The national supervisory authorities should take appropriate measures to ensure a high level of safety including the possibility of issuing an individual certificate for each type of air navigation service, while respecting the need for cost-efficiency and consistency and avoiding duplication.

(18) The functional airspace blocks are key enablers for enhancing cooperation between air navigation service providers in order to improve performance and create synergies. Member States should establish functional airspace blocks within a reasonable time-frame. For that purpose and in order to optimise the interface of functional airspace blocks in the single European sky, the Member States concerned should cooperate with each other and where appropriate they should also cooperate with third countries.

(19) When Member States establish a functional airspace block, other Member States, the Commission and other interested parties have an opportunity to submit their observations with the aim of facilitating an exchange of views. Those observations should be merely of an advisory nature for the Member State(s) concerned.

(20) In case of difficulties in the negotiation process with regard to the setting up of functional airspace blocks, the Commission may designate a Functional Airspace Blocks System Coordinator (the Coordinator). The tasks of the Coordinator should aim at providing assistance in overcoming such difficulties without interfering with the sovereignty of the Member State(s) concerned and, where appropriate, that of third countries taking part in the same functional airspace block. Costs incurred for the activities of the Coordinator should not have any impact on Member States' national budgets.

(21) The reports of the Eurocontrol Performance Review Commission and the final report of the High Level Group confirm that the route network and airspace structure cannot be developed in isolation, as each individual Member State is an

integral element of the European Air Traffic Management Network (EATMN), both inside and outside the Community. A progressively more integrated operating airspace should therefore be established for general air traffic.

(22) In view of the creation of functional airspace blocks and the setting up of the performance scheme, the Commission should determine and take into account the necessary conditions for the Community to create a Single European Flight Information Region (SEFIR), to be requested by the Member States from the ICAO in accordance with both the established procedures of that organisation and the rights, obligations and responsibilities of Member States under the Convention on International Civil Aviation, signed in Chicago on 7 December 1944 (the Chicago Convention). By encompassing the airspace under the responsibility of the Member States, the SEFIR should facilitate common planning and integrated operations in order to overcome regional bottlenecks. Such a SEFIR should include the necessary flexibility to reflect specific needs such as traffic density and the level of complexity required.

(23) Airspace users face disparate conditions of access to, and freedom of movement within, Community airspace. This is due to the lack of harmonised Community rules of the air, and, in particular, the lack of a harmonised classification of airspace. The Commission should therefore harmonise such rules on the basis of ICAO standards.

(24) The EATMN should be designed and implemented with a view to achieving the safety, environmental sustainability, capacity enhancement and improved cost-efficiency of the whole air transport network. As highlighted in the Eurocontrol performance review Commission's report entitled "Evaluation of functional airspace block initiatives and their contribution to performance improvement" of 31 October 2008, this could be best ensured through coordinated air transport network management at Community level.

(25) In line with the Statement by the Member States on military issues related to the single European sky accompanying Regulation (EC) No 549/2004, civil-military cooperation and coordination should play a fundamental role in the implementation of the single European sky, in order to move towards an enhanced flexible use of airspace for the achievement of the single European sky performance objectives, having due regard to military mission effectiveness.

(26) It is essential to achieve a common, harmonised airspace structure in terms of routes, to base the present and future organisation of airspace on common principles, to ensure the progressive implementation of the ATM Master Plan, to optimise the use of scarce resources to avoid unnecessary equipage costs, and to design and manage airspace in accordance with harmonised rules. To this end, the Commission should be responsible for adopting the necessary rules and implementing decisions with legally binding effect.

(27) The list of functions for network management and design should be amended to integrate, if necessary, future network functions defined by the ATM Master

Plan. In doing so, the Commission should make the best possible use of the expertise of Eurocontrol.

(28) The High Level Group has recommended building new or enhanced functions upon existing foundations and enhancing the role of Eurocontrol, while positioning the Community as the single regulator and respecting the principle of separation of regulation from service provision. Accordingly, the Commission should entrust a reformed Eurocontrol, which has new governance arrangements in place, with the execution of tasks related to various functions, which do not involve the adoption of binding measures of a general scope or the exercise of political discretion. The execution of these tasks by Eurocontrol should be done in an impartial and cost-effective manner and with the full involvement of the airspace users and air navigation service providers.

(29) Adequate measures should be introduced to improve the effectiveness of air traffic flow management in order to assist existing operational units, including the Eurocontrol Central Flow Management Unit, to ensure efficient flight operations. Furthermore, the Commission communication on an action plan for airport capacity, efficiency and safety in Europe highlights the need to ensure operational consistency between flight plans and airport slots. In addition, the Community Observatory on Airport Capacity could help in providing Member States with objective information in order to align airport capacity with ATM capacity, without prejudice to their competences in this area.

(30) The provision of modern, complete, high-quality and timely aeronautical information has a significant impact on safety and on facilitating access to Community airspace and freedom of movement within it. Taking account of the ATM Master Plan, the Community should take the initiative to modernise this sector in cooperation with Eurocontrol and ensure that users are able to access those data through a single public point of access, providing a modern, user-friendly and validated integrated briefing.

(31) For the electronic portal on meteorological information, the Commission should take into account the various sources of information including from designated service providers, where relevant.

(32) To avoid unnecessary administrative burden and overlapping verification procedures, certificates issued in accordance with Regulation (EC) No 216/2008 of the European Parliament and of the Council of 20 February 2008 on common rules in the field of civil aviation and establishing a European Aviation Safety Agency should be accepted for the purposes of this Regulation, where they apply to constituents or systems.

(33) A certificate issued in accordance with Regulation (EC) No 216/2008 and used to demonstrate an alternative means of compliance with the essential requirements of Regulation (EC) No 552/2004, should be accompanied by a technical file as required for the purposes of certification by the European Aviation Safety Agency (EASA).

(34) Certain requirements of Regulation (EC) No 552/2004 should not apply to systems put into operation before 20 October 2005. National supervisory authorities and air navigation service providers should have the freedom to agree, at national level, the procedures and documentation required to demonstrate compliance of ATM systems in operation before 20 October 2005 with the essential requirements of Regulation (EC) No 552/2004. Implementing rules and Community specifications adopted after the adoption of this Regulation should take account of this arrangement and this should not result in a retroactive requirement for documentary evidence.

(35) The High Level Group recommended in its final report to the Commission that the SESAR programme should address specifically the definition of interoperable procedures, systems and information exchange within Europe and with the rest of the world. This should also include the development of relevant standards and the identification of new implementing rules or Community specifications in the context of the single European sky.

(36) When adopting implementing measures including standards laid down by Eurocontrol, the Commission should ensure that the measures include all necessary improvements to the original standards and take full account of the need to avoid double regulation.

(37) The simultaneous pursuit of the goals of augmentation of air traffic safety standards and improvement of the overall performance of ATM and ANS for general air traffic in Europe require that the human factor be taken into account. Therefore the Member States should consider the introduction of "just culture" principles.

(38) In view of the proposed extension of the competences of the EASA to include air traffic management safety, consistency should be ensured between Regulations (EC) No 549/2004, (EC) No 550/2004, (EC) No 551/2004, (EC) No 552/2004 and (EC) No 216/2008.

(39) The measures necessary for the implementation of this Regulation should be adopted in accordance with Council Decision 1999/468/EC of 28 June 1999 laying down the procedures for the exercise of implementing powers conferred on the Commission. Those measures should be adopted within a suitable time-frame in order to meet the deadlines set out in this Regulation and Regulations (EC) No 549/2004, (EC) No 550/2004, (EC) No 551/2004, (EC) No 552/2004 and (EC) No 216/2008.

(40) In particular, the Commission should be empowered to update measures due to technical or operational developments as well as to lay down the basic criteria and procedures for the exercise of certain network management functions. Since those measures are of a general scope and are designed to amend non-essential elements of Regulations (EC) No 549/2004, (EC) No 550/2004, (EC) No 551/2004 and (EC) No 552/2004 by supplementing them with new non-essential elements,

they must be adopted in accordance with the regulatory procedure with scrutiny provided for in Article 5a of Decision 1999/468/EC.

(41) When on imperative grounds of urgency the normal time limits for the regulatory procedure with scrutiny cannot be complied with, the Commission should be able to use the urgency procedure provided for in Article 5a(6) of Decision 1999/468/EC.

(42) The Ministerial Statement on Gibraltar Airport, agreed in Córdoba on 18 September 2006 (the Ministerial Statement), during the first Ministerial meeting of the Forum of Dialogue on Gibraltar, will replace the Joint Declaration on the Airport made in London on 2 December 1987, and the full compliance with that Statement will be deemed to constitute compliance with the 1987 Declaration.

(43) This Regulation applies in full to Gibraltar Airport in the context and by virtue of the Ministerial Statement. Without prejudice to the Ministerial Statement the application to Gibraltar Airport and all the measures related to its implementation shall conform fully with that Statement and all the arrangements contained therein.

(44) Regulations (EC) No 549/2004, (EC) No 550/2004, (EC) No 551/2004 and (EC) No 552/2004 should therefore be amended accordingly,

HAVE ADOPTED THIS REGULATION:

Regulation (EC) No 549/2004 of the European Parliament and of the Council of 10 March 2004 laying down the framework for the creation of the single European sky (the framework Regulation)

(Text with EEA relevance)

THE EUROPEAN PARLIAMENT AND THE COUNCIL OF THE EUROPEAN UNION,

Having regard to the Treaty establishing the European Community, and in particular

Article 80(2) thereof,

Having regard to the proposal from the Commission,

Having regard to the opinion of the European Economic and Social Committee, Having regard to the opinion of the Committee of the Regions,

Acting in accordance with the procedure laid down in Article 251 of the Treaty, in the light of the joint text approved by the Conciliation Committee on 11 December 2003,

Whereas:

(1) Implementation of the common transport policy requires an efficient air transport system allowing safe and regular operation of air transport services, thus facilitating the free movement of goods, persons and services.

(2) At its Extraordinary Meeting in Lisbon on 23 and 24 March 2000, the European Council called on the Commission to put forward proposals on airspace management, air traffic control and air traffic flow management, based on the work of the High Level Group on the single European sky set up by the Commission. This Group, made up largely of the civil and military air navigation authorities in the Member States, submitted its report in November 2000.

(3) Smooth operation of the air transport system requires a consistent, high level of safety in air navigation services allowing optimum use of Europe's airspace and a consistent, high level of safety in air travel, in keeping with the duty of general interest of air navigation services, including public service obligations. It should therefore be carried out to the highest standards of responsibility and competence.

(4) The single European sky initiative should be developed in line with the obligations stemming from the membership of the Community and its Member States of Eurocontrol, and in line with the principles laid down by the 1944 Chicago Convention on International Civil Aviation.

(5) Decisions relating to the content, scope or carrying out of military operations and training do not fall within the sphere of competence of the Community.

(6) The Member States have adopted a general statement on military issues related to the single European sky. According to this statement, Member States should, in particular, enhance civil-military cooperation and, if and to the extent deemed necessary by all Member States concerned, facilitate cooperation between their armed forces in all matters of air traffic management.

(7) Airspace constitutes a limited resource, the optimum and efficient use of which will be possible only if the requirements of all users are taken into account and where relevant, represented in the whole development, decision-making process and implementation of the single European sky, including the Single Sky Committee.

(8) For all these reasons, and with a view to extending the single European sky to include a larger number of European States, the Community should, while taking into account the developments occurring within Eurocontrol, lay down common objectives and an action programme to mobilise the efforts by the Community, the Member States and the various economic stakeholders in order to create a more integrated operating airspace: the single European sky.

(9) Where Member States take action to ensure compliance with Community requirements, the authorities performing verifications of compliance should be sufficiently independent of air navigation service providers.

(10) Air navigation services, in particular air traffic services which are comparable to public authorities, require functional or structural separation and are organised according to very different legal forms in the various Member States.

(11) Where independent audits are required relating to providers of air navigation services, inspections by the official auditing authorities of the Member States where those services are provided by the administration, or by a public body subject to the supervision of the abovementioned authorities, should be recognised as independent audits, whether the audit reports drawn up are made public or not.

(12) It is desirable to extend the single European sky to European third countries, either within the framework of participation by the Community in the work of Eurocontrol, after the accession by the Community to Eurocontrol, or by means of agreements concluded by the Community with these countries.

(13) The accession of the Community to Eurocontrol is an important component in the creation of a pan-European airspace.

(14) In the process of creating the single European sky, the Community should, where appropriate, develop the highest level of cooperation with Eurocontrol in order to ensure regulatory synergies and consistent approaches, and to avoid any duplication between the two sides.

(15) In accordance with the conclusions of the High Level Group, Eurocontrol is the body that has the appropriate expertise to support the Community in its role as regulator. Accordingly, implementing rules should be developed, for matters falling within the remit of Eurocontrol as a result of mandates to that organisation, subject to the conditions to be included in a framework of cooperation between the Commission and Eurocontrol.

(16) The drafting of the measures necessary in order to create the single European sky requires broad-based consultations of economic and social stakeholders.

(17) The social partners should be informed and consulted in an appropriate way on all measures having significant social implications. The Sectoral Dialogue Committee set up under Commission Decision 1998/500/EC of 20 May 1998 on the establishment of Sectoral Dialogue Committees promoting the dialogue between the social partners at European level should also be consulted.

(18) Stakeholders such as air navigation service providers, airspace users, airports, manufacturing industry and professional staff representative bodies should have the possibility to advise the Commission on technical aspects of the implementation of the single European sky.

(19) The performance of the air navigation services system as a whole at European level should be assessed on a regular basis, with due regard to the maintenance of a high level of safety, to check the effectiveness of the measures adopted and to propose further measures.

(20) The sanctions provided for with respect to infringements of this Regulation and of the measures referred to in Article 3 should be effective, proportional and dissuasive, without reducing safety.

(21) The impact of the measures taken to apply this Regulation should be evaluated in the light of reports to be submitted regularly by the Commission.

(22) This Regulation does not affect the power of Member States to adopt provisions in relation to the organisation of their armed forces. This power may lead Member States to adopt measures to ensure that their armed forces have sufficient airspace for adequate education and training purposes. Provision should therefore be made for a safeguards clause to enable this power to be exercised.

(23) Arrangements for greater cooperation over the use of Gibraltar airport were agreed in London on 2 December 1987 by the Kingdom of Spain and the United Kingdom in a joint declaration by the Ministers of Foreign Affairs of the two countries. Such arrangements have yet to enter into operation.

(24) Since the objective of this Regulation, namely the creation of the single European sky, cannot be sufficiently achieved by the Member States, by reason of the transnational scale of the action, and can therefore be better achieved at Community level, while allowing for detailed implementing rules that take account of specific local conditions, the Community may adopt measures in accordance with the principle of subsidiarity as set out in Article 5 of the Treaty. In accordance with the principle of proportionality as set out in that Article, this Regulation does not go beyond what is necessary in order to achieve this objective.

(25) The measures necessary for the implementation of this Regulation should be adopted in accordance with Council Decision 1999/468/EC of 28 June 1999 laying down the procedures for the exercise of implementing powers conferred on the Commission.

(26) Article 8(2) of the Standard Rules of Procedure for committees established in application of Article 7(1) of Decision 1999/468/EC provides a standard rule according to which the Chairman of a committee may decide to invite third parties to a meeting of that committee. If appropriate, the Chairman of the Single Sky Committee should invite representatives of Eurocontrol to take part in meetings as observers or experts,

HAVE ADOPTED THIS REGULATION:

Article 1

Objective and scope

1. The objective of the single European sky initiative is to enhance current air traffic safety standards, to contribute to the sustainable development of the air transport system and to improve the overall performance of air traffic management (ATM) and air navigation services (ANS) for general air traffic in Europe, with a view to meeting the requirements of all airspace users. This single European sky shall comprise a coherent pan-European network of routes, network management and air traffic management systems based only on safety, efficiency and technical

considerations, for the benefit of all airspace users. In pursuit of this objective, this Regulation establishes a harmonised regulatory framework for the creation of the single European sky.

2. The application of this Regulation and of the measures referred to in Article 3 shall be without prejudice to Member States' sovereignty over their airspace and to the requirements of the Member States relating to public order, public security and defence matters, as set out in Article 13. This Regulation and the measures referred to in Article 3 do not cover military operations and training.

3. The application of this Regulation and of the measures referred to in Article 3 shall be without prejudice to the rights and duties of Member States under the 1944 Chicago Convention on International Civil Aviation (the Chicago Convention). In this context, an additional objective of this Regulation is, in the fields it covers, to assist Member States in fulfilling their obligations under the Chicago Convention, by providing a basis for a common interpretation and uniform implementation of its provisions, and by ensuring that these provisions are duly taken into account in this Regulation and in the rules drawn up for its implementation.

4. The application of this Regulation to the airport of Gibraltar is understood to be without prejudice to the respective legal positions of the Kingdom of Spain and the United Kingdom of Great Britain and Northern Ireland with regard to the dispute over sovereignty over the territory in which the airport is situated.

Article 2

Definitions

For the purpose of this Regulation and of the measures referred to in Article 3, the following definitions shall apply:

1. "air traffic control (ATC) service" means a service provided for the purpose of:

    (a) preventing collisions:
    - between aircraft, and
    - in the manoeuvring area between aircraft and obstructions; and

    (b) expediting and maintaining an orderly flow of air traffic;

2. "aerodrome control service" means an ATC service for aerodrome traffic;

3. "aeronautical information service" means a service established within the defined area of coverage responsible for the provision of aeronautical information and data necessary for the safety, regularity, and efficiency of air navigation;

4. "air navigation services" means air traffic services; communication, navigation and surveillance services; meteorological services for air navigation; and aeronautical information services;

5. "air navigation service providers" means any public or private entity providing air navigation services for general air traffic;

6. "airspace block" means an airspace of defined dimensions, in space and time, within which air navigation services are provided;

7. "airspace management" means a planning function with the primary objective of maximising the utilisation of available airspace by dynamic time-sharing and, at times, the segregation of airspace among various categories of airspace users on the basis of short-term needs;

8. "airspace users" means operators of aircraft operated as general air traffic;

9. "air traffic flow management" means a function established with the objective of contributing to a safe, orderly and expeditious flow of air traffic by ensuring that ATC capacity is utilised to the maximum extent possible, and that the traffic volume is compatible with the capacities declared by the appropriate air traffic service providers;

10. "air traffic management (ATM)" means the aggregation of the airborne and ground-based functions (air traffic services, airspace management and air traffic flow management) required to ensure the safe and efficient movement of aircraft during all phases of operations;

11. "air traffic services" means the various flight information services, alerting services, air traffic advisory services and ATC services (area, approach and aerodrome control services);

12. "area control service" means an ATC service for controlled flights in a block of airspace;

13. "approach control service" means an ATC service for arriving or departing controlled flights;

13a. "ATM Master Plan" means the plan endorsed by Council Decision 2009/320/EC [(*)], in accordance with Article 1(2) of Council Regulation (EC) No 219/2007 of 27 February 2007 on the establishment of a Joint Undertaking to develop the new generation European air traffic management system (SESAR) [(**)];

14. "bundle of services" means two or more air navigation services;

15. "certificate" means a document issued by a national supervisory authority in any form complying with national law, which confirms that an air navigation service provider meets the requirements for providing a specific service;

16. "communication services" means aeronautical fixed and mobile services to enable ground-to-ground, air-to-ground and air-to-air communications for ATC purposes;

17. "European air traffic management network" (EATMN) means the collection of systems listed in Annex I to Regulation (EC) No 552/2004 of the European

---

(*). OJ L 95, 9.4.2009, p. 41.
(**).OJ L 64, 2.3.2007, p. 1.

Parliament and of the Council of 10 March 2004 on the interoperability of the European air traffic management network (the interoperability Regulation) enabling air navigation services in the Community to be provided, including the interfaces at boundaries with third countries;

18. "concept of operation" means the criteria for the operational use of the EATMN or of part thereof;

19. "constituents" means tangible objects such as hardware and intangible objects such as software upon which the interoperability of the EATMN depends;

20. Eurocontrol is the European Organisation for the Safety of Air Navigation set up by the International Convention of 13 December 1960 relating to Cooperation for the Safety of Air Navigation;

[Point 21 is deleted]

22. "flexible use of airspace" means an airspace management concept applied in the European Civil Aviation Conference area on the basis of the "Airspace management handbook for the application of the concept of the flexible use of airspace" issued by Eurocontrol;

23. "flight information region" means an airspace of defined dimensions within which flight information services and alerting services are provided;

23a. "flight information service" means a service provided for the purpose of giving advice and information useful for the safe and efficient conduct of flights;

23b. "alerting service" means a service provided to notify relevant organisations regarding aircraft in need of search and rescue aid, and to assist such organisations as required;

24. "flight level" means a surface of constant atmospheric pressure which is related to the specific pressure datum of 1013.2 hectopascals and is separated from other such surfaces by specific pressure intervals;

25. "functional airspace block" means an airspace block based on operational requirements and established regardless of State boundaries, where the provision of air navigation services and related functions are performance-driven and optimised with a view to introducing, in each functional airspace block, enhanced cooperation among air navigation service providers or, where appropriate, an integrated provider;

26. "general air traffic" means all movements of civil aircraft, as well as all movements of State aircraft (including military, customs and police aircraft) when these movements are carried out in conformity with the procedures of the ICAO;

27. "ICAO" means the International Civil Aviation Organisation, as established by the 1944 Chicago Convention on International Civil Aviation.

28. "interoperability" means a set of functional, technical and operational properties required of the systems and constituents of the EATMN and of the procedures for its operation, in order to enable its safe, seamless and efficient operation. Interoperability is achieved by making the systems and constituents compliant with the essential requirements;

29. "meteorological services" means those facilities and services that provide aircraft with meteorological forecasts, briefs and observations as well as any other meteorological information and data provided by States for aeronautical use;

30. "navigation services" means those facilities and services that provide aircraft with positioning and timing information;

31. "operational data" means information concerning all phases of flight that are required to take operational decisions by air navigation service providers, airspace users, airport operators and other actors involved;

32. "procedure", as used in the context of the interoperability Regulation, means a standard method for either the technical or the operational use of systems, in the context of agreed and validated concepts of operation requiring uniform implementation throughout the EATMN;

33. "putting into service" means the first operational use after the initial installation or an upgrade of a system;

34. "route network" means a network of specified routes for channelling the flow of general air traffic as necessary for the provision of ATC services;

35. "routing" means the chosen itinerary to be followed by an aircraft during its operation;

36. "seamless operation" means the operation of the EATMN in such a manner that from the user's perspective it functions as if it were a single entity;

[Point 37 is deleted]

38. "surveillance services" means those facilities and services used to determine the respective positions of aircraft to allow safe separation;

39. "system" means the aggregation of airborne and ground-based constituents, as well as space-based equipment, that provides support for air navigation services for all phases of flight;

40. "upgrade" means any modification that changes the operational characteristics of a system.

41. "cross-border services" means any situation where air navigation services are provided in one Member State by a service provider certified in another Member State.

Article 3

Fields for action by the Community

1. This Regulation establishes a harmonised regulatory framework for the creation of the single European sky in conjunction with:

(a) Regulation (EC) No 551/2004 of the European Parliament and of the Council of 10 March 2004 on the organisation and use of the airspace in the Single European Sky (the airspace Regulation);
(b) Regulation (EC) No 550/2004 of the European Parliament and of the Council of 10 March 2004 on the provision of air navigation services in the Single European Sky (the service provision Regulation); and
(c) Regulation (EC) No 552/2004 of the European Parliament and of the Council of 10 March 2004 on the interoperability of the European Air Traffic Management network (the interoperability Regulation);

and with the implementing rules adopted by the Commission on the basis of this Regulation and the regulations referred to above.

2. The measures referred to in paragraph 1 shall apply subject to the provisions of this Regulation.

Article 4

National supervisory authorities

1. Member States shall, jointly or individually, either nominate or establish a body or bodies as their national supervisory authority in order to assume the tasks assigned to such authority under this Regulation and under the measures referred to in Article 3.

2. The national supervisory authorities shall be independent of air navigation service providers. This independence shall be achieved through adequate separation, at the functional level at least, between the national supervisory authorities and such providers.

3. National supervisory authorities shall exercise their powers impartially, independently and transparently. This shall be achieved by applying appropriate management and control mechanisms, including within the administration of a Member State. However, this shall not prevent the national supervisory authorities from exercising their tasks within the rules of organisation of national civil aviation authorities or any other public bodies.

4. Member States shall ensure that national supervisory authorities have the necessary resources and capabilities to carry out the tasks assigned to them under this Regulation in an efficient and timely manner.

5. Member States shall notify the Commission of the names and addresses of the national supervisory authorities, as well as changes thereto, and of the measures taken to ensure compliance with paragraphs 2, 3 and 4.

Article 5

Committee procedure

1. The Commission shall be assisted by the Single Sky Committee, hereinafter referred to as "the Committee", composed of two representatives of each Member State and chaired by a representative of the Commission. The Committee shall ensure an appropriate consideration of the interests of all categories of users.

2. Where reference is made to this paragraph, Articles 3 and 7 of Decision 1999/468/EC shall apply, having regard to the provisions of Article 8 thereof.

3. Where reference is made to this paragraph, Articles 5 and 7 of Decision 1999/468/EC shall apply, having regard to the provisions of Article 8 thereof. The period referred to in Article 5(6) of Decision 1999/468/EC shall be set at one month.

4. Where reference is made to this paragraph, Article 5a(1) to (4) and Article 7 of Decision 1999/468/ECshall apply, having regard to the provisions of Article 8 thereof.

5. Where reference is made to this paragraph, Article 5a(1), (2), (4), (6) and Article 7 of Decision1999/468/EC shall apply, having regard to the provisions of Article 8 thereof.

Article 6

Industry consultation body

Without prejudice to the role of the Committee and of Eurocontrol, the Commission shall establish an "industry consultation body", to which air navigation service providers, associations of airspace users, airport operators, the manufacturing industry and professional staff representative bodies shall belong. The role of this body shall solely be to advise the Commission on the implementation of the single European sky.

Article 7

Relations with European third countries

The Community and its Member States shall aim at and support the extension of the single European sky to countries which are not members of the European Union. To that end, they shall endeavour, either in the framework of agreements concluded with neighbouring third countries or in the context of agreements on functional airspace blocks, to extend the application of this Regulation, and of the measures referred to in Article 3, to those countries.

Article 8

Implementing rules

1. For the development of implementing rules the Commission may issue mandates to Eurocontrol or, where appropriate, to another body, setting out the tasks to

be performed and the timetable for this and taking into account the relevant deadlines laid down in this Regulation. The Commission shall act in accordance with the advisory procedure referred to in Article 5(2).

2. When the Commission intends to issue a mandate in accordance with paragraph 1 it shall endeavour to make the best use of existing arrangements for the involvement and consultation of all interested parties, where these arrangements correspond to Commission practices on transparency and consultation procedures and do not conflict with its institutional obligations.

Article 9

Penalties

The penalties that Member States shall lay down for infringements of this Regulation and of the measures referred to in Article 3 in particular by airspace users and service providers shall be effective, proportionate and dissuasive.

Article 10

Consultation of stakeholders

1. The Member States, acting in accordance with their national legislation, shall establish consultation mechanisms for appropriate involvement of stakeholders, including professional staff representative bodies, in the implementation of the single European sky.

2. The Commission shall establish a consultation mechanism at Community level. The specific Sectoral Dialogue Committee set up under Decision 98/500/EC shall be involved in the consultation.

3. Consultation of stakeholders shall cover, in particular, the development and introduction of new concepts and technologies in the EATMN.

The stakeholders may include:

- air navigation service providers,
- airport operators,
- relevant airspace users or relevant groups representing airspace users,
- military authorities,
- manufacturing industry, and,
- professional staff representative bodies.

Article 11

Performance scheme

1. To improve the performance of air navigation services and network functions in the single European sky, a performance scheme for air navigation services and network functions shall be set up. It shall include:

(a) Community-wide performance targets on the key performance areas of safety, the environment, capacity and cost-efficiency;
(b) national plans or plans for functional airspace blocks, including performance targets, ensuring consistency with the Community-wide performance targets; and
(c) periodic review, monitoring and benchmarking of the performance of air navigation services and network functions.

2. In accordance with the regulatory procedure referred to in Article 5(3), the Commission may designate Eurocontrol or another impartial and competent body to act as a "performance review body". The role of the performance review body shall be to assist the Commission, in coordination with the national supervisory authorities, and to assist the national supervisory authorities on request in the implementation of the performance scheme referred to in paragraph 1. The Commission shall ensure that the performance review body acts independently when carrying out the tasks entrusted to it by the Commission.

3. (a) The Community-wide performance targets for the air traffic management network shall be adopted by the Commission in accordance with the regulatory procedure referred to in Article 5(3), after taking into account the relevant inputs from national supervisory authorities at national level or at the level of functional airspace blocks.

(b) The national or functional airspace block plans referred to in point (b) of paragraph 1 shall be drawn up by national supervisory authorities and adopted by the Member State(s). These plans shall include binding national targets or targets at the level of functional airspace blocks and an appropriate incentive scheme as adopted by the Member State(s). Drafting of the plans shall be subject to consultation with air navigation service providers, airspace users' representatives, and, where relevant, airport operators and airport coordinators.
(c) The consistency of the national or functional airspace block targets with the Community-wide performance targets shall be assessed by the Commission using the assessment criteria referred to in point (d) of paragraph 6.

In the event that the Commission identifies that one or more national or functional airspace block targets do not meet the assessment criteria, it may decide, in accordance with the advisory procedure referred to in Article 5(2), to issue a recommendation that the national supervisory authorities concerned propose revised performance target(s). The Member State(s) concerned shall adopt revised performance targets and appropriate measures which shall be notified to the Commission in due time.

Where the Commission finds that the revised performance targets and appropriate measures are not adequate, it may decide, in accordance with the regulatory procedure referred to in Article 5(3), that the Member States concerned shall take corrective measures.

Alternatively, the Commission may decide, with adequate supporting evidence, to revise the Community-wide performance targets in accordance with the regulatory procedure referred to in Article 5(3).

(d) The reference period for the performance scheme shall cover a minimum of three years and a maximum of five years. During this period, in the event that the national or functional airspace block targets are not met, the Member States and/or the national supervisory authorities shall apply the appropriate measures they have defined. The first reference period shall cover the first three years following the adoption of the implementing rules referred to in paragraph 6.

(e) The Commission shall carry out regular assessments of the achievement of the performance targets and present the results to the Single Sky Committee.

4. The following procedures shall apply to the performance scheme referred to in paragraph 1:

(a) collection, validation, examination, evaluation and dissemination of relevant data related to the performance of air navigation services and network functions from all relevant parties, including air navigation service providers, airspace users, airport operators, national supervisory authorities, Member States and Eurocontrol;

(b) selection of appropriate key performance areas on the basis of ICAO Document No 9854 'Global air traffic management operational concept', and consistent with those identified in the Performance Framework of the ATM Master Plan, including safety, the environment, capacity and cost-efficiency areas, adapted where necessary in order to take into account the specific needs of the single European sky and relevant objectives for these areas and definition of a limited set of key performance indicators for measuring performance;

(c) establishment of Community-wide performance targets that shall be defined taking into consideration inputs identified at national level or at the level of functional airspace blocks;

(d) assessment of the national or functional airspace block performance targets on the basis of the national or functional airspace block plan; and

(e) monitoring of the national or functional airspace block performance plans, including appropriate alert mechanisms.

The Commission may add to the list of procedures referred to in this paragraph. These measures designed to amend non-essential elements of this Regulation, by supplementing it, shall be adopted in accordance with the regulatory procedure with scrutiny referred to in Article 5(4).

5. The establishment of the performance scheme shall take into account that en route services, terminal services and network functions are different and should be treated accordingly, if necessary also for performance-measuring purposes.

6. For the detailed functioning of the performance scheme, the Commission shall by 4 December 2011 and within a suitable time-frame with a view to meeting the relevant deadlines laid down in this Regulation, adopt implementing rules in accordance with the regulatory procedure referred to in Article 5(3). These implementing rules shall cover the following:

(a) the content and timetable of the procedures referred to in paragraph 4;
(b) the reference period and intervals for the assessment of the achievement of performance targets and setting of new targets;
(c) criteria for the setting up by the national supervisory authorities of the national or functional airspace block performance plans, containing the national or functional airspace block performance targets and the incentive scheme. The performance plans shall:
  (i) be based on the business plans of the air navigation service providers;
  (ii) address all cost components of the national or functional airspace block cost base;
  (iii) include binding performance targets consistent with the Community-wide performance targets;
(d) criteria to assess whether the national or functional airspace block targets are consistent with the Community-wide performance targets during the reference period and to support alert mechanisms;
(e) general principles for the setting up by Member States of the incentive scheme;
(f) principles for the application of a transitional mechanism necessary for the adaptation to the functioning of the performance scheme not exceeding 12 months following the adoption of the implementing rules.

Article 12

Supervision, monitoring and methods of impact assessment

1. The supervision, monitoring and methods of impact assessment shall be based on the submission of annual reports by the Member States on implementation of the actions taken pursuant to this Regulation and to the measures referred to in Article 3.

2. The Commission shall periodically review the application of this Regulation and of the measures referred to in Article 3, and shall firstly report to the European Parliament and to the Council by 4 June 2011, and at the end of each reference period referred to in Article 11(3)(d) thereafter. When justified for this purpose, the Commission may request from the Member States information additional to the information contained in the reports submitted by them in accordance with paragraph 1 of this Article.

3. For the purposes of drafting the reports referred to in paragraph 2, the Commission shall request the opinion of the Committee.

4. The reports shall contain an evaluation of the results achieved by the actions taken pursuant to this Regulation including appropriate information about

developments in the sector, in particular concerning economic, social, environmental, employment and technological aspects, as well as about quality of service, in the light of the original objectives and with a view to future needs.

Article 13

Safeguards

This Regulation shall not prevent the application of measures by a Member State to the extent to which these are needed to safeguard essential security or defence policy interests. Such measures are in particular those which are imperative:

- for the surveillance of airspace that is under its responsibility in accordance with ICAO Regional Air Navigation agreements, including the capability to detect, identify and evaluate all aircraft using such airspace, with a view to seeking to safeguard safety of flights and to take action to ensure security and defence needs,
- in the event of serious internal disturbances affecting the maintenance of law and order,
- in the event of war or serious international tension constituting a threat of war,
- for the fulfilment of a Member State's international obligations in relation to the maintenance of peace and international security,
- in order to conduct military operations and training, including the necessary possibilities for exercises.

Article 13a

European Aviation Safety Agency

When implementing this Regulation and Regulations (EC) No 550/2004, (EC) No 551/2004, (EC) No 552/2004 and Regulation (EC) No 216/2008 of the European Parliament and of the Council of 20 February 2008 on common rules in the field of civil aviation and establishing a European Aviation Safety Agency, Member States and the Commission, in accordance with their respective roles as provided for by this Regulation, shall coordinate as appropriate with the European Aviation Safety Agency to ensure that all safety aspects are properly addressed.

Article 14

Entry into force

This Regulation shall enter into force on the twentieth day following that of its publication in the Official Journal of the European Union.

This Regulation shall be binding in its entirety and directly applicable in all Member States.

(*). OJ L 79, 19.3.2008, p. 1.

Regulation (EC) No 550/2004 of the European Parliament and of the Council of 10 March 2004 on the provision of air navigation services in the single European sky (the service provision Regulation)

(Text with EEA relevance)

THE EUROPEAN PARLIAMENT AND THE COUNCIL OF THE EUROPEAN UNION,

Having regard to the Treaty establishing the European Community, and in particular

Article 80(2) thereof,

Having regard to the proposal from the Commission,

Having regard to the opinion of the European Economic and Social Committee, Having regard to the opinion of the Committee of the Regions,

Acting in accordance with the procedure laid down in Article 251 of the Treaty, in the light of the joint text approved by the Conciliation Committee on 11 December 2003,

Whereas:

(1) Member States have restructured, to varying degrees, their national air navigation service providers by increasing their level of autonomy and freedom to provide services. It is increasingly necessary to ensure that minimum public-interest requirements are satisfied under this new environment.

(2) The report of the High Level Group on the single European sky of November 2000 has confirmed the need for rules at Community level to distinguish between regulation and service provision and to introduce a system of certification aimed at preserving public interest requirements, most notably in terms of safety, and to improve charging mechanisms.

(3) Regulation (EC) No 549/2004 of the European Parliament and of the Council of 10 March 2004 (the framework Regulation) lays down the framework for the creation of the single European sky.

(4) In order to create the single European sky, measures should be adopted to ensure the safe and efficient provision of air navigation services consistent with the organisation and use of airspace as provided for in Regulation (EC) No 551/2004 of the European Parliament and of the Council of 10 March 2004 on the organisation and use of the airspace in the single European sky (the airspace Regulation). The establishment of a harmonised organisation for the provision of such services is important in order to respond adequately to the demand of airspace users and to regulate air traffic safely and efficiently.

(5) The provision of air traffic services, as envisaged by this Regulation, is connected with the exercise of the powers of a public authority, which are not of an economic nature justifying the application of the Treaty rules of competition.

(6) Member States are responsible for monitoring the safe and efficient provision of air navigation services and for the control of compliance by air navigation service providers with the common requirements established at Community level.

(7) Member States should be permitted to entrust to recognised organisations, which are technically experienced, the verification of compliance of air navigation service providers with the common requirements established at Community level.

(8) Smooth operation of the air transport system also requires uniform and high safety standards for air navigation service providers.

(9) Arrangements should be made to harmonise the licensing systems for controllers, in order to improve the availability of controllers and to promote the mutual recognition of licences.

(10) Whilst guaranteeing the continuity of service provision, a common system should be established for certifying air navigation service providers, which constitutes a means for defining the rights and obligations of those providers and for regular monitoring of compliance with such requirements.

(11) Conditions attached to certificates should be objectively justified and should be non-discriminatory, proportionate and transparent, and compatible with relevant international standards.

(12) The certificates should be mutually recognised by all Member States in order to allow air navigation service providers to provide services in a Member State other than the country in which they obtained their certificates, within the limits of the safety requirements.

(13) The provision of communication, navigation and surveillance services, as well as aeronautical information services, should be organised under market conditions whilst taking into account the special features of such services and maintaining a high level of safety.

(14) In the interest of facilitating the safe handling of air traffic across the boundaries of the Member States for the benefit of the airspace users and their passengers, the system of certification should provide for a framework to enable Member States to designate providers of air traffic services, regardless of where they have been certified.

(15) On the basis of their analysis of safety considerations, Member States should be able to designate one or more providers of meteorological services in respect of all or part of the airspace under their responsibility, without the need to organise a call for tenders.

(16) Air navigation service providers should establish and maintain close cooperation with military authorities responsible for activities that may affect general air traffic, through appropriate arrangements.

(17) The accounts of all air navigation service providers should provide for maximum transparency.

(18) The introduction of harmonised principles and conditions for access to operational data should facilitate the provision of air navigation services and the operation of airspace users and airports under a new environment.

(19) Charging conditions applying to airspace users should be fair and transparent.

(20) User charges should provide remuneration for the facilities and services provided by air navigation service providers and Member States. The level of user charges should be proportionate to the cost, taking into consideration the objectives of safety and economic efficiency.

(21) There should be no discrimination between airspace users as to the provision of equivalent air navigation services.

(22) Air navigation service providers offer certain facilities and services directly related to the operation of aircraft, the costs of which they should be able to recover according to the "user pays" principle, which is to say that airspace users should pay for the costs they generate at, or as close as possible to, the point of use.

(23) It is important to ensure the transparency of the costs to which such facilities or services give rise. Accordingly, any changes made to the system or level of charges should be explained to airspace users; such changes or investment proposed by air navigation service providers should be explained as part of an exchange of information between their management bodies and airspace users.

(24) There should be scope for modulating charges that contribute to maximising system-wide capacity. Financial incentives may be a useful way of accelerating the introduction of ground-based or airborne equipment that increases capacity, of rewarding high performance or of offsetting the inconvenience of choosing less desirable routings.

(25) In the context of those revenues raised to provide a reasonable return on assets, and in direct correlation with the savings made from efficiency improvements, the Commission should study the possibility of establishing a reserve aimed at reducing the impact of a sudden increase in charges to airspace users at times of reduced levels of traffic.

(26) The Commission should examine the feasibility of organising temporary financial aid for measures to increase the capacity of Europe's air traffic control system as a whole.

(27) The establishment and imposition of charges on airspace users should be reviewed by the Commission on a regular basis, in cooperation with Eurocontrol, and with national supervisory authorities and airspace users.

(28) Owing to the particular sensitivity of information concerning air navigation service providers, national supervisory authorities should not disclose information covered by the obligation of professional secrecy, without prejudice to the organisation of a system for monitoring and publishing the performance of those providers,

HAVE ADOPTED THIS REGULATION:

CHAPTER I

General

Article 1

Scope and objective

1. Within the scope of the framework Regulation, this Regulation concerns the provision of air navigation services in the Single European Sky. The objective of this Regulation is to establish common requirements for the safe and efficient provision of air navigation services in the Community.

2. This Regulation shall apply to the provision of air navigation services for general air traffic in accordance with and within the scope of the framework Regulation.

Article 2

Tasks of the national supervisory authorities

1. The national supervisory authorities referred to in Article 4 of the framework Regulation shall ensure the appropriate supervision of the application of this Regulation, in particular with regard to the safe and efficient operation of air navigation service providers which provide services relating to the airspace falling under the responsibility of the Member State which nominated or established the relevant authority.

2. To this end, each national supervisory authority shall organise proper inspections and surveys to verify compliance with the requirements of this Regulation, including human resources requirements for the provision of air navigation services. The air navigation service provider concerned shall facilitate such work.

3. In respect of functional airspace blocks that extend across the airspace falling under the responsibility of more than one Member State, the Member States concerned shall conclude an agreement on the supervision provided for in this Article with regard to the air navigation service providers providing services relating to those blocks.

4. National supervisory authorities shall cooperate closely to ensure adequate supervision of air navigation service providers holding a valid certificate from one Member State that also provide services relating to the airspace falling under the responsibility of another Member State. Such cooperation shall include arrangements for the handling of cases involving non-compliance with the applicable common requirements set out in Article 6 or with the conditions set out in Annex II.

5. In the case of cross-border provision of air navigation services, such arrangements shall include an agreement on the mutual recognition of the supervisory

tasks set out in paragraphs 1 and 2 and of the results of these tasks. This mutual recognition shall apply also where arrangements for recognition between national supervisory authorities are made for the certification process of service providers.

6. If permitted by national law and with a view to regional cooperation, national supervisory authorities may also conclude agreements regarding the division of responsibilities regarding supervisory tasks.

Article 3

Qualified entities

1. National supervisory authorities may decide to delegate in full or in part the inspections and surveys referred to in Article 2(2) to qualified entities that fulfil the requirements set out in Annex I.

2. Such a delegation granted by a national supervisory authority shall be valid within the Community for a renewable period of three years. National supervisory authorities may instruct any of the qualified entities located in the Community to undertake these inspections and surveys.

Article 4

Safety requirements

The Commission shall, in accordance with the regulatory procedure referred to in Article 5(3) of the framework Regulation, adopt implementing rules incorporating the relevant provisions of the Eurocontrol safety regulatory requirements (ESARRs) and subsequent amendments to those requirements falling within the scope of this Regulation, where necessary with appropriate adaptations

CHAPTER II

RULES FOR THE PROVISION OF SERVICES

[Article 5 is deleted]

Article 6

Common requirements

Common requirements for the provision of air navigation services shall be established in accordance with the procedure referred to in Article 5(3) of the framework Regulation. The common requirements shall include the following:

- technical and operational competence and suitability,
- systems and processes for safety and quality management,
- reporting systems,
- quality of services,
- financial strength,
- liability and insurance cover,

- ownership and organisational structure, including the prevention of conflicts of interest,
- human resources, including adequate staffing plans,
- security.

Article 7

Certification of air navigation service providers

1. The provision of all air navigation services within the Community shall be subject to certification by Member States.

2. Applications for certification shall be submitted to the national supervisory authority of the Member State where the applicant has its principal place of operation and, if any, its registered office.

3. National supervisory authorities shall issue certificates to air navigation service providers where they comply with the common requirements referred to in Article 6. Certificates may be issued individually for each type of air navigation service as defined in Article 2 of the framework Regulation, or for a bundle of such services, inter alia where a provider of air traffic services, whatever its legal status, operates and maintains its own communication, navigation and surveillance systems. The certificates shall be checked on a regular basis.

4. Certificates shall specify the rights and obligations of air navigation service providers, including non-discriminatory access to services for airspace users, with particular regard to safety. Certification may be subject only to the conditions set out in Annex II. Such conditions shall be objectively justified, non-discriminatory, proportionate and transparent.

5. Notwithstanding paragraph 1, Member States may allow the provision of air navigation services in all or part of the airspace under their responsibility without certification in cases where the provider of such services offers them primarily to aircraft movements other than general air traffic. In those cases, the Member State concerned shall inform the Commission and the other Member States of its decision and of the measures taken to ensure maximum compliance with the common requirements.

6. Without prejudice to Articles 8 and 9, the issue of certificates shall confer on air navigation service providers the possibility of offering their services to Member States, other air navigation service providers, airspace users and airports within the Community.

7. National supervisory authorities shall monitor compliance with the common requirements and with the conditions attached to the certificates. Details of such monitoring shall be included in the annual reports to be submitted by Member States pursuant to Article 12(1) of the framework Regulation. If a national supervisory authority finds that the holder of a certificate no longer satisfies such requirements or conditions, it shall take appropriate measures while ensuring

continuity of services on condition that safety is not compromised. Such measures may include the revocation of the certificate.

8. A Member State shall recognise any certificate issued in another Member State in accordance with this Article.

9. In exceptional circumstances, Member States may postpone compliance with this Article beyond the date resulting from Article 19(2) by six months. Member States shall notify the Commission of such postponement, giving their reasons therefor.

Article 8

Designation of air traffic service providers

1. Member States shall ensure the provision of air traffic services on an exclusive basis within specific airspace blocks in respect of the airspace under their responsibility. For this purpose, Member States shall designate an air traffic service provider holding a valid certificate in the Community.

2. For the provision of cross-border services, Member States shall ensure that compliance with this Article and Article 10(3) is not prevented by their national legal system requiring that air traffic service providers providing services in the airspace under the responsibility of that Member State:

(a) be owned directly or through a majority holding by that Member State or its nationals;
(b) have their principal place of operation or registered office in the territory of that Member State; or
(c) use only facilities in that Member State.

3. Member States shall define the rights and obligations to be met by the designated air traffic service providers. The obligations may include conditions for the timely supply of relevant information enabling all aircraft movements in the airspace under their responsibility to be identified.

4. Member States shall have discretionary powers in choosing an air traffic service provider, on condition that the latter fulfils the requirements and conditions referred to in Articles 6 and 7.

5. In respect of functional airspace blocks established in accordance with Article 9a that extend across the airspace under the responsibility of more than one Member State, the Member States concerned shall jointly designate, in accordance with paragraph 1 of this Article, one or more air traffic service providers, at least one month before implementation of the airspace block.

6. Member States shall inform the Commission and other Member States immediately of any decision within the framework of this Article regarding the designation of air traffic service providers within specific airspace blocks in respect of the airspace under their responsibility.

Article 9

Designation of providers of meteorological services

1. Member States may designate a provider of meteorological services to supply all or part of meteorological data on an exclusive basis in all or part of the airspace under their responsibility, taking into account safety considerations.

2. Member States shall inform the Commission and other Member States without delay of any decision within the framework of this Article regarding the designation of a provider of meteorological services.

Article 9a

Functional airspace blocks

1. By 4 December 2012, Member States shall take all necessary measures in order to ensure the implementation of functional airspace blocks with a view to achieving the required capacity and efficiency of the air traffic management network within the single European sky and maintaining a high level of safety and contributing to the overall performance of the air transport system and a reduced environmental impact. Member States shall cooperate to the fullest extent possible with each other, in particular Member States establishing neighbouring functional airspace blocks, in order to ensure compliance with this provision. Where relevant, cooperation may also include third countries taking part in functional airspace blocks.

2. Functional airspace blocks shall, in particular:

(a) be supported by a safety case;
(b) enable optimum use of airspace, taking into account air traffic flows;
(c) ensure consistency with the European route network established in accordance with Article 6 of the airspace Regulation;
(d) be justified by their overall added value, including optimal use of technical and human resources, on the basis of cost-benefit analyses;
(e) ensure a smooth and flexible transfer of responsibility for air traffic control between air traffic service units;
(f) ensure compatibility between the different airspace configurations, optimising, inter alia, the current flight information regions;
(g) comply with conditions stemming from regional agreements concluded within the ICAO;
(h) respect regional agreements in existence on the date of entry into force of this Regulation, in particular those involving European third countries; and
(i) facilitate consistency with Community-wide performance targets.

3. A functional airspace block shall only be established by mutual agreement between all the Member States and, where appropriate, third countries who have responsibility for any part of the airspace included in the functional airspace block. Before notifying the Commission of the establishment of a functional

airspace block, the Member State(s) concerned shall provide the Commission, the other Member States and other interested parties with adequate information and give them an opportunity to submit their observations.

4. Where a functional airspace block relates to airspace that is wholly or partly under the responsibility of two or more Member States, the agreement by which the functional airspace block is established shall contain the necessary provisions concerning the way in which the block can be modified and the way in which a Member State can withdraw from the block, including transitional arrangements.

5. Where difficulties arise between two or more Member States with regard to a cross- border functional airspace block that concerns airspace under their responsibility, the Member States concerned may jointly bring the matter to the Single Sky Committee for an opinion. The opinion shall be addressed to the Member States concerned. Without prejudice to paragraph 3, the Member States shall take that opinion into account in order to find a solution.

6. After having received the notifications by Member States of the agreements and declarations referred to in paragraphs 3 and 4 the Commission shall assess the fulfilment by each functional airspace block of the requirements set out in paragraph 2 and present the results to the Single Sky Committee for discussion. If the Commission finds that one or more functional airspace blocks do not fulfil the requirements it shall engage in a dialogue with the Member States concerned with the aim of reaching a consensus on the measures necessary to rectify the situation.

7. Without prejudice to paragraph 6, the agreements and declarations referred to in paragraphs 3 and 4 shall be notified to the Commission for publication in the *Official Journal of the European Union*. Such publication shall specify the date of entry into force of the relevant decision.

8. Guidance material for the establishment and modification of functional airspace blocks shall be developed by4 December 2010 in accordance with the advisory procedure referred to in Article 5(2) of the framework Regulation.

9. The Commission shall, by 4 December 2011 and in accordance with the regulatory procedure referred to in Article 5(3) of the framework Regulation, adopt implementing rules regarding the information to be provided by the Member State(s) concerned before establishing and modifying a functional airspace block in accordance with paragraph 3 of this Article.

Article 9b

Functional airspace blocks system coordinator

1. In order to facilitate the establishment of the functional airspace blocks, the Commission may designate a natural person as functional airspace blocks system coordinator (the Coordinator). The Commission shall act in accordance with the regulatory procedure referred to in Article 5(3) of the framework Regulation.

2. Without prejudice to Article 9a(5) the Coordinator shall facilitate at the request of all Member States concerned and, where appropriate, third countries taking part in the same functional airspace block, overcoming of difficulties in their negotiation process in order to speed up the establishment of functional airspace blocks. The Coordinator shall act on the basis of a mandate from all Member States concerned and, where appropriate, third countries taking part in the same functional airspace block.

3. The Coordinator shall act impartially in particular with regard to Member States, third countries, the Commission and the stakeholders.

4. The Coordinator shall not disclose any information obtained whilst performing his function except where authorised to do so by the Member State(s) and, where appropriate, third countries concerned.

5. The Coordinator shall report to the Commission, to the Single Sky Committee and to the European Parliament every three months after his designation. The report shall include a summary of negotiations and their results.

6. The remit of the Coordinator shall expire when the last functional airspace block agreement is signed but no later than 4 December 2012.

Article 10

Relations between service providers

1. Air navigation service providers may avail themselves of the services of other service providers that have been certified in the Community.

2. Air navigation service providers shall formalise their working relationships by means of written agreements or equivalent legal arrangements, setting out the specific duties and functions assumed by each provider and allowing for the exchange of operational data between all service providers in so far as general air traffic is concerned. Those arrangements shall be notified to the national supervisory authority or authorities concerned.

3. In cases involving the provision of air traffic services, the approval of the Member States concerned shall be required. In cases involving the provision of meteorological services, the approval of the Member States concerned shall be required if they have designated a provider on an exclusive basis in accordance with Article 9(1).

Article 11

Relations with military authorities

Member States shall, within the context of the common transport policy, take the necessary steps to ensure that written agreements between the competent civil and military authorities or equivalent legal arrangements are established or renewed in respect of the management of specific airspace blocks.

Article 12

Transparency of accounts

1. Air navigation service providers, whatever their system of ownership or legal form, shall draw up, submit to audit and publish their financial accounts. These accounts shall comply with the International Accounting Standards adopted by the Community. Where, owing to the legal status of the service provider, full compliance with the International Accounting Standards is not possible, the provider shall endeavour to achieve such compliance to the maximum possible extent.

2. In all cases, air navigation service providers shall publish an annual report and regularly undergo an independent audit.

3. When providing a bundle of services, air navigation service providers shall identify and disclose the costs and income deriving from air navigation services, broken down in accordance with the charging scheme for air navigation services referred to in Article 14 and, where appropriate, shall keep consolidated accounts for other, non-air-navigation services, as they would be required to do if the services in question were provided by separate undertakings.

4. Member States shall designate the competent authorities that shall have a right of access to the accounts of service providers that provide services within the airspace under their responsibility.

5. Member States may apply the transitional provisions of Article 9 of Regulation (EC) No 1606/2002 of the European Parliament and of the Council of 19 July 2002 on the application of international accounting standards to air navigation service providers that fall within the scope of that Regulation.

Article 13

Access to and protection of data

1. In so far as general air traffic is concerned, relevant operational data shall be exchanged in real-time between all air navigation service providers, airspace users and airports, to facilitate their operational needs. The data shall be used only for operational purposes.

2. Access to relevant operational data shall be granted to appropriate authorities, certified air navigation service providers, airspace users and airports on a non-discriminatory basis.

3. Certified service providers, airspace users and airports shall establish standard conditions of access to their relevant operational data other than those referred to in paragraph 1. National supervisory authorities shall approve such standard conditions. Detailed rules relating to such conditions shall be established, where appropriate, in accordance with the procedure referred to in Article 5(3) of the framework Regulation.

CHAPTER III

CHARGING SCHEMES

Article 14

General

In accordance with the requirements of Articles 15 and 16,the charging scheme for air navigation services shall contribute to greater transparency in the determination, imposition and enforcement of charges to airspace users and shall contribute to the cost efficiency of providing air navigation services and to efficiency of flights, while maintaining an optimum safety level. This scheme shall also be consistent with Article 15 of the 1944 Chicago Convention on International Civil Aviation and with Eurocontrol's charging system for en-route charges.

Article 15

Principles

1. The charging scheme shall be based on the account of costs for air navigation services incurred by service providers for the benefit of airspace users. The scheme shall allocate these costs among categories of users.

2. The following principles shall be applied when establishing the cost-base for charges:

(a) the cost to be shared among airspace users shall be the determined cost of providing air navigation services, including appropriate amounts for interest on capital investment and depreciation of assets, as well as the costs of maintenance, operation, management and administration. Determined costs shall be the costs determined by the Member State at national level or at the level of functional airspace blocks either at the beginning of the reference period for each calendar year of the reference period referred to in Article 11 of the framework Regulation, or during the reference period, following appropriate adjustments applying the alert mechanisms set out in Article 11 of the framework Regulation;

(b) the costs to be taken into account in this context shall be those assessed in relation to the facilities and services provided for and implemented under the ICAO Regional Air Navigation Plan, European Region. They may also include costs incurred by national supervisory authorities and/or qualified entities, as well as other costs incurred by the relevant Member State and service provider in relation to the provision of air navigation services. They shall not include the costs of penalties imposed by Member States according to Article 9 of the framework Regulation nor the costs of any corrective measures imposed by Member States according to Article 11 of the framework Regulation;

(c) in respect of the functional airspace blocks and as part of their respective framework agreements, Member States shall make reasonable efforts to agree on common principles for charging policy;

(d) the cost of different air navigation services shall be identified separately, as provided for in Article 12(3);
(e) cross-subsidy shall not be allowed between en-route services and terminal services. Costs that pertain to both terminal services and en-route services shall be allocated in a proportional way between en-route services and terminal services on the basis of a transparent methodology. Cross-subsidy shall be allowed between different air navigation services in either one of those two categories only when justified for objective reasons, subject to clear identification;
(f) transparency of the cost-base for charges shall be guaranteed. Implementing rules for the provision of information by the service providers shall be adopted in order to permit reviews of the provider's forecasts, actual costs and revenues. Information shall be regularly exchanged between the national supervisory authorities, service providers, airspace users, the Commission and Eurocontrol.

3. Member States shall comply with the following principles when setting charges in accordance with paragraph 2:

(a) charges shall be set for the availability of air navigation services under non-discriminatory conditions. When imposing charges on different airspace users for the use of the same service, no distinction shall be made in relation to the nationality or category of the user;
(b) exemption of certain users, especially light aircraft and State aircraft, may be permitted, provided that the cost of such exemption is not passed on to other users;
(c) charges shall be set per calendar year on the basis of the determined costs, or may be set under conditions established by Member States for determining the maximum level of the unit rate or of the revenue for each year over a period not exceeding five years;
(d) air navigation services may produce sufficient revenues to provide for a reasonable return on assets to contribute towards necessary capital improvements;
(e) charges shall reflect the cost of air navigation services and facilities made available to airspace users, taking into account the relative productive capacities of the different aircraft types concerned;
(f) charges shall encourage the safe, efficient, effective and sustainable provision of air navigation services with a view to achieving a high level of safety and cost-efficiency and meeting the performance targets and they shall stimulate integrated service provision, whilst reducing the environmental impact of aviation. To that end, and in relation to the national or functional airspace block performance plans, national supervisory authorities may set up mechanisms, including incentives consisting of financial advantages and disadvantages, to encourage air navigation service providers and/or airspace users to support improvements in the provision of air navigation services such as increased capacity, reduced delays and sustainable development, while maintaining an optimum safety level.

4. The Commission shall adopt detailed implementing rules for this Article in accordance with the regulatory procedure referred to in Article 5(3) of the framework Regulation.

Article 15a

Common projects

1. Common projects may assist the successful implementation of the ATM Master Plan. Such projects shall support the objectives of this Regulation to improve the performance of the European aviation system in key areas such as capacity, flight and cost efficiency as well as environmental sustainability, within the overriding safety objectives.

2. The Commission may, in accordance with the regulatory procedure referred to in Article 5(3) of the framework Regulation, develop guidance material concerning the way in which such projects can support the implementation of the ATM Master Plan. Such guidance material shall not prejudice mechanisms for the deployment of such projects concerning functional airspace blocks as agreed upon by the parties of those blocks.

3. The Commission may also decide, in accordance with the regulatory procedure referred to in Article 5(3) of the framework Regulation, to set up common projects for network-related functions which are of particular importance for the improvement of the overall performance of air traffic management and air navigation services in Europe. Such common projects may be considered eligible for Community funding within the multiannual financial framework. To this end, and without prejudice to Member States' competence to decide on the use of their financial resources, the Commission shall carry out an independent cost-benefit analysis and appropriate consultations with Member States and with relevant stakeholders in accordance with Article 10 of the framework Regulation, exploring all appropriate means for financing the deployment thereof. The eligible costs of deployment of common projects shall be recovered in accordance with the principles of transparency and non-discrimination.

Article 16

Review of compliance

1. The Commission shall provide for the ongoing review of compliance with the principles and rules referred to in Articles 14 and 15, acting in cooperation with the Member States. The Commission shall endeavour to establish the necessary mechanisms for making use of Eurocontrol expertise and shall share the results of the review with the Member States, Eurocontrol and the airspace users' representatives.

2. At the request of one or more Member States that consider that the principles and rules referred to in Articles 14and 15 have not been properly applied, or on its own initiative, the Commission shall carry out an investigation into any allegation of non-compliance or non-application of the principles and/or rules concerned. Without prejudice to Article 18(1), the Commission shall share the results of the investigation with the Member States, Eurocontrol and the airspace users'

representatives. Within two months of receipt of a request, after having heard the Member State concerned and after consulting the Single Sky Committee in accordance with the advisory procedure referred to in Article 5(2) of the framework Regulation, the Commission shall take a decision on the application of Articles 14 and 15 of this Regulation and as to whether the practice concerned may continue.

3. The Commission shall address its decision to the Member States and inform the service provider thereof, in so far as it is legally concerned. Any Member State may refer the Commission's decision to the Council within one month. The Council, acting by a qualified majority, may take a different decision within a period of one month.

CHAPTER IV

FINAL PROVISIONS

Article 17

Revision of Annexes

Measures, designed to amend non-essential elements of the Annexes in order to take into account technical or operational developments, shall be adopted in accordance with the regulatory procedure with scrutiny referred to in Article 5(4) of the framework Regulation.

On imperative grounds of urgency, the Commission may use the urgency procedure referred to in Article 5(5) of the framework Regulation.

Article 18

Confidentiality

1. Neither the national supervisory authorities, acting in accordance with their national legislation, nor the Commission shall disclose information of a confidential nature, in particular information about air navigation service providers, their business relations or their cost components.

2. Paragraph 1 shall be without prejudice to the right of disclosure by national supervisory authorities or the Commission where this is essential for the fulfilment of their duties, in which case such disclosure shall be proportionate and shall have regard to the legitimate interests of air navigation service providers, airspace users, airports or other relevant stakeholders in the protection of their business secrets.

3. Information and data provided pursuant to the charging scheme referred to in Article 14 shall be publicly disclosed.

Article 18a

Review

The Commission shall submit a study to the European Parliament and to the Council no later than 4 December 2012evaluating the legal, safety, industrial, economic and social impacts of the application of market principles to the provision of communication, navigation, surveillance and aeronautical information services, compared to existing or alternative organisational principles and taking into account developments in the functional airspace blocks and in available technology.

Article 19

Entry into force

1. This Regulation shall enter into force on the twentieth day following that of its publication in the Official Journal of the European Union.

2. However, Articles 7 and 8 shall enter into force one year after publication of the common requirements, as referred to in Article 6, in the Official Journal of the European Union.

This Regulation shall be binding in its entirety and directly applicable in all Member States.

ANNEX I

REQUIREMENTS FOR QUALIFIED ENTITIES

The qualified entities must:

- be able to document extensive experience in assessing public and private entities in the air transport sectors, In particular air navigation service providers, and in other similar sectors in one or more of the fields covered by this Regulation,
- have comprehensive rules and regulations for the periodic survey of the abovementioned entities, published and continually upgraded and improved through research and development programmes,
- not be controlled by air navigation service providers, by airport management authorities or by others engaged commercially in the provision of air navigation services or in air transport services,
- be established with significant technical, managerial, support and research staff commensurate with the tasks to be carried out,
- be managed and administered in such a way as to ensure the confidentiality of information required by the administration,
- be prepared to provide relevant information to the national supervisory authority concerned,
- have defined and documented its policy and objectives for and commitment to quality and have ensured that this policy is understood, implemented and maintained at all levels in the organisation,
- have developed, implemented and maintained an effective internal quality system based on appropriate parts of internationally recognised quality standards and in compliance with EN 45004 (inspection bodies) and with EN 29001, as interpreted by the IACS Quality System Certification Scheme Requirements,

– be subject to certification of its quality system by an independent body of auditors recognised by the authorities of the Member State in which it is located.

ANNEX II

CONDITIONS TO BE ATTACHED TO CERTIFICATES

1. Certificates shall specify:

(a) the national supervisory authority issuing the certificate;
(b) the applicant (name and address);
(c) the services which are certified;
(d) a statement of the applicant's conformity with the common requirements, as defined in Article 6 of this Regulation;
(e) the date of issue and the period of validity of the certificate.

2. Additional conditions attached to certificates may, as appropriate, be related to:

(a) non-discriminatory access to services for airspace users and the required level of performance of such services, including safety and interoperability levels;
(b) the operational specifications for the particular services;
(c) the time by which the services should be provided;
(d) the various operating equipment to be used within the particular services;
(e) ring-fencing or restriction of operations of services other than those related to the provision of air navigation services;
(f) contracts, agreements or other arrangements between the service provider and a third party and which concern the service(s);
(g) provision of information reasonably required for the verification of compliance of the services with the common requirements, including plans, financial and operational data, and major changes in the type and/or scope of air navigation services provided;
(h) any other legal conditions which are not specific to air navigation services, such as conditions relating to the suspension or revocation of the certificate.

Regulation (EC) No 551/2004 of the European Parliament and of the Council of 10 March 2004 on the organisation and use of the airspace in the single European sky (the airspace Regulation)

(Text with EEA relevance)

THE EUROPEAN PARLIAMENT AND THE COUNCIL OF THE EUROPEAN UNION,

Having regard to the Treaty establishing the European Community, and in particular

Article 80(2) thereof,

Having regard to the proposal from the Commission,

Having regard to the opinion of the European Economic and Social Committee, Having regard to the opinion of the Committee of the Regions,

Acting in accordance with the procedure laid down in Article 251 of the Treaty, in the light of the joint text approved by the Conciliation Committee on 11 December 2003,

Whereas:

(1) The creation of the single European sky requires a harmonised approach for regulation of the organisation and the use of airspace.

(2) In the report of the High Level Group on the single European sky in November 2000 it is considered that airspace should be designed, regulated and strategically managed on a European basis.

(3) The Communication of the Commission on the creation of the single European sky of 30 November 2001 calls for structural reform to permit the creation of the single European sky by way of a progressively more integrated management of airspace and the development of new concepts and procedures of air traffic management.

(4) Regulation (EC) No 549/2004 of the European Parliament and of the Council of 10 March 2004 (the framework Regulation) lays down the framework for the creation of the single European sky.

(5) In Article 1 of the 1944 Chicago Convention on Civil Aviation, the Contracting States recognise that "every State has complete and exclusive sovereignty over the airspace above its territory". It is within the framework of such sovereignty that the Member States of the Community, subject to applicable international conventions, exercise the powers of a public authority when controlling air traffic.

(6) Airspace is a common resource for all categories of users that needs to be used flexibly by all of them, ensuring fairness and transparency whilst taking into account security and defence needs of Member States and their commitments within international organisations.

(7) Efficient airspace management is fundamental to increasing the capacity of the air traffic services system, to providing the optimum response to various user requirements and to achieving the most flexible use of airspace.

(8) The activities of Eurocontrol confirm that the route network and airspace structure cannot realistically be developed in isolation, as each individual Member State is an integral element of the European air traffic management network (EATMN), both inside and outside the Community.

(9) A progressively more integrated operating airspace should be established for en-route general air traffic in the upper airspace; the interface between upper and lower airspace should be identified accordingly.

(10) A European upper flight information region (EUIR) encompassing the upper airspace under the responsibility of the Member States within the scope of this Regulation should facilitate common planning and aeronautical information publication in order to overcome regional bottlenecks.

(11) Airspace users face disparate conditions of access to, and freedom of movement within, the Community airspace. This is due to the lack of harmonisation in the classification of airspace.

(12) The reconfiguration of airspace should be based on operational requirements regardless of existing boundaries. Common general principles for creating uniform functional airspace blocks should be developed in consultation with and on the basis of technical advice from Eurocontrol.

(13) It is essential to achieve a common, harmonised airspace structure in terms of routes and sectors, to base the present and future organisation of airspace on common principles, and to design and manage airspace in accordance with harmonised rules.

(14) The concept of the flexible use of airspace should be applied effectively; it is necessary to optimise the use of sectors of airspace, especially during peak periods for general air traffic and in high-traffic airspace, by cooperation between Member States in respect of the use of such sectors for military operations and training. To that end, it is necessary to allocate the appropriate resources for an effective implementation of the concept of the flexible use of airspace, taking into account both civil and military requirements.

(15) Member States should endeavour to cooperate with neighbouring Member States to apply the concept of flexible use of airspace across national borders.

(16) Differences in the organisation of civil-military cooperation in the Community restrict uniform and timely airspace management and the implementation of changes. The success of the single European sky is dependent upon effective cooperation between civil and military authorities, without prejudice to the prerogatives and responsibilities of the Member States in the field of defence.

(17) Military operations and training should be safeguarded whenever the application of common principles and criteria is detrimental to their safe and efficient performance.

(18) Adequate measures should be introduced to improve the effectiveness of air traffic flow management in order to assist existing operational units, including the Eurocontrol Central Flow Management Unit, to ensure efficient flight operations.

(19) It is desirable to reflect upon the extension of upper airspace concepts to the lower airspace, in accordance with a timetable and appropriate studies,

HAVE ADOPTED THIS REGULATION:

CHAPTER I

GENERAL

Article 1

Objective and scope

1. Within the scope of the framework Regulation, this Regulation concerns the organisation and the use of airspace in the Single European Sky. The objective of this Regulation is to support the concept of a progressively more integrated operating airspace within the context of the common transport policy and to establish common procedures for design, planning and management ensuring the efficient and safe performance of air traffic management.

2. The use of airspace shall support the operation of the air navigation services as a coherent and consistent whole in accordance with Regulation (EC) No 550/2004 of the European Parliament and of the Council of 10 March 2004 on the provision of air navigation services in the Single European Sky (the service provision Regulation).

3. Without prejudice to Article 10, this Regulation shall apply to the airspace within the ICAO EUR and AFI regions where Member States are responsible for the provision of air traffic services in accordance with the service provision Regulation. Member States may also apply this Regulation to airspace under their responsibility within other ICAO regions, on condition that they inform the Commission and the other Member States thereof.

4. The Flight Information Regions comprised within the airspace to which this Regulation applies shall be published in the Official Journal of the European Union.

CHAPTER II

AIRSPACE ARCHITECTURE

[Article 2 is deleted]

Article 3

European Upper Flight Information Region (EUIR)

1. The Community and its Member States shall aim at the establishment and recognition by the ICAO of a single EUIR. To that effect, for matters which fall within the competence of the Community, the Commission shall submit a recommendation to the Council in accordance with Article 300 of the Treaty at the latest by 4 December 2011.

2. The EUIR shall be designed to encompass the airspace falling under the responsibility of the Member States in accordance with Article 1(3) and may also include airspace of European third countries.

3. The establishment of the EUIR shall be without prejudice to the responsibility of Member States for the designation of air traffic service providers for the airspace under their responsibility in accordance with Article 8(1) of the service provision Regulation.

4. Member States shall retain their responsibilities towards the ICAO within the geographical limits of the upper flight information regions and flight information regions entrusted to them by the ICAO on the date of entry into force of this Regulation.

Article 3a

Electronic aeronautical information

1. Without prejudice to the publication by Member States of aeronautical information and in a manner consistent with that publication, the Commission, working in cooperation with Eurocontrol, shall ensure the availability of electronic aeronautical information of high quality, presented in a harmonised way and serving the requirements of all relevant users in terms of data quality and timeliness.

2. For the purpose of paragraph 1, the Commission shall:

(a) ensure the development of a Community-wide aeronautical information infrastructure in the form of an electronic integrated briefing portal with unrestricted access to interested stakeholders. That infrastructure shall integrate access to and provision of required data elements such as, but not limited to aeronautical information, air traffic services reporting office (ARO) information, meteorological information and flow management information;
(b) support the modernisation and harmonisation of the provision of aeronautical information in its broadest sense in close cooperation with Eurocontrol and the ICAO.

3. The Commission shall adopt detailed implementing rules for this Article in accordance with the regulatory procedure referred to in Article 5(3) of the framework Regulation.

Article 4

Rules of the air and airspace classification

The Commission shall, in accordance with the regulatory procedure referred to in Article 5(3) of the framework Regulation, adopt implementing rules in order to:

(a) adopt appropriate provisions on rules of the air based upon ICAO standards and recommended practices;
(b) harmonise the application of the ICAO airspace classification, with appropriate adaptation, in order to ensure the seamless provision of safe and efficient air traffic services within the single European sky.

[Article 5 is deleted]

Article 6

Network management and design

1. The air traffic management (ATM) network functions shall allow optimum use of airspace and ensure that airspace users can operate preferred trajectories, while allowing maximum access to airspace and air navigation services. These network functions shall be aimed at supporting initiatives at national level and at the level of functional airspace blocks and shall be executed in a manner which respects the separation of regulatory and operational tasks.

2. In order to achieve the objectives referred to in paragraph 1 and without prejudice to the responsibilities of the Member States with regard to national routes and airspace structures, the Commission shall ensure that the following functions are carried out:

(a) design of the European route network;
(b) coordination of scarce resources within aviation frequency bands used by general air traffic, in particular radio frequencies as well as coordination of radar transponder codes.

The functions listed in the first subparagraph shall not involve the adoption of binding measures of a general scope or the exercise of political discretion. They shall take into account proposals established at national level and at the level of functional airspace blocks. They shall be performed in coordination with military authorities in accordance with agreed procedures concerning the flexible use of airspace.

The Commission may, after consultation of the Single Sky Committee and in conformity with the implementing rules referred to in paragraph 4, entrust to Eurocontrol, or another impartial and competent body, the tasks necessary for the execution of the functions listed in the first subparagraph. These tasks shall be executed in an impartial and cost-effective manner and performed on behalf on Member States and stakeholders. They shall be subject to appropriate governance, which recognises the separate accountabilities for service provision and regulation, taking into consideration the needs of the whole ATM network and with the full involvement of the airspace users and air navigation service providers.

3. The Commission may add to the list of the functions in paragraph 2 after proper consultation of industry stakeholders. Those measures, designed to amend non-essential elements of this Regulation by supplementing it, shall be adopted in accordance with the regulatory procedure with scrutiny referred to in Article 5(4) of the framework Regulation.

4. Detailed rules for the implementation of the measures referred to in this Article, except for those referred to in paragraphs 6 to 9, shall be adopted in accordance

with the regulatory procedure referred to in Article 5(3) of the framework Regulation. Those implementing rules shall address in particular:

(a) the coordination and harmonisation of processes and procedures to enhance the efficiency of aeronautical frequency management including the development of principles and criteria;
(b) the central function to coordinate the early identification and resolution of frequency needs in the bands allocated to European general air traffic to support the design and operation of European aviation network;
(c) additional network functions as defined in the ATM Master Plan;
(d) detailed arrangements for cooperative decision-making between the Member States, the air navigation service providers and the network management function for the tasks referred to in paragraph 2;
(e) arrangements for consultation of the relevant stakeholders in the decision-making process both at national and European levels; and
(f) within the radio spectrum allocated to general air traffic by the International Telecommunication Union, a division of tasks and responsibilities between the network management function and national frequency managers, ensuring that the national frequency management functions continue to perform those frequency assignments that have no impact on the network. For those cases which do have an impact on the network, the national frequency managers shall cooperate with those responsible for the network management function to optimise the use of frequencies.

5. Aspects of airspace design other than those referred to in paragraph 2 shall be dealt with at national level or at the level of functional airspace blocks. This design process shall take into account traffic demands and complexity, national or functional airspace block performance plans and shall include full consultation of relevant airspace users or relevant groups representing airspace users and military authorities as appropriate.

6. Member States shall entrust Eurocontrol or another impartial and competent body with the performance of air traffic flow management, subject to appropriate oversight arrangements.

7. Implementing rules for air traffic flow management, including the necessary oversight arrangements, shall be developed in accordance with the advisory procedure referred to in Article 5(2) of the framework Regulation and adopted in accordance with the regulatory procedure referred to in Article 5(3) of the framework Regulation, with a view to optimising available capacity in the use of airspace and enhancing air traffic flow management processes. These rules shall be based on transparency and efficiency, ensuring that capacity is provided in a flexible and timely manner, consistent with the recommendations of the ICAO Regional Air Navigation Plan, European Region.

8. The implementing rules for air traffic flow management shall support operational decisions by air navigation service providers, airport operators and airspace users and shall cover the following areas:

(a) flight planning;
(b) use of available airspace capacity during all phases of flight, including slot assignment; and
(c) use of routings by general air traffic, including:
  - the creation of a single publication for route and traffic orientation,
  - options for diversion of general air traffic from congested areas, and
  - priority rules regarding access to airspace for general air traffic, particularly during periods of congestion and crisis.

9. When developing and adopting the implementing rules the Commission shall, as appropriate and without prejudice to safety, take into account consistency between flight plans and airport slots and the necessary coordination with adjacent regions.

CHAPTER III

FLEXIBLE USE OF AIRSPACE IN THE SINGLE EUROPEAN SKY

Article 7

Flexible use of airspace

1. Taking into account the organisation of military aspects under their responsibility, Member States shall ensure the uniform application within the Single European Sky of the concept of the flexible use of airspace as described by the ICAO and as developed by Eurocontrol, in order to facilitate airspace management and air traffic management in the context of the common transport policy.

2. Member States shall report annually to the Commission on the application, in the context of the common transport policy, of the concept of the flexible use of airspace in respect of the airspace under their responsibility.

3. Where, in particular following the reports submitted by Member States, it becomes necessary to reinforce and harmonise the application of the concept of the flexible use of airspace within the Single European Sky, implementing rules within the context of the common transport policy shall be adopted in accordance with the procedure under Article 8 of the framework Regulation.

Article 8

Temporary suspension

1. In cases where the application of Article 7 gives rise to significant operational difficulties, Member States may temporarily suspend such application on condition that they inform without delay the Commission and the other Member States thereof

2. Following the introduction of a temporary suspension, adjustments to the rules adopted under Article 7(3) may be worked out for the airspace under the responsibility of the Member State(s) concerned, in accordance with the procedure under Article 8 of the framework Regulation.

[Article 9 is deleted]

CHAPTER IV

FINAL PROVISIONS

Article 10

Review

In the context of the periodical review referred to in Article 12(2) of the framework Regulation, the Commission shall finalise a prospective study on the conditions for future application of the concepts referred to in Articles 3, 5 and 6 to lower airspace.

On the basis of the study's conclusions and in the light of the progress achieved, the Commission shall submit at the latest by 31 December 2006 a report to the European Parliament and the Council accompanied, if appropriate, by a proposal to extend the application of these concepts to lower airspace, or to determine any other steps. In the event of such an extension being envisaged, the relevant decisions should preferably be taken before 31 December 2009

Article 11

Entry into force

This Regulation shall enter into force on the twentieth day following that of its publication in the Official Journal of the European Union.

This Regulation shall be binding in its entirety and directly applicable in all Member States.

Regulation (EC) No 552/2004 of the European Parliament and of the Council of 10 March 2004 on the interoperability of the European Air Traffic Management network (the interoperability Regulation)

(Text with EEA relevance)

THE EUROPEAN PARLIAMENT AND THE COUNCIL OF THE EUROPEAN UNION,

Having regard to the Treaty establishing the European Community, and in particular

Article 80(2) thereof,

Having regard to the proposal from the Commission,

Having regard to the opinion of the European Economic and Social Committee, Having regard to the opinion of the Committee of the Regions,

Acting in accordance with the procedure laid down in Article 251 of the Treaty, in the light of the joint text approved by the Conciliation Committee on 11 December 2003,

Whereas:

(1) In order to create the Single European Sky, measures should be adopted in relation to systems, constituents and associated procedures with the objective of ensuring the interoperability of the European air traffic management network (EATMN) consistent with the provision of air navigation services as provided for in Regulation (EC) No 550/2004 of the European Parliament and of the Council of 10 March 2004 on the provision of air navigation services in the Single European Sky (the service provision Regulation) and the organisation and use of airspace as provided for in Regulation (EC) No 551/2004 of the European Parliament and of the Council of 10 March 2003 on the organisation and use of the airspace in the Single European Sky (the airspace Regulation).

(2) The report of the High Level Group on the Single European Sky has confirmed the need to establish technical regulation on the basis of the "new approach" in accordance with the Council resolution of 7 May 1985 on a new approach to technical harmonisation and standards where essential requirements, rules and standards are complementary and consistent.

(3) Regulation (EC) No 549/2004 of the European Parliament and of the Council of 10 March 2004 (the framework Regulation) lays down the framework for the creation of the Single European Sky.

(4) The report of the High Level Group has confirmed that even though progress has been achieved during the last few years towards seamless operation of the EATMN, the situation still remains unsatisfactory, with a low level of integration between national air traffic management systems and a slow pace in the introduction of new concepts of operation and technology necessary to deliver the additional required capacity.

(5) Enhancing the level of integration at Community level would result in better efficiency and lower costs for system procurement and maintenance and in improved operational coordination.

(6) The predominance of national technical specifications used in procurement has led to fragmentation of the systems market and does not facilitate industrial cooperation at Community level; as a result, industry is particularly affected since it needs to considerably adapt its products for each national market; these practices render development and implementation of new technology unnecessarily difficult and slow down the introduction of new operational concepts that are required to increase capacity.

(7) It is therefore in the interest of all those involved in air traffic management to develop a new partnership approach allowing the balanced involvement of all parties and stimulating creativity and the sharing of knowledge, experience and

risks; such partnership should aim at defining, in cooperation with industry, a coherent set of Community specifications that can fulfil the widest possible range of needs.

(8) The internal market is a Community objective and therefore measures taken under this Regulation should contribute to its progressive development in this sector.

(9) It is therefore appropriate to define essential requirements which should apply to the European air traffic management network, its systems, constituents and associated procedures.

(10) Implementing rules for interoperability should be drawn up for systems whenever necessary to complement or further refine the essential requirements; those rules should also be drawn up where necessary to facilitate the coordinated introduction of new, agreed and validated concepts of operation or technologies; compliance with those rules should be permanently maintained; those rules should rely on rules and standards developed by international organisations such as Eurocontrol or ICAO.

(11) The development and adoption of Community specifications concerning EATMN, its systems and constituents and associated procedures is an appropriate means of defining the technical and operational conditions necessary to meet the essential requirements and relevant implementing rules for interoperability; compliance with published Community specifications, which remains voluntary, creates a presumption of conformity with the essential requirements and the relevant implementing rules for interoperability.

(12) Community specifications should be established by the European standardisation bodies in conjunction with the European Organisation for Civil Aviation Equipment (Eurocae) and by Eurocontrol, in accordance with general Community standardisation procedures.

(13) The procedures governing the assessment of conformity or suitability for use of constituents should be based on the use of the modules covered by Council Decision 93/465/EEC of 22 July 1993 concerning the modules for the various phases of the conformity assessment procedures and the rules for the affixing and use of the CE conformity marking, which are intended to be used in the technical harmonisation directives(9); as far as necessary, these modules should be expanded to cover specific requirements of the industries concerned.

(14) The market concerned is of small size and consists of systems and constituents used almost exclusively for air traffic management purposes and not intended for the general public; it would be therefore excessive to affix the CE mark to constituents as, on the basis of the assessment of conformity and/or suitability for use, the manufacturer's declaration of conformity is sufficient;

that should not affect the obligation on manufacturers to affix the CE mark to certain constituents in order to certify their compliance with other Community legislation relating to them.

(15) The putting into service of air traffic management systems should be subject to verification of compliance with the essential requirements and relevant implementing rules for interoperability; use of Community specifications creates a presumption of conformity with the essential requirements and relevant implementing rules for interoperability.

(16) The full application of this Regulation should be accomplished by means of a transitional strategy designed to attain the objectives of this Regulation while not creating unjustified cost-benefit barriers to preservation of the existing infrastructure.

(17) Within the framework of the relevant Community legislation, due account should be taken of the need to ensure:

- harmonised conditions with regard to the availability and efficient use of radio spectrum necessary for the implementation of the Single European Sky, including electromagnetic compatibility aspects,
- protection of the safety-of-life services from harmful interference,
- efficient and appropriate use of frequencies allocated to and managed exclusively by the aviation sector.

(18) Council Directive 93/65/EEC of 19 July 1993 on the definition and use of compatible technical specifications for the procurement of air traffic management equipment and systems(10) is limited to obligations of awarding entities; this Regulation is more comprehensive in that it addresses obligations of all actors, including air navigation service providers, airspace users, industry and airports, and provides both for rules applicable to all and for the adoption of Community specifications which, while being voluntary, creates a presumption of conformity with the essential requirements. Therefore, Directive 93/65/EEC, Commission Directive 97/15/EC of 25 March 1997 adopting Eurocontrol standards and amending Council Directive 93/65/EEC on the definition and use of compatible technical specifications for the procurement of air-traffic-management equipment and systems(11) and Commission Regulations (EC) No 2082/2000 of 6 September 2000 adopting Eurocontrol standards and amending Directive 97/15/EC(12) and (EC) No 980/2002 of 4 June 2002 amending Regulation (EC) No 2082/2000 should be repealed after a transitional period.

(19) For reasons of legal certainty it is important to ensure that the substance of certain provisions of Community legislation adopted on the basis of Directive 93/65/EEC remains in force unchanged. The adoption under this Regulation of the implementing rules corresponding to such provisions will necessitate a certain amount of time,

HAVE ADOPTED THIS REGULATION:

CHAPTER I

GENERAL PROVISIONS

Article 1

Objective and scope

1. Within the scope of the framework Regulation, this Regulation concerns the interoperability of the EATMN.

2. This Regulation shall apply to the systems, their constituents and associated procedures identified in Annex I.

3. The objective of this Regulation is to achieve interoperability between the different systems, constituents and associated procedures of the EATMN, taking due account of the relevant international rules. This Regulation aims also at ensuring the coordinated and rapid introduction of new agreed and validated concepts of operations or technology in air traffic management.

CHAPTER II

ESSENTIAL REQUIREMENTS, IMPLEMENTING RULES FOR INTEROPERABILITY AND COMMUNITY SPECIFICATIONS

Article 2

Essential requirements

The EATMN, its systems and their constituents and associated procedures shall meet essential requirements. The essential requirements are set out in Annex II.

Article 3

Implementing rules for interoperability

1. Implementing rules for interoperability shall be drawn up whenever necessary to achieve in a coherent way the objectives of this Regulation.

2. Systems, constituents and associated procedures shall comply with the relevant implementing rules for interoperability throughout their lifecycle.

3. Implementing rules for interoperability shall in particular:

(a) determine any specific requirements that complement or refine the essential requirements, in particular in terms of safety, seamless operation and performance; and/or
(b) describe, where appropriate, any specific requirements that complement or refine the essential requirements, in particular regarding the coordinated introduction of new, agreed and validated concepts of operation or technologies; and/or
(c) determine the constituents when dealing with systems; and/or

(d) describe the specific conformity assessment procedures involving, where appropriate, notified bodies as referred to in Article 8, based on the modules defined in Decision 93/465/EEC to be used to assess either the conformity or the suitability for use of constituents as well as the verification of systems; and/or
(e) specify the conditions of implementation including, where appropriate, the date by which all relevant stakeholders are required to comply with them.

4. The preparation, adoption and review of implementing rules for interoperability shall take into account the estimated costs and benefits of technical solutions by means of which they may be complied with, with a view to defining the most viable solution, having due regard to the maintenance of an agreed high level of safety. An assessment of the costs and benefits of those solutions for all stakeholders concerned shall be attached to each draft implementing rule for interoperability.

5. Implementing rules for interoperability shall be established in accordance with the procedure under Article 8 of the framework Regulation.

Article 4

Community specifications

1. In pursuit of the objective of this Regulation, Community specifications may be established. Such specifications may be:

(a) European standards for systems or constituents, together with the relevant procedures, drawn up by the European standardisation bodies in cooperation with Eurocae, on a mandate from the Commission in accordance with Article 6(4) of Directive 98/34/EC of the European Parliament and of the Council of 22 June 1998 laying down a procedure for the provision of information in the field of technical standards and regulations and pursuant to the general guidelines on cooperation between the Commission and the standardisation bodies signed on 13 November 1984; or
(b) specifications drawn up by Eurocontrol on matters of operational coordination between air navigation service providers, in response to a request from the Commission in accordance with the procedure referred to in Article 5(2) of the framework Regulation.

2. Compliance with the essential requirements and/or the implementing rules for interoperability shall be presumed for systems, together with the associated procedures, or constituents that meet the relevant Community specifications and whose reference numbers have been published in the Official Journal of the European Union.

3. The Commission shall publish the references to the European standards referred to in subparagraph 1(a) in the Official Journal of the European Union.

4. The references to Eurocontrol specifications referred to in paragraph 1(b), shall be published by the Commission in the Official Journal of the European Union in accordance with the procedure referred to in Article 5(2) of the framework Regulation.

5. Where a Member State or the Commission considers that conformity with a published Community specification does not ensure compliance with the essential requirements and/or implementing rules for interoperability which the said Community specification is intended to cover, the procedure referred to in Article 5(2) of the framework Regulation shall apply.

6. In the case of shortcomings of published European standards, partial or total withdrawal of the standards concerned from the publications containing them, or amendments thereto, may be decided upon in accordance with the procedure referred to in Article 5(2) of the framework Regulation after consultation of the committee set up under Article 5 of Directive 98/34/EC.

7. In the case of shortcomings of published Eurocontrol specifications, partial or total withdrawal of the specifications concerned from the publications containing them, or amendment thereof, may be decided upon in accordance with the procedure referred to in Article 5(2) of the framework Regulation.

CHAPTER III

VERIFICATION OF COMPLIANCE

Article 5

EC declaration of conformity or suitability for use of constituents

1. Constituents shall be accompanied by an EC declaration of conformity or suitability for use. The elements of this declaration are set out in Annex III.

2. The manufacturer, or its authorised representative established in the Community, shall ensure and declare, by means of the EC declaration of conformity or suitability for use, that he has applied the provisions laid down in the essential requirements and in the relevant implementing rules for interoperability.

3. Compliance with the essential requirements and the relevant implementing rules for interoperability shall be presumed in relation to those constituents that are accompanied by the EC declaration of conformity or suitability for use.

4. The relevant implementing rules for interoperability shall identify, where appropriate, the tasks pertaining to the assessment of conformity or suitability for use of constituents to be carried out by the notified bodies referred to in Article 8.

Article 6

EC declaration of verification of systems

1. Systems shall be subject to an EC verification by the air navigation service provider in accordance with the relevant implementing rules for interoperability, in order to ensure that they meet the essential requirements of this Regulation and the implementing rules for interoperability, when integrated into the EATMN.

2. Before a system is put into service , the relevant air navigation service provider shall establish an EC declaration of verification, confirming compliance, and shall

submit it to the national supervisory authority together with a technical file. The elements of this declaration and of the technical file are set out in Annex IV. The national supervisory authority may require any additional information necessary to supervise such compliance.

3. The relevant implementing rules for interoperability shall identify, where appropriate, the tasks pertaining to the verification of systems to be carried out by the notified bodies as referred to in Article 8.

4. The EC declaration of verification shall be without prejudice to any assessments that the national supervisory authority may need to carry out on grounds other than interoperability.

*Article 6a**

Alternative verification of compliance

A certificate issued in accordance with Regulation (EC)No 216/2008 of the European Parliament and of the Council of 20 February 2008 on common rules in the field of civil aviation and establishing a European Aviation Safety Agency, where it applies to constituents or systems, shall be considered, for the purposes of Articles 5 and 6 of this Regulation, as an EC declaration of conformity or suitability for use, or as an EC declaration of verification, if it includes a demonstration of compliance with the essential requirements of this Regulation and the relevant implementing rules for interoperability.

Article 7

Safeguards

1. Where the national supervisory authority ascertains that:

(a) a constituent accompanied by an EC declaration of conformity or suitability for use, or
(b) a system accompanied by the EC declaration of verification,

does not comply with the essential requirements and/or relevant implementing rules for interoperability, it shall, with due regard to the need to ensure safety and continuity of operations, take all measures necessary to restrict the area of application of the constituent or the system concerned or to prohibit its use by the entities under the responsibility of the authority.

2. The Member State concerned shall immediately inform the Commission of any such measures, indicating its reasons and, in particular, whether in its opinion non-compliance with the essential requirements is due to:

(a) failure to meet the essential requirements;
(b) incorrect application of the implementing rules for interoperability and/or Community specifications;

(*). OJ L 79, 19.3.2008, p. 1.

(c) shortcomings in the implementing rules for interoperability and/or Community specifications.

3. As soon as possible, the Commission shall consult the parties concerned. After such consultation, the Commission shall inform the Member State of its findings and of its opinion as to whether the measures taken by the national supervisory authority are justified.

4. Where the Commission establishes that the measures taken by the national supervisory authority are not justified, it shall request the Member State concerned to ensure that they are withdrawn without delay. It shall forthwith so inform the manufacturer or its authorised representative established in the Community.

5. Where the Commission establishes that non-compliance with the essential requirements is due to incorrect application of the implementing rules for interoperability and/or the Community specifications, the Member State concerned shall take appropriate measures against the originator of the declaration of conformity or suitability for use or the EC declaration of verification and shall inform the Commission and the other Member States thereof.

6. Where the Commission establishes that non-compliance with the essential requirements is due to shortcomings in the Community specifications, the procedures referred to in Article 4 (6) or (7) shall apply.

Article 8

Notified bodies

1. Member States shall notify the Commission and the other Member States of the bodies they have appointed to carry out tasks pertaining to the assessment of conformity or suitability for use referred to in Article 5, and/or the verification referred to in Article 6, indicating each body's area of responsibility and its identification number obtained from the Commission. The Commission shall publish in the Official Journal of the European Union the list of bodies, their identification numbers and areas of responsibility, and shall keep the list updated.

2. Member States shall apply the criteria provided for in Annex V for the assessment of the bodies to be notified. Bodies meeting the assessment criteria provided for in the relevant European standards shall be deemed to meet the said criteria.

3. Member States shall withdraw notification of a notified body which no longer meets the criteria provided for in Annex V. It shall forthwith inform the Commission and the other Member States thereof.

4. Without prejudice to the requirements referred to in paragraphs 1, 2 and 3, Member States may decide to appoint organisations recognised in conformity with Article 3 of the service provision Regulation as notified bodies.

CHAPTER IV

FINAL PROVISIONS

Article 9

Revision of Annexes

Measures, designed to amend non-essential elements of the Annexes, in order to take into account technical or operational developments, shall be adopted in accordance with the regulatory procedure with scrutiny referred to in Article 5(4) of the framework Regulation.

Article 10

Transitional arrangements

1. Starting from 20 October 2005, the essential requirements shall apply to the putting into service of systems and constituents of the EATMN, if not otherwise specified by the relevant implementing rules for interoperability.

2. Compliance with the essential requirements shall be required for all systems and constituents of the EATMN currently in operation by 20 April 2011, if not otherwise specified by the relevant implementing rules for interoperability.

2a. For the purposes of paragraph 2 of this Article, Member States may declare systems and constituents of the EATMN as compliant with the essential requirements and exempt from the provisions of Articles 5 and 6.

3. Where systems of the EATMN have been ordered or binding contracts to that effect have been signed

- before the date of entry into force of this Regulation, or, where appropriate,
- before the date of entry into force of one or more relevant implementing rules for interoperability,

so that compliance with the essential requirements and/or the relevant implementing rules for interoperability cannot be guaranteed within the time limit mentioned in paragraph 1, the Member State concerned shall communicate to the Commission detailed information on the essential requirements and/or implementing rules for interoperability where uncertainty of compliance has been identified.

The Commission shall enter into consultation with the parties concerned, after which it shall take a decision in accordance with the procedure referred to in Article 5(3) of the framework Regulation.

Article 11

Repeal

Directives 93/65/EEC and 97/15/EC and Regulations (EC) Nos 2082/2000 and 980/2002 shall be repealed on 20 October 2005.

Article 12

Entry into force

This Regulation shall enter into force on the twentieth day following that of its publication in the Official Journal of the European Union.

This Regulation shall be binding in its entirety and directly applicable in all Member States.

ANNEX I

LIST OF SYSTEMS FOR AIR NAVIGATION SERVICES

For the purpose of this Regulation the EATMN is subdivided into eight systems.

1. Systems and procedures for airspace management.
2. Systems and procedures for air traffic flow management.
3. Systems and procedures for air traffic services, in particular flight data processing systems, surveillance data processing systems and human-machine interface systems.
4. Communications systems and procedures for ground-to-ground, air-to-ground and air-to-air communications.
5. Navigation systems and procedures.
6. Surveillance systems and procedures.
7. Systems and procedures for aeronautical information services.
8. Systems and procedures for the use of meteorological information.

ANNEX II

ESSENTIAL REQUIREMENTS

Part A: General requirements

These are network-wide requirements that are generally applicable to each one of the systems identified in Annex I.

1. *Seamless operation*

Air traffic management systems and their constituents shall be designed, built, maintained and operated using the appropriate and validated procedures, in such a way as to ensure the seamless operation of the EATMN at all times and for all phases of flight. Seamless operation can be expressed, in particular, in terms of information- sharing, including the relevant operational status information, common understanding of information, comparable processing performances and the associated procedures enabling common operational performances agreed for the whole or parts of the EATMN.

2. *Support for new concepts of operation*

The EATMN, its systems and their constituents shall support, on a coordinated basis, new agreed and validated concepts of operation that improve the quality, sustainability and effectiveness of air navigation services, in particular in terms of safety and capacity.

The potential of new concepts, such as collaborative decision-making, increasing automation and alternative methods of delegation of separation responsibility, shall be examined taking due account of technological developments and of their safe implementation, following validation.

3. *Safety*

Systems and operations of the EATMN shall achieve agreed high levels of safety. Agreed safety management and reporting methodologies shall be established to achieve this.

In respect of appropriate ground-based systems, or parts thereof, these high levels of safety shall be enhanced by safety nets which shall be subject to agreed common performance characteristics.

A harmonised set of safety requirements for the design, implementation, maintenance and operation of systems and their constituents, both for normal and degraded modes of operation, shall be defined with a view to achieving the agreed safety levels, for all phases of flight and for the entire EATMN.

Systems shall be designed, built, maintained and operated, using the appropriate and validated procedures, in such a way that the tasks assigned to the control staff are compatible with human capabilities, in both the normal and degraded modes of operation, and are consistent with required safety levels.

Systems shall be designed, built, maintained and operated using the appropriate and validated procedures, in such a way as to be free from harmful interference in their normal operational environment.

4. *Civil-military coordination*

The EATMN, its systems and their constituents shall support the progressive implementation of civil/military coordination, to the extent necessary for effective airspace and air traffic flow management, and the safe and efficient use of airspace by all users, through the application of the concept of the flexible use of airspace.

To achieve these objectives, the EATMN, its systems and their constituents shall support the timely sharing of correct and consistent information covering all phases of flight, between civil and military parties.

Account should be taken of national security requirements.

5. *Environmental constraints*

Systems and operations of the EATMN shall take into account the need to minimise environmental impact in accordance with Community legislation.

6. *Principles governing the logical architecture of systems*

Systems shall be designed and progressively integrated with the objective of achieving a coherent and increasingly harmonised, evolutionary and validated logical architecture within the EATMN.

7. *Principles governing the construction of systems*

Systems shall be designed, built and maintained on the grounds of sound engineering principles, in particular those relating to modularity, enabling interchangeability of constituents, high availability, and redundancy and fault tolerance of critical constituents.

Part B: Specific requirements

These are the requirements that are specific to each one of the systems and that complement or further refine the general requirements.

1. *Systems and procedures for airspace management*

1.1. Seamless operation

Information relating to pre-tactical and tactical aspects of airspace availability shall be provided to all interested parties in a correct and timely way so as to ensure an efficient allocation and use of airspace by all airspace users. This should take into account national security requirements.

2. *Systems and procedures for air traffic flow management*

2.1. Seamless operation

Systems and procedures for air traffic flow management shall support the sharing of correct, coherent and relevant strategic, pre-tactical and tactical, as applicable, flight information covering all phases of flight and offer dialogue capabilities with a view to achieving optimised use of airspace.

3. *Systems and procedures for air traffic services*

3.1. Flight data processing systems

3.1.1. Seamless operation

Flight data processing systems shall be interoperable in terms of the timely sharing of correct and consistent information, and a common operational understanding of that information, in order to ensure a coherent and consistent planning process and resource-efficient tactical coordination throughout the EATMN during all phases of flight.

In order to ensure safe, smooth and expeditious processing throughout the EATMN, flight data processing performances shall be equivalent and appropriate for a given environment (surface, terminal manoeuvring area (TMA), en-route), with known traffic characteristics and exploited under an agreed and validated operational concept, in particular in terms of accuracy and error tolerance of processing results.

3.1.2. Support for new concepts of operation

Flight data processing systems shall accommodate the progressive implementation of advanced, agreed and validated concepts of operation for all phases of flight, in particular as envisaged in the ATM Master Plan.

The characteristics of automation-intensive tools must be such as to enable coherent and efficient pre-tactical and tactical processing of flight information in parts of the EATMN.

Airborne and ground systems and their constituents supporting new, agreed and validated concepts of operation shall be designed, built, maintained and operated, using appropriate and validated procedures, in such a way as to be interoperable in terms of timely sharing of correct and consistent information and a common understanding of the current and predicted operational situation.

3.2. *Surveillance data processing systems*

3.2.1. Seamless operation

Surveillance data processing systems shall be designed, built, maintained and operated using the appropriate and validated procedures, in such a way as to provide the required performance and quality of service within a given environment (surface, TMA, en-route) with known traffic characteristics, in particular in terms of accuracy and reliability of computed results, correctness, integrity, availability, continuity and timeliness of information at the control position.

Surveillance data processing systems shall accommodate the timely sharing of relevant, accurate, consistent and coherent information between them to ensure optimised operations through different parts of the EATMN.

3.2.2. Support for new concepts of operation

Surveillance data processing systems shall accommodate the progressive availability of new sources of surveillance information in such a way as to improve the overall quality of service, in particular as envisaged in the ATM Master Plan.

3.3. *Human-machine interface systems*

3.3.1. Seamless operation

Human-machine interfaces of ground air traffic management systems shall be designed, built, maintained and operated using the appropriate and validated procedures, in such a way as to offer to all control staff a progressively harmonised working environment, including functions and ergonomics, meeting the required performance for a given environment (surface, TMA, en-route), with known traffic characteristics.

3.3.2. Support for new concepts of operation

Human-machine interface systems shall accommodate the progressive introduction of new, agreed and validated concepts of operation and increased automation, in such a way as to ensure that the tasks assigned to the control staff remain compatible with human capabilities, in both the normal and degraded modes of operation.

4. *Communications systems and procedures for ground-to-ground, air-to-ground and air-to-air communications*

4.1. Seamless operation

Communication systems shall be designed, built, maintained and operated using the appropriate and validated procedures, in such a way as to achieve the required performances within a given volume of airspace or for a specific application, in particular in terms of communication processing time, integrity, availability and continuity of function.

The communications network within the EATMN shall be such as to meet the requirements of quality of service, coverage and redundancy.

4.2. Support for new concepts of operation

Communication systems shall support the implementation of advanced, agreed and validated concepts of operation for all phases of flight, in particular as envisaged in the ATM Master Plan.

5. *Navigation systems and procedures*

5.1. Seamless operation

Navigation systems shall be designed, built, maintained and operated using appropriate and validated procedures in such a way as to achieve the required horizontal and vertical navigation performance, in particular in terms of accuracy and functional capability, for a given environment (surface, TMA, en-route), with known traffic characteristics and exploited under an agreed and validated operational concept.

6. *Surveillance systems and procedures*

6.1. Seamless operation

Surveillance systems shall be designed, built, maintained and operated using appropriate and validated procedures in such a way as to provide the required performance applicable in a given environment (surface, TMA, en-route) with known traffic characteristics and exploited under an agreed and validated operational concept, in particular in terms of accuracy, coverage, range and quality of service.

The surveillance network within the EATMN shall be such as to meet the requirements of accuracy, timeliness, coverage and redundancy. The surveillance network shall enable surveillance data to be shared in order to enhance operations throughout the EATMN.

7. *Systems and procedures for aeronautical information services*

7.1. Seamless operation

Accurate, timely and consistent aeronautical information shall be provided progressively in an electronic form, based on a commonly agreed and standardised data set.

Accurate and consistent aeronautical information, in particular concerning airborne and ground-based constituents or systems, shall be made available in a timely manner.

7.2. Support for new concepts of operation

Increasingly accurate, complete and up-to-date aeronautical information shall be made available and used in a timely manner in order to support continuous improvement of the efficiency of airspace and airport use.

8. *Systems and procedures for the use of meteorological information*

8.1. Seamless operation

Systems and procedures for the use of meteorological information shall improve the consistency and timeliness of its provision and the quality of its presentation, using an agreed data set.

8.2. Support for new concepts of operation

Systems and procedures for the use of meteorological information shall improve the promptness of its availability and the speed with which it may be used, in order to support continuous improvement of the efficiency of airspace and airport use.

ANNEX III

CONSTITUENTS

EC declaration

- of conformity
- of suitability for use

1. *Constituents*

The constituents will be identified in the implementing rules for interoperability in accordance with the provisions of Article 3 of this Regulation.

2. *Scope*

The EC declaration covers:

- either the assessment of the intrinsic conformity of a constituent, considered in isolation, with the Community specifications to be met, or
- the assessment/judgment of the suitability for use of a constituent, considered within its air traffic management environment.

The assessment procedures implemented by the notified bodies at the design and production stages will draw upon the modules defined in Decision 93/465/EEC, in accordance with the conditions set out in the relevant implementing rules for interoperability.

3. *Contents of the EC declaration*

The EC declaration of conformity or suitability for use and the accompanying documents must be dated and signed.

That declaration must be written in the same language as the instructions and must contain the following:

- the Regulation references,
- the name and address of the manufacturer or its authorised representative established within the Community (give trade name and full address and, in the case of the authorised representative, also give the trade name of the manufacturer),
- description of the constituent,
- description of the procedure followed in order to declare conformity or suitability for use (Article 5 of this Regulation),
- all of the relevant provisions met by the constituent and in particular its conditions of use,
- if applicable, name and address of notified body or bodies involved in the procedure followed in respect of conformity or suitability for use and date of examination certificate together, where appropriate, with the duration and conditions of validity of the certificate,
- where appropriate, reference to the Community specifications followed,
- identification of signatory empowered to enter into commitments on behalf of the manufacturer or of the manufacturer's authorised representative established in the Community.

ANNEX IV

SYSTEMS

EC declaration of verification of systems

Verification procedure for systems

1. *Contents of EC declaration of verification of systems*

The EC declaration of verification and the accompanying documents must be dated and signed. That declaration must be written in the same language as the technical file and must contain the following:

- the Regulation references,
- name and address of the air navigation service provider (trade name and full address),

- a brief description of the system,
- description of the procedure followed in order to declare conformity of the system (Article 6 of this Regulation),
- name and address of the notified body which carried out tasks pertaining to the verification procedure, if applicable,
- the references of the documents contained in the technical file,
- where appropriate, reference to the Community specifications,
- all the relevant temporary or definitive provisions to be complied with by the systems and in particular, where appropriate, any operating restrictions or conditions,
- if temporary: duration of validity of the EC declaration,
- identification of the signatory.

2. *Verification procedure for systems*

Verification of systems is the procedure whereby an air navigation service provider checks and certifies that a system complies with this Regulation and may be put into operation on the basis of this Regulation.

The system is checked for each of the following aspects:

- overall design,
- development and integration of the system, including in particular constituent assembly and overall adjustments,
- operational system integration,
- specific system maintenance provisions if applicable.

Where involvement of a notified body is required by the relevant implementing rule for interoperability, the notified body, after having carried out the tasks incumbent upon it in accordance with the rule, draws up a certificate of conformity in relation to the tasks it carried out. This certificate is intended for the air navigation service provider. This provider then draws up the EC declaration of verification intended for the national supervisory authority.

3. *Technical file*

The technical file accompanying the EC declaration of verification must contain all the necessary documents relating to the characteristics of the system, including conditions and limits of use, as well as the documents certifying conformity of constituents where appropriate.

The following documents shall be included as a minimum:

- indication of the relevant parts of the technical specifications used for procurement that ensure compliance with the applicable implementing rules for interoperability and, where appropriate, the Community specifications,
- list of constituents as referred to in Article 3 of this Regulation,
- copies of the EC declaration of conformity or suitability for use with which the above mentioned constituents must be provided in accordance with Article 5 of this Regulation accompanied, where appropriate, by a copy

of the records of the tests and examinations carried out by the notified bodies,
- where a notified body has been involved in the verification of the system(s), a certificate countersigned by itself, stating that the system complies with this Regulation and mentioning any reservations recorded during performance of activities and not withdrawn,
- where there has not been involvement of a notified body, a record of the tests and installation configurations made with a view to ensuring compliance with essential requirements and any particular requirements contained in the relevant implementing rules for interoperability.

4. *Submission*

The technical file must be attached to the EC declaration of verification which the air navigation service provider submits to the national supervisory authority.

A copy of the technical file must be kept by the provider throughout the service life of the system. It must be sent to any other Member States which so request.

ANNEX V

NOTIFIED BODIES

1. The body, its Director and the staff responsible for carrying out the checks may not become involved, either directly or as authorised representatives, in the design, manufacture, marketing or maintenance of the constituents or systems or in their use. This does not exclude the possibility of an exchange of technical information between the manufacturer or constructor and that body.

2. The body and the staff responsible for the checks must carry out the checks with the greatest possible professional integrity and the greatest possible technical competence and must be free of any pressure and incentive, in particular of a financial type, which could affect their judgment or the results of their inspection, in particular from persons or groups of persons affected by the results of the checks.

3. The body must employ staff and possess the means required to perform adequately the technical and administrative tasks linked with the checks; it should also have access to the equipment needed for exceptional checks.

4. The staff responsible for inspection must have:

- sound technical and vocational training,
- satisfactory knowledge of the requirements of the inspections they carry out and adequate experience of such operations,
- the ability required to draw up the declarations, records and reports to demonstrate that the inspections have been carried out.

5. The impartiality of the inspection staff must be guaranteed. Their remuneration must not depend on the number of inspections carried out or on the results of such inspections.

6. The body must take out liability insurance unless its liability is assumed by the Member State in accordance with national law, or the Member State itself is directly responsible for the inspections.

7. The staff of the body must observe professional secrecy with regard to all information acquired in carrying out their tasks under this Regulation.

Annex 3

The FAB information Regulation No 176/2011

COMMISSION REGULATION (EU) No 176/2011 of 24 February 2011 on the information to be provided before the establishment and modification of a functional airspace block

(Text with EEA relevance)

THE EUROPEAN COMMISSION,

Having regard to the Treaty on the Functioning of the European Union,

Having regard to Regulation (EC) No 550/2004 of the European Parliament and of the Council of 10

March 2004 on the provision of air navigation services in the single European sky (the service provision Regulation[1]and in particular Article 9a(9) thereof,

Whereas:

(1) The functional airspace blocks are key enablers for enhancing cooperation between Member States in order to improve performance and create synergies. For that purpose and in order to optimise the interface of functional airspace blocks in the single European sky, the Member States concerned should cooperate with each other and where appropriate they may also cooperate with third countries.

(2) Member States have to comply with the requirements of Article 9a of Regulation (EC) No 550/2004 when establishing a functional airspace block.

1. OJ L 96,31.3.2004,p.10.

(3) Member States that establish a functional airspace block have to provide information to the Commission, the European Aviation Safety Agency, other Member States and other interested parties, giving them an opportunity to submit their observations with the aim of facilitating an exchange of views. However, the Member States should not provide classified information, business secrets or otherwise confidential information.

(4) The information to be provided under this Regulation should reflect compliance with the objectives for the functional airspace blocks and assist Member States in ensuring consistency with other measures of the single European sky.

(5) In order to facilitate such exchange of information and submission of observations, the information which is considered as 'adequate' to be provided to Member States, the Commission, the European Aviation Safety Agency (EASA) and other interested parties should be clearly laid out as well as the procedures for this exchange of information.

(6) In particular, the Member States concerned should jointly provide the information and accordingly provide one set of information and documentary evidence per functional airspace block.

(7) The establishment of a functional airspace block should be considered as the legal process through which Member States must enhance cooperation between their respective airspace blocks. Member States should take the necessary measures to comply with this requirement at the latest by 4 December 2012, in accordance with Regulation (EC) No 550/2004.

(8) The determination whether a functional airspace block has been modified should be made on the basis of the same criteria for all Member States and should be limited to those changes which have a considerable impact on the functional airspace block and/or the neighbouring functional airspace blocks or Member States.

(9) According to Article 13a of Regulation (EC) No 549/2004 of the European Parliament and of the Council[2] Member States and the Commission should coordinate with the EASA to ensure that all safety aspects are properly addressed when implementing the single European sky.

(10) This Regulation does not affect the security or defence policy interests of Member States and related confidentiality needs according to Article 13 of Regulation (EC) No 549/2004.

(11) Pursuant to Article 83 of the Chicago Convention, Member States that establish a functional airspace block will have to register agreements or arrangements for functional airspace blocks and any subsequent amendment thereto with the International Civil Aviation Organisation (ICAO).

2. OJ L 96,31.3.2004,p.1.

(12) The establishment of functional airspace blocks which would result in changes to the ICAO flight information region (FIR) boundaries or to the facilities and services provided within those boundaries should continue to be the subject of the ICAO air navigation planning process and the procedure for amendment of the ICAO air navigation plans.

(13) Member States should ensure that they fulfil their safety responsibilities effectively when establishing a functional airspace block. They should demonstrate and provide the necessary assurance that the functional airspace block will be established and managed safely and address the Member States and the air navigation service providers safety management elements associated with the functional airspace block establishment, with a focus on their respective safety roles and responsibilities.

(14) The measures provided for in this Regulation are in accordance with the opinion of the Single Sky Committee,

HAS ADOPTED THIS REGULATION:

Article 1

Subject matter and scope

This Regulation lays down the requirements for:

(1) the information to be provided by the Member States concerned to the Commission, the European Aviation Safety Agency (EASA), other Member States and interested parties before the establishment and modification of a functional airspace block;

(2) the procedures for the provision of the information to and submission of observations from the parties referred to in point (1), before notification of the functional airspace block is made to the Commission.

Article 2

Definitions

For the purpose of this Regulation, the definitions in Article 2 of Regulation (EC) No 549/2004 shall apply.

In addition the following definitions shall apply:

(1) 'Member States concerned' means the Member States having mutually agreed to establish a functional airspace block under Regulation (EC) No 550/2004.

(2) 'Interested parties' means the neighbouring third countries to a functional airspace block, relevant airspace users or groups of airspace users and staff representative bodies as well as adjacent air navigation service providers to those in a functional airspace block.

Article 3

Demonstration of compliance

The Member States concerned shall jointly provide the information set out in the Annex to this Regulation to demonstrate fulfilment of the requirements of Article 9a of Regulation (EC) No 550/2004.

Article 4

Procedure for exchange of information for new functional airspace blocks

1. The Member States concerned shall provide the information set out in the Annex to the Commission at the latest by 24 June 2012. The Commission shall make it available for observations to the EASA, other Member States and interested parties at the latest one week after receipt of the information.
2. The observations of the EASA, other Member States and interested parties shall be submitted to the Commission at the latest two months after receipt of the information. The Commission shall without delay communicate the observations received and its own observations to the Member States concerned.
3. The Member States concerned shall duly consider the observations received before establishing their functional airspace block.

Article 5

Modification of an established functional airspace block

1. For the purpose of this Regulation, an established functional airspace block shall be considered as modified when a proposed modification shall result in changes to the defined dimensions of the functional airspace block.
2. At least six months before a modification is implemented, the Member States concerned shall jointly notify the Commission of the proposed changes and provide information supporting the changes, updating as appropriate the information provided for the establishment of the functional airspace block. The Commission shall make it available for observations to the EASA, other Member States and interested parties at the latest one week after receipt of the information.
3. The observations of the EASA, other Member States and interested parties shall be submitted to the Commission at the latest two months after receipt of the information. The Commission shall without delay communicate the observations received and its own observations to the Member States concerned.
4. The Member States concerned shall duly consider the observations received before modifying their functional airspace block.

Article 6

Functional airspace blocks already established

Member States concerned which have already established a functional airspace block prior to the entry into force of this Regulation shall ensure that the required information laid out in the Annex, which has not been already submitted as part of their notification, is provided to the Commission at the latest by 24 June 2012.

Article 7

Entry into force

This Regulation shall enter into force on the 20th day following its publication in the Official Journal of the European Union.

This Regulation shall be binding in its entirety and directly applicable in all Member States.

ANNEX

INFORMATION TO BE PROVIDED

PART I

General information

1. The Member States concerned shall specify:
   (a) the point of contact for the functional airspace block;
   (b) the defined dimensions of the functional airspace block;
   (c) the jointly designated air traffic service providers and meteorological service providers, if applicable, and their respective areas of responsibility;
   (d) the providers of air traffic services providing services without certification in accordance with Article 7(5) of Regulation (EC) No 550/2004 and their respective areas of responsibility.
2. The Member States concerned shall provide the following information on the arrangements concluded regarding the establishment or modification of the functional airspace block, including:
   (a) copy of the documents which reflect the mutual agreement of the Member States concerned to establish the functional airspace block;
   (b) information on the arrangements between the national supervisory authorities in the functional airspace block;
   (c) information on the arrangements between the air traffic service providers in the functional airspace block;
   (d) information on arrangements between competent civil and military authorities in respect of their involvement in the governance structures of the functional airspace block.

3. Member States concerned may refer to information already provided to the Commission as part of the implementation of the single European sky.

PART II

Requirements of Article 9a(2) of Regulation (EC) No 550/2004

The Member States concerned shall provide information, including supporting documentation, pertaining to the requirements of Article 9a(2) of Regulation (EC) No 550/2004.

1. Functional airspace block safety case

With regard to the functional airspace block safety case, the following information shall be provided:

(a) the common safety policy or plans to establish a common safety policy;
(b) a description of the arrangements dealing with accident and incident investigation and plans on how to address safety data collection, analysis and exchange;
(c) a description of the way in which safety is being managed to avoid degradation in safet y performance within the functional airspace block;
(d) a description of the arrangements clearly identifying and allocating the responsibilities and interfaces with relation to the setting of safety targets, safety oversight and the accompanying enforcement measures in regard to the provision of air navigation services within the functional airspace block;
(e) documentation and/or statements that the safety assessment including hazard identification, risk assessment and mitigation has been conducted before introducing operational changes resulting from the establishment or modification of the functional airspace bloc.

2. Optimum use of airspace, taking into account air traffic flows

The Member States concerned shall provide the following information:

(a) a description of the relations with the relevant network functions for airspace management and air traffic flow management referred to in Article 6 of Regulation (EC) No 551/2004 of the European Parliament and of the Council[3] including the coordination, arrangements and procedures to achieve optimised use of the airspace;
(b) in respect of airspace management within the functional airspace block not covered by the network functions referred to in Article 6 of Regulation (EC) No 551/2004, information on:
   - the arrangements for an integrated airspace management,
   - the provisions for sharing of airspace management data,
   - the arrangements for an effective cooperative decision-making;

3. OJ L 96, 31.3.2004, p. 20.

(c) in respect of real time coordination within the functional airspace block:
  — a description of how cross-border activities are managed if new areas are created resulting from the establishment or modification of the functional airspace block.

3. Consistency with the European route network

The Member States concerned shall provide information to demonstrate that route design and implementation for the functional airspace block is consistent with, and completed within, the established process for overall coordination, development and implementation of the European route network referred to in Article 6 of Regulation (EC) No 551/2004.

Member States concerned may refer to information already provided to the Commission as part of the implementation of the single European sky.

4. Overall added value based on cost-benefit analyses

The Member States concerned shall provide statements confirming that:

(a) the cost-benefit analysis was conducted according to industry standard practice, using among others discounted cash flow analysis;
(b) the cost-benefit analysis provides a consolidated view of the impact of the establishment or modification of the functional airspace block on the civil and military airspace users;
(c) the cost-benefit analysis demonstrates an overall positive financial result (net present value and/or internal rate of return) for the establishment or modification of the functional airspace block;
(d) the functional airspace block contributes to a reduction of the aviation environmental impact; values for costs and benefits, their sources and the assumptions made to develop the cost-benefit analysis were documented;
(e) the main stakeholders were consulted and provided feedback on the costs and benefit estimates which are applicable to their operations.

5. Ensure smooth and flexible transfer of responsibility for air traffic control between air traffic service units

The Member States concerned shall provide information to demonstrate that the transfer of responsibilit y for air traffic control is smooth and flexible within the functional airspace block. This shall include the following information on the changes introduced by the establishment or modification of the functional airspace block:

(a) a description of the arrangements for cross border provision of air traffic services;
(b) the arrangements concluded to enhance coordination procedures between the concerned air traffic service providers within the functional airspace block and further planned initiatives to enhance coordination;

(c) a description of the arrangements concluded to enhance coordination procedures between the concerned civil and military air traffic service providers and further planned initiatives to enhance coordination in line with the concept of flexible use of airspace;
(d) a description of the arrangements concluded to enhance coordination procedures with the concerned adjacent air traffic service providers, and further planned initiatives to enhance coordination.

6. Ensure compatibility between the different airspace configurations, optimising, inter alia, the current flight information regions

The Member States concerned shall provide information on the available plans how to achieve harmonised organisation and classification of different airspace configurations within the functional airspace block. The plans shall include:

(a) the principles for airspace classification and airspace organisation for the functional airspace block;
(b) the changes of airspace configuration resulting from the harmonisation within the functional airspace block.

7. Regional agreements concluded within the ICAO

The Member States concerned shall provide the list of existing regional agreements concluded in compliance with the framework established by Annex 11 to the Convention on International Civil Aviation which are of relevance with respect to the establishment and operations of the functional airspace block.

8. Regional agreements in existence

The Member States concerned shall provide a list of existing agreements concluded by one or more of the Member States concerned, including those with third countries, which are of relevance with respect to the establishment and operations of the functional airspace block.

9. European Union-wide performance targets

The Member States concerned shall provide information on the arrangements concluded in order to facilitate consistency with the European Union-wide performance targets referred to in Article 11 of Regulation (EC) No 549/2004.

Member States concerned may refer to information already provided to the Commission under the provision of Article 5 of Commission Regulation (EU) No 691/2010[4].

4. (1) OJL 201, 3.8.2010, p. 1.

Index

B

C

F

G

H

I

J

K

L

AVIATION LAW AND POLICY SERIES

1. Erwin von den Steinen, *National Interest and International Aviation* (ISBN 90-411-2455-1).
2. Ludwig Weber, *International Civil Aviation Organisation: An Introduction* (ISBN 978-90-411-2622-1).
3. Niels van Antwerpen, *Cross-Border Provision of Air Navigation Services with Specific Reference to Europe: Safeguarding Transparent Lines of Responsibility and Liability* (ISBN 978-90-411-2688-7).
4. Brian F. Havel, *Beyond Open Skies: A New Regime for International Aviation* (ISBN 978-90-411-2389-3).
5. Jiefang Huang, *Aviation Safety through the Rule of Law: ICAO's Mechanisms and Practices* (ISBN 978-90-411-3115-7).
6. Marian Hoeks, *Multimodal Transport Law: The Law Applicable to the Multimodal Contract for the Carriage of Goods* (ISBN 978-90-411-3246-8).
7. George N. Tompkins, Jr., *Liability Rules Applicable to International Air Transportation as Developed by the Courts in the United States: From Warsaw 1929 to Montreal 1999* (ISBN 978-90-411-2646-7).
8. Daniel Calleja Crespo and Pablo Mendes de Leon (eds), *Achieving the Single European Sky: Goals and Challenges* (ISBN 978-90-411-3730-2).